"We give a copy of *Fundraising for Social Change* to each participant in the Fundraising Academy for Communities of Color because it provides grounding in donor development that is relevant in each of our cultures. People love Kim's fundraising wisdom and her keen ability to connect fund development with what matters in our communities. I always recommend it to organizations in need of a book with ideas they can use right away as well as information about how to build a successful long-term fundraising program."

—Steve Lew, senior projects director, CompassPoint Nonprofit Services

"I used *Fundraising for Social Change* as a textbook for my class for many years and often recommend it to grassroots organizations as a primer for developing a fundraising strategy. Kim's years of experience and her own broad knowledge of the field give the book heft and credibility. Her pragmatism and sense of humor make it readable and engaging."

—Maria Mottola, executive director, New York Foundation

"The information and inspiration we have received from Kim Klein's books have been key to our grassroots fundraising efforts. Some people go back to Proust; I go back to her specifics about how to write a fundraising plan that actually works!"

—Bob Fulkerson, state director, Progressive Leadership Alliance of Nevada (PLAN)

"Kim makes me a believer again whenever I am in her presence—be it through her spoken or written word. While she provides the basics of raising money in an accessible form, what I truly value is the deep sense of purpose she reawakens in me as a fundraiser-activist."

—Miguel Gavaldón, fundraising coach and trainer, Grassroots Institute for Fundraising Training

"Over the past 25 years, I have been a fundraiser, grantmaker, board member, and consultant. Whatever role I am in, I turn to *Fundraising for Social Change*. Working with Kim to present *Fundraising for Social Change* workshops in communities changes lives—both professional and personal—including mine. She offers hands-on experience and extraordinary human values to the nonprofit sector, as well as skilled expertise in teaching others how to make fundraising fun and meaningful to our whole life."

—Jaune Evans, development chair, Yerba Buena Center for the Arts

The Instructor's Guide for the sixth edition of *Fundraising for Social Change* includes a course description and syllabus, with week-by-week questions for discussion, writing assignments, small-group exercises, and case studies of ethical dilemmas. It also describes in detail the eight-week field placement component of the class. If you would like to download and print a copy of this guide, please visit:

www.wiley.com/college/klein

Kim Klein's Fundraising Series

I believe in creating a society in which the primary question is always, "What promotes the common good?" Enacting this vision of social justice requires mobilizing significant resources, including money. For that reason, effective, diversified fundraising must be part of every organization's organizing, advocacy, and service work.

The Kim Klein Fundraising Series is committed to supporting the common good by producing practical, reliable, and easy-to-understand materials on fundraising and philanthropy. We hope these works help people who are committed to social justice to build strong, financially healthy, mission-driven organizations.

Kim Klein, Series Editor

Additional Titles from Kim Klein's Fundraising Series

The Power of Legacy and Planned Gifts: How Nonprofits and Donors Work Together to Change the World, Kevin Johnson

Reliable Fundraising in Unreliable Times: What Good Causes Need to Know to Survive and Thrive, Kim Klein

Change Philanthropy: Candid Stories of Foundations Maximizing Results Through Social Justice, Alicia Epstein Korten

Inspired Philanthropy: Your Step-by-Step Guide to Creating a Giving Plan and Leaving a Legacy, 3rd Edition, Tracy Gary with Nancy Adess

The Accidental Fundraiser: A Step-by-Step Guide to Raising Money for Your Cause, Stephanie Roth, Mimi Ho

Grassroots Grants: An Activist's Guide to Grantseeking, 2nd Edition, Andy Robinson

Selling Social Change (Without Selling Out): Earned Income Strategies for Nonprofits, Andy Robinson

Raise More Money: The Best of The Grassroots Fundraising Journal, Kim Klein, Stephanie Roth, Editors

Kim Klein

FUNDRAISING

for
SOCIAL CHANGE

Sixth Edition

JOSSEY-BASS
A Wiley Imprint
www.josseybass.com

Published by Jossey-Bass
A Wiley Imprint
989 Market Street, San Francisco, CA 94103-1741—www.josseybass.com

Jossey-Bass books and products are available through most bookstores. To contact Jossey-Bass directly call our Customer Care Department within the U.S. at 800-956-7739, outside the U.S. at 317-572-3986, or fax 317-572-4002.

Jossey-Bass also publishes its books in a variety of electronic formats. Some content that appears in print may not be available in electronic books.

Library of Congress Cataloging-in-Publication Data

Klein, Kim.
   Fundraising for social change / Kim Klein. — 6th ed.
      p. cm. — (Kim Klein's Fundraising series)
   Includes bibliographical references and index.
   ISBN 978-0-470-88717-2 (pbk.); ISBN 978-1-118-01934-4 (ebk); ISBN 978-1-118-01936-8(ebk); ISBN 978-1-118-01937-5
   1. Fund raising—United States.   2. Nonprofit organizations—United States—Finance.   I. Title.
HV41.9.U5K57 2011
361.7068'1—dc22

2011007469

Printed in the United States of America
SIXTH EDITION
PB Printing   10 9 8 7 6 5 4 3 2 1

CONTENTS

PREMIUM WEB CONTENT

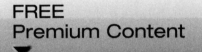

This book includes premium content that can be accessed from our Web site when you register at **www.josseybass.com/go/fundraisingforsocialchange** using the password *professional*.

Donor Bill of Rights, Association of Fundraising Professionals

Suggested books and Web sites

Chapter 9: Special Event Evaluation Form

Chapter 14: Institute for Conservation Leadership Report, *Reality Check: How Grassroots Environmental Groups Are (or Are Not) Raising Money On-Line* by Andy Robinson

Chapter 14: *How Five Trends Will Reshape the Social Sector* by La Piana and Associates, published for the James Irvine Foundation

Chapter 23: "How to Raise $50,000 in Six Weeks," by Kim Klein, *Grassroots Fundraising Journal*

Chapter 27: Sample Feasibility Study Report

Chapter 27: Sample Feasibility Study Surveys: Capital and Endowment

Chapter 27: Case Study of the Use of a Feasibility Study

PREFACE TO THE SIXTH EDITION

I love doing new editions of this book because it helps me (in fact, forces me) to figure out what is new in fundraising that I need to share with the people who read my books and what has stayed the same. For most editions I have added huge amounts of material (the first edition of this book, published in 1988, was a little more than two hundred pages long; by this edition we are close to five hundred pages with strategies not even imagined in the first edition. For the first edition, I learned to use a computer; for this sixth edition I learned to tweet. This edition will not be very much longer than the previous one because some reference material is being moved to the Web and because some things that were true are no longer true and have to be taken out.

Many things in the world have gotten far worse since 2006, when I did the fifth edition of this book. The United States remains embroiled in what is now the longest war we have ever been in. The gap between rich and poor is now greater than it has ever been, and recent census data show that America's poverty level has returned to the heights it was at when President Lyndon Johnson declared the "War on Poverty." Our oceans are rapidly acidifying; Glacier National Park will soon have no glaciers at all; and global warming is finally being acknowledged, even as it gets exponentially worse. We have been in a deep recession with high unemployment for almost three years.

It is easy to focus on all that is wrong and bad. But I see a lot of reason for hope. The Millennial Generation (born 1977–1997) is looking to be the most generous and engaged generation ever. Social media has allowed grassroots non-profits to get their message out far more widely than was ever possible before. That we were able to elect Barack Obama president gave many of us hope that racial justice is a goal we may someday attain. In the meantime, children from all income and racial groups can really think, "I could be president."

Alice Walker said recently, "Now is the best time to be alive, because so much is at stake." I completely agree. And to accomplish what we all want to accomplish, we must raise the money required. Organizations must focus on raising money, not on cutting their budgets. Change can happen very quickly, and our job is to make these changes work for the common good. This book is dedicated to helping organizations raise the money they need to do the work that we all know must be done.

ACKNOWLEDGMENTS

In my experience writing all the editions of this book, there have been people who made it possible for me to keep writing, be accurate, incorporate new ideas, and state them clearly. First are all the people I have met in my work who gave me the knowledge that I have. Second is my best friend and long-time editor, Nancy Adess. Nancy has edited everything I have written since 1981, and I can't imagine getting through any manuscript without her.

Third, my partner in life and work, Stephanie Roth, who shares her own vast knowledge of fundraising and organizational development with me, helps me flesh out new ideas and discard old or unworkable ones, and makes me laugh every day.

Fourth, all the animals I have had through these many editions. Today, I thank my cats, Jack Daniels and Ruby Tuesday, and my dear ancient dog, Brooklyn.

Fourth, as always, the team at Jossey-Bass has been terrific.

For this edition, special thanks go to Anne Ryan, a recent college graduate who volunteered to read a number of the chapters to keep my references to modern technology real. Her insights were invaluable. I also thank the staff of the Institute for Conservation Leadership and Andy Robinson for letting me use their article on online fundraising, which appears in the Premium Web Content.

Some of the information in this book first appeared in article form in the *Grassroots Fundraising Journal,* a bimonthly periodical that I published from 1981 through 2006, and that now belongs to the Grassroots Institute for Fundraising Training (GIFT).

THE AUTHOR

Kim Klein is an internationally known fundraising trainer who has worked in all aspects of fundraising: as staff, as volunteer, as board member, and as consultant. She is best known for adapting traditional fundraising techniques, particularly major donor campaigns, to the needs of organizations with small budgets that are working for social justice.

Kim is the author of five books. *Fundraising for Social Change,* now in this sixth edition, has become a classic text widely used in the field and in university degree programs. Kim is also the author of *Reliable Fundraising in Unreliable Times,* which won the Terry McAdam Book Award in 2010. Kim is featured in the fundraising video "Ready, Set, Raise," produced by the Grassroots Institute for Fundraising Training (GIFT), and answers readers' fundraising questions in the "Dear Kim" column of the GIFT e-newsletter.

Kim is a member of the Building Movement Project (www.buildingmovement. org), where her current work is helping nonprofits understand the need for fair and just tax policy and revenue solutions to our fiscal crises. She writes a blog for the Building Movement Project, www.kimkleinandthecommons.blogspot.com. She is a lecturer at the School of Social Welfare at the University of California, Berkeley, and was the Resident Resource Person at Concordia University in Montreal, Quebec. Widely in demand as a keynote speaker, trainer, and consultant, Kim has provided training and consultation in all fifty states in the United States and in twenty-one other countries. Kim lives in Berkeley, California. She can be reached at www.KleinandRoth.com.

INTRODUCTION

This is a how-to book. Its goal is to provide organizations that have budgets of less than $2,500,000, which describes most nonprofits, with the information they need to establish, maintain, and expand a successful fundraising program that is based on individual donors. Creating and maintaining a large number of individual donors gives organizations maximum freedom to pursue their mission. They can then use foundation, corporate, or government grants for special programs, startup costs, technical assistance, capital or endowment projects, or other time-limited needs. This book will be particularly helpful to nonprofits with one or two staff people and a large volunteer base.

Organizations with small to medium-size budgets, particularly those working for social change, need to keep in mind that the context in which their fundraising efforts take place is different from that of large organizations such as universities, urban hospitals, well-established museums, or multi-pronged social service agencies.

First, the name of your organization is not a household word. And even when they hear about you, many people will not understand what you are trying to do. Many of those who do understand your mission may disagree with it, particularly if you are trying to challenge the status quo. Even those in sympathy with your mission may think your aims are hopelessly naïve or idealistic; you may often be told to "face reality."

Second, you probably have little or no front money and not enough staff, so you don't have the funds to invest in strategies that take a long time to come to fruition, and you must always be adapting strategies to work on a smaller scale.

Third, your board of directors, volunteers, and staff are likely to be unfamiliar with fundraising strategies and may not be comfortable with the idea of asking for money.

For organizations such as yours, traditional fundraising strategies need to be rethought and translated into workable terms. This book does that. All of the strategies explained and recommended here have been successful for small nonprofits. Not every strategy will work for every organization, but the discussion of each strategy will allow you to decide which strategies will work for your organization and how to expand the strategies you are already using.

Fundraising without planning; without a strong, committed group of volunteers to help; without a workable organizational structure; or without an understanding of the basic components of all fundraising plans is impossible to sustain over a period of more than a few months. The appropriate staff, whether paid or unpaid, of every organization should read the first two sections of this book to learn the context for successful fundraising.

The subsequent sections present detailed descriptions of how to carry out strategies to acquire, retain, and upgrade donors to your organization. These proceed from the more impersonal solicitation of large groups of people at once, such as by direct mail, online, or through large special events, to the most personal—one person asking someone they know for a gift in person. The book gives special attention to the difficulties most people have asking for money and offers concrete ways to overcome these difficulties. Also discussed are some long-term strategies, such as legacy giving, and some large-scale strategies, such as capital campaigns. These discussions are included because I have seen small groups raise big money, and I believe most organizations have far more access to money than they realize.

Except in passing, this book does not discuss raising money from foundations, governments, or corporations. There are many books about those strategies. Most important, though, in my opinion, is that all organizations ought to have a base of individual support even if they then seek most of their money from governments (which might be completely appropriate depending on their mission) or from foundations (which will always be risky).

This book also covers the crucial nuts and bolts of fundraising: how to create a budget and a fundraising plan, the rudiments of setting up a fundraising office, managing donor data, the working relationships of fundraising staff with an executive director, and hiring fundraising staff or consultants. Finally, it discusses special circumstances for fundraising, such as raising money in rural communities or raising money for coalitions. Although this book is focused on the United

States, organizations in other countries will find many of the strategies explained here to be useful to their fundraising programs.

Throughout the book, you will see references to Premium Web Content—free resources that you can access on the Web. In addition to specific articles and examples, the Premium Web Content also includes a list of suggested books, periodicals, and Web sites for further information and the Association of Fundraising Professionals' Donor Bill of Rights.

If you find this book helpful, I encourage you to buy my other books and to subscribe to the *Grassroots Fundraising Journal,* a bimonthly publication that will help you keep up with fundraising strategies and developments in the field.

But ultimately, after you have read about how to raise money and gone to workshops on how to do it, the only thing left is actually to do it. As with driving a car or learning to swim, all the theory and explanation will not help until you get behind the wheel or into the pool and try it for yourself. With practice and attention, you can become an excellent driver or a strong swimmer. Likewise, putting your all into becoming a successful fundraiser will reap the money your organization needs to do its important work.

Few people give money without being asked. Make this your motto: "Today somebody has to ask somebody for money."

PART ONE

Fundraising Framework

When I hand out the agenda for a fundraising workshop, participants are often surprised to see that the section on personal solicitation is in the afternoon. Many have said, "I came to learn how to identify prospects and ask for money, not how to create a case statement or build a board of directors." Successful fundraisers know, however, that fundraising doesn't start with asking for money: it starts with understanding how fundraising and philanthropy work and what an organization needs to have in place in order to be successful when it asks for money.

This first section starts with what, for me, are the two most important facts I have ever learned about fundraising: the bulk of money given away to nonprofits comes from individuals, and the majority of people who give are not rich. The corollary to these facts is this: fundraising starts with who you know, and you already know all the people you need to know to begin your fundraising efforts.

The section continues by describing what an organization should have in place before it can begin asking for money in earnest and finishes with the group of people that is going to be key to a successful fundraising effort: the board of directors.

The Landscape of the Nonprofit Sector

The word *nonprofit* is used to distinguish organizations that work for the public good without seeking profit. Unlike businesses and corporations, which may work for the public good, nonprofit organizations are not beholden to individuals or shareholders to deliver a profit, even though they still have to operate in a businesslike manner and pay attention to their financial health. Over the past thirty years, the word *nonprofit* has gradually replaced the word *charity*, as more and more nonprofit organizations do work that is not strictly "charitable," such as community organizing, advocacy, arts, or environmental protection. The word *charity* also carried a whiff of noblesse oblige—upper-class, "fortunate" people helping the "less fortunate." This whole concept and way of doing business has been rejected by progressive nonprofits, which seek more to work "with" people than "for" them.

Many have argued that *nonprofit* is an unfortunate word, as it describes an entire sector by what it is not, and have suggested using the term *community benefit organization* (CBO) instead. In most countries other than the United States, nonprofits are referred to as "nongovernmental organizations" (NGOs) to distinguish them from the work of government. In this book, I use the term *nonprofit* most of the time. While recognizing its limitations, I also know that it is the most commonly used and commonly understood word to describe the sector in the United States. To describe an individual nonprofit entity, I mostly use the word *organization* or *agency*. To remind ourselves that we are organizations set up to benefit the community, and that we do not take the place of government, I will occasionally use NGO.

The word *philanthropy* comes from two Greek words that together mean "love of people." In modern times, this goodwill or humanitarianism is often expressed in donations of property, money, or volunteer time to worthy causes. Similarly, the word *charity* comes from a Latin word meaning *love* in the sense of unconditional loving kindness, compassion, and seeking to do good. The roots of these words remind us of the fundamental reasons for the work of most nonprofit organizations.

Measured as a share of total employment, the nonprofit sector in the United States is the fifth largest in the world. The Netherlands has the largest proportional nonprofit sector, followed by Canada, Belgium, and Ireland. (For more information on nonprofit sectors in other countries, see *Global Civil Society: Dimensions of the Nonprofit Sector* by Lester Salomon and others and *The Canadian Nonprofit and Voluntary Sector in Comparative Perspective* by Michael Hall and others, both of which can be found at ImagineCanada.ca.)

If the nonprofit sector in the United States were a single industry, it would rank as the nation's largest industry, accounting for about 10 percent of the workforce and about 5 percent of the gross domestic product. As of 2010, more than 1,800,000 organizations in the United Sates were listed on the Guidestar Web site (which collects information on nonprofits) as organizations recognized as nonprofits by the Internal Revenue Service.

Several million more small, grassroots organizations are not registered with the government and have no formal tax status. These include organizations just getting started; organizations that use very little money, such as neighborhood block clubs; organizations that come together for a one-time purpose, such as cleaning up a vacant lot or protesting something; and organizations that don't wish to have a structural relationship with the state or federal government.

Because of the size and growing sophistication of the nonprofit sector, it has increasingly drawn government attention, as well as that of researchers, academics, and many members of the general public. Although recognized nonprofits are regulated by federal, state, and local government laws and regulations, public awareness coupled with the role of individuals in funding nonprofits means that voluntary compliance with accepted ethical standards of accounting, personnel, and fundraising practices provides an added, and usually sufficient, layer of self-regulation. Nonprofit status is a public trust, and tax exemption is, in effect, a public expense. Even if an organization has no formal tax status, if it seeks to raise money from the public it has the same moral duty as registered nonprofits to operate ethically, be truthful with donors, and provide the highest quality of services to clients.

THE FOUNDATION AND CORPORATE GIVING MYTH

As with many endeavors that are critically important and use the resources of millions of people, it is not surprising that a number of misconceptions have grown up about philanthropy and charities.

The most serious misconception for fundraising is many people's belief that most money given to nonprofits comes from foundations and corporations. The truth is far different. About half of all the income of all nonprofits is earned income: that is, it comes from fees for service or products for sale. About 30 percent of nonprofit income is derived from government funding programs (collectively known as "the public sector"). Extensive cutbacks in government funding starting in the 1980s and continuing to the present day have reduced government funding a great deal, but it remains a significant source for many organizations. The final 20 percent of nonprofit income is from the private sector: individuals, foundations, and corporations. For most of the organizations using this book, the private sector will supply the majority of your funding. Surprisingly to most people, individuals give the bulk of private-sector funding, far more than all donated foundation and corporate money combined.

This book focuses almost entirely on how to raise money from that enormous market of individual donors.

I said earlier that there is now an enormous body of research on philanthropy, both in the United States and in other countries, and most of this research tries to determine who gives, why they give, and to what they give. The most widely used report is *Giving USA,* compiled yearly by the American Association of Fund Raising Counsel. Every year since 1935, Counsel authors have calculated just how much money was given away to nonprofits and which sources gave how much. They have identified four sources of gifts from the private (nongovernmental) sector: living individuals, bequests (a cash or other donation an individual arranges to be given to a nonprofit on his or her death), foundations, and corporations. Their research shows that the proportion of giving from each of these sources remains constant, varying from year to year by only two or three percentage points, with gifts from individuals (living or deceased) exceeding the rest by 9 to 1.

A look at the numbers brings this reality out starkly. The chart shows private-sector giving for the year 2009.

Sources of Contributions, 2009		
From	Amount in Billions	Percentage of Total
Individuals	227.41	75.0
Bequests	23.80	8.0
Foundations	38.44	13.0
Corporations	14.10	4.0
Totals	303.75	100.0

Given these facts, an organization should have no trouble knowing where to go for money: individuals provide the vast bulk of private support to nonprofits.

WHO GIVES AWAY MONEY?

The logical follow-up question—Who are these people?—is more difficult to answer because there are many complex variables that make it difficult to draw a single profile of givers. One way to begin to answer the question is to look at how and what data are collected on giving.

There are three main ways to collect data on giving:

- Analyze tax returns of people who itemize and extrapolate from the results

- Survey a random sample of the population and extrapolate from their responses

- Compare either or both of the results from these methods with what is reported from charities either in their reports to the IRS on their income (these reports are on the IRS Form 990 and are often referred to simply as 990s) or in polls and surveys

Further research can done by demographic variables, such as age or income, or by carrying out longitudinal studies (following the same people over several years) comparing donors and non-donors via surveys, detailed focus groups, or other methods.

Discrepancies in reports about who gives away money and how much they give largely turn on the study methodology employed. *Giving USA* looks at itemized tax returns, which limits its results because only 30 percent of Americans file an itemized return. The 70 percent of Americans who file a "short form" do not exceed the standard deduction and therefore receive no special tax benefits from their giving. Estimating how much people who do not itemize gifts on their tax return give is done with an econometric model, and there is no reason to think it is wildly inaccurate. However, it is probably conservative, undercounting a lot of giving. Independent Sector, a coalition of approximately six hundred nonprofit organizations that speaks for the sector, bases its data about giving on telephone and written surveys. Arguments can be made for and against all of these methods. Do people who itemize lie on their taxes and exaggerate their giving? Probably. By how much? It's hard to say. Do people exaggerate their generosity to a phone surveyor? Probably. By how much? Again, it's hard to say. People also underreport on their taxes, as a number of studies have shown, and certainly people often forget how much they have given to a nonprofit when they have no incentive, such as a tax deduction, to help them remember. Possibly the exaggerators cancel out the underreporters. Add to that mix that rules about what is tax deductible are confusing even to nonprofits, and we can safely say that it is difficult to say with great accuracy exactly who gives away money and how much they give every year.

There are some other variables that make knowing who gives away money difficult:

- Although the majority of people give money from their annual income, the wealthy minority give from their assets. Some studies looking at who is generous relative to their ability to give only judge generosity by level of income; others look at net worth. These two factors can yield very different results. For example, a family with little income could be wealthy in terms of assets (such as ownership of homes, businesses, art, and the like), or it could be very poor.

- Studies that calculate which region of the country is the most generous usually fail to take into account cost of living. For example, two states may both have a median income of $40,000 per family, but the median cost of housing per year in one state may be $20,000 and in the other twice as much. The people living in the second state might well give less money away than those in the first state; however, factoring in cost of living may reveal that both groups are equally generous.

- Almost all studies try to focus on formal philanthropic giving, but if we were to count the numerous acts of unrecorded kindness—money donated to homeless people on the street, or sent as remittances to family members in other countries, or help given to a friend to go to college or to a poor family to pay rent for a few months—our studies not only would show much more giving but might yield even more demographic differences among givers.

Looking at what nonprofits declare as income would seem to give the most accurate data, and those figures are helpful to a point. However, giving to religious organizations, which make up a full third of the nonprofit sector, is obscured because these organizations are not required to file 990s, in accordance with the separation of church and state. Likewise, organizations with annual budgets of less than $25,000 are not required to file a 990, which leaves out thousands more organizations.

So you can see the problem of knowing who gives away money and how much: the majority of people are not declaring their giving on their taxes, and a vast number of nonprofits are not reporting their income sources, requiring a good deal of sleuthing on the part of researchers to figure out what might be true.

A final compounding factor is how the U.S. economy has changed over the past ten years. For many years, the vast majority of money given away in the United States came from middle-class and working-class people. In 1998, Independent Sector's research showed that about 82 percent of all giving came from households with incomes of $65,000 or less—the majority of people. Now we have a slightly different reality: *Giving USA* for 2009 reports that households with a gross income of $100,000 or less—92 percent of all households, according to the IRS—contribute approximately 52 percent of all giving, still the majority of giving, but no longer the bulk of giving. The 1 percent of households that have a net worth of $5 million or more, they say, contribute 28 percent of all gifts. Of course the share of private wealth that these households own is more than the bottom 90 percent of all households combined, so they are not particularly generous. (This gap reflects two decades of tax policy that redistributes money to the wealthy.) Bill Gates himself has as much wealth as the total of the bottom 40 percent of households. Other studies looking at the question of just who gives away all this money provide more detail and sometimes more contradictory findings. Some of the most common sources of studies are Independent Sector's biannual study, *Giving and Volunteering in the USA*; the Center on Philanthropy Panel Study (COPPS) at Indiana University; the Center on Wealth and Philanthropy at Boston College; the Foundation Center; the National Center for Charitable Statistics; the NewTithing Group; and empty tomb (for research on religion), just to name a few.

Giving USA notes, "The researchers suggest that the trend toward increasing inequality in income in the past two decades paired with different giving patterns to charitable organizations by income level will affect the overall distribution of contributions among nonprofit organizations in the coming years." Further, as United for a Fair Economy (UFE) points out, as of 2007, that inequality in income is increasing: the pay ratio of the average CEO among the Standard and Poors's 500 companies in the United States (average $10.5 million per CEO) to production worker pay (average $30,617 per worker) is 344 to 1. "Thirty years ago," UFE comments, "chief executives averaged only 30 to 40 times the average American worker paycheck."[1] To put this in perspective, if the minimum wage had risen as fast as CEO pay since 1990, the lowest-paid workers in the United States would be earning $23.03 an hour today, not $5.15 an hour.[2] We have the largest gap between rich and poor of any country in the world, with a shrinking middle class.

WHAT IS TRUE ABOUT WHO GIVES

Despite the difficulties inherent in research about who gives, there are some facts that are found in a number of studies, remain constant year after year, and are borne out by the experience of development professionals all over the world.

- About seven out of ten adults in the United States give away money. Where these numbers have been studied more closely on a local level, we see some interesting variations. For example, in Hawai'i, nine out of ten adults give away

---

[1] Sarah Anderson and others, Institute for Policy Studies, and Mike Lapham, United for a Fair Economy, *Executive Excess 2008*, August 25, 2008.

[2] United for a Fair Economy.

money, compared to Alaska, where six out of ten give. In Boulder, Colorado, where I grew up, a smaller percentage of the population gives away money than in nearby Denver. Eight out of ten Canadians give away money, but more people give away money in Nova Scotia than in British Columbia. (Here's a fun sampling from around the world: in Holland, almost 90 percent of the population gives away money, despite paying very high taxes. In South Korea, 64 percent give; in the Philippines, 80 percent.)

- Middle- and lower-income donors are responsible for a significant percentage of the money given—from 50 to 80 percent—and are the majority of givers.

- The vast majority of donations come from families with annual incomes of less than $90,000.

- Most people who give to nonprofits give to at least five and as many as fifteen groups.

- About 20 percent of people on welfare give away money (average gift of $74) and about 97 percent of millionaires give away money.

- Volunteers are more likely to be donors than are people who don't volunteer.

- More people give away money than vote.

- The majority of people who give away money describe themselves as religious or spiritual, whether or not they are involved in a formal religious or spiritual community.

- And finally, a theme I will return to a thousand times: people give when they are asked.

In the United States, the lion's share of private-sector giving, according to all studies, goes to religion. Religious organizations also make up the majority of nonprofits in the United States. Religion has lost market share over the years. When I entered the field of fundraising in 1976, religious giving was 50 percent of all giving; now it is just over 30 percent.

Regardless of the methodology used or the variables considered, study after study gives us a picture of a generous country, with most people making donations and feeling good about doing so. They also give us a picture of middle- and lower-income donors making up a significant percentage of all money given away and of a constantly increasing amount of money given every year.

Foundations and corporations, which have the false reputation of keeping charity alive, are overrated as a source of funds, and the help they can provide is often misunderstood. Although foundation and corporate giving will always play a vital role in the nonprofit sector, the limitations of that role must be clearly understood.

FOUNDATIONS

Foundations give away relatively little money compared to individuals, and that money is in very great demand. Many of the larger foundations report receiving a hundred proposals for every two they are able to fund. As more information about foundations is easily available, the demand is increasing. Online databases help potential grantees identify more and more sources. Most foundations that publish guidelines and annual reports post them on the Internet, and increasingly ask to receive proposals by e-mail. Some progressive foundations have adopted a standard grant application form, allowing grantees to submit exactly the same proposal for many different foundations. The very things that thus make foundations more accessible also make them inundated with requests.

Although many nonprofits, especially new or small organizations, think foundation funding would be the answer to their money problems, in fact foundation funding is designed to be used only for short-term projects. These include the startup of a new organization and its first few years of operation; capital improvements; new programs; one-time projects, such as studies or conferences; capacity building; or help through a particularly rough period in the life of an organization for which it has a good excuse and a recovery plan. More recently, foundations have been creating "initiatives," for which they focus most or all of their grant-making on one area, such as preschools, youth organizing, or immigrants' rights. These initiatives are often helpful for bringing together a number of organizations working on the same issue, allowing them to share ideas and create joint strategies. Sometimes several foundations join an initiative. However, the foundation funding invariably dries up before the problems identified by the initiatives have been solved, leaving organizations that have relied heavily on this funding unable to continue programs that may just have been starting to show success. Many foundations, recognizing the limits of their funding, have provided capacity-building grants, which are largely efforts to help organizations move away from the foundation to a more diverse set of income streams.

If an organization has come to rely on foundation funding, decreasing reliance should be an important part of its financial planning. If an organization has never become reliant on foundation funding, it should plan not to. And all organizations should guard against making the mistake common to many small organizations of seeking more foundation funding as the years pass rather than less.

CORPORATIONS

Corporations are different from foundations in a key way: unlike foundations, whose job is to give money away, corporations exist to make money. Giving money away is primarily an activity that a corporation hopes will directly or indirectly help it to make more money. Even so, only 11 percent of corporations give away any money at all, and the average amount these companies give away is a mere 1 percent of their pretax profits, even though they are allowed to give away up to 10 percent of those profits.

Corporations generally give money to the following types of organizations or activities:

- Organizations that improve the life of the community where their employees live (symphonies, parks, museums, libraries)

- Organizations that help their employees be more productive by addressing common employee problems (alcohol and drug rehabilitation, domestic violence, stress reduction, wellness)

- Organizations that provide volunteer opportunities for employees, or to which employees make donations

- Research activities that will help the company invent products or market existing products (various departments in universities get much of their research funding from corporations)

- Education programs for young people to ensure an adequate future workforce for the company (literacy programs, innovative schools, scholarships, internships)

More frequent and generous is corporate giving to match employee donations. Although many corporations have had matching gift programs for some time, the scale of today's matching programs has come to be called "employee-driven philanthropy." For this reason it is important to know where your donors work and whether their corporation will match their gift.

Corporations also make valuable donations besides money, such as expertise (loaning a worker to help a nonprofit with accounting, marketing, or personnel), space (free use of conference or meeting rooms), printing, furniture, office equipment (computers, printers, fax machines, copy machines), building materials, and so on.

The past couple of decades have seen many corporations joining with nonprofits in what is called "cause-related marketing" efforts, in which a corporation donates a certain percentage of its profits from a particular item or a certain amount of each sale to its partner nonprofit. The agency and the corporation advertise the arrangement and encourage people who may be choosing among similar products to choose the one that also benefits the nonprofit. Variations on this theme include corporations that offer to give a percentage of profits to a certain kind of organization (environmental, progressive, feminist) or that allow customers to nominate groups that should receive corporate funding. Cause-related marketing has benefited many organizations by allowing shoppers to feel that their spending can also serve a charitable purpose, but it does not serve to build a donor base.

Some organizations using this book will not be able to get corporate funding because their work is too controversial, others are not located near any corporate headquarters, and others will not seek corporate funding because they wish to avoid appearing to endorse a corporate product or a particular corporation's way of doing business. However, for those who do wish to seek corporate funding, keep in mind that the key element is knowing someone in the corporation. Having "a friend at the bank"—literally and figuratively—is important, and the many ways a corporation can help you should not be overlooked. Just like foundation giving, however, corporate giving should not be relied on.

THE POWER OF INDIVIDUAL GIVING

It should be clear by now that a broad base of individual donors provides the only reliable source of funding for a nonprofit year in and year out, and the growth of individual donations to an organization is critical to its growth and self-sufficiency. Further, relying on a broad base of individuals for support increases an organization's ability to be self-determining: it does not need to base program priorities on what foundations, corporations, or government agencies will fund.

Recipients of Charitable Giving

To really understand private-sector giving, it is important to look at not only who gives this money but also who receives it. Again, with only a few percentage points of variation from year to year, *Giving USA* has reported a consistent pattern of where gifts go. A little more than one-third of all the money given away in the United States goes to religious organizations, with education a distant second, followed by human services, health, the arts, and five other categories that receive small percentages of giving.

Uses of Contributions, 2009		
Contributions to	**Amount in Billions**	**Percentage of Total**
Religion	100.95	33.0
Education	40.01	13.0
Health	22.46	7.0
Human services	27.08	9.0
Arts, culture, humanities	12.34	4.0
Public-society benefit*	22.77	8.0
Environment or animals	6.15	2.0
International affairs	8.89	3.0
Gifts to foundations**	31.00	10.0
Foundation grants to individuals	3.51	1.0
Unallocated giving***	28.59	10.0
Totals	303.75	100.0

*This category includes organizations that work in the areas of community organizing and civil rights and civil liberties as well as United Way, Jewish Federation, and other combined funds, such as the Combined Federal Campaign.

**This category includes giving to community and private foundations.

***This category includes deductions carried over, which are amounts claimed for a gift made up to five years earlier. These deductions apply when charitable contributions exceed 50 percent of a taxpayer's gross adjusted income and for grants made by foundations to organizations outside the United States. Most interesting to anyone concerned about privatization, these deductions also apply to deductible gifts individuals give to government entities, such as public schools, public libraries, public health departments, and the like. Government entities are not required to report private gifts, mostly because no one ever thought public agencies would be raising money privately.

Source: Giving USA, 2010

Giving to Religion

Religion as a category receives one-third of every charitable dollar; only a small percentage of giving to religion is from foundations and virtually none of it is from corporations. Until recently, because of the constitutional separation of "church" and state, religious activity received little government funding either, except for when providing a specific social service. President George W. Bush created an office called Faith-Based and Neighborhood Partnerships that provided some money to religious organizations and helped programs run by faith-based organizations or houses of worship know what federal grant dollars might be available to them. Today this office does not administer federal grant programs but still provides assistance in identifying grant opportunities (whitehouse.gov/administration/oep.ofnp). Many religious groups opted not to apply for this money because they did not believe religious organizations should do the work of government; those that did receive funding often found the process onerous for the amount of money that was actually available. Even with this money, the vast majority of funding that religious organizations receive is from their own members.

We can learn a lot by examining what makes fundraising for religious institutions so successful. At first glance, many people think that religious institutions receive so much money because of their theology: the reward of heaven, the blessing of giving, the threat of eternal damnation for those who do not give. Although these enticements may play a role in some people's giving, it is clear that in the wide variety of religious expression, these motives are not enough. Some religious traditions do not believe in any form of eternal life; some don't even believe in God. Even in traditions that encompass some of these beliefs, mature adults can be given more credit than to think that their behavior is based simply on a desire for rewards or a fear of punishment.

So, why do religious organizations receive almost one-third of all private-sector dollars? Although religious institutions offer ideas and commitments that are of great value, the reason they get money—and this is key to understanding successful fundraising—is that they ask for it.

Let's take as an example a Protestant or Catholic church. (If you are of a different religious tradition, compare your own tradition to what follows.) Here is how they raise money:

- They ask every time worshippers are assembled, which is at least once a week.

- They make it easy to give: a basket is passed to each person in the service and all gifts are acceptable, from loose change to large checks. Everyone—whether out-of-town visitor, occasional churchgoer, or loyal and generous congregant—is given the same opportunity to give. The ushers are not concerned about offending someone by asking. They would never say, "Don't pass the basket to Phyllis Frontpew—she just bought the new carpet," or "Skip over Joe because he just lost his job."

- They make it easy to give, even if you are not a regular congregant. Once a year, most houses of worship have some kind of stewardship drive or all-member canvass; in many churches, someone will come to your house and ask you how much you will be pledging this year. You can pay your pledge by the week, month, or quarter or give a one-time gift. The option of pledging and paying over time allows people to give a great deal more over the course of a year than most could in a single lump sum.

- They provide a variety of programs to which you can give as you desire. If you are particularly interested in the youth program you can give to that, or you can buy flowers for the altar, support the music program, or help fund overseas missions. Many churches have scholarships, homeless shelters, food banks, or other social programs. And of course, if you are a "bricks and mortar" person, you can contribute to any number of capital improvements: new hymnals, a new window, a better organ, or a whole new sanctuary.

Finally, religious institutions approach fundraising with the attitude that they are doing you as much of a favor to ask as you will be doing them to give. In other words, they recognize that fundraising allows an exchange to happen between a person who wants to see a certain kind of work get done and an institution that can do that work. If one of your values and beliefs is that a house of worship and the work it does are important, then in order for that institution to exist, you will need to help pay for it. Giving money allows you to express your desire and commitment to be part of a faith community and allows your commitment to be realized.

All organizations should institute the diversity of fundraising methods that characterizes most religious institutions. In the chapters that follow, I will show you how.

chapter TWO

Key Principles of Fundraising

This chapter lays out several key principles that apply to all fundraising: why we do fundraising, where the money should come from, why people give to nonprofits, and who can raise funds.

Let's start with a question: "What does an organization want from fundraising?" The answer: donors. Not donations, but donors, not gifts, but givers. We do fundraising in order to build relationships with a broad cross-section of people who will do some or all of the following: give themselves, ask others to give, open doors to institutional giving, volunteer, say nice things about our organization, and so on. You want people to make donations and to feel so good about how they were treated and what you did with the money they gave that they want to give again and again.

Focusing on building a donor base rather than on simply raising money means that sometimes you will undertake a fundraising strategy that does not raise money in the first year, such as direct mail, or that may not raise money for several years, such as legacy giving. It means that you will relate to your donors as individual human beings rather than as ATMs that you engage when you want money but whom you otherwise ignore. It means you will plan your fundraising for both the short term and the long term and look at the results of any fundraising strategy not only for the next month but also for the next few years.

DIVERSIFYING SOURCES

Focusing on raising donors means that an organization systematically diversifies its sources of funding, increases the number of people helping raise money, and diversifies these people's skills. The need for diversity is not a new lesson. People with only one skill have a more difficult time finding employment than those with a variety of skills. Investors put their money in a variety of financial instruments. Thousands of organizations have had to cut back or even close because they relied too heavily on one or two foundations or one government contract.

Yet many organizations continue to look for the ideal special event that will fund their entire budget, or they search for one person, foundation, or corporation that will give most of the money they need, or they try to hire the perfect fundraiser who will bring in all their income without the help of anyone else in the organization. These organizations reason that if they could use one fundraising strategy that was absolutely certain, tried and true, or hire the one fundraising staff person who could do it all—their money worries would be over. Unfortunately, no fundraising strategy or person fits that description. In fact, only if it maintains a diversity of sources will an organization survive for the long term.

Organizations should not receive more than 30 percent of their funding from any one source for more than one or two years. An organization could lose 30 percent of its funding and probably survive, though it would be difficult, but to lose more than 30 percent of one year's funding would be catastrophic for all but the biggest organizations. This guideline about diversifying sources of income means that although you could have more than 30 percent of income coming from membership (and many nonprofits do), you cannot have one member providing 30 percent of this money. The IRS recognizes this principle with its "one-third rule," which states that an organization with one-third or more of its total income from one person, foundation, or corporation for more than three years does not meet the test of a public charity; if this condition persists for several years, an organization risks losing its 501(c)(3) status. Public charities are to be supported by a cross-section of the public and not to be hobbies of one or two people while operating with the tax advantages of public charities.

There is no set number of sources that constitutes healthy diversity. Much will depend on the size of your budget as well as on your location and your work. However, for organizations that seek to raise a significant amount of money from individuals, clearly, the more people who give you money, and the more ways you have of raising money, the better off you are.

WHY PEOPLE GIVE

To build that broad base of donors, it useful to understand what motivates people to give. As I noted in Chapter One, about 70 percent of adults in the United States regularly make donations to nonprofits, and most of those who give support between five and eleven organizations. Fundraising efforts should therefore go toward trying to become one of the organizations that these givers give to. Unless your focus is on bringing young people into your organization with their first donation, do not spend a lot of effort trying to be the first organization that someone gives to who has never given money before. In general, people who don't give away money are unlikely to change this habit: it is not that they just haven't found the right NGO yet, it is that they are not givers. People who give money are going to give it away. They will give it to your organization or to another organization, and they are not denying their family food or their children shoes when they do so. Your organization's job is to become one of the nonprofits they support. To do that you first must examine what makes a person a giver, and while you are reading this, think about what makes you a giver, assuming that you are part of the majority of people around the world who give away money.

THE MULTIPLE REASONS WHY PEOPLE GIVE AWAY MONEY

There are many reasons why people give to nonprofit organizations. The most common reason by far why people give to a particular nonprofit is that they were asked. People are more likely to remember how they were asked than the name of the organization they gave to. In addition to responding to being asked, there are many other motives for giving, which vary from consumerism to tradition to deeply held beliefs. Some people give because they like the organization's newsletter or because they will receive a free tote bag, bumper sticker, or some other tangible item. Some give to a certain organization because everyone in their social circle gives to that group or because it is a family tradition. Some give because it is the only way to get something the organization offers (classes, theater seats, access to a swimming pool).

At a more altruistic level, there are more reasons for giving. People give because they care about the issue and because they believe the organization's analysis of a problem and vision for a solution are correct. Often people give because they or someone they know were once in the position of the people the agency serves (alcoholics, abused women or children, unemployed, homeless) or because they are thankful that neither they nor anyone they know is in that position.

Sometimes people give because they feel guilty about how much they have or what they have done in their own life, or in order to feel more assured of forgiveness.

People give because the nonprofit expresses their own ideals and enables them to reinforce their image of themselves as a principled and generous person—for example, "I am a feminist, environmentalist, pacifist, equal rights advocate, good parent, concerned citizen," or whatever values are important to them. Through their giving, they can say in truth, "I am a caring person," "I have deep feelings for others," "I am helping others."

When people are asked personally by a friend or someone they admire to give to a particular organization, in addition to feeling good about giving to the organization, they get to show themselves as kind and open-hearted to someone whose opinion they value.

Although these motivations for giving are what impel most people to give, most nonprofit organizations do not specifically appeal to them. Instead, they focus on two other reasons they think will motivate people to give but that are not very persuasive. These are, "We need the money" and "Your gift is tax deductible." Neither of these reasons distinguishes your organization from all the others. All nonprofit organizations claim to need money, and most of them do. The fact that the gift is tax deductible is a nice touch, but gifts to more than one million other nonprofits are tax deductible too. Further, 71 percent of Americans file a "short form" (meaning they don't have enough deductions to exceed the standard deduction), so they actually receive no tax benefits for their giving. Neither need nor tax advantage makes your organization special or particularly worthy of a gift.

The 70 percent of Americans who give away money pay nonprofits to do work that can only be accomplished by group effort. There is very little one person can do about racism or pollution or world hunger. There are few services, such as child care, after-school enrichment, or health care, that a single person can offer. Only as part of an organization can an individual make a difference in these or any other pressing social problems. Certainly, one person cannot be a theater or a museum or an alternative school—but many people can be entertained or educated by these organizations. Donors need the organization as much as the organization needs them, and the money is given in exchange for work performed. In a way, donations are a form of fee for service.

ANYONE CAN DO FUNDRAISING

Most important for small organizations, it is critical to understand that fundraising is easy to learn. In the past thirty years, there has been an increasing emphasis on fundraising as a "discipline." Colleges and universities offer courses on various aspects of fundraising, sometimes as part of degree programs in nonprofit management, and professional organizations offer fundraising certification programs. More and more people are professional fundraisers. All of these developments contribute to the health and well-being of the nonprofit sector. But a course, a degree, or certification is not required for a person to be good at fundraising, and they will never take the place of the only three things you really need to be a successful fundraiser: simple common sense, a commitment to a cause, and a basic affection for people.

No one says at the age of twelve, "When I grow up, I want to be in fundraising." Instead, a person is drawn to an idea or cause and to an organization working on that issue. The organization needs money in order to pursue the cause, so the person decides to help with fundraising even though it is not her first choice of how to be involved and even though she initially has found the idea of raising money slightly distasteful or a little frightening. With time and experience, many people find that fundraising is not as difficult as they had imagined; and many others even begin to like it. They realize that people feel good about themselves when they give money to a cause they believe in and that to ask someone for money actually means to give that person an opportunity to express traditions or beliefs that are important to them.

People asked to raise money often project the distaste they may feel about asking for money and assume that those being asked feel the same about giving money. In fact, there is a significant difference between the two. Rarely do people feel good when they ask for money until they get used to it, but people almost always feel good about giving money. In asking situations, potential donors are more than likely flattered, pleased to be included, and thinking about what amount they could give.

The feelings of discomfort in asking for money are normal; in Chapter Six I talk about them and how to deal with them. For now, be clear that asking and giving are two very different experiences, even when they happen in the same conversation. When people are recruited to ask for money, they must reflect on what they like about giving, not on what they hate about asking.

When an organization has a diverse number of ways to raise money, it can use the talents and abilities of all the people in the group to help with fundraising. As volunteers and board members learn more about fundraising and experience success doing it, they will be willing to learn new strategies and they will begin to like asking for money. Further, an organization that has only one or two people raising its funding is not much better off than an organization that has only one or two sources of money. Many small organizations have suffered more from having too few people doing the fundraising than from having too few sources of funds. In the chapters that follow, I discuss how to identify appropriate fund-raising strategies and how to build a team of volunteer fundraisers.

chapter THREE

Matching Fundraising Strategies with Financial Needs

O rganizations have three financial needs: the money they need to operate every year, not surprisingly called *annual* needs; the money they need to improve their building or upgrade their capacity to do their work, called *capital* needs; and a permanent income stream to ensure financial stability and assist long-term planning, the source of which is either an *endowment* or a *reserve fund*.

ANNUAL NEEDS

Most organizations spend most of their time raising money for the program needs of the current year. This kind of fundraising is often referred to as the "annual fund" or the "annual drive" or, to cover all tracks, the "annual fund drive." The annual fund uses several strategies, such as online fundraising, direct mail, special events, phoning, and personal visits. The purpose of the annual fund is to acquire new donors and to encourage current donors to give again and, if possible, to give bigger gifts.

Because the overall purpose of fundraising is to build a base of donors who give you money every year, it is helpful to analyze how a person becomes a donor to an organization and how, ideally, that person increases his or her loyalty to the group and expresses that increased loyalty with a steady increase in giving.

In moving from having never given to a particular group to giving regularly year after year and sometimes several times a year, a person goes through three phases. The first phase starts when a person is asked to give to an organization she hears or reads about and likes the sound of and decides on the spur of the moment to make a donation. That first gift is called an "impulse" gift. Even if an impulse gift is fairly large, it will rarely reflect what the donor could really afford and it is generally based on little knowledge or commitment to the organization. This is the moment at which the organization seeks to move this donor to the second phase. The donor is thanked as soon as possible; then, several times during the course of the year, she is asked for additional gifts to different areas of the organization's work. Ideally, the donor is asked in a few different ways, such as by phone, at an event, or with a personal letter. Each year the donor is asked and, if she continues to give, after three or more years she has become what is called a "habitual" donor. Habitual donors see themselves as part of the organization and identify with the work and the victories of the organization. Some habitual donors have a bigger commitment to the organization than their gift reflects and have the capacity to make a bigger gift. Identifying and asking these people to increase their gift forms the basis of a major donor program.

Once donors are giving larger gifts than they give to most other nonprofits, they have entered the third phase, called "thoughtful" giving. Instead of just giving what they are in the habit of giving, they now think about what they can afford and how making a large gift to one group will affect their other giving.

The process of moving people from nondonor to donor, then to habitual donor, and then to thoughtful donor is the main focus in planning the annual fund. To maintain its annual income, an organization has to recruit a certain number of new donors every year, upgrade a certain number of regular donors into major donors, and give all their donors three or four chances to give extra gifts.

Here are some thoughts on the subject of asking several times a year. Some people say they dislike receiving several appeals a year from a group. But because one donor doesn't like to be asked more than once a year, it doesn't mean that most people are like that. Many people don't even notice how often they are asked, particularly if you are using a few different strategies. Some donors give every time they are asked, and many donors find being asked a few times a year a good way to keep up with the work of the organization. However, since fundraising is a process of building relationships, if a donor says to you, "I only give once a year, so please only ask me once a year," then you will go into your database and suppress that person's name for any extra appeals. If a donor says, "Don't ever call me on the phone," you similarly note in his or her file not to call that person.

An organization can expect to retain about two-thirds of its individual donors every year, with the greatest proportion of the one-third loss being people who give once and not again. In planning fundraising strategies, then, you need a few strategies for the sole purpose of replacing lost donors. Organizations that lose a lot fewer than one-third of their donor base most likely do not have enough donors—almost any organization can keep a small group of donors renewing year in and year out. You want to grow big enough that you are bringing in a lot of new donors, knowing that up to one-third of them will not stay. Organizations that lose more than one-third of their donors are not doing enough to keep them; in the case of most grassroots organizations, this situation usually means they are not asking donors for money often enough or thanking them when they do give. Remember, every organization a donor belongs to is asking several times a year, and donors are also being solicited by organizations they haven't given to. If you only ask once a year, yours becomes a minuscule percentage of the solicitations the donor receives. In fact, many lapsed donors report that they don't remember receiving any requests from the organization, and that it was not their intent for their membership to lapse. To retain your donors, you need to use a few strategies designed just for them.

Finally, you need to have some strategies to get current donors to give more money—these are called upgrading strategies. Sections Two and Three discuss a wide variety of retention and upgrade strategies and their uses.

CAPITAL NEEDS

In addition to the money an organization needs each year and what strategies will be used to raise that money, organizations occasionally need to raise extra money for capital improvements. Capital needs can range from new computers to the cost of buying and refurbishing an entire building. A capital expense is a one-time or infrequent expense that is too large for the annual budget. Most donors who give capital gifts have given thoughtfully to an annual fund. They know your organization, they believe in your cause, and they have the resources to help you with a special gift. These resources could be stocks, bonds, real estate, or any very large source of income. These gifts are given only a few times in a donor's lifetime, and they are almost always requested in person (see Chapter Twenty-Six, "Capital Campaigns").

ENDOWMENT AND RESERVE FUNDS

An endowment or a reserve fund is a glorified savings account in which an organization invests money and uses the interest from that investment to augment its annual budget; the invested amount, or principal, is not spent. Endowment funds are raised in many ways, but the most common source is legacy gifts, such as bequests. A gift from a person's estate is in some ways the most thoughtful gift of all and usually reflects a deep and abiding commitment to an organization. It also reflects the donor's belief that the organization will continue to exist and do important work long after the donor is dead. The idea of making an endowment gift can be introduced to donors in a variety of ways, but most often a person making such a gift has a personal relationship with the organization. An endowment is much more permanent than a reserve fund, and organizations that hope that someday their work will no longer be needed (which is what most social change groups are working toward) will want to think carefully about having an endowment. A reserve fund allows you to put money aside, use the interest, and occasionally use the principal. (How to set up an endowment is discussed in Chapter Twenty-Four, "Setting Up an Endowment").

THE STORY OF GINA GENEROUS

To understand how a person might move from not giving at all to becoming a thoughtful donor and then to leaving the organization a bequest, imagine the following scenario:

Gina Generous comes home from work tired and frustrated. It's been a long day. She feeds her cats, kicks off her shoes, and sits down to glance through what little snail mail she still gets now that most correspondence is online. Most of this postal mail she characterizes as "junk" and throws away, but one piece of direct mail catches her eye. It's not fancy or even very well designed, but it is from a local program for women previously on welfare. Gina is attracted to the agency's mission statement, "We believe in the power of women to change and the potential of each woman to give all women power." Gina generally supports women's causes. She opens the letter, reads it quickly, and decides to send a small gift. As she waits for her dinner to cook, she writes out a check for $35 and puts it in the return envelope that came with the appeal. She mails it the next day and forgets about the group.

This impulse gift does not represent Gina's true giving ability or say very much about her commitment to or even knowledge of that particular organization. Now the program must try to get Gina to give again so that she begins to be a regular or "habitual" donor.

In a few days Gina again comes home tired, and again feeds her cats and starts her dinner. In her mail, she finds a short, personal thank you note from the program. "Wow. How nice," she thinks. She again feels good about her gift and the name of the organization is more firmly planted in her mind.

Over the next few months, Gina receives a copy of the program's newsletter. She looks at its Web site and becomes a "friend" on its Facebook page. One day she drives by the organization's office and is amazed at how many people are going in and out of the front door. About three months after her first gift, Gina receives another letter from the program. This letter thanks her again for her previous gift and asks if she can make a special, extra gift to help buy some playground equipment so that children of the women at the program have a nice place to play while their mothers take classes and receive coaching on job skills. Gina is touched by the request and sends $50. Again, she is personally thanked with a note that specifically mentions her gift, "Thanks so much for your extra gift of $50." Gina appreciates that the organization notices these extra gifts. Three months later, she is asked again for a special extra gift—this one to help defray the costs of a job training program that will partially be funded by the city. Although Gina thinks this is an important program, she has also had to replace two tires on her car, so does not give in response to this appeal.

Three months after that—now nine months since her first gift—she is invited to an open house and tour of the program. She attends and meets the director and some board members, including some graduates of the program. Everyone who attends the open house is asked to leave a check in a jar by the door if possible. Gina gives another $25.

Over the next two years, this pattern is repeated. Gina comes to a few events. In response to an e-mail, she volunteers to help with the phone-a-thon. Having signed onto the organization's action alert e-mail list, from time to time Gina calls her Congressperson or signs a petition to advocate for better services and more funding for welfare-to-work programs.

By now, Gina has moved from being an impulse donor to being a habitual donor to the program. Whenever she receives a request for funds, she gives unless she really can't afford to. She now sees herself as a part of this organization. She forwards e-mails from the organization to friends and recommends that her family give donations to the program instead of buying her birthday presents.

After two years of giving small gifts two or three times a year, now mostly online or at a special event, Gina receives a personal letter signed by a board member asking her to consider joining the "Sustainer Circle" by contributing $25 per month. The letter thanks her for her past support, reminds her of how important the programs are, and asks her not to make a decision until the board member calls her. Gina now has to think about the organization: How important is it to her? Does she care enough to have $25 charged to her credit card every month? Can she afford it? What will she want to find out from the board member to help make her decision?

Whatever her decision, Gina has moved to the next level, a thoughtful donor. She may decide to give $25 a month, or she may decide to give a one-time gift of $100, or she may continue to give small gifts a few times a year, but she has had to think about her giving to the organization. After talking with the board member, she decides to join the monthly donor program.

Over the course of about three years, Gina's relationship to the organization went from impersonal (giving by mail) to a little more personal (attending events and volunteering for short-term projects) to very personal (being solicited by a member of the board).

Over the next few years, Gina is asked to give both time and money; after ten years of being a regular donor to the organization, she is giving $2,000 a year. That year, the group decides to buy a new building. The building will cost $1,500,000 and will become a model for this type of program as well as saving money for the program by enabling it to bring all its services on-site. The group receives $950,000 in state and federal funding for the purchase of the building and $250,000 total from two foundations, along with $50,000 from corporate donors. The group must raise the remaining $250,000 from individuals. The group launches a campaign to ask each current donor for a capital gift in addition to their annual gift. Because she is both a reliable volunteer and a steady major donor, Gina is asked to serve on the capital campaign committee. She now knows several board members and the executive director and development director. Gina agrees to serve and decides to give $15,000 that she inherited from an aunt to the capital campaign. She is happy to find a meaningful way to use this money that she had received unexpectedly.

After the campaign is completed, Gina is invited onto the organization's board. The next year, when the organization institutes a legacy giving program, Gina changes her will so that the program is the beneficiary of the bulk of her estate.

The progression to this stage of highly committed donor is natural and Gina feels good about it, but it is the result of careful planning on the part of the organization and reflects its commitment to developing relationships with donors.

THREE GOALS FOR EVERY DONOR

An organization has three goals for every donor. The first is for that person to get to the point of being a thoughtful donor—to give the biggest gift he or she can afford on a yearly basis. Annual gifts usually come from the donor's annual income. The second goal is for as many donors as possible to give gifts to a capital or other special campaign. These do not have to be connected to capital improvements, but they are gifts that are unusual in some way and are only given a few times (or possibly only once) during the donor's lifetime. Capital gifts are usually given from the donors' assets, such as savings, inheritance, or property. A donor cannot afford to give assets every year, so will only give such a gift for a special purpose. The third goal is for every donor to remember the organization in his or her will or to make some kind of arrangement benefiting the organization from his or her estate. An estate gift is arranged during the donor's lifetime but wholly received by the organization on the donor's death. Obviously, these gifts are made only once.

Most small organizations will do well if they can plan a broad range of strategies to acquire, maintain, and upgrade annual gifts, but over time organizations need to think about capital and endowment gifts and learn to use fundraising strategies that will encourage such gifts. Grassroots organizations do receive bequests and gifts of property, art, appreciated stock, and the like. Only by asking will you find out what your donors might be willing and able to do for your organization.

Matching Organizational Needs to Donor Giving

Organization Needs	Donor Helps Using
Annual gifts	Yearly income
Capital gifts	Assets (savings, property, stocks)
Endowment	Estate

THREE TYPES OF STRATEGIES

Because all strategies are directed toward building relationships with funding sources—whether these sources are individuals, as this book stresses, or foundations, corporations, or government—it is important to understand the types of strategies that create or improve relationships with donors. There are three broad categories of strategies—acquisition strategies, retention strategies, and upgrading strategies—that directly relate to the cycles that donors follow: giving impulsively, giving habitually, and giving thoughtfully.

Acquisition Strategies.   The main purpose of acquisition strategies is to get people who have not given to your group before to give for the first time. Direct mail appeals, online appeals, or some kinds of special events are the most common acquisition strategies. Acquisition strategies seek impulse donors, and the income from them is generally used for the organization's annual fund. The main purpose of getting a donor to give for the first time is to be able to ask him or her for a second gift. The income from the first gift is rarely significant, and the cost of getting the gift may be as much or more as the gift itself (see Chapter Eleven, "Using Direct Mail," to see how this works).

Retention Strategies.   Retention strategies seek to get donors to give a second time, a third time, and so on, until they are donors of habit. The income from retention strategies is also used for annual needs. Donors who give regularly, year in and year out, are the bread and butter of individual donor programs. During downturns in the economy, if these donors remain employed, they will continue to give and may even give more. These donors tend to be low maintenance—they will continue to give in return for information about what their gift does for the organization and some minimal personal recognition in the form of a thank you note or call.

Upgrading Strategies.   Upgrading strategies aim to get donors to give more than they have given previously—to give a bigger gift regularly, and later to give gifts of assets and a gift of their estate. Upgrading is done almost entirely through personal solicitation, although it can be augmented by e-mail, mail, or phone contact or through certain special events. Upgrading strategies seek to move habitual donors to thoughtful donors. The income from thoughtful donors is used for annual, capital, and endowment needs, depending on the nature of the gift or the campaign for which the gift was sought.

As you create a fundraising plan, note beside each strategy you intend to use whether you are using it for acquiring, retaining, or upgrading donors, and make sure it is the best strategy for that purpose.

HOW ONE ORGANIZATION LEARNED TO USE A STRATEGY CORRECTLY

Eastern Counties Native Plant Society decides to hold some house parties to raise money. Seven board members will invite friends to their homes and ask them for money for the group. The remaining five board members, none of whom want to have a party at their house, will help with invitations, food, cleanup, and so on.

No thought is given to the purpose of these parties beyond the goal of raising money. No one thinks about whether these parties should be used for acquiring, keeping, or upgrading donors. Consequently, each board member has a hodgepodge of people they have invited to the event—some are donors, some never heard of the group but came with a friend who is a donor, and some came because they are neighbors and it seemed that there would be free food. Because there is no attempt to sort lists ahead of time and because many of these board members travel in the same circles, several people are invited to more than one house party.

The parties make a total of about $6,000, so they are not a waste of time and effort, but some donors complain about being invited to so many events, and many people come to the parties but do not make a gift.

The following year, the organization decides to use the same strategy but to be more thoughtful in their fundraising approach. First, they compile a master list of everyone who is going to be invited to ensure that no one is invited to more than one party. Then they designate some parties as being only for people who have not given before, with a sprinkling of current donors to encourage those who aren't donors to give.

They also vary the way they ask for money at the parties. One board member charges people $35 to come to his party so that every person who is there will have made a donation, and he does not do another pitch at the party. Another feels that her friends will give more if she gives a pitch at the party, and she aims for first gifts of $50 to $250 from most of the guests. One board member with a particularly fancy house has an elegant party for current donors; this party is used specifically as an upgrade strategy. The donors who are invited are capable of giving more than they currently do. They are introduced to members of the board and given an opportunity to discuss a political issue related to this group's work and to make recommendations for action. The party is limited to fifteen people; in a follow-up solicitation after the party, each person is asked for $500.

By determining which parties are for which purpose, the organization now increases its earnings from these parties by more than 400 percent, to $25,000, acquires forty new donors, upgrades fifteen donors, and does not receive any complaints. As an unexpected side benefit, three donors offer to give their own house parties.

YOU CAN'T SAVE TIME

For small organizations, the ultimate reason to be thoughtful about fundraising strategies is to work smarter, not harder. The organization in the house party example raised 400 percent more money in their second year of house parties by spending a little more time to think about the strategy more thoroughly. There is a Buddhist saying, "Make haste slowly." This adage applies to fundraising—and especially to the fundraising programs of small organizations with tight budgets, which have little room for errors that result from carelessness and lack of thought.

It is clear to me from years of working with nonprofit organizations that you can never save time. You can put time in on the front end, planning, thinking things through, and doing things right; or you can "save time" on the front end, only to have to spend the time during the middle of the campaign trying to fix what is not working and calm frustrated volunteers and board members; or you can put the time in at the end, clearing up the mess, figuring out who is to blame, grumbling, and having to do more fundraising because what you have done did not raise the money you need. This book will help you be a front-end time user!

chapter FOUR

Creating a Case Statement

The previous two chapters discussed the framework for fundraising, the logic of the fundraising process, and the fact that an organization will ultimately be supported not so much by money itself, but by relationships with individuals who give money because of their increasing commitment to the organization and its work. This chapter presents the first step in successful fundraising—creating a case statement.

Before you can begin to raise money, your organization must state clearly why it exists and what it does. This statement is put in a written document that describes in some detail the need the organization was set up to meet, the way the organization will meet that need, and the capacity of the organization to do so. This is an internal document for use by staff, board, and key volunteers. It is called your "internal case" and, although it is not a secret document, it will have more information than someone at any distance from the organization would want to read. Language and ideas that come from this internal case will be used for developing material on your Web site, in brochures, proposals, reports, speeches—any time you are making a case for supporting your organization to an external source. All materials that are sent out represent the "external case." Everyone close to the organization should agree with the information presented in the internal case statement, and nothing produced by the organization for external use should contradict it. The internal case can be thought of as the original writing, and all the external versions are summaries, restatements, and other kinds of explanations.

THE CONTENTS OF THE CASE STATEMENT

The easiest way to understand a case statement is to imagine the questions a person truly interested in the kind of work you do would ask about your organization. The answers to these questions all have formal names, indicated in parentheses:

"Why do you exist?" (Mission statement)

"What do you do?" (Goals)

"How do you accomplish those goals?" (Objectives or outcomes)

"What have you accomplished?" (Results or history)

"Who is involved in this group and how does it run?" (Structure)

"How much does it cost for your organization to function, and where do you get your money?" (Budget and fundraising plan)

Your internal case statement will have clear, concise explanations for each of these elements: mission, goals, objectives, history, structure, and budget and funding. Some organizations also like to have a statement of vision that describes what the world would be like if your organization completely succeeded in its work. Such a vision statement will often be the first element of a case statement, or will follow the mission statement.

Having this information in one document, with key people in the organization all having copies of it, saves a great deal of time and helps guarantee that information and philosophies that are presented by board members, staff, or volunteers in their personal fundraising letters, in speeches, or in conversations with funders or donors are consistent. Further, it reminds people of why they are raising money—to do the important work of the organization. A good case statement rallies people to the cause and reinvigorates staff and volunteers. Much of the case statement—objectives, history, budget, funding plans—needs to be updated every year, and the entire document should be reviewed at least annually to ensure that everyone is still in agreement with its premises and that the words used still accurately describe what the organization is doing. Many organizations open each board meeting with a recitation of the mission statement and goals, a practice that they find helps keep the meeting on track and focused.

The following sections present an explanation of each of the components of the case statement.

The Mission Statement

The statement of mission, sometimes called the "statement of purpose," answers the question, "Why does your organization exist?" In other words, what does your organization most believe in? What will you not compromise on? This statement is your basic premise and should describe the one thing that unites everything you do. People in an organization will often claim, "We know why we exist," and then describe their programs, but it may not be clear to a listener that the programs meet any particular need or that there is a problem to be solved. For example, an organization that buys run-down or abandoned apartment buildings and then fixes up and rents each unit well below market rates to elderly poor people has this mission statement: "Housing for Seniors believes that everyone should have decent and affordable housing. We work to ensure that there is quality housing for seniors in our community who are living in substandard housing or are homeless." At this time, the program's goal is to buy run-down homes or apartments, rehabilitate them, and then rent them at affordable rates to seniors. However, its mission statement allows it to have a wide variety of goals, such as advocating with the city to provide housing, helping seniors stay in their current homes, educating the public about the housing shortage, or providing loans to seniors so they can purchase affordable housing. Organization members intend to pursue all these goals as the program grows, but they will not need to change their mission statement as the reach of their work expands. Their commitment to go beyond simply providing housing is the result of long discussion among board and staff members during the creation of their mission statement. Some board members wanted the statement to read, "We provide quality housing for seniors." Others felt that promising that Housing for Seniors could actually provide a significant amount of housing for all needy seniors was unrealistic and that such a mission did not hold government agencies, landlords, or even other senior-serving organizations accountable for finding more permanent solutions to the problem of lack of housing for an increasingly elderly population. The desire of some board and staff to do advocacy, pass strict rent control laws, and create policies to keep seniors from losing their homes eventually won over the group, and these efforts are reflected in the mission statement where the word *ensure* replaces *provide*. These can seem like small things, but they have big implications.

Here's another example. An educational organization that primarily teaches economic literacy has this lofty mission: "Authentic human freedom begins with every person living free of economic compulsion. Understanding how economic forces work and how they can be changed is fundamental to this freedom." Its goals include teaching that practices that are unhealthy for people, such as unsafe workplaces, wage discrimination, toxic dumping, substandard housing, and poverty itself, are not unavoidable by-products of a functioning economy, and how societies can be structured to eliminate these injustices. This organization, too, went through a major change in focus while working within its mission. At first it was only teaching people the practical skills of how to live within a budget or how to set up a savings plan; now it includes broader issues of economic literacy, such as understanding how public schools and roads are paid for, what kinds of taxes are fair, and what kinds are not. The organization has also expanded to the much broader work of advocating for changes in the country's basic economic structure. It still teaches very practical classes, but the students are also introduced to much larger ideas. As the organization's work became bigger, its mission became larger.

Organizations need to take the creation and maintenance of a mission statement very seriously. It has an impact on all your programs and the direction of your organization, and when its wording is neglected or hurriedly put together, disagreements in program direction, goals, and even staffing are far more likely to arise and will take far longer to resolve.

A mission statement should be only one or two sentences long. Its purpose is to catch the attention of potential donors so that they will want to learn more. The mission should be passionate, keeping in mind the old saying, "People buy with their hearts first, then their heads." The statement has to be short because people who are delivering it, as well as people you are reaching out to, like you, have a lot on their minds. Your organization and its needs are not foremost, at least at the beginning of a conversation. Further, we live in a world of constant messages—advertising, warnings, directions, prompts, signals. Our conscious mind doesn't even take in most of these messages. We are constantly screening and filtering messages. Your mission statement is one of hundreds of messages coming in, and you don't want people filtering it out. To get through, it has to be brief, compelling, and intriguing. It has to make a person with a lot on their mind stop thinking about all other cares and focus on your organization for a few minutes.

In fact, a good mission statement does only two things: it is a summary of the basic belief of the organization and the people in the organization, and it makes the person hearing or reading it want to ask for more information: "Well, that's very nice, but how are you going to accomplish that mission?" This question allows the organization to describe its goals.

A hint about writing a mission statement: start with "Because" or "We believe" or with a noun, such as "People," "Children," "The future." Avoid using infinitive verbs such as to do, to provide, to help. Infinitive language is goal language.

Goals

Goal statements tell what your organization is going to do about what you believe and indicate the organization's philosophy, which may be expanded in the section on history. The goals are what really distinguish one organization from another, since organizations may have similar missions but very different agendas. For example, two organizations whose missions concern the health of children can have opposite goals. Nonetheless, their mission statements are remarkably similar. Organization A reads, "We believe that the best public policy promotes children's health and well-being." Organization B states, "We believe the health of our children is the highest priority in creating public policy."

The first mission statement belongs to an organization that seeks to ensure that all children receive immunizations. The parents of most of the children who are not immunized in the county are undocumented workers. Despite the fact that the county offers free immunization to all children, some parents are afraid to take their children to be immunized because they have heard that one of the clinics had been raided by the Immigration and Naturalization Service; other parents do not understand the immunization process. Organization A believes that immigration status should not be questioned in the context of immunizing children and works to have immunization administered in schools, in houses of worship, and in a mobile van that travels to communities where many migrants live. Organization B believes that some vaccines used to immunize children are the cause of the rising rate of autism. This organization is opposed to all immunization because it believes that the risk from immunization is higher than the risk of contracting diseases such as diphtheria, typhoid, and polio, which are now rare in the United States and Canada. Two organizations with the same concern about children's health, with very similar mission statements, both governed and staffed by thoughtful people, but with very different goals.

Goal statements almost always start with infinitives: to provide, to ensure, to monitor, to educate. For example, "To ensure that old-growth forests are protected forever" or "To teach conflict resolution skills to all elementary school children" or "To find a cure for breast cancer."

Objectives

Objectives are statements describing how the group intends to accomplish its goals. Good objectives can be easily created and ensured of being successful if they are written to conform to the principles of the acronym "SMART": Specific, Measurable, Achievable, Realistic, and Time-limited. More recently, the idea of working toward *objectives* has been replaced with the idea of striving for *outcomes*, and many foundations are using a process called "outcome-based evaluation" to compare what an organization said it would do with what it actually achieved, and then to base its funding decisions on the results. Objectives and outcomes are not dissimilar, and for some organizations "outcomes" might be a better expression of their objectives. For the sake of the internal case statement, it is most important to answer the question, "How do we intend to meet our goals?" In external versions of your case or more detailed descriptions of programs, you can decide whether to use the word *outcome, objective, method,* or whatever is most appropriate.

The main difference between a goal and an objective is that goals last as long as they need to, but objectives last for one year at the most. Objectives are evaluated yearly or in whatever time frame is specified in the objective. For example, here is an objective from the economic literacy group: "We will teach ten weekend courses for teenagers during the months of September and October. Two courses will be presented in Spanish, one in Cantonese, and seven in English. Each course will have a minimum attendance of fifteen students and maximum of twenty-five. A pretest and post-test will be given to document learning, and the curriculum will be modified for use in the next round as indicated by the evaluations." The outcomes for this objective might be expressed differently: "Participants will understand the fundamentals of budgeting, how credit cards work, what simple and compound interest are, and what taxes they pay and what that money is used for. In general, participants will feel confident in their ability to make wise financial choices."

History

The history section summarizes when the organization was formed and by whom and narrates major program accomplishments, including any major program changes. In describing your accomplished objectives, you have the chance to provide further documentation of the work your organization was set up to do and your ability to do it. The more specific your objectives or outcomes are, the more dramatic your history will be. Your track record is one of the most important elements for attracting donors, so making sure you have a way to measure, document, and publish your accomplishments is key to fundraising.

"WE ARE BRAND NEW. WHAT ARE WE SUPPOSED TO DO ABOUT HISTORY?"

If yours is a new organization, you may think you have no history to report. However, you have the history of other organizations like yours and what you have learned from them, and the history of the people involved in getting your organization started. You can also use this section of the case statement to discuss any new thinking about how to address the issue that you are working on, and why you have decided to go the route of forming a new organization instead of linking up with something that already exists. Because there is some frustration amongst donors and funders with the sheer number of nonprofits that exist, a new organization may want to create a separate section in its case statement titled, "The Need for a New Organization."

There are donors who like to give to new organizations, and many will not stay with you much past five years—they like being at the beginning, they like thinking of themselves as innovators, cutting-edge thinkers, risk takers. Thus, although new organizations have a different appeal than more established ones, they still must use the insights and claims derived from historical precedents to establish credibility.

For example: "Homes for Seniors originally focused on providing permanent homes for homeless seniors until we discovered that hundreds of seniors who have housing live in homes that are substandard, with poor insulation and dangerous wiring and sometimes without running water. Every year since our founding in 1990, we have refurbished or upgraded between 20 and 30 housing units that seniors were living in; we are continually expanding our programs to upgrade seniors' substandard housing. This program has benefited more than 2,000 seniors who had housing, in addition to the 500 homeless seniors we serve each year."

There are no set rules for the length of the historical piece. A summary of high points will do, with a reference to a longer document, such as an annual report or Web site, for people who are interested in more details.

The Structure

The structure section shows that the way you are organized is consistent with your overall mission. This section discusses staffing and board size, composition, and governance. Here are some examples: "We have four staff who work collectively" or "Our board of eleven members is composed of three current clients, five former clients, and three former staff people, so that all decisions about the organization are made by the people most interested in and knowledgeable about the effects of our work." This section should be long enough to explain a complicated or nontraditional structure, but brief if the organizational structure is fairly straightforward.

The way an organization is structured is a key to its accountability. For example, an organization that claims it is committed to the full participation of all members of a multiracial community but has only white people on its board raises questions about its understanding or commitment to being truly "multiracial." An organization that claims to organize in low-income communities but whose board members are all well-paid professionals, none of whom are from the communities the organization serves, raises questions about the organization's philosophy of power.

Sophisticated donors often request information on structural issues to help determine if the group understands the implications of its mission and goals. This section can also include brief biographical sketches of board members and resumes of staff, along with statistics on members, volunteers, and chapters, if applicable.

A Fundraising Plan

The fundraising plan shows whether the organization has a diversity of funding sources and an understanding of the fundraising process. The fundraising plan shows all of the organization's prospective sources of income and describes in a narrative fashion how this income will be raised or how these financial goals will be reached. Like the section on structure, the fundraising plan will show whether the organization operates consistently with its mission. For example, an environmental organization primarily supported by oil or timber corporations or a community-based organization with only foundation funding raises questions about how its financing can be consistent with its mission. In contrast, an organization that works to reduce high school drop-out rates that has significant support from parents and alumnae of the program or a downtown preservation and beautification project that is supported entirely by business and residents of the community appears to be wanted and needed by the people who most benefit from it.

A Financial Statement and a Budget

A financial statement provides proof that the organization spends money wisely and monitors its spending—both in total amount and by category. The financial statement consisting of an audited financial report, if available, or a balance sheet is usually part of an annual report. The budget is an estimate of expenses and income for the current fiscal year and should include a description of how finances are monitored, such as "The finance committee of the board reviews financial reports monthly, and the full board reviews such reports quarterly. We compare our income and expenses with other organizations and with industry standards and are committed to raising enough money to do our work properly and making sure that all our money is spent wisely and prudently" (see also Chapter Thirty-Eight, "Developing a Budget").

CREATING A STRATEGIC PLAN

People often ask, "What is the difference between a case statement and a strategic plan?" The answer is that the case statement is a basic blueprint of what the organization is and how it operates. It must be in place before you can make long-range plans. A strategic plan is a projection of the organization's work into the future—generally, two, three, or five years. To embark on a strategic planning process without an internal case statement is similar to building your house on the proverbial sand. In other words, the case statement provides the foundation for a strategic plan. A strategic plan also looks at both internal and external realities (the so-called SWOT test is classic: strengths, weaknesses, opportunities, and threats) and uses research on demographic trends, the results of outside evaluation, and a variety of other information to help set realistic, ambitious, and mission-fulfilling goals. Some elements of the strategic plan are already in place in a well-done case statement, especially some of the thinking about goals and objectives and some of the evaluation of the organization's track record to date. And the strategic planning process may help the organize refine and sometimes redefine its goals going forward. Thus the case statement and strategic plan work together nicely, but they are not interchangeable.

DEVELOPING THE CASE STATEMENT

A case statement is usually developed by a small committee, but the board, staff, and key volunteers must all agree on its contents, particularly the mission and goals. If the people who must carry out the plans don't like them or don't believe they are possible, they will not do good work for the group. Therefore, it is worth spending a good amount of time on developing the case statement. Hurrying a statement of mission or a set of goals through the board approval process in order to save time or "get on with the job" will come back to haunt you in the form of commitments not kept and half-hearted fundraising efforts.

Elements of the Case Statement

Section On	Establishes
Mission	Why the organization exists
Goals	What it will do about why it exists
Objectives	How it will accomplish the goals
History	Its credibility, showing which objectives have been accomplished already
Structure	Who is involved, showing consistency of personnel with the goals
Fundraising plan	That the organization has a number of well-managed and appropriate income streams that will enable it to fulfill its mission over the long term
Budget	That salaries, benefits, rent, and other costs are consistent with the mission, and that the organization knows how much it will cost to do the job it has set out to do

---

chapter FIVE

The Board of Directors

All over the world, nongovernmental organizations (NGOs) play increasingly critical roles in the development and maintenance of a healthy society. In countries such as the United States, NGOs provide much of the available social services, arts and culture, shelter, research, education, advocacy, religion, free legal services, health care, and so on. In addition, nonprofits are leading the charge on saving the environment, ending racism, protecting and expanding our understanding of civil rights and civil liberties, creating art, preserving history, advocating, educating, organizing on any number of issues—in fact, almost everything that is creative, is humane, and promotes justice is brought to us by a nonprofit. In many other countries, the government provides services directly (such as universal health care). This chapter focuses particularly on the United States and the place of nonprofits in this country. Organizations in other countries are encouraged to research laws and structures that pertain to them. Even so, they will find many similarities, as there is a certain logic in the way NGOs are structured and regulated around the world.

Countries that have laws pertaining to NGOs start with the recognition that a nonprofit cannot exist in a for-profit economy without some financial help, and the help the government gives nonprofits is tax relief. Over the past several decades, here in the United States, a body of law has developed creating various forms of tax relief for organizations and tax credits or tax avoidance (not to be confused with tax evasion, which is illegal) for donors—both of which help nonprofits survive financially. This body of law is under the Internal Revenue Service code 501. The most advantageous status for groups doing educational, religious, or charitable work is 501(c)(3). This is the designation that most nonprofits using this book will either have or aspire to. Organizations with 501(c)(3) status are exempt from many corporate taxes, can offer donors tax deductibility for their gifts, have access to foundation and corporate funding that individuals and small businesses do not, receive lower rates for sending bulk mail with the U.S. Postal Service, and enjoy a host of other exemptions from tax at both the federal and state levels. Because these exemptions from taxes and the subsidies such organizations receive are provided by tax revenue that costs all taxpayers money, the government has also created a structure to hold nonprofits accountable for these tax advantages. An organization's board of directors is the group of people that is responsible to the government for the actions of the nonprofit.

The broad purpose of a board of directors is to run the organization effectively. To qualify for tax-exempt status an organization must file a list of the names of people who have agreed to fulfill the legal requirements of board membership. The board members are bound to ensure that the organization meets the following obligations:

• Operates within state and federal laws

• Earns its money honestly and spends it responsibly

• Adopts programs and procedures most conducive to carrying out its mission

The best summary of a board member's responsibility is contained in the State of New York's Not-for-Profit Corporation Law, the language of which has since been adopted by many other states. According to this law, board members must act "in good faith and with a degree of diligence, care and skill which ordinarily prudent people would exercise under similar circumstances and in like positions." The key here is the "diligence, care and skill" that "prudent people" would observe. These are serious responsibilities, and board members must take them seriously.

Board members, in effect, own the organization. They are chosen because of their commitment to the organization and long-term vision for it. As the Council of Better Business Bureaus points out, "Being part of the official governing body of a nonprofit, soliciting organization is a serious responsibility and should never be undertaken with the thought that this is an easy way to perform a public service."

The responsibilities of board members fall into several broad categories. How any specific organization chooses to have board members carry out these responsibilities will depend on the number of board members, the number of paid staff, the sources of the organization's funding, and the history of the organization. There are few right or wrong ways to manage an organization, but there are ways that work better in some situations than in others.

With that in mind, let's look at board member responsibilities.

RESPONSIBILITIES OF THE BOARD

Board members are responsible for six areas of the organization's functioning:

1. Ensuring organizational continuity. The board develops leadership within both board and staff to maintain a mix of old and new people in both spheres.

2. Setting organizational policy, and reviewing and evaluating organizational plans. The board ensures that the organization's programs are always in keeping with its statement of mission, and that the statement of mission continues to reflect a true need.

3. Doing strategic planning. The board forms long-range plans with reference to the case statement, focusing on the following types of questions:

    Where does the organization want to be in six months, two years, five years? How big does the organization want to become? If it is a local organization, does it want to become regional or national? What are the implications of world events for the organization's work, and what is its response? How can the group become more proactive rather than reactive? These and other questions are usually answered using a strategic planning process based on a solid case statement. Some organizations find it helpful to have a board-level strategic planning committee that raises and researches appropriate questions and brings recommendations to a strategic planning retreat for discussion and decisions.

4. Maintaining fiscal accountability. The board approves and closely monitors the organization's expenses and income. The board makes certain that all the organization's resources (including the time of volunteers and staff) are used wisely and that the organization has enough money to operate.

5. Overseeing personnel. The board sets and reviews personnel policies, and hires, evaluates, and if necessary, fires staff. For staff positions other than the executive director, these tasks are usually delegated to the executive director. She or he then takes the place of the board in human resource issues. The board hires the executive director and evaluates her or his performance regularly. The board is also the final arbiter of internal staff disputes and grievances and is ultimately responsible for maintaining good staff-board relationships.

6. Funding the organization. The board is responsible for the continued funding and financial health of the organization. With regard to fundraising, board members have two responsibilities: give money and raise money.

BOARD STRUCTURE AND SIZE

There is no evidence that any particular board structure works better than another. Each structure will have its strengths and weaknesses. The structure your organization chooses will probably stem from past history and the experience and desires of the present board members. Some organizations work best with a collective structure, including open meetings, informal discussion, and decision by consensus. Other organizations do better with a hierarchical structure, including a parliamentarian who will help the group follow Robert's Rules of Order in meetings, and a formal method of discussion and decision making. The only rule is that everyone has to understand the structure you have. If one person thinks that she should raise her hand and wait to be called on before speaking while another person simply shouts out what he thinks, the board will have communication problems.

The size of the board also depends on many variables, but there is evidence that the ideal size is between eleven and twenty-one members. A board of fewer than eleven members will probably have too much work, and one of more than twenty-one members is likely to be unwieldy, with work divided unevenly. If you already have a large board, work can be most effectively accomplished through small committees and few full board meetings. A small board can also be divided into committees, which can be fleshed out with non-board representatives recruited to participate.

STATEMENT OF AGREEMENT

For a board to operate successfully each member must understand and respect the organization's structure and decision-making process, as well as the mission of the organization, and feel that she or he can participate fully in it. One technique that many groups have found helpful to achieve this understanding is to develop a statement of agreement for board members. This statement serves as a job description and clarifies board responsibilities and authority.

A generic example of such a statement is presented here.

Statement of Agreement

As a board member of _____, I believe in the mission and goals of this organization, which can be summarized as follows: _____

I understand being a board member means that I have fiduciary responsibility for this organization. My duties and responsibilities include the following:

1. I am fiscally responsible, with the other board members, for this organization. We need to make sure that the organization has enough money to do the work our mission compels us to do and to make sure that the money we raise is spent properly. It is my duty to know what our budget is and to take an active part in planning the budget and the fundraising to meet it.

2. I am legally responsible, along with the other board members, for this organization. I am responsible to know and approve all policies and programs and to oversee their implementation.

3. I must show my confidence in the organization by making a donation that is significant for me. I may give this as a one-time donation each year, or I may pledge to give a certain amount several times during the year.

4. I will actively engage in fundraising for this organization in whatever ways are best suited to me. These may include individual solicitation, undertaking special events, writing proposals or appeals, and the

(Continued)

---

like. I will work with the staff and other board members to determine which tasks I will take on. There is no set amount of money that I must raise because I am making a good faith agreement to do my best and to bring in as much money as I can.

5. I will attend (#) _____ board meetings every year and be available for committee work and phone consultation, where appropriate. I understand that commitment to this board will involve a good deal of time, probably a minimum of _____ hours per month.

6. I understand that no quotas have been set, that no rigid standards of measurement and achievement have been formed. Every board member is making a statement of faith about every other board member. We are trusting each other to carry out the agreements above to the best of our ability, each in our own way, with the knowledge, approval, and support of all. I know that if I fail to act in good faith I must resign, or someone from the board may ask me to resign.

In its turn, this organization is responsible to me in a number of ways:

1. The organization will send me, without request, quarterly financial reports that allow me to act in good faith and with the degree of diligence, care, and skill that ordinarily prudent people would exercise under similar circumstances and in like positions.

2. Paid staff will make themselves available to me to discuss programs, policies, goals, and objectives.

3. Board members and staff will respond in a straightforward and thorough fashion to any questions I have that I feel are necessary to carry out my fiscal, legal, and moral responsibilities to this organization.

This kind of agreement defines understandings that may never before have been articulated. In doing so, it helps channel board members' motivation to serve the organization. It also improves relations between board and staff by making clear to staff the limits of board members' responsibilities and letting board members know when they can say, "No, this is not my responsibility."

Once a board has developed this type of contract, the statement can be read at regular intervals to remind people of their commitments. It can also be used for internal evaluation and to recruit new board members.

THE BOARD AND FUNDRAISING

The reluctance of board members to take responsibility for fundraising can usually be traced to two sources: (1) board members don't understand the importance of taking a leadership role in fundraising, and (2) they are afraid of asking for money. Board members cannot give themselves wholeheartedly to the process of fundraising unless these two problems are resolved.

The reason that board members must take a leadership role in fundraising is simple: they own the organization. They have to show that they think the group is worth supporting by setting an example. They are responsible for the well-being of the organization and for its successes. Furthermore, the organization's supporters and potential supporters see board members as the people most committed and dedicated to the organization. If they, who care the most about the group, will not take a lead role in fundraising, why should anyone else? When the board does take the lead, its members and the staff can go to individuals, corporations, and foundations and say, "We have 100 percent commitment from our board. All board members give money and raise money." This position strengthens the fundraising case a great deal. Both individual donors and foundations often ask organizations about the role of the board in fundraising and look more positively on groups whose board plays an active part.

Board members are often reluctant to participate in fundraising activities because they fear they will be required to ask people for money. It's true that many fundraising strategies require board members to make face-to-face solicitations. This is a skill and thus can be learned, and all board members should have the opportunity to attend a training session on asking for money (see Chapter Six, "Getting Comfortable with Asking for Money").

In a diversified fundraising plan, however, some board members can participate in fundraising strategies that do not require asking for money directly. While some can solicit large gifts, others can conduct special events, write mail appeals, approach small businesses, give talks at service clubs and houses of worship, market products for sale, write thank you notes or make thank you calls, enter information into a database, and so on. Everyone's interests and skills can be used. Board members inexperienced in fundraising can start with an easy task ("Help set minimum bids for the silent auction items") and gradually move on to more difficult fundraising tasks ("Ask this person for $1,000"). Some fundraising strategies will use all the board members (selling tickets to the movie benefit), whereas others will require the work of only one or two people (speaking to service clubs or sending thank you notes).

People often bring to their board service two mistaken beliefs that hamper their participation in fundraising. First, they feel that because they give time they should not be called on to give money. "Time is money," they will argue. Second, if an organization has paid development staff, board members may feel that it is the staff's job to do the fundraising. Let us quickly dispel both of these myths.

Time and Money

Time is not money. We all have exactly the same amount of time—twenty-four hours every day. But we have vastly unequal amounts of money. Time is a non-renewable resource—when a day is gone, you cannot get it back. Money is a renewable resource. You earn it, spend it, and earn more. Further, you cannot go to the telephone company and ask to volunteer your time in order to pay your phone bill. You cannot pay your staff or buy your office supplies with your time. Finally, people are rarely anxious about asking someone for their time, but most people are quite reluctant to ask someone for their money, even though for many people, time is the more precious resource. In trainings, I often use this example: "If a board member is assigned to call three people and tell them about a meeting on Wednesday night, he or she will do it. If two people can come to the meeting and one can't, the board member does not take this personally and feel like a failure. However, if this same board member is assigned to ask these same three people for $100 each, he or she will probably have to go to a training in how to ask for money before being comfortable carrying out that assignment." I have conducted thousands of trainings in how to ask for money, but I have never been asked to lead a training in how to ask for time.

Comparing time and money is like comparing apples and asphalt. We waste the time of our creative volunteers when we don't have enough money, and we waste the money of our donors when we don't use volunteers appropriately. Board members must understand that contributions of time and money are very different, although equally important, parts of their role. People who want to give only one or the other are valuable to an organization, but are not suitable to be board members.

The Role of Paid Staff

Paid staff has specific roles in fundraising. These are to help plan fundraising strategies; coordinate fundraising activities; keep records; take care of routine fundraising tasks such as renewal appeals; and assist board members by writing letters for them, forming fundraising plans with them, accompanying them to solicitation meetings, and so on. Generally, fundraising staff handle most or all of the process of approaching foundations or government entities for funding, and they provide the backup needed for others in the organization to do effective fundraising. It is clearly impossible, however, for one person or even several people to do all the work necessary to maintain a diversified fundraising plan. Just as it is foolish for an organization to depend on one or two sources of funding, it is equally unwise for it to depend on one or two people to do fundraising.

The final reason for all board members to participate in fundraising is to ensure that the work is evenly shared. Fundraising is rarely anyone's favorite task, so it is important that each board member knows that the other members are doing their share. If some members do all the fundraising while others only make policy, resentments are bound to arise. The same resentments will surface if some board members give money and others don't. Those who give may feel that their donation buys them out of some work or that their money entitles them to more power. Those who do not give money may feel that they do all the work or that those who give money have more power. When board members know that everyone is giving their best effort to fundraising according to their abilities—including making their own gift—the board will function most smoothly and members will be more willing to take on fundraising tasks.

COMMON BOARD PROBLEMS AND SUGGESTED SOLUTIONS

Although each board of directors will have its own problems and tensions to be resolved, many boards have a number of problems in common. Those problems are discussed here, along with some solutions.

Board Members Are Overworked—Too Much Is Expected of Them. Nonprofit organizations use all of their volunteers to augment paid staff. The smaller the organization, the more responsibility volunteers will have, becoming more and more like paid staff. To a certain point this is fine. But there comes a time when board members are taking on much more work than they had agreed to. When board members find themselves attending three or four meetings each month and spending hours reading and answering e-mail, or spending a lot of time on the telephone on behalf of the organization, they begin to dread hearing from anyone in the organization and to count the days until their term is up.

This dynamic can be changed or averted altogether by adhering to the following principles:

1. Board members should understand that they can say no to tasks that go beyond their original commitment.

2. Staff and board members should ensure that tasks given to the board have a clear beginning and end. Thus, when additional work is essential, board members should be assured that extra meetings will be called for no more than a month or two and that once that task is accomplished they will not be asked to do more than the minimum for a few months.

3. A careful eye should be kept on what the whole board does with its time. Board members (particularly the executive or steering committee) should ask, "Are all these meetings necessary? Can one person do what two have been assigned to do, or can two people do what four have committed to do?" Consider having some meetings by conference call and doing routine business by e-mail.

4. Boards should not be asked to make decisions or take on tasks for which they are unqualified. Sometimes consultants need to be brought in to make recommendations, or the board needs to be trained to handle tasks related to management and fundraising.

Individual Board Members Feel Overworked. Even if the board is attentive to the time limitations of board members, this problem can arise either because those people were given the wrong impression of the amount of work involved beyond attending regular board meetings, or because they are already overcommitted in the rest of their lives. In the latter case they cannot completely fulfill the expectations of any part of their lives, so they feel overworked even while not doing very much for the organization.

A clear and precise statement of agreement, as discussed earlier in this chapter, will help with this problem. The statement can be used to screen out people who are overextended and to call current board members into accountability. A tip: don't try to talk anyone into being on the board. When you ask people to serve on the board, tell them why they would be a good addition to the board and what you would expect from them. If their response is less than enthusiastic, let them go. We would not offer a job to someone who said, "I don't know if I have the time." A board role is a job—and it needs to be approached as such.

The Board Avoids Making Decisions.   In this instance board members never seem to have enough information to commit themselves to a course of action and constantly refer items back to committees or to staff for further discussion and research. This problem is generally the result of inadequate board leadership. The board chair or president must set an example of decisiveness. He or she needs to point out that the board can never know all the factors surrounding a decision and yet must act despite factors changing on a daily or weekly basis.

The person facilitating a meeting should always establish time limits for each item on the agenda. This can be done at the beginning of the meeting. Close to the end of the time allotted for an item, the chair should say, "We are almost at the end of time for discussion on this item. What are the suggestions for a decision?" If the chair or facilitator of the meeting does not take this role, individual board members should take it on themselves to call for a time limit on discussion and a deadline for a decision.

Very few decisions are irrevocable. Decisions can be modified, expanded, or scrapped altogether once they are made and put into action if they are not working out.

Decisions Are Made, Then Forgotten.   When this shortcoming is at work, the board both fails to implement its decisions and ends up discussing the same issue again in a few months or years. Further, board members feel that they are not taking themselves seriously and that their work is for nothing. Three methods can be used to avoid this problem. One method is to appoint a member to keep track of decisions and remind the board of them. The secretary of the board can serve this function, or someone designated as board "historian." A second, complementary method is for decisions from board meetings (as distinct from meeting minutes) to be kept in a notebook or an internal Web page, such as Google Docs, that can be easily accessed when setting the agenda, or even during a meeting. The decisions can be categorized and indexed so that they can be easily found. The chair and executive committee should review decisions frequently so that they are familiar with them.

Finally, each board member should read and keep a copy of the minutes of every meeting. Don't rush through the process of approving minutes, particularly if they are recording anything that was contentious. At the board meetings the board chair or secretary should ask members questions such as, "Rob, I want to make sure I captured your amendment accurately," or "Mary, can you make sure that I got all the budget modifications?" The board members then know they might be called on to review parts of the minutes and so will be more likely to read them thoroughly.

A Few Board Members Do All or Most of the Work.   When this situation happens, those who do the work resent those who are not carrying their share. Those who don't work resent those who do because they imagine them to have all the power. Inevitably, some people will work harder than others, and some will work better. Nonetheless, the board should plan for work to be evenly shared and for everyone to take an active role, assuming that all members will work equally hard and equally effectively. People rise to the standards set for them. Mediocre work should not be accepted. Above all, board members must value everyone's contribution. The person who stuffs envelopes is as valuable as the person whose friend gives $5,000.

Staff or Board Members Don't Want to Share Power Evenly.   Sometimes people take and keep power because they enjoy having power and building empires. More often, though, they take power because they are afraid to let go, afraid that others will not do as well as they have. This situation is likely to occur when some board members have served for many years or when a person on staff has seen a lot of turnover on the board. Whoever perceives that someone is hoarding power or refusing to delegate tasks (either staff or board) should address their concerns to the appropriate committee or the board chair. That person should use examples, so that people can have a clear sense of what they are doing wrong and change their behavior accordingly. Generally, people will share power in an organization as others prove reliable.

There Are No Consequences for Behavior. Of all the problems that plague boards, this is the most serious. I have worked with hundreds of boards over the past thirty years, most of them here in the United States but also in Canada, Korea, Brazil, Australia, and Africa. I have watched as board members thoroughly discussed their responsibilities, solemnly signed their board agreements, enthusiastically endorsed the mission and goals of the organization, and then one after another, board members didn't do what they said they would do, and nothing happened. Board members are like any group of human beings—classes, families, workplaces. Let's say in your workplace you have a rule that everyone must clean up after him- or herself. But consistently, predictably, Gary does not. People see him leave dishes and cups in the sink. At the staff meeting, people indirectly call attention to the problem: "Someone has been leaving dishes in the sink" or "I am tired of doing other people's dishes," with meaningful glances in Gary's direction. Behind his back, people say, "Can you believe him? I can't believe his wife/partner/ mother puts up with this at home." But no one ever says, "Gary, are these your dishes? Can you please wash them?" Before long, other people will start leaving their dishes in the sink and Gary will not be the only culprit. Ditto board members. June says she will get all the food donated from her cousin's store, but doesn't, and the organization has to buy food for their meeting. Bob says he will ask five people to renew their donations, but he doesn't, and the donors don't renew until one of the staff asks them. Marge, who always does what she says, notices that June and Bob are still on the board and except for some grumbling about them, nothing happens. So pretty soon Marge isn't fulfilling her commitments either.

Accountability on a board is actually a very simple thing to put in place: when people say they will do something, it is written down, someone else reminds them to do it (reminding people of their tasks is a task), they are thanked when they get it done, and they are praised in front of the board. If, after one or two reminders, the job is still not done, the board chair or someone else on the board calls and asks, "What happened? What could have been done differently? What would have allowed you to do your work?" And when, like Gary, a person establishes a pattern of saying they will do something and not doing it, the board chair meets with them privately and asks if they really want to be on the board. Accountability is not to punish the Garys of the world—it is ensure that the work of the group gets done, in part by rewarding people who do what they say they will do and by surrounding them with other reliable people. If you set a tone of expecting people to keep their commitments, being appreciative, and making sure work is divided relatively evenly, you won't have to have very many difficult conversations.

A LESSON IN ACCOUNTABILITY

I learned a great deal about accountability from my late friend Vicki Quatmann, who was the chair of the board of the Appalachian Community Fund when I served as its first executive director from 1986 to 1989. We formed a board representative of the four states whose Appalachian counties we served: West Virginia, Virginia, Kentucky, and Tennessee. The board included coal miners, long-time civil rights and anti-poverty activists, artists, school teachers, community organizers, a librarian, and a legal aid lawyer. Some people were very well educated and some could barely read. Most had never served on a board before. Two were very wealthy and several were very poor. Vicki said, "This will only work if all the rules are clear to everyone, agreed on by everyone, and enforced." One agreement we had made ahead of the first board meeting was to start meetings on time. So the first meeting of the board, and the first time many of these people were to meet each other, started at 10:00 AM, and most people were there. Three stragglers showed up at about 11:15. Vicki instructed the minute taker to note who was present, who was absent (just one person), and who was late. I was shocked and said to her after the meeting, "You can't put who is late in the minutes." She said, "Watch me. I'll never need to do it again." And she didn't. No one was ever late while she was the board chair.

In the first three meetings, if she thought that someone had not read through the materials that were sent out well in advance, she would ask them quietly, "Were you able to prepare for this meeting before you got here?" If people said no, she would say, "That's OK. We all get busy. You'll have to sit out the decision making." In the board meeting she would say, "Those who can vote, please do so now." And after the third meeting at which someone had been told they couldn't vote, people very rarely came unprepared. Vicki set a high bar for that board. She believed that this unlikely collection of people could be a working and active board, and she made it so. I learned from her that when we tolerate lateness, not keeping commitments, and so on, we show that we never believed in the people in the first place. That is the fastest way to demoralize a board that I know.

MOVING PAST BOARD PROBLEMS

All of the dynamics described so far, as well as others such as personality conflicts, deep political disagreements, or staff-board conflicts, can be serious enough to immobilize an organization. The board and staff may not be able to resolve whatever the problem is themselves. Sometimes they can't even figure out what the problem is. Board or staff members should not hesitate to seek help in such cases. A consultant in organizational development or a mediator can help the group articulate and solve its problems. Although for a board to find itself in such an extreme situation is unfortunate, it is usually no one person's fault. Not to ask for help in getting out of the situation, however, constitutes a failure of board or staff members to be fully responsible. I believe that conflict resolution training for board and staff is important, particularly before any conflicts arise.

Some conflict can be creative, and board members and staff should not shun difficult discussions or disagreements. There is built-in tension between program and finance committees, new and old board members, and staff and board personnel. As Karl Mathiasen, a veteran board member and consultant, states in his book *Confessions of a Board Member*, "My own feeling is that if you go to a Board meeting and never during that meeting have a time during which you are tense and your heart beats faster and you know that something is at stake—if you lack that feeling two or three meetings in a row, there is something wrong with the organization."

RECRUITING AND INVOLVING NEW BOARD MEMBERS

Once an organization has a clear sense of the board's roles and responsibilities, has defined the type of structure it wants (collective, hierarchy, or

Current Board Evaluation

Board Needs	Name of Board Member			
	Montoya	Murphy	Hong	Burger
Demographic:*				
Women		X	X	
Men	X			X
GLBTQ			X	
Latino	X			
African American				X
White		X		
Asian			X	
Other			X	
Budgeting			X	
Financial management				X
Personnel		X		
Fundraising:				
Personal asking	X	X		
Events				
Planned giving				
Marketing				
Web 2.0				
Evaluation			X	
Public policy				
Organizing				X
Other:				

*Note: Although it is important to be very thoughtful about having diversity on your board, an organization must keep in mind that one or two people will not represent a whole constituency, and the work of becoming ethnically diverse, for example, does not end (and in fact, may just begin) with having one or two people from each ethnic category on your board.

other), and has developed a statement of understanding or similar agreement, it can begin the formal process of recruiting additional board members. There are two key tenets of board composition: board members need to represent a diversity of opinion and skill, while sharing a sense of commitment to the organization's mission and goals, and, ideally, the combination of all the people on the board will provide all the skills required to run the organization.

To recruit board members, the current board should appoint two or three people to form a nominating committee. This small group will assess the present board's strengths and decide what skills or qualities are needed to overcome the board's weaknesses. The chart shown here is an example of a way to evaluate the current board and quickly spot the gaps. Each group should fill it in with the board membership criteria it has established.

There is a common belief that a board should have "movers and shakers" on it. Bank presidents, successful business people, politicians, corporate executives, and the like are thought to be people with power and connections to money, making them ideal board members. An organization needs to define who are the "movers and shakers" *for its work*. Many of the people perceived to be most powerful in a community would be terrible board members, even if they would agree to serve, because they would have neither the passion nor the interest in serving the organization. There are hundreds of successful organizations whose board members are neither rich nor famous and who have no access to the traditional elite, but whose connections are exactly what the organization needs. Belief in the mission of the organization and willingness to do the work required are of far greater importance than being part of the traditional power elite or being wealthy.

First and foremost, board members and new recruits must understand, appreciate, and desire to further the goals and objectives of the organization. Enthusiasm, commitment, and a willingness to work are the primary qualifications. Everything else required of a board member can be learned, and the skills needed can be brought to the board by a wide variety of people and taught to others on the board.

In assessing what skills and qualifications your board lacks, then, don't just go for the obvious recruits. For example, suppose that no one on your board understands budgeting. An obvious solution would be to recruit an accountant, someone with an MBA, or a corporate executive to meet this need. If you know someone in one of these areas who shares the commitments and ideals of your nonprofit, then certainly invite her or him to be a board member. But if you don't know anyone whose profession involves budgeting, use your imagination to see what other kind of person might have those skills. In one organization, a self-described housewife does all the budgeting and evaluation of financial reports. Her experience of managing a large family has taught her all the basics of financial management; she is completely self-taught. Anyone who has had to keep within a budget may have excellent budgeting skills: ministers, directors of other non-profit organizations, people who own small businesses, and seniors living on fixed incomes.

Another example: if the gap on your board is in getting publicity, an obvious choice would be someone who works in the media or has a job in public relations. However, as many groups know, anyone willing to tell the story of his or her personal experience with a group or who is articulate about the issues can get media attention if a staff person lays the groundwork. A staff member can arrange an interview, send a press release, and put together a press packet. A volunteer can then do the follow-up required to get the media coverage.

The Recruitment

Prospective board members are found among friends and acquaintances of current board members, staff members, former board and staff members, and current donors and clients. Ideally, a prospective board member is someone who already gives time and money to the organization.

The chair of the board should send a letter to each prospective board member asking the person if she or he is interested in serving on the board and giving a few details of what that would mean. The letter should state that someone will call in a few days to make an appointment to discuss the invitation in detail. Even if the prospect is a friend of a board or staff member or is themselves a long-time volunteer, a formal invitation will convey that being on this board is an important responsibility and a serious commitment and that it is a privilege to be invited. Whoever knows the board prospect can follow up on the letter by talking to the person about being on the board. If no one knows the prospect, two people from the board should see the person. If the prospective board member does not have time to meet and discuss the board commitment, this is a clue that he or she will not have time to serve and should be removed from the list of prospects.

Whoever meets with the prospective board member should go over the board's statement of agreement point by point. The current members should share their experiences in fulfilling their commitment and discuss what others have done to fulfill theirs. It is particularly important to discuss the amount of time board participation requires as well as expectations of board members in the area of fundraising. Do not make the board commitment sound easier than it is. It is better for a person to join the board and discover that it is not as much work as he or she originally thought than to find that it is much more work and resent having had the commitment misrepresented.

The contact person should feel free to ask the prospective board member how he or she feels about the organization or what experience he or she has had in working on this issue, working in other nonprofits, working with people crossing class and race lines, or whatever you think you need to know to assess someone's likely contribution to the board. Considering someone to join the board is as serious as finding a new roommate, interviewing potential staff, or deciding to take a job. Do not expect people to change once they are on the board. What you see is what you get.

Tell the person why you are asking him or her to join the board, and that the nominating committee has given a great deal of thought to this choice. Give the person a few days to think it over, and encourage him or her to call for more information or with further questions. Let this be an informed and considered choice. It is better for ten people to turn you down than to get ten half-hearted new board members.

The Orientation

After a person has accepted nomination to the board and been elected, a current board member should be assigned to act as the new person's "buddy." The current board member should bring the new board member to the first meeting, meet with him or her (perhaps for lunch or dinner) once a month for the first two or three months, and be available to answer questions or discuss any issues regarding board functioning or responsibilities and the organization's work. New board members have many questions that they are often too embarrassed or shy to raise at a full board meeting. They will be incorporated into the life of the organization much faster if they can easily get the answers they need.

Before their first meeting, new board members should receive a packet of information, including a copy of the statement of understanding, the organization's by-laws, the case statement, and anything else that would be helpful to their understanding of the organization, such as an organizational chart, the current annual budget, brochures and other promotional information, and the names, addresses, phone numbers, and profiles of the other board members and of staff members.

Board members work best when they feel both needed and accountable. They will be more likely to keep their commitments when they know that doing so is expected and that others are keeping theirs. When this tone is established at the beginning, the board will function smoothly.

ADVISORY BOARDS

In addition to a board of directors, small organizations often find it helpful to form advisory boards made up of people who can help with various parts of the organization's program, including fundraising. Although it involves a good deal of work and does not take the place of a board of directors, an advisory board can be helpful for getting advice from a particular group of people (such as doctors, researchers, journalists, clergy) or in expanding your fundraising team (bringing on non-board members to do a special event or to help solicit major gifts), or to serve as an editorial board for your publications. In some ways an advisory board is an administrative fiction. Unlike a board of directors, an advisory board has no legal requirements, no length of time to exist, and no purposes that must be fulfilled. Such a board can consist of one person or two hundred.

Advisory boards are variously named depending on their functions. An advisory board may be called a community board, auxiliary, task force, committee, or advisory council. Some advisory boards meet frequently; others never meet. Sometimes advisory board members serve the group by lending their names to the organization's letterhead. In at least one case an organization's advisory board was called together, met for the first time, then disbanded all in the same day, having accomplished what they had been asked to do.

You can form an advisory board for the sole purpose of fundraising. Since this board has no final responsibility for the overall management of the organization, its members do not have to meet the recruitment requirements of the board of directors. Furthermore, the advisory board can be completely homogeneous—something a group tries to avoid in its board of directors.

People like to be on advisory boards. It gives them a role in an organization without taking on the full legal and fiscal responsibilities of a member of the board of directors.

When to Form an Advisory Board

Organizations sometimes see an advisory board as a quick fix to their fundraising problems. They may reason, "Next year our group has to raise three times as much money as it did this year. Our board can't do it alone and we don't want to add new board members. So, we'll just ask ten rich people to be on a fundraising advisory board and they'll raise the extra money we need."

There are two main problems here. First, finding "ten rich people" is not that simple. If it were, the organization would already have a successful major gifts program. Second, a wealthy person doesn't necessarily have an easier time asking for and getting money than someone who is not wealthy. Nor will he or she necessarily be more willing to give money than would a "not rich" person.

There are, however, several conditions under which an advisory board is a solution to a fundraising need:

- Although the board of directors is already doing as much fundraising as it can, it is not enough. An advisory board works best when it is augmenting the work of an active and involved board of directors.

- An organization has a specific and time-limited project that needs its own additional funding. This can be a capital campaign, an endowment project, or a time-limited program requiring extra staff and other expenses. The advisory board commits to raise a certain amount of money overall or a certain amount every year, usually for no more than three years.

- An organization needs help to run a small business or put on a large special event every year. The type of advisory board that runs a small business is usually called an "auxiliary," as it does not have a time-limited function.

- An organization wants help in raising money from a particular part of the private sector, such as corporations, businesses, service clubs, or houses of worship. The advisory board, composed of representatives from these particular sectors, plans the campaign, and the members solicit their own colleagues.

Forming the Advisory Board

If you decide that an advisory board is a good tool for your group, be sure to write out clearly your expectations of this group. Use the same specificity and thoroughness here as in drawing up a statement of agreement for your board of directors. In terms of fundraising, set an amount that you want the group to raise as a goal, the number of hours you expect each person on the board to work (per month, per event), and the number of meetings each will need to attend. Also suggest ways for them to raise money. (If you are forming this board because you don't know how to raise the money needed, let them know this at the outset.)

Be straightforward with prospects for your advisory board. Tell them your goals and choose people who can work to meet those goals. Use the same priorities in choosing members as when forming a board of directors. Of primary importance is the members' commitment to your organization and their willingness to express that commitment by fundraising.

Once you have formed an advisory board, the staff of the organization must provide backup support as needed and guide the board as much as necessary. The chair of the board of directors or another designated representative should receive reports from the advisory board and frequently call or write the advisory board's chair to express the organization's appreciation for the advisory board's work. Advisory board members should receive minutes from the meetings they hold, a staff person should phone each member from time to time in between meetings to seek their advice or to tell them some news about the organization, and they should generally be treated like major donors to the organization (which they are).

Allow the advisory board to develop a direction. The first few months may be slow, but once an advisory board begins to work well and carry out its commitments, its members can raise a substantial amount of money every year.

USING OTHER VOLUNTEERS FOR FUNDRAISING

In addition to, or instead of, forming an Advisory Committee, many organizations have gone to a structure with a smaller board (five to eleven members) and then used volunteers who are not board members to augment committees as needed. In this structure, there are no standing committees; instead, each committee is put together for a specific time and task. For example, two board members take on a major gifts campaign. They recruit five other people to help them for six weeks to meet a goal of raising $50,000 from major gifts. These five people care a lot about the organization but can't or don't want to take on full board responsibility. They are willing to work hard for a short period of time. In these organizations, most or all future board members have first served on one of these ad hoc committees. Coming on the board becomes a reward for work well done.

PART TWO

Strategies for Acquiring and Keeping Donors

The work of asking people who have not given to an organization to give a first time, and then if they give, asking them to give again and again forms the bulk of what fundraising is about. As I noted in Chapter One, most people who give one gift will not give a second time. About two-thirds of those who give a second time, however, will give a third time. Each year a person gives increases the chances that he or she will give the following year. Thus a higher percentage of donors will give for a fifth consecutive year than will give for a third consecutive year. Many organizations report donors giving to them for twenty-five or thirty years. Some of those donors become major donors, some provide capital gifts, and some include the organization in their will.

Building a donor base is a labor-intensive task that requires persistence and minute attention to detail along with a healthy sense of risk and willingness to spend money in order to make money. Not all strategies suit all organizations, and every organization will need to figure out which strategies work best for it. At the same time, organizations need to resist the temptation to fly from strategy to strategy looking for the magic one that will solve all their financial problems. Strategies that work well have usually been honed over many years, with lots of evaluation and planning each year.

The strategies in the next thirteen chapters are the most commonly used strategies for acquisition and retention of individual donors, ranging from personal solicitation to special events, phone banking to voluntary fees for service.

Although it requires the most nerve, asking someone in person for a donation is the most effective way to raise money, so the section begins with that strategy. The concluding chapter is on writing thank you notes. I devote an entire chapter to this topic because thanking people for what they give to your organization is the best way, besides running your organization soundly and honestly, to get them to give again.

chapter SIX

Getting Comfortable with Asking for Money

Asking someone you know for money in person is the most effective way to raise funds. If you ask all the people who you know give away money to give a gift they can afford to a cause they like, half of them will give something. (People who fit this description are called "prospects." Not everyone you know will meet all three criteria.) Of the half who say "yes" to your request, half of those people will give you the amount you asked for; the other half will give you less.

The response rate you get from personal asking is much higher than you can get from any other kind of fundraising. (For example, you can expect 1 percent of people to respond to a direct mail solicitation and 5 percent to give when asked by phone.) Moreover, you can ask for much larger amounts in person. It is rare, and usually silly, to ask for a $5,000 or $10,000 gift by e-mail or phone, because a substantial gift needs to be requested respectfully and responded to thoughtfully. So although an e-mail request for such an amount without follow-up is out of the question, it is appropriate to ask for such a sum in person if you think the prospect is someone who gives away money, can make such a gift, and has an interest in your cause. Personal solicitation is also used when asking a donor to increase his or her gift or when asking a major donor to consider a capital gift in addition to an annual gift.

In studies in which people are asked why they made their most recent donation, 80 percent will say, "Because someone asked me." Of course, millions of smaller fundraising requests are done in person—canvassing, Girl Scout cookie sales, raffle ticket sales, Salvation Army buckets, panhandling, and so on all have a strong element of personal asking. These forms of personal solicitation will not have the 50 percent rate of success unless the solicitor is known to each potential donor, but they will have a higher rate of success than methods that don't use a face-to-face approach. Strategies to raise more substantial gifts for nonprofits, including major gifts programs, capital campaigns, and endowment drives, rely for success on personal solicitation. The success of "street canvassing" (stopping strangers on the street to ask for donations for a cause, usually with an opening line such as, "Got a minute to save the planet?") speaks to how important face-to-face solicitation is.

Despite these facts, personal solicitation is one of the most difficult strategies to implement. It requires that people engage in an activity—asking for money—that most of us have been taught is rude or just not done. It requires that all of us get comfortable with people turning down our requests. However, for organizations that are serious about fundraising, and particularly for organizations that would like to increase the number of people in their donor base who give at least $500 annually, learning how to ask for money in person is imperative.

WHY WE'RE AFRAID TO ASK FOR MONEY

If the idea of asking for money fills you with anxiety, disgust, dread, or some combination of these feelings, you are among the majority of people. If asking for money does not cause you any distress, either you have let go of your fear about it, you grew up in a household of unusually liberated attitudes toward money, or you may have come from a country or a culture that does not consider talking about money taboo.

To identify the sources of our fears we must look at both the role of money in American society and the attitudes about asking for anything that are the legacy of the strong Puritan ethic that is our American heritage.

Most of us were taught that money, sex, religion, death, and politics are all taboo topics for discussion with anyone other than perhaps one's most intimate friends or family. Mental illness, age, race, and related topics are often added to this list of inappropriate topics, and are broached with more or less discomfort in some parts of the country or among some generations.

The taboo on talking about money, however, is far stronger than any of the others. Many of us were taught to believe that inquiring about a person's salary or asking how much he or she paid for a particularly large purchase, such as a house or a car, is rude. Even today, it is not unusual for one spouse not to know how much the other spouse earns, for children not to know how much their parents earn, or for close friends not to know each other's income. Further, few people really understand how the economy works. They don't know the meaning of things they hear and read about every day—the stock market, for example, including the difference between a bear and a bull market or what the rising or falling of the various stock market indices mean. In the past thirty years, more and more social justice groups have recognized that economic literacy is a key component in community organizing, but it will take decades to reverse the general ignorance about how the economy works and, more important, how it could work better for all.

Many people justify their aversion to dealing with money by misquoting from the Christian New Testament, saying, "Money is the root of all evil." In fact, the correct quote from Paul's Letter to Timothy is, "For the love of money is the root of all evil. Some people, in their passion for it, have strayed from the faith and have come to grief amid great pain" (Timothy 6:10, *Inclusive New Testament*). In another part of the Bible, the Letter of James to the Apostles makes a very different case: "You have not because you ask not" (James 4:2, *English Standard Version*).

In truth, money in itself has no good or evil qualities. It is a substance made of paper or metal. It has no constant value, and it has no morality. It can be used well or badly. It can buy guns or flowers. Good people need it just as much as evil people do. It is simply a means of exchange.

People will also say, "Money doesn't buy happiness," but of course, poverty doesn't buy anything. Moreover, we listen to stories of unhappy rich people and secretly think we would be happier if we had their money! Most people are curious about the salary levels of their friends, how much money their neighbors have inherited, how the superrich live. How much money you have and how long you have had it denote class distinctions and help each of us place ourselves in relation to others—even while we maintain the myth that our country is a classless meritocracy. Consequently, people speculate a great deal about the place of money in others' lives. Money is like sex and sexuality in this regard: kept in secrecy and therefore alluring. But just as much of what we learned as children and teenagers about sex turned out to be untrue, so it is with money. The comedian Kate Clinton says she was raised to think about sex like this: "Sex is dirty. Save it for someone you love." Most of us can relate to that, and can see much of what we learned about money in that same light. "Money is evil. Get a lot of it."

Over the past two decades our concepts and understanding about money have been changing, giving us more mixed messages than ever. For example, people are often told they must have at least a million dollars saved in order to retire with any degree of comfort, even though putting away that amount is completely unrealistic for the majority of the population. People who have very high incomes compare themselves to people with even higher incomes and feel disadvantaged. They never compare themselves to the more than one-third of the world's population who live on less than $2 a day. Concepts about money that we really don't understand have entered our vocabulary and leave us feeling increasingly helpless to deal with how money moves in our society: for example, the news is full of terms such as derivatives, subprime mortgages, hedge funds, and "toxic assets," all of which underlay the economic disaster that came to light in 2008 that has had to be bailed out with billions of taxpayer dollars and has caused the financial devastation of millions of people who have lost their homes and their jobs. We have learned that few, if any, people understood these financial products—to the ruin of many.

One major effect of money being a taboo topic and learning how money is handled being out of bounds—even at a more mundane level of everyday financial transactions—is that only those willing to learn about it can control it. In the United States, an elite and fairly hidden class controls most of the nation's wealth, either by earning it, having inherited it, or both. It serves the interest of this ruling class for the rest of us not to know who controls money and how to gain control of it ourselves. As long as we cannot ask about other people's salaries, we will not be able to find out that someone is being paid more because she is white or less because she is a woman. As long as we do not understand basic economics, we will not be able to advocate for or even know what the most progressive tax structure is, finance our nonprofits adequately, or create a society in which wealth is more fairly and equally distributed—which is, after all, the main underlying goal of social justice movements.

Political activists and participants in social change must learn how to raise money effectively and ethically, how to manage it carefully, and how to spend it wisely. In fact, activists who refuse to learn about money, including how to ask for it, wind up collaborating with the very system that the rest of their work is designed to change.

The idea of asking for money raises another set of hindering attitudes, which are largely the inheritance of a predominantly Protestant culture infused with a Puritan ethic that affects most Americans, including those who are not Protestants. This set of values conveys a number of messages that influence our feelings and actions. For example, a Puritan ethic implies that if you are a good person and you work hard you will get what you deserve. It further implies that if you have to ask for something you are a weak person because strong people are self-sufficient. Further, most likely you have not worked hard enough and you probably don't deserve whatever you are asking for. Rounding out this series of beliefs is our deep distrust in the ability of government to solve social problems and a general conviction that the government wastes our money in unnecessary and inefficient bureaucratic red tape.

All of these beliefs can be found among people on both the left and right sides of the political spectrum as well as across age and race lines and different religious orientations. Where these beliefs will not be found is in two places:

- Other countries. Although many countries have various taboos related to money, none have as many contradictory ones as the United States. Our taboos about talking and learning about money are not universal.

- Children. Children have no trouble asking for money. They do not subscribe to the idea that self-sufficiency means not asking or that polite people don't ask. They ask, and they ask again and again. Our taboos about money are not natural—we are not born with them.

Our beliefs about money are learned, and therefore they can be unlearned. The wonderful writer Ursula Le Guin once said in a lecture, "I never learned much from my teachers, but I learned a great deal from my un-teachers: the people who said to me, 'You shouldn't have learned that and you don't need to think it anymore.'"

Fundraising for social change is in part about raising the money we need, but over a longer period of time it is also about creating healthy attitudes toward money, and many people find that aspect of fundraising to be most fascinating.

To get over your own anxieties about money, it is helpful to reflect on how you were raised to think about money and about how you want to relate to money now that you are an adult. It takes time and work, but you can adopt new and healthier attitudes toward money.

SPECIFIC FEARS

With these very strong taboos operating against asking for money, it is a wonder that anyone ever does it! Understanding the source of our discomfort is the first step toward overcoming it. The next step is to examine our fears of what will happen to us when we do ask for money. When people look at their fears rationally they often find that most of them disappear or at least become manageable.

Fears about asking for money fall into three categories:

- Those that will almost never happen ("The person will hit me"; "I'll die of a heart attack during the solicitation")

- Those that could be avoided with training and preparation ("I won't know what to say"; "I won't know my facts; the person will think I am an idiot")

- Those that definitely will happen sometimes, maybe as much as half the time ("The person will say no"; "It will negatively affect our friendship and create obligations")

In the last category—things that will happen—most people do not fear only the possible outcome that the person will say no; many also fear that asking will have a negative effect on a friendship and that a gift from a friend will obligate them to give to the friend's cause in turn. Let's look at each of these more closely.

"The Person Will Say No."   Rejection is the number-one fear. Unfortunately, being told no will happen at least as often as being told yes. Therefore it is important to get to the point where you don't feel upset when someone says no. You do this by realizing that when you ask someone for a gift, you are seeing that person at a single moment in his or her life. A thousand things have happened to the person prior to your request, none of which has anything to do with you but many of which will affect the person's receptiveness to your request. For example, the person may have recently found out that one of his children needs braces, that his car needs new tires, that a client is not able to pay a bill on time, or that he has lost an important contract. This news may affect the prospect's perception of what size donation he can make at that time. A person may wish your organization success, but may already have given away all the money she can at this time or determined other priorities for her giving this year. Events unrelated to money can also cause the prospect to say no: a divorce proceeding, a death in the family, a headache. None of these things is your fault as the solicitor. Many of them you could not have known ahead of time, and you may never learn them because the prospect keeps them private. By feeling personally rejected you misinterpret the prospect's response and flatter yourself that you had something to do with it.

As the asker, you have to remember that, above all, the person being asked has the right to say no to a request without offering a reason. Most of the time you will not know exactly why your request was turned down. Your job is not to worry about why this prospect said no, but to go on, undaunted, to the next prospect.

"Asking a Friend for Money Will Have a Negative Effect on Our Friendship."   Many people feel that friendship is outside the realm of money. They feel that to bring money into a friendship is to complicate it and perhaps to ruin it. Friends are usually the best prospects, however, because they share our commitments and values. They are interested in our lives and wish us success and happiness. To many people's surprise, friends are more likely to be offended or hurt when they are *not* asked. They can't understand why you don't want to include them in your work.

Further, if it is truly acceptable to you for a person to say no to your request for a donation, your friend will never feel put on the spot. Your friend will not feel pressured by your request, as if your whole friendship hung on the answer. When asking friends, make clear that yes is the answer you are hoping for, but no is also acceptable. Say something like, "I don't know what your other commitments are, but I wanted to invite you to be part of this if you can."

"If the Person Says Yes to My Request, I Will Be Obligated to Give to His or Her Cause Whether I Want to or Not."   This quid pro quo situation ("this for that") does happen from time to time, and it happens frequently with some people. Giving money to a cause at the request of a friend so that you can ask him or her later for your own cause, or feeling you must give because your friend gave to your cause is not fundraising. It is simply trading money; it would be cheaper and easier for you just to give to your cause and let your friend give to his or hers. Also, people who give out of obligation to a friend will not become habitual donors. They will cease to give as soon as their friend is no longer involved.

If someone you ask for money gives to your organization, you are not obligated to that person, except to make sure that the organization uses the money wisely and for the purpose you solicited. The obligation is fulfilled if the organization is honest and does its work. The solicitor does not materially benefit from a solicitation. They present the cause, and if the prospect is sympathetic, he or she agrees to help support it. The cause was furthered. Beyond a thank you note, a gracious attitude, and reasonable assurance that the organization will use the money to further its mission, the solicitor owes the donor nothing. If the donor then asks you to support his or her cause, you consider the request without reference to your previous request or its result. You may wish to support the person or the cause, but you are not obligated to do so. If you think that someone is going to attach strings to a gift, don't ask that prospect. There are hundreds of prospects who will give freely.

Far from being a horrible thing to do, asking someone for money actually does them a favor. People who agree with your goals and respect the work of your group will want to be a part of it. Giving money is a simple and effective way to be involved, to be part of a cause larger than oneself.

Many volunteers find that it takes practice to overcome their fears about asking for money. To begin soliciting donations does not require being free of fear; it only requires having your fear under control. Ask yourself if what you believe in is bigger than what you are afraid of. An old fundraising saying is that if you are afraid to ask someone for a gift, "Kick yourself out of the way and let your cause do the talking." The point is this: if you are committed to an organization, you will do what is required to keep that organization going, which includes asking for money.

chapter SEVEN

The Logistics of Personal Solicitation

It takes time to work through all your anxieties about asking, and some people never do feel completely comfortable with the process. That's OK—you can ask even if you feel nervous about it. In this chapter, we look at the process you use to identify whom to ask and how you go about asking.

ASK A PROSPECT

Because personal solicitation is, by definition, done on a person-by-person basis, it takes more time than most strategies. On the other hand, with an e-mail you can reach hundreds or thousands of people just by pushing the "send" button, and a direct mail appeal can reach hundreds or thousands of people through one letter, duplicated and stuffed into envelopes. And even factoring in the effort it takes to maintain an accurate database, which is significant, to do these large-scale mailings, personal solicitation is more time consuming. Whereas volume is the key to those mass strategies, personal solicitation is done strictly person by person. For that reason, we are looking for people who are worth that much time.

In larger organizations, personal solicitation is generally used to ask for gifts of at least $1,000 and often $2,500 or more. For smaller organizations, however, donors who could give a gift of $500 or more are worth the time a personal solicitation takes, and defining a major gift as $250 or more opens the possibility to more people of becoming a major donor.

The question that determines whether a person is a prospect could be phrased this way: "What evidence do I have that if I asked this person for thirty to sixty minutes of her time to meet with me, thus also investing thirty to sixty minutes of my time (plus preparation), this person would be likely to make a gift that is significantly bigger than one she might have made if approached through a less time-consuming and less personal strategy?"

Three broad qualifications determine if someone is a prospect and therefore worth your time:

- **A**bility to make a gift of the size you are looking for

- **B**elief in the cause or something similar

- **C**ontact with someone in the group who is either willing to ask this person or willing to allow their name to be used in the asking

When you have positive, verifiable evidence of A, B, and C, you have a prospect. If one of the criteria is missing, or more, you have a potential prospect, usually called a "suspect." Let's look at each of these criteria in depth, beginning with the most important.

Contact

Contact is the most important of the three criteria and also the most overlooked. Do you know the prospect? Does anyone in your network know the prospect? Without contact, you cannot proceed with a personal solicitation because there is no link between your organization and this person.

There are three ways for a person to have contact with your organization:

1. A board member, staff person, or volunteer knows the person.

2. A board member, staff person, or volunteer knows someone who knows this person, and that someone is either willing to let you use his or her name in the approach ("Mary Jones suggested I call …") or, better yet, is willing to call on your behalf ("Joe, this is Mary. I'm giving money to a really amazing group and was hoping you would be willing to see a couple of their representatives, let them tell you about the group, and ask you to join").

3. The person is currently a donor to your organization, but no one close to the group knows the person. In that case, when you call you will say, "We don't know each other, but we share a commitment to _____ and I want to talk with you about an exciting project we are about to undertake."

Belief

In thinking through why someone who is not already a donor might believe in your organization, return to your case statement (discussed in Chapter Four). What values does your group espouse? What organizations have similar values even if their goals are different? Be broad-minded and creative in assessing potential linkage. For example, people who give to children's organizations are often interested in environmental issues because they are concerned about the kind of world children are growing up in and will inherit as adults. People giving to environmental groups are likely to be interested in health issues; people who give to libraries often will support literacy programs or creative educational projects that help people appreciate the value of reading. But people who give to community organizing may also give to symphonies, and people who give to human rights programs may be big supporters of museums. In other words, most of us have multiple interests, and it is important not to make a lot of assumptions about a prospect's interest or lack of interest in your cause. In addition to reviewing the case statement for your underlying values, ask staff, volunteers, and board members to write down all the values they hold dear and what beliefs of theirs tie in with your group. This should provide a broad list that you can use to help screen potential prospects.

For example, a reproductive justice organization working to educate beauty salons about the health effects, particularly reproductive damage, of the chemicals in nail polish and remover, hair dye, and other products used routinely by salon workers, who are mostly women, discovered some surprises in its list of underlying values. In addition to what one would imagine, such as workplaces should be safe and toxin free, or workers should understand what they are being exposed to and what their rights are, they also said that standards of beauty, which drive women to be customers of these salons, need to be questioned. Small salons are often owned and run by immigrant families, and this organization said these entrepreneurs should be given tax incentives to start other kinds of businesses that provide more important and needed products. This led the organization to look for donors to programs that address sex stereotyping in schools and to a coalition of small business owners who were interested in creating a master plan for development of neighborhood shopping areas to include fresh fruit and vegetable vendors, bike shops, recycle programs, and the like. It had been focusing on helping liquor store owners convert to other kinds of products, but found a receptive audience in some of the salon owners. By broadening its definitions beyond the already broad health and worker justice values, it brought in a new set of donors and the possibility of new approaches to its work.

In addition to looking for similar values, look for other things that might link a person to your cause. Do you serve a neighborhood that the person's family comes from? If your organization has clients, do those clients patronize the prospect's business?

Try not to draw conclusions from facts about people that could lead you to assume they won't be sympathetic to your cause. Many donors to the arts are concerned about censorship, so they are also likely to give to organizations working to protect civil liberties. People who support environmental organizations may give to anti-poverty programs, recognizing that poverty is a result and a cause of environmental destruction. People may strongly disagree with aspects of traditions they otherwise support or beliefs they otherwise hold: for example, many Catholics are pro-choice, and many Jews are critical of Israel. People live in a context that is bigger than any one aspect of their identity, and drawing conclusions based on one piece of information may lead you away from a prospect if you are not careful.

Ability

Although first in the A-B-C order, ability is actually the least important factor in identifying prospects. We can safely assume that if a volunteer or staff person in an organization has friends or colleagues who give away money and believe in the cause, those same people have the ability to make some kind of gift even if it is very small. The question is, how much should they be asked for?

One of the biggest mistakes fundraisers make is assuming that how much a person can give will be related to how much money she has. Obviously, how much money a person has influences how much that person can give at one time, but sometimes people will give more than they could have given in one gift by giving over time through monthly donations off a credit card or through their bank. Many wealthy people could afford to give much more than they do, while many poor people give a high proportion of what little they have. Stockbrokers, bankers, and financial planners are interested in how much people have, because they are selling the idea that they can help them have more. Fundraisers are interested in how much people give, so giving is the behavior to focus on, not having.

In terms of identifying how much a person can give, first you need to figure out if that person gives away money. To do so, ask the contact what other groups the prospect supports and look at lists of donors printed in other organizations' newsletters, annual reports, and programs. Listen closely to what people say. Do they complain about getting a lot of direct mail? ("I seem to be on everyone's list.") This is probably a person who gives by mail. Do they complain about how many phone calls they receive? ("Just when we're sitting down to dinner, the phone rings, and it's the disabled, or the theater or global warming.") These calls are rarely random—they are made to people who give by phone. Is the person very busy? With what? Board meetings at the legal aid society? Organizing a special event for International Women's Day? Volunteering with the PTA? Being a docent at the art museum? Working for a political candidate? These involvements all signal someone who participates actively in nonprofit causes.

Next, to determine the size of a possible gift, the following guidelines are useful. All of them assume some evidence that the person is interested in your cause.

To determine whether someone could give $100 to $499, you need to know little more than that he is employed in a job that pays a living wage, that he is not supporting very many other people (children, partner, elderly relative), and that he has given in that range to some other nonprofit.

To determine if someone could give in the $500 to $1,000 range will require knowing that the person has a well-paying job or some inheritance or a healthy retirement income, or that the person is married to or living with someone who has any of these advantages. People who give in this range usually are not the sole support of their household or the household is not very large.

To determine if someone could give more than $1,000 will require a little more knowledge, particularly that the person has given in this range to other nonprofits, but most important as you get to these larger gifts, that the person is already a donor of some size to your organization. No matter how wealthy and generous someone is, that person will rarely start giving to a small organization with such a large gift. (I discuss these larger gifts in Part Three, "Strategies for Upgrading Donors.")

Ultimately, you will not know with any certainty how much any person can give because you can't know all their circumstances and because their perception of what they can afford can change from day to day. You make your best guess and you ask. People are rarely insulted to be asked for more money than they can afford; it's flattering to have people think you are that successful financially.

STEPS IN CREATING A PROSPECT LIST

Now that you know how to define a prospect, your group can begin to create a list of people who qualify as prospects you will ask for gifts. The first step is for the people who are going to be involved in the personal solicitation strategy to meet and create a Master Prospect List. Having all the names in one place ensures that no one gets asked by more than one person and that the right person does the asking in each case. Also, in a group setting people get more excited about the process and come up with more names and more enthusiasm for asking than they would on their own. Moreover, when more than one person knows a prospect, more information can be collected and verified.

The easiest way to create a Master Prospect List for donors who might give more than $250 was developed by fundraising consultant Stephanie Roth. Here's how it works. Each person at the meeting first creates her or his own personal list, set up as in the accompanying illustration that follows, of all the people they know or who would recognize them if they were to call. People should not censor themselves by saying, "He hates me" or "She's a tightwad" or "I can't ask *her*!" Each person just makes the list of people they know, some of whom will be prospects. Also, people should remember that just because they are the contact does not mean that they will be the solicitor. Who will solicit the gift will be decided for each prospect once they are identified.

Prospect Identification List			
Contact Name:			
Person I Know	**Believes in Cause**	**Gives Away Money**	**Amount to Ask For:**
			$
			$
			$
			$
			$
			$
			$
			$
			$

Beside each name the contact notes whether or not the potential prospect believes in the cause. If contacts don't know what the person believes in, they put a question mark. Next, they cross off all the people whom they know don't believe in the cause. Next to the names of the people who believe in the cause, they make a note of whether they know for a fact that this person gives away money. If they don't know, they put a question mark. They cross off anyone they know for a fact does not give away money. Next to all the people who remain—that is, people they know, who they know believe in the cause, and who they know give away money, they put what amount of money they think the prospect could give. This can be any amount, but this exercise is generally used to find people who can give between $250 and $2,500. If the contacts don't have any idea how much the prospect could give, they put a question mark. When everyone in the meeting has created his or her own list, they each then read their list of firm prospects aloud. Firm prospects are those people for whom contacts were able to answer affirmatively in all categories. One person then enters these names on a spreadsheet program to construct a Master Prospect List. If anyone else knows the prospects, they can confirm the information or add other information. The Master Prospect List will look like the example shown here.

Master Prospect List				
Name of Prospect	Contact	Solicitor	Amount to Be Solicited	Other Info

Next, each person reads aloud the names of people on their list that have question marks concerning belief in the cause or whether they give money to see if anyone else filled in this information. If no one else knows the person, he or she is not a prospect. If someone does know them, they are either moved to the Master Prospect List or crossed off on the basis of the additional information.

Once there is a final Master List of people whom someone knows, who believe in the cause, and who could make this size of gift, then a decision is made as to who is going to ask each person for a gift. The decision about who asks is based on who has the best relationship with the prospect, who is willing to ask, and by whom the prospect would feel most comfortable being solicited. For example, let's say the choice of solicitor is between a close friend of the prospect and a business colleague whom the prospect likes and admires. At first blush, one might think that the friend should ask, but it might be better to go with the business colleague who can present the case in a businesslike way. Another option is for the two people to go together. Ultimately, the best solicitor is the person most likely to do a good job.

Each solicitor now ends up with his or her own Prospect List. From the Master Prospect List, a database of prospect records will be developed, with each prospect record containing more detailed information about that person. The solicitor for each prospect is given a copy of the prospect record.

The Prospect Record shown here is a generic sample of what you need to know about individual prospects. Keep in mind that you need to know less about someone you are asking for $500 than about someone you will approach for $2,500. This information is kept in the database and added to or corrected as you learn more. Eventually, as at least half of the prospects become donors, it will be helpful to have information recorded for each of them. The following types of information should be discovered and recorded for each prospect.

It is imperative for one or two people to take on the task of collecting this information and recording it systematically. This is the job of development staff. If your organization does not have staff, one or two people from the board should take on this task. The information must be accurate and confidential. Nothing should appear that is only known from gossip or that is not helpful in seeking a gift. ("Had an affair with the Methodist minister" may be interesting, but is not prospect information.) Some kinds of information will be more useful to some organizations than to others. An agency working with

```
┌─────────────────────────────────────────────────────────────────┐
│                       Prospect Record                           │
│                                                                 │
│  Date:_____ │
│  Name:_____ │
│  Address (work):_____ │
│  Address (home):_____ │
│  Phone: (work)_____ (home) _____ (cell) _____ │
│  Fax: (work) _____ (home)_____ │
│  E-mail: _____ │
│  Contact(s):_____ │
│  Interest or involvement in nonprofits (be specific): _____ │
│  Donations to nonprofits:_____ │
│  Evidence of interest in our work:_____ │
│  Occupation:_____ │
│  Employer:_____ Matching gift possible?___ │
│  Household composition: _____ │
│  Other interests/hobbies:_____ │
│  Suggested gift range:_____ │
│     Anything else we should know (for example, lives half-time here and │
│  half-time in Cuba, more likely to respond to e-mail than phone, makes │
│  all decisions with partner): _____ │
│  Suggested solicitor:_____ │
│  Relationship to solicitor:_____ │
│  Result:_____ │
└─────────────────────────────────────────────────────────────────┘
```

prisoners may wish to know if anyone in the prospect's family has spent time in prison. Otherwise, that would probably not be appropriate information. People working in historic preservation may want to know how long someone has lived in a community, whereas people working on animal welfare issues will be more interested in knowing whether the person has pets or livestock or likes animals.

The most helpful tip for putting together lists of prospects is to put yourself at the top of the list. In fundraising we say that the first time you ask someone for money in person, you should always get a yes, because the first person you ask should be yourself. Once you test the proposition that the group is worth supporting against your own bank account, you will have a much clearer sense of who else you know who might give and what amount they might consider.

After all the solicitors have made their own donations, and appropriate and adequate information has been gathered about the prospects, the solicitors should each have a list of people they are going to approach. They should plan to approach the people most likely to say yes first. These do not have to be your potentially biggest donors—what is important is to have two or three good experiences before you encounter anyone saying no. In our "Brussels sprouts before dessert" culture, solicitors sometimes start with the hardest people "to get them over with." Don't do that. You need the experience of hearing someone respond positively early on to carry you through some of the harder requests.

HOW TO APPROACH THE PROSPECT

The solicitors are now ready to approach their prospects. The most formal approach involves three steps:

1. An e-mail or letter describing the organization or the specific need, including a sentence or two indicating that you wish to ask the prospect for a gift and requesting a meeting to discuss it further, followed by

2. A phone call or e-mail to set up a meeting, and then

3. The meeting itself, in which the gift is actually solicited

Obviously, if you are approaching your spouse or your best friend you can skip the letter and perhaps even the phone call. In other cases, particularly for smaller gifts, the letter may be enough and there will be no need for a phone call. In others, the letter and a phone call will be enough, and there will be no need for a meeting. Deciding whether a meeting or follow-up phone call is necessary will depend on your knowledge of the prospect and how much money you are requesting. Some people are very comfortable giving $250, $500, or even $1,000 in response to a phone call from someone they know. If the prospect lives far away from the organization or the solicitor, she or he may be more willing to have an extended phone conversation than to expect the solicitor to visit them.

Regardless of how generous, easygoing, or committed your prospects are, they will be more likely to give if you follow up your letter with a phone call, and they will almost always give more in a meeting than when asked over the phone. Remember, you are requesting a thoughtful gift—a gift that is big enough that a person needs to think about whether they can afford it and whether they wish to give your organization a gift that big. You want sufficient time with prospects to answer all their questions and concerns. It takes about thirty minutes to have the conversation you need to have, and a thirty-minute meeting seems a lot shorter than a thirty-minute phone call.

THE E-MAIL OR LETTER

The letter should raise the prospect's interest, giving some information but not enough for a truly informed decision. If a letter, it should not be longer than one page. An e-mail may even be shorter. Its purpose is to get the prospect to be open to the phone call in which the solicitor requests a meeting. In other words, the letter introduces the fact that you will be asking for a large gift for your organization and that you want the prospect to be willing to give a short amount of time to hear why you want this gift and why you think this prospect will be interested. No commitment to give or to be involved in any way is asked for in this opening correspondence—only a request for the prospect to discuss the proposition of a gift with the solicitor. A sample letter is shown here:

Ms. Concerned Activist with Good-Paying Job
Professional Office Building
City, State, ZIP

Dear Connie,

For several years you have heard me talk about the Downtown Free Clinic. As you know, I have recently been elected to serve on the board, which I am really excited about! At a recent meeting, we decided to launch a major gifts campaign, the main purpose of which is to help the clinic become financially self-sufficient. In the future, we want to depend on a broad base of donors rather than on foundations and government grants, which have proven most unreliable.

The goal of the campaign is $50,000 the first year. All of us on the board have made our own commitments, which total $15,000. We are now turning to other caring people in the community to raise the rest. We need some lead gifts in the range of $1,000 to $2,000 from people of standing in the community whose word and example carry weight. I am hoping you will consider being one of the leaders in the campaign because of your long-time activism in community health care.

(Include one more brief paragraph on the current programs of the organization.)

I know this is a big request, and I don't expect you to decide on the basis of my letter alone, so I am hoping we can meet and talk. I am very excited about the direction the Downtown Free Clinic is taking, and I can't really do it justice in this letter.

I'll call you next week to set up a time. Hope you are well. Enjoyed seeing you and your family at the baseball game last week.

Best always,
Annie
Another Concerned Activist

The letter is straightforward. Connie knows what the request will be, including the amount. She knows what the money is for. If giving anything to this organization is out of the question for her, she can decide that now. If giving a lead gift is out of the question, it is implicit from the letter that a smaller gift is an option. Her importance to the campaign has been stated, which is flattering, but there is nothing she needs to do at this point except wait for the phone call. No action has been requested—in fact, she has specifically only been asked not to decide.

An e-mail would have most of the same content, with various choices of subject line, such as "Free Clinic hat on," "A request," "Starting an exciting campaign."

The last paragraph of the e-mail would probably say, "Let me know what would be a good time to get together next week." There are a number of advantages to e-mail; one of the biggest is that the meeting can often be set up without a phone call. A return e-mail or texting about a time and place to meet may be the next step.

THE PHONE CALL

If you are the solicitor and you say you are going to call, you must call. Rehearse the phone call beforehand to anticipate questions or objections the prospect may have. Be sure you know exactly what you are going to say from the very first hello. Many people find it useful to write down what they will say, in the same way that one writes a script for a phone-a-thon (see Chapter Thirteen, "Fundraising by Telephone").

The phone call is the most difficult part of the solicitation. You need it in order to arrange a meeting, and if you are not going to ask for a meeting, the phone conversation will make a difference as to whether the person gives at all. There is a lot of pressure on this call. Also, you have no body language to help you infer what the prospect is thinking and feeling. You can't tell if he or she is frowning, smiling, in a hurry, or doing something else while talking with you. You can't rely on how people sound on the phone. People who are easygoing may sound brusque or harried on the phone. Increasingly, we reach people on their cell phones. People on a cell phone can, quite literally, be anywhere. I often hear people making hurried plans while waiting for a plane to take off, while walking down the street, or while standing outside a restaurant. It may be hard to hear them, and your conversation may be dropped before you are finished. Some people simply do not like to talk on the phone, and their dislike of being on the phone may come across to you as a dislike of talking to you or a reluctance to discuss a gift. Finally, a phone call is always an interruption, even if the prospect really likes you.

All of these things can make a solicitor anxious; anxiety, unfortunately, makes for poor phone calls. Anxious people have a hard time listening to others because they are too absorbed in thinking about what they are going to say next. Practicing the phone call a few times with other people in your organization will help you be less anxious.

There are two things that can happen when you make this phone call: either you won't reach the prospect, or you will.

You Don't Reach the Prospect.   About 90 percent of the time that you phone someone you will get some kind of gatekeeper—an answering machine, voice mail, a secretary, someone else in the household. When this happens, leave a brief message that includes a good time to call you back and say that you will try again.

Leave at least three such messages before you give up on this prospect. Messages are not reliable. Voice mail gets erased accidentally, messages written on pieces of paper get lost, numbers get transposed, names are spelled wrong and the prospect cannot recognize who called, prospects try to call you back and get a busy signal or carry your message around with them meaning to call but never find the time, and so on. Many people find that leaving their e-mail address in addition to their phone number increases the chance of the person getting back to them. Again, don't assume that because you can't reach the prospect the answer is no. However, your time is valuable also, and leaving more than three messages for one person is not as useful as moving on to the next prospect.

If you have made a serious effort to reach a prospect and have not succeeded, you may want to ask the contact for more information about the prospect. You may find out that the prospect is out of the country or is tending to a sick relative, or that you can make an appointment with the prospect through her personal assistant, or even that the assistant has the authority to handle these requests.

You Do Reach the Prospect.   If you do reach the prospect, first ensure that you have not caught her or him at a bad time by asking if this is a good time to talk. Once that is established, get right to the purpose of the call. If you have sent the prospect a letter, inquire about whether the prospect received it and had a chance to review it. Be clear about the purpose of the phone call, which is to ask for some time to discuss the possibility of the prospect making a gift—not to ask for the gift. The prospect does not need to decide about his or her gift until the meeting.

Be sure not to read meaning into statements the prospect may make that can be taken at face value. For example, do not hear, "I don't want to give" in a statement such as "I'm very busy this month" or "I have to talk to my spouse before making any decision." Instead, in the first instance say, "I can understand that. How about if I call you next month, when things might have slowed down for you?" In the second instance say, "Would it be possible for me to see you both in that case?" Hear everything the prospect says as being literally true. If she says, "I've already given away all the money I am going to give this year," then ask if you can meet so that your organization can be considered for next year. If she says, "I need more information before I can meet," ask what information would be most helpful, tell her you will send it today, and then suggest penciling in a meeting for a later time after the prospect has had time to review the information.

If the prospect tries to put you off, do not assume that he or she is saying no. In fact, people who make a lot of big gifts will often use put-offs to determine whether you are serious about the organization and whether the organization can really do its work. This is particularly true for community organizing projects. It is hard to believe that a group will really face down corporate intimidation or stand up to political power if its members fold at the first sign of resistance from someone they have identified as a person who believes in their cause!

There's one more logistical item to consider before you pick up the phone: where to try to reach the prospect. In the older and simpler days, fundraisers chose between calling someone at home or at work. A general rule is to call people where you know them. Where would you call them if the topic weren't money? You would probably call neighbors at home. Friends you can often call anywhere, including on their cell phone. Colleagues are generally approached through work. Wherever you call, always ask this question first: "Is this a good time to talk?" Or "Do you have a few minutes to talk right now?" If you are able, stand up while making these calls and smile while you are talking. You will breathe more deeply and sound less anxious. Don't talk too fast, and pause between sentences.

THE MEETING

Once you have set up an appointment, you are ready to prepare for the face-to-face solicitation. This is not so frightening as it seems. First of all, the prospect knows from your e-mail or your phone call that you will be talking about making a contribution. Since he or she has agreed to see you, the answer to your request is not an outright no. The prospect is considering saying yes. Your job is to move the prospect from consideration to commitment.

The purpose of the meeting is to request a specific gift and get some kind of answer from the prospect. As the solicitor, you must appear poised, enthusiastic, and confident. If you are well prepared, this will not be too difficult. Board members and volunteers can go with each other or bring a staff person to such a meeting to provide any information the solicitor doesn't have. If you do go in pairs, be sure you know who is going to begin the meeting and who is going to actually ask for the gift. Make sure each of you has something to say so that one of you doesn't do all the talking, and remember that going in pairs means that each person has less time to talk.

The solicitor's job is to ask for the gift. The prospect's job is to decide; among possible decisions are whether to give the gift requested or a smaller gift, whether to take time to think about it, or whether to say no. It is important that the solicitor does not get personally caught up in the prospect's response. You are not a good fundraiser if someone says yes, nor are you a poor fundraiser if someone says no. If you are asking enough people, a certain percentage of them will say no. In fact, a sign that you are not asking enough people is when you go for a long time without anyone saying no.

Meeting Etiquette

Regardless of how well you know this prospect, the subject of this meeting is business. You should begin the meeting with pleasantries, catch up on family and friends briefly, but avoid the temptation to have a long chat before getting down to the subject at hand. It is often helpful to say early in the meeting, "Well, you know why we are here, which is to ask you to consider making a gift to Important Group. Before we get to that, however, I wanted to hear how your grandson likes kindergarten/if you found homes for those kittens that showed up in your yard/if you liked the play the other night. . . ." Don't ask wide-open questions, such as "How is your summer going?" or "What's new in your life?" You want a question that can be easily answered so you can move into the business at hand.

Show genuine interest in the answers to your questions, or the person will think you were just asking out of some sense of protocol, but do move into the business at hand as soon as you can. "We are doing some really exciting stuff this summer, and I wanted to have a chance to tell you about it." Or "Our capital campaign is almost done, and now we can expand our programs, which is mostly why we are here today." This moves everyone into the conversation about the organization and its fundraising goals.

Next, keep in mind that the more the prospect is encouraged to talk, the more likely he or she is to give. No one likes to be talked at or lectured. Ask the prospect what she knows about your group, how she keeps up with the issues your group works on, and other open-ended questions. Share your own experience with the group and tell stories that illustrate facts rather than just giving a dry exposition of what the group does. Sentences that begin, "I am most excited by . . ." or, "I got involved with Important Group because of my own situation/commitment/longstanding interest in . . ." are much more likely to be listened to than "We started in 1997 with funding from the Havelots Foundation."

In addition to asking questions, pause for a few seconds between every few sentences. Wait to see if the prospect wants to add anything or has any questions or objections. If the prospect says something you don't understand, ask for clarification or say, "Tell me more about that." If the prospect says something that offends you or that you don't agree with, don't pretend to agree. Don't sacrifice your integrity for this gift, but see if you can find a way to counter what the prospect said without getting into an argument. You can use phrases such as, "I can see why you say that because that is the impression that the media gives, but in fact . . ." or "We have discovered that fact-fact-fact, which is why we have designed the program the way we have." Said without rancor or defensiveness, statements like these can allow the prospect to change his mind without looking ignorant.

After about half an hour, when the prospect seems satisfied with what you have said, you should be ready to close—that is, to ask for the gift. Repeat the goal of the campaign and the importance of the cause in one or two sentences. Then, looking directly at the prospect, ask for a specific gift: "Will you join me and give $2,000?" or, "I'm hoping you can give a gift in the range of $1,500," or, "Do you think you could consider a gift of $5,000?" There are no magic words for the close—what is important is that you figure out a phrase that suits your personality and that includes the range or the specific gift you want. Then be quiet. At this moment, you give up control of the interaction. At last, you are asking the prospect to make a decision. Wait for the prospect to speak, even if you have to wait for what seems like several minutes. If you are anxious, time will seem to pass very slowly. Keep looking at the prospect without staring. You can breathe easy now, because you have said everything you need to say and you have put your best foot forward. Take a deep breath in and release it slowly. Smile a little and don't frown. You want to look relaxed and confident.

The Prospect's Response

At this point the prospect will say one of six things, or some variation on these responses:

1. "Yes, I'll help." Thank the prospect. Be grateful and pleased, but don't be overly effusive or you will give the impression you didn't think the prospect was really a generous person. Arrange for how the gift will be made (by check, by pledge, online, by stock transfer; now, later). The easiest way to do that is to ask, "How would you like to pay that?" Once those arrangements are made, thank the prospect again and leave.

2. "I'd like to help, but the figure you name is too high." This is a yes answer but for a smaller gift. You can say, "Would you like to pledge that amount and contribute it in quarterly installments over a year's time?" Or you can say, "What would you feel comfortable giving?" or "What would you like to give?" Avoid the temptation to bargain with the prospect. Once the prospect has decided on an amount, follow the procedure in answer 1.

3. "That's a lot of money." This statement is generally a stall. The prospect feels he can give what you have asked, which is a big gift for him. He wants to be sure that your organization agrees that the gift is large. Your answer: "It is a lot of money. There are not many people we could ask for that amount." Or "It is a lot of money. That's why I wanted to talk to you about it in person." Or "It is a lot of money. It would be a big help." Then be quiet again and let the prospect decide.

4. "I need to think about it." Some people truly cannot make up their mind on the spot and if pushed for an answer will say no. Reassure the prospect that you don't need an answer today: "That's fine. I know it is a big request." Then ask the prospect, "What else can I tell you that will help you in your thinking?" and answer any remaining questions. End by saying, "May I call you in a few days to see what your decision is?" or "Should we be in touch by e-mail?" Set a time when the prospect will be finished thinking and will give you an answer.

5. "I need to talk to my spouse/partner/other party." This probably does mean the person needs to talk to someone else; however, it is surprising that the prospect didn't say that when you set up the meeting, so it probably also means the person needs more time. Often it means that the person has another question or objection but is embarrassed to say it. This is called the "shadow question," and you need to surface what it is. You will do that by saying, "That makes sense. Is there anything your partner will want to

know that I can tell you now?" The prospect may then tell you what's bothering him or her. "My accountant will want to know why you spend so much on office space" or "My wife will want to know why you take money from Possibly Bad Corporation and will wonder if that affects your work." You can then answer these objections. You will end this solicitation by getting some agreement as to when the prospect can talk to the person they need to consult and when you should get back to them.

6. *"No, I can't help you."* Although this is an unlikely response at this point, it should be treated with respect. Nod your head and wait silently for a longer explanation. Generally, the prospect will expand to provide a reason. "I just don't agree with your approach. I thought when I heard more about it I might understand and agree, but I don't." Or, "I just can't get past the fact that Person I Hate is the chair of your board." Don't join in trashing this person, but don't spend a lot of time defending them either, unless your defense is confined to discussing their work for your organization. "He has done really good work for us, but I know he is controversial."

In the highly unlikely situation that you have remained silent for at least a full minute and the prospect hasn't volunteered any explanation for saying no, you can ask for one. "Would you say a little bit about why you are saying no?" Or "I am going to be asking other people as well. Are there any ways I can improve?" If you ask nondefensively, the prospect will answer. If the answer is a misunderstanding, clear it up and you may get a yes, or at least, "I'll think about it." Don't spend much time trying to change the prospect's mind or you will seem disrespectful. Often, people who say no to a request like this later say yes as they learn more or have time to think more about what you have said. Try to end the meeting with a question the prospect can say yes to. "Would you like to stay on our e-mail list?" Or "When Person You Hate leaves the board, can I call you?" Or just, "What is the best way to get downtown from here?" Thank the prospect for his or her time and leave. Remember that you have an unspoken but very important agreement with all the people you ask for money: if they agree to be asked, you will respect their right to say no.

Immediately after the interview send a thank you note regardless of the response you got at the meeting. "Thanks for your pledge of $5,000. I can't wait to tell the executive director. Your generosity makes a BIG difference." Or "Thanks for your candid and helpful observations about our new program. I will bring them back to the staff and let you know how we decide to proceed." If the prospect made a gift, another thank you note should come from the organization when the gift is received.

Although it can be anxiety-producing to ask someone for a large gift, it is also thrilling when a prospect says yes, and it is not a big deal when someone says no. Most of the time people say no for understandable reasons that have nothing to do with you. With practice, asking for money becomes easier and easier. Most people are encouraged by being able to set aside their own discomfort about asking for money for the greater purpose of meeting the needs of the organization.

chapter EIGHT

Using Special Events Correctly

Special events, also often called "fundraising benefits," are social gatherings of many sorts that expand the reputation of the organization; give those attending an amusing, interesting, or moving time; and possibly make money for the organization sponsoring the event. The variations among special events are practically limitless, as are the possibilities for money earned or lost, amount of work put in, number of people participating, and so on. Special events are arguably the oldest fundraising strategy and certainly the most common around the world. In every country where I have taught fundraising or read about fundraising, special events have played a big role. Because of their variety and flexibility, special events are excellent strategies for acquiring, retaining, or upgrading donors, and organizations that are serious about building a broad base of individual donors need to have at least one or two special events every year.

Events are often misunderstood and misused. Organizations hope that they will raise lots of money, but that is not what events do well. Instead, special events should have the following three goals:

- To generate publicity for the organization
- To raise the visibility of the organization
- To bring in (new) money

Generating publicity means getting a particular audience to pay attention to the organization for a limited time by means of advertising the event and by the quality of the event.

Enhancing visibility raises the overall profile of the organization in the community. Visibility is the cumulative effect of publicity. With each successive event, and in combination with other fundraising and organizing efforts, the organization becomes known to more and more of the people who should know about it (which is usually not everyone in a community). You can assess the visibility of your group by asking this question: Of the people who should know about you, what percentage do? This percentage is called your *visibility quotient.* Assessing a visibility quotient requires thinking through what types of people should know about your organization and what mechanisms reach those potential donors. For example, if you are regularly featured in the local newspaper, you may be well known to those who read the paper, but you also need to reach people who don't read the newspaper, which today is a majority of young people and larger and larger numbers of all people. In that case, getting more print publicity will not help you, and you may need to move to the Internet, radio, speaking engagements at houses of worship, or a door-to-door canvass in order to reach new constituencies. Events are excellent publicity-generating tools because they give the media a hook around which to focus attention on the group. A newspaper or radio station may be interested in discussing the event or even doing a profile of it—an auction, a self-defense class, or a concert—and will mention the sponsoring group's name, thus raising visibility. Getting someone to mention your event in her blog or on her Facebook page may attract people you otherwise have little access to. People can send an announcement about your event to all their friends or to a subset of those friends. Ditto with announcing your event on Twitter. Other people will then "like" that announcement or retweet it, and it will be sent further.

Raising money is a secondary goal for a special event because there are many faster and easier ways to raise money than this one. An organization that simply needs money (perhaps from being in a cash flow bind or having an unexpected expense) will find that the slowest ways to raise that money are seeking government funding or having an event. On the other hand, an organization that wants to raise its profile, bring in new people, and possibly make money will find a special event an ideal strategy. In many cases special events can lose money or barely break even and still be successful because of the publicity and visibility they produced.

TYPES OF PEOPLE WHO ATTEND SPECIAL EVENTS

There are two categories of people who attend events: those who come because of the event itself and those who come both for the event and to support your group. In the first category are people who would come to a particular event no matter who sponsored it. These people attend flea markets, dances, movie benefits, decorator showcases, auctions, and the like. Many times these people will not even know the name of the nonprofit sponsoring the event. In a similar vein are small businesses or corporations that will buy ads in an adbook, donate raffle prizes, buy tables at luncheons, or even underwrite an event, but would not give the organization money under other circumstances. They want the advertising and resulting goodwill the event gives them, along with the chance to target a specific audience inexpensively. Raising money from a person or a business that would not give you money otherwise does not constitute donor "acquisition," but it is a smart use of an event and provides another income stream. Of course, the event should also be designed to draw people who are interested in your organization. However, for organizations in rural communities or serving a very small constituency and unable to build a large base of donors, events that draw people to the event rather than to the cause will be important for raising money.

The second kind of people who attend events are those who are both interested in the event and believe in your cause. They may not have heard of your organization before learning of this event, or they may already know of your organization and want to support it while getting something important to them. For example, women wanting to take a self-defense class may choose one sponsored by the local rape crisis program rather than a commercial gym in order to support the rape crisis program. After the classes, some of the participants may want to join the program as volunteers and paying members. People who buy all their holiday presents at a crafts fair that benefits a public radio station or who enter marathons sponsored by organizations they believe in are good prospects to follow up with using another strategy such as e-mail or direct mail.

Among the second type are people who appreciate your organization's work but can't afford or don't want to donate more than a small sum. For them, buying a $2 raffle ticket or attending a $10 movie benefit is a perfect way to show their support.

CHOOSING A FUNDRAISING EVENT

Several criteria should be considered in choosing a fundraising event: the appropriateness of the event, the image of the organization created by the event, the amount of volunteer energy required, the amount of front money needed, the repeatability and the timing of the event, and how the event fits into the organization's overall fundraising plan.

Appropriateness of the Event

To decide if an event is appropriate, ask yourself, "If people knew nothing about our organization except that it had sponsored this event, what would they think of us?" If you think their thoughts would be neutral or good, then the event is appropriate. If you think that you would want them to know more about your work than just what the event implies about it, you should think again. Examples of inappropriate events abound. In the extreme, if you are the symphony you don't sponsor a pie-eating contest; if you run an alcohol recovery program you don't have a wine tasting. Often, however, the question of appropriateness is more subtle than in those examples, as shown here in two case studies.

A QUESTION OF CONSISTENCY

An organization working to end sweatshop conditions in garment factories around the world plans a luncheon to which it will invite a thousand people in the hope that three hundred will attend. The development director asks a large print shop to print their invitations and adbook as an in-kind donation. Soon after, a member of a union that has been trying to organize the workers at the print shop calls the development director of the anti-sweatshop organization and asks him not to use this shop. She explains that working conditions there are terrible—the workers are exposed to toxic fumes, they are paid minimum wage with no benefits, and they are laid off during slow periods, then rehired when business picks up—and she points out the lack of consistency for an organization whose mission is to stand up for workers everywhere to take their business to such a shop. However, the lure of free printing for a thousand invitations and 750 copies of an adbook, saving the organization as much as $3,000, proves too much for this development director to pass up. He thanks the union organizer for her comments, but says that his using this print shop will not worsen conditions there and that not using it will not improve conditions.

The union knows that this organization's events get a lot of publicity and often attract powerful people. They decide to organize an information line outside the event. The line is not a picket line and not intended to ask people to boycott the event, but union members and volunteers hand out information about the print shop outside the hotel during the time the event is held there. The workers at the hotel, members of a different union, spontaneously decide to join the information line. As a result, the event becomes a public relations nightmare from which the organization does not recover quickly. It learned the hard way the importance of political consistency.

A QUESTION OF JUDGMENT

A women's health organization in a large West Coast city offered as a top raffle prize a case of fine, expensive wine. During its promotion, a number of studies were released showing the high rate of alcoholism among women and the dangers to a developing fetus when a pregnant woman drinks alcohol. An internal debate ensued in the organization over whether it was appropriate for an NGO working to prevent dangerous drugs and devices from being given to women to offer alcohol—a potentially dangerous drug—as a raffle prize. Proponents argued that only 10 percent of the population are alcoholics and that alcohol does not harm most people who use it. The chance of an alcoholic winning that prize was slim compared to how many people would be attracted to the raffle because of this prize. However, opponents won by reasoning that they would not approve of a contraceptive that hurt only 10 percent of its users. The organization withdrew the prize, not wanting to promote a drug with any potential for harm.

Image of the Organization

In addition to being appropriate, the event as much as possible should be in keeping with the image of the organization or should promote the image the organization wishes to have. Although considerations of appropriateness sometimes include those of image, image is also a distinct issue. Many events that are appropriate for a group do not promote a memorable image of it. For example, a library would choose a book sale over a garage sale, even though both are appropriate. An environmental organization would use a white water rafting trip over season tickets to the ballet as a door prize, even though both are nice prizes. An organization promoting awareness of high blood pressure might choose a health fair over a dance. The idea is to attract people to your event who might become regular donors to your organization by linking the event to your mission.

Energy of Volunteers

The volunteer energy required to plan and mount an event involves several considerations. How many people are required to put on this event? What would these volunteers be doing if they were not working on this event? Are there enough volunteers who have the time required to produce this event—not only to manage the event on the day of its occurrence but to take care of all the details that must be done beforehand?

Volunteer time is a resource to be cultivated, guided, and used appropriately. For example, don't use someone with connections to major donor prospects and who is comfortable asking for money in person to hand address invitations to the gala. Similarly, a friendly, outgoing person should be the solicitor of auction items rather than asked to bake brownies for the food booth at the county fair. Obviously, what the volunteer wants to do should be of primary concern. People generally like to do what they are good at and be involved where they can be most useful.

Front Money

Most special events require that some money be spent before there is assurance that any money will be raised. The front money needed for an event should be an amount your organization could afford to lose if the event had to be canceled. This money should already be available—you should not, for example, use funds from advance ticket sales to rent the place where the event will be held. If the event is canceled some people will want their money back, but you may not get your whole rent deposit back. Events that require a lot of front money can create a cash flow problem in the organization if the need for this money is not taken into account.

Repeatability

The best event is one that becomes a tradition in your community, so that every year people look forward to the event that your group sponsors. Using this criterion can save you from discarding an event simply because the turnout was small the first time you did it. Perhaps you got too little publicity and only a handful of people came. If each of those people had a great time and you heard them saying, "I wish I had brought Juan" or "I wish Tiffany had known about this," then it may be worth having the event again next year. To decide if an event is repeatable, evaluate whether the same number of people working the same number of hours would raise more money producing this event again.

Timing

You need to find out what else is happening in your community at the time you want to hold your event. You don't want to conflict with the major fundraising event of a similar organization, nor do you want to be the tenth dance or auction in a row. If you are appealing to a particular constituency, you need to think of their timing. Farmers are mostly unavailable during planting and harvest seasons, Muslims will not appreciate being invited to a food festival during Ramadan, gay men and lesbians may not come to a day-long meditation scheduled during the local Pride Parade, and so on.

The Big Picture

The final consideration is the place of the event in the overall fundraising picture. If you find that the same people attend all your organization's events as well as give money by mail, you are "eating your own tail" and need to rethink how you are using events. If you cannot seem to get publicity for your events or you are unable to find an event to reach new constituencies, then maybe holding special events is not the right approach. If after analyzing your donor base you decide that your organization needs to increase its number of thoughtful donors, then you won't do as many events whose main purpose is acquisition. In other words, the results of special events (new names, publicity, new volunteers) must be fed into the overall effort to build a donor base or the effort of the event will have mostly been wasted.

chapter NINE

How to Plan a Special Event

Special events require more planning time than one would imagine. Because so much can go wrong, and because many things often hinge on one thing so that one mistake can throw off weeks of work, events must be planned with more attention to minute detail than in almost any other fundraising strategy. While different kinds of events require different kinds of planning and longer or shorter timelines, there are some things that every event requires, and they are detailed here.

THE COMMITTEE FOR SPECIAL EVENTS

There must be a small committee of volunteers overseeing the work for the event. If an event is so complicated that it is unrealistic for volunteers to be able to manage (a conference, a giant gala, a multiday fair), then hire an event planner. Using your own paid staff to plan and carry out a special event is not a good use of their time. Presumably, this is not what they were hired to do, it is not their expertise, and if you factor in the cost of their time on the event and the opportunity cost of what they are not doing while they are working on the event, you will see that your event is costing a much larger amount of money than the budget for it indicates.

The job of the committee is to plan and coordinate the event, not to do every task. After planning the event, most of the committee's work is delegating as many tasks as possible. Keep the committee to between five and seven people. Larger committees are unwieldy and can be counterproductive. With a larger committee planning the event, it is likely that the planning process will take longer, that the committee meetings will be like special events themselves, and the committee members will burn out and not want to help with this or any other event again. It is also likely that a large committee, for example of fifteen people, will have only five real workers.

Each special event should have its own committee, although there can be overlap from one event to another. Special events are labor intensive, however, and people need to have a rest period between events and a chance not to participate in every one. The committee must have staff and board support, and everyone must agree that the chosen event is a good idea.

TASKS OF THE COMMITTEE

There are three simple steps a special events committee should take to ensure the success of the event: detail a master task list, prepare a budget, and develop a timeline.

Detail a Master Task List

On a piece of paper or a spreadsheet, create columns with the following labels: "What," "When," "Who," and "Done." Under "What" list all the tasks that must be accomplished. Include everything—even those things you are sure no one would ever forget, such as "pick up tickets at printer" or "send invitations to the board." Every minute detail should be on this list. Under the column "When" note beside each task when it must be finished. Now put the list into chronological order, so that you have a list of things that must be done and the order in which to do them. Next, complete the "Who" column—to whom the task is assigned, and note the date the task is to be completed under "Done."

Putting this information on a spreadsheet means that each year you can easily update it and that updates or parts of the Master Task List can be e-mailed to anyone who needs to see them. Keeping the Master Task List on Google Docs or another shared space means people can access it from anywhere, note what has been done and what needs to be done, and ask questions or propose ideas for the whole committee to respond to without everyone having to get together in person.

Master Task List			
What	**When**	**Who**	**Done**

Prepare a Budget

Using a spreadsheet program (or a piece of paper, if the event is relatively simple) create two sets of three columns as shown in the example.

Event Budget		
Expenses	**Estimated**	**Actual**
Item	$	$
Item	$	$
Item	$	$
Total expenses	$	$
Income	**Estimated**	**Actual**
Item	$	$
Item	$	$
Item	$	$
Total income	$	$
Net	$	$

Look at the Master Task List. Enter anything from that list that will cost money in the column marked "Expenses" and anything that will raise money in the column marked "Income." When you have listed everything, subtract expenses from income to find the projected "net income," or financial goal, of the event. The budget should be simple but thorough, so that all costs are accounted for and planned on. As actual costs come in, you can enter those and that way you will have a thorough record for evaluating your event, and for helping the committee plan the event next year.

As you budget, remember that an estimate is not a guess. If someone says, "The estimate for food is . . ." or "The estimate for printing is . . . ," this means he or she has called several vendors for prices, bargained, and is satisfied that the estimate will be the price or very close to the price you will actually pay. As costs are incurred they can be noted in the column "Actual" for each item. As much as possible, put off paying for anything until after the event is over and be sure you work in cancellation clauses for rentals or other contracts. For example, if a hall rents for $600, with $300 required as a deposit, try to reserve the right to cancel as close to the date of the event as possible and still get all or part of that $300 back.

Ideally, of course, you will aim to get as many things as possible given as in-kind donations, but don't budget to get anything for free. Always put down a price in the budget. Estimating its cost will protect you in case you do have to pay for something you had planned to get donated, and it will also give you a cushion in case you have an unexpected expense.

Develop a Timeline

To ensure that you have thought of everything that should be done and that you have allowed enough time to do everything, think backward from the target date of your event. If you want to have a dance the evening of August 10, what would you have to do the morning of August 10? How about on August 9? To do those things, what would you have to do in early August? What would have to be in place by July 15? Work back in this way to the day you are starting from. By this backward planning the committee may find out that it is impossible to put on the event in the time allowed. In that case they must either modify the event or change the date. Thinking through each week's tasks for the time line may also surface expenses you hadn't thought of or make clear some additional tasks. Add these to your task list and budget.

As you plan, remember to take into account that, although there may be ninety days between now and the event, there may be only sixty "working" days because of schedule conflicts, weekends, and so on. For example, if a number of your volunteers have children, you should check a school calendar to make sure you don't need anything done on the first or last day of school, during a vacation, or on commencement day. Few organizations can have a New Year's party as a fund-raiser simply because they cannot get anyone to work during the two weeks preceding New Year's Day.

Establish "go or no-go" dates. On your timeline, you will notice that there are periods of intense activity as well as lulls throughout the time leading up to the event. The periods of intense activity, when several tasks must be accomplished and each is related to the other (for example, design, layout, proofread, print, and mail invitations), are called "task clusters." These groups of tasks must be accomplished as projected on your timeline. The date by which each cluster must be accomplished is a "go or no-go" date. At those dates, evaluate your progress and decide if you are going to proceed with the event or if you are too hopelessly behind or too many things have gone wrong and you would be better off to cancel or modify the event. Go or no-go dates are also set for when expenses will be incurred. The night before you send your invitations to the printer is a go or no-go date because you will owe the printer the money whether you do the event or not.

Once the committee has prepared the task list, the budget, and the timeline, it is ready to assign tasks to other volunteers. When you ask volunteers or vendors to do things, give them a due date that is sooner than the one in the "When" column of your task list. That way, in the best case you will always be ahead of your schedule; in the worst case—if the task is not completed—you will have some time to get it done.

WHAT NOT TO FORGET

Here is a checklist of commonly forgotten items in planning an event:

- Liquor license. Whether this is required, and whether the requirement is strictly enforced, will vary by municipality, but keep in mind that your organization carries some liability for people driving after drinking at your event. Many organizations find that their events are successful either without alcohol or with just a cash bar, so don't feel obligated to serve wine or beer. Generally speaking, don't serve hard liquor.

- Insurance (on the hall, for the speaker, for participants). Contracts vary on this item. It often happens that a hall or auditorium is inexpensive because insurance is not included but is required of the renting organization. A one-night insurance policy or a rider on an existing policy can cost as much as $2,000.
- Logistics (and the costs) of transporting food, drink, speakers, performers, sound equipment, and the like to and from the event.
- Lodging for performers or speaker.
- Parking: either in a well-lit lot or available on well-lit streets.
- If there is going to be food: platters, plates, utensils, and napkins. Don't forget things such as salt and pepper, hot and cold cups, cream and sugar.
- Heat or air conditioning: is it available, does it cost extra, will you need to bring your own fans or space heaters?
- Receipt books for people who pay at the door or who buy anything sold at the event.

Here are some questions you need to ask before the event:

- Is the venue wheelchair accessible? Make sure that all rooms are accessible, especially the men's and women's bathroom doors, stalls, toilet paper dispenser, and sinks. Sometimes a building will be labeled "wheelchair accessible" when only the front door and one area of seating are actually accessible.
- Where and how to dispose of trash. Are there clearly marked compost and recycling bins and trash cans?
- If smoking is allowed outside, make sure the area is clearly marked. Rarely, if ever, should smoking be allowed inside the venue.
- Does the invitation's reply card fit into the return envelope?
- Has everything (online and off-line) been proofread at least five times?
- Is the organization's address, Web site URL, Facebook page, and phone number on the reply card, flier, poster, invitation, and everything else?

- Is the event advertised on the Web site, can people buy tickets online, is there an announcement of it on your voice mail?
- Who should add the event's name and date as part of their e-mail signature?
- Are the price, date, time, place, directions, and RSVP instructions for the event on all advertising and on your Web site?
- Have you considered the necessity of child care or language translation, including sign language translation?
- How safe is the neighborhood? Will women feel safe coming to the event alone?
- Can you see and hear from every seat? (Sit in a number of seats to make sure.)
- Who will open the room or building for you? Do you need a key?
- Where are the fire exits?
- Do you know how all the lights work?
- Do you have a person who understands the sound system?
- What has to be done for cleanup? Do you know where the trash goes?

THE EVALUATION

The final step in planning a special event is evaluation. Within a few days after the event, the planning committee should fill out an evaluation form, like the one illustrated here. Save this evaluation along with copies of the advertising, the invitations, and any other information that would be useful for next year's planning committee.

The evaluation will allow you to decide whether or not to do the event again, and it will also ensure that the same number of people working the same amount of time will raise more and more money every year. It should not be necessary to create the planning documents described in this chapter more than once. Once you have created them, every year a new committee can modify and add to them, with each committee building on the knowledge and experience of previous committees.

Special Event Evaluation Form

Approximately how much time did the committee spend on this event? (In evaluating the time spent, try to subtract time spent fooling around, but be sure to count time members spent driving on errands and speaking on the phone.)_____

Did this event bring in any new donors? How many?_____

Can people who came to this event be invited to be donors?_____

Did this event bring in new money?_____

Does this event have the capacity to grow every year?_____

What would you do exactly the same next time?_____
_____

What would you do differently?_____
_____

List sources of free or low-cost items and who solicited them and indicate whether you think these items will be available next year:

_____   _____

_____   _____

What kind of follow-up needs to be done (such as thank you notes to people who went out of their way to help, bills to be paid, prizes to be sent to those who weren't at the drawing, tablecloths or platters to be returned to those who loaned them)?

_____   _____

_____   _____

Which committee members did what work?

_____   _____

_____   _____

Which committee members would be willing to work on this event next year?

_____   _____

_____   _____

Other comments:

_____   _____

_____   _____

(*Note:* You can also download this form from Premium Web Content: "Premium Content: Special Event Evaluation Form.")

chapter TEN

Details of Two Prototypical Events

This chapter discusses two events: a house party and an annual dinner. It also covers two important components of many events: a raffle and an adbook. These four activities have been chosen because they are relatively easy to organize in the sense that they follow a formula and, taken as a whole, they demonstrate all the principles of fundraising that are discussed in this book.

HOW TO PUT ON A HOUSE PARTY

One of the easiest special events, and sometimes one of the most lucrative, is the common house party. It seems ludicrous to describe how to do a house party since anyone who has ever put on a birthday party, school picnic, or anniversary celebration, let alone a small wedding or bat-mitzvah, already knows most of what there is to know about putting on a house party. However, because sometimes the most seemingly simple events are fraught with pitfalls, I describe here both the obvious and not-so-obvious details about giving a house party.

First, the basic definition of a house party: someone involved in a nonprofit group invites their friends to a party at their house. The purpose of the party is to educate the friends about the work of the nonprofit group and ask them to make a contribution. The party is also a place for those attending to meet new people, see old friends, and eat good food, so it sets up a cordial atmosphere for the request. Finally, a house party allows someone not familiar with the group to learn a lot about it, ask questions, and get some personal attention without being obligated to make a donation. People can either give a very small gift or not give at all without feeling embarrassed, and they can usually attend the house party without having to pay to get in.

House parties are a useful venue for an organization to explain a complicated issue to many people at once, allowing the listeners to ask questions and get more information. A house party can be used to discover what questions friendly people may have about an issue or strategy, and thus help prepare the group for more hostile audiences. It can also be a safe place for gathering for people to discuss an issue in a way that a more public event would not be. House parties have been widely used over the past half century to raise awareness and money for unions, peace and justice work, tenants' rights, and racial justice organizing, as well as for hundreds of political initiatives and candidates.

In addition to providing an opportunity for explaining an issue, a house party can be the venue for a group of people to meet someone famous or important or who brings interesting information about the issue your organization is working on. Recently released political prisoners, journalists who have witnessed atrocities, academics discussing their research, or activists of various kinds can tell their story to an audience that is then moved to help. The host then describes what people can do to respond (vote, give money, boycott, give money, demonstrate, give money).

No matter what else you ask people to do at a house party, ask them to give money. It is the only thing they can do right on the spot, and it is usually the most passive action, requiring the least amount of work. The final use of a house party, which underlies all the other uses, is to expand the organization's donor base.

There are five steps to putting on a house party:

1. Finding people willing to host a party at their house and take on other responsibilities related to the event
2. Preparing the list of people to be invited
3. Designing and sending the invitation
4. Choreographing the event, particularly the pitch
5. Following up and evaluating

Finding the Host(s)

The host of a house party has several responsibilities, the least of which is providing the house and the food. The host invites anyone he or she thinks might be interested in the organization or the topic being discussed. At the party, the host or another person gives an appropriate description of the organization and the issues. Then the host makes a pitch for money. Because the host is asking her or his guests to join them in making a significant gift, she or he (or they) must have already made a donation that is significant. Even if the host does not want to be the person making the pitch (in which case the host introduces the person making the pitch, such as a staff person or another board member), she or he must have the conviction of having made a meaningful donation in order to be a credible host.

The ideal host is someone close enough to the organization to understand the importance of the organization and to be willing to conquer their fear of asking friends for money, but not so close that all their friends are already donors. A major flaw of house parties is that the same people attend several house parties for the same organization. Those people may enjoy each party, but wind up feeling "nickel and dimed to death," and the donor base of the group is not expanded.

Whom to Invite

Once someone has volunteered to host the party, the organization's staff can help that person decide who should be invited. A house party can have any number of people, but it generally works best when there are at least twelve guests and not more than fifty. Figure out how many people the house or apartment can comfortably accommodate. If you are planning a presentation, you will need to make sure most of the people can sit down at that time. If the pitch will be short, then having enough seats will not be so important.

As a general rule, you need to invite three times as many people as you want to attend the party. There should be one person from the organization such as a board member, volunteer, or staff person for every ten guests, so include them in the numbers.

Obviously, start with the host's friends. Don't forget neighbors. Sometimes a house party is also a way to meet neighbors. For example, a member of an organization working to end the death penalty had a house party at his apartment. Knowing how emotional some people can be about this issue, he was nervous to invite people he didn't know well. Nevertheless, he decided to take a risk and invite his entire apartment building. A neighbor from another floor, whom he had never met, gave $2,500 that night!

Suggest that the host think about people from her religious or spiritual center, social clubs, work, the Web 2.0 networks she is part of, and her relatives. Except for those people specifically invited to mingle and represent the organization, don't include very many people who are already donors. The exception is donors whose gifts you want to upgrade; in that case, focus on those who could be asked to give more money than they currently do.

The Invitation

The invitation can be done as an e-vite or, if paper, can be printed at an instant-print copy shop, so expense shouldn't be an issue. Desktop publishing programs mean that good-looking invitations can be turned out inexpensively.

Whether virtual or paper, the invitation should reflect something about the host and the crowd being invited that will make people want to attend. Whether your invitation is serious or light, educational or assuming knowledge on the part of the invitee, always include the following elements:

- An indication that people will be asked for money. "Bring your checkbook or your credit card" is the most direct way to make this known. You might also say, "Bring your questions and your checkbook," or "Find out how your contribution can be instrumental in starting (or stopping, ending, creating, propelling, saving) X." One lighthearted invitation said, "Of course, you'll be asked for money. Come anyway. The worst thing that will happen is you'll have to listen to something you don't agree with, but you'll get free food!"

- A way for people to give without coming to the party. On the invitation's return card include the option, "I can't come, but I want to help. Enclosed is my donation." On the e-vite, create a link to the organization's Web site so people can give online.

- Encourage people to bring friends. Require an RSVP so you will know how many people are coming.

- Give people clear directions to the house. If finding the place is at all confusing, draw a map. Include the phone number and e-mail address of the host.

- Send the invitation at least three weeks before the party so you have plenty of time to hear from people and to make follow-up calls.

Choreographing the Event

Where most parties fail is in not having thought through exactly how the event will go. To avoid this danger, imagine yourself a guest at the event and play over in your mind what will happen.

You walk or drive up to the house. Is it obvious where to park? This can be important if the host shares a driveway with people not attending the party, if there is a hidden ditch near the house, or if the neighbors are the kind that are likely to call the police about a guest parked too near the crosswalk. Is the house obvious? Is there a porch light? Is there a sign saying, "Marvin's house party here"? This is especially important in rural communities where homes can be hard to see, and in big apartment complexes where it may be confusing to find the right unit.

You come in to the house or apartment. Is it obvious where to put your coat? If not, someone needs to be stationed at the door to provide that information. Ditto for the bathroom. Is there a place where people will sign in and pick up literature about the group? There should be a guest book for everyone to sign their name, postal and e-mail addresses, and phone numbers.

You look around for people you know and make your way to the food. Is there a traffic jam at the food table? Pull the table out from the wall so people can serve themselves from all sides of it. Put the drinks on a separate table removed from the food table to force people to move on from the food or from the drinks. If possible, have several small platters of food in a few locations rather than two or three large platters. Are the plates big enough? You don't want people to have to come back for five helpings to feel satisfied or to stay hungry because they are too embarrassed to keep going back for more food. People returning to the food table creates a traffic jam; people feeling hungry or frustrated creates a non-money-giving atmosphere. On the other hand, it is a house party and not an "all-you-can-eat" buffet, so don't use dinner plates.

If the house allows it, there can be several food tables in different rooms serving different kinds of food. Serve things that are easy to eat while standing up—finger food rather than items that need a fork and knife. Don't serve anything that would be a disaster if spilled (barbecue sauce on light-colored carpeting, chili on the beige couch).

Once you get your food, you look for a place to sit. Are there enough chairs? Make sure no chair is sitting alone or obstructing people coming in and out of the entrance, the bathroom, or the kitchen. When you are done with your food, where will you put your empty dish? Make sure there are obvious places for people to put dishes, utensils, and glasses needing to be washed and a container for recyclables.

The Special Moment: The Pitch

Everything at the house party should be built around the pitch. Make arrangements ahead of time with a couple of people so that when the host says, "I hope you will make a donation," they pull out checkbooks. They don't have to be ostentatious about it, but a few people have to break the ice and show that this is the time to give money.

Some people object to this practice, claiming that it is both manipulative and imposes too much pressure. However, a little more thought will show that it is the considerate thing to do. Few people have the self-confidence to be the first to do anything. When the host asks for money, many people are prepared to give, but everyone has a brief attack of anxiety. "Perhaps this isn't when you give the money" or "Perhaps I am the only person in the room who believes in this cause" or "Perhaps everyone else already turned in their money and I will look odd if I give my money now." Having some people go first gives permission for everyone else who wants to give to do it now. Much like ushers at plays who show you to your seat without being asked, or clerks in clothing stores who hand you the appropriate accessory (without you having to reveal that you wouldn't have known what to put on with that outfit), the people who make the first donation show that giving is the right thing to do at this time.

Time the pitch so that the most people will be present when it is made. This is usually forty-five minutes to an hour into the party. The host calls for people's attention. The members of the organization discreetly get envelopes ready and the "plants" space themselves around the room. The host introduces himself or herself and welcomes everyone. If there is a presentation, the host introduces the presenter. (If there is more than one host, such as a couple or a group, they should take turns talking so it is clear that both or all are involved.)

After the presentation, the host should be the one who gives the pitch. If the presenter is a famous person or somehow special to the work of the group, that person can sometimes make a formal request for money, followed by the host saying, "I hope you will join me in helping this important cause." It doesn't matter if the host is nervous or doesn't like asking for money. Your proceeds will be reduced by at least half without a pitch—or at least a strong indication of support—from the party sponsor.

Sometimes people argue that doing the party—loaning the house, arranging for the food, giving the time—should indicate the host's interest. Indeed it does. It shows that the host helped save the organization the cost of renting a conference room or arranging for catering. But in order for the guests to give money, the host must also say that he or she gives money and wants anyone who agrees with him or her to do the same.

How the pitch is made determines how the money will be collected. This detail is also decided ahead of time. The best way to get the most money at the party is to pass around envelopes immediately after the host speaks. If you would prefer, the host can say, "Please put your donation in the basket over there," and point to a place. Or the host can say, "You can hand me your check, or give it to any of the people wearing a Youth Now T-shirt." In any case, tell people how and when to give the money.

After the pitch is made, the host should remain standing in front of the group and give people a few moments to write their checks. A very effective method is to say, "Let's just have a moment of silence right now so that everyone can write a check or make a pledge. For those who have already given, just sit quietly for a moment while everyone else has a chance to catch up with you." Then wait a minute and say, "When you have finished writing your check and putting it in the envelope, pass it to . . . " and then tell people whom to give their envelope to. This method ensures that no one who wants to give will leave without making a gift but gives those who do not wish to give a way to sit quietly without being embarrassed.

House parties often fail at the moment right after the pitch. For example, at one house party the host said, "I hope you will all think about making a gift to this group, which is my favorite." Then, without missing a beat he said, "Now that the fundraising part is over, eat up and drink up! Let's have fun." People did exactly as they were told. For a few seconds they thought about giving a gift, then headed for the food. No envelopes were present, and no method of collection was obvious.

At another party, the hosts showed a brief video about the organization, and when it was over, they went into the kitchen. People sat around chatting about the video and then got up to get drinks and food. After a while, the hosts re-emerged and went on with the party. People could be heard asking, "Are we supposed to give money?" or "What are you supposed to do with the money?" Perhaps out of fear of being rude, they did not ask the hosts.

In those cases, the parties raised almost no money and left people feeling that house parties are a waste of time. They are if not done properly.

Evaluation and Follow-Up

After each party, take some time to evaluate what went well and what could have been done better. Particularly if you have a regular presentation, think about the length, the relevance, how to get a discussion going, and so on.

Be sure to write thank you notes to everyone who gave money, and put those people on the organization's mailing list. If the host failed to make a pitch, then immediately send the guest list an appeal letter. If people gave, go over the list of donors with the host, and if there are people missing from it who the host thinks would have given but didn't take the opportunity or forgot, he or she should call them. If the host does not want to make those calls, then send them an appeal letter as soon as possible.

Like all fundraising strategies, house parties only work if someone actually asks for the money. Otherwise a house party is just a party—fun but no funds.

THE ANNUAL DINNER

In Chapter Eight, I said that one of the criteria to consider in choosing an event is that the event is repeatable. Many organizations find that creating an event that is associated with them and occurs every year is the most lucrative way to use the strategy of special events. This annual event becomes their "signature" event. They may or may not do other events during the year, but they will always do this one. A relatively easy and malleable signature event is the annual dinner.

An annual dinner is a banquet generally held at a hotel or other venue that can accommodate a large number of guests. During the dinner, the organization presents a short program, often honoring someone or having a great speaker, comedian, or singer, and certainly including bragging briefly about the group's accomplishments. The dinner may include a silent auction or dancing, but the main reason that people come is that they have come every year. Many of the people who come know each other. They bring new friends with them and have the most fun when the program is brief and the time for mingling and eating is long.

An annual dinner takes two or three years to really reach its stride, but it is worth the investment. The first year people close to the organization come and have a good time. Perhaps there are only 50 people at the dinner. The next year, many of them bring friends and the ranks grow to 100, and the following year to 150, then 200. When the event draws an audience of 200 to 300 people, it does not need to grow and does not need to rely on all of the same people coming back every year. There are dozens of grassroots organizations that have 500 people come to their signature event: some come every year, some every two years, some have come once but continue to give to the event, some always bring friends, others always say they are going to come and don't show up, but in all cases the event is noticed.

A well-organized annual dinner takes at least six months to plan. It is a lot of work, but the work is predictable and generally proceeds in the following pattern.

Form an Annual Dinner Committee

Identify four or five volunteers who will shepherd the event. They will set a date for the event and prepare the master task list, budget, and timeline detailed in Chapter Eight. The ideal members of the committee include at least one or two volunteers who have organized an event of comparable complexity in the past. It could have been an anniversary party or commitment ceremony, the grand opening of a business, or something similar—it does not have to have been for a nonprofit, but it should have been a large event with a lot of details. People with this experience know the importance of keeping on schedule, and they expect that some things will not go according to plan so they are able to be flexible and solve problems quickly. In addition, people on this committee need to be able to spend weekday time on the event: making calls, visiting venues, interviewing caterers, and the like.

If the income stream for the event includes other mini-events, such as a raffle or adbook (described further on), silent or live auction, or reception ahead of time, the committee will need to form subcommittees to take care of each of these components. In other words, the Dinner Committee will serve as the Master or Oversight Committee; then there will be an adbook committee, a raffle committee, and so on. These subcommittees operate fairly autonomously, but they must be included in the overall planning so that they don't step on each other's toes in arranging prizes, underwriting, or auction items, and they must make sure that no one is accidentally solicited for more than one thing. The first year of an annual dinner there should be no more than one other component in addition to the dinner.

Recruiting Volunteers

Once the Master Committee has completed the task list, budget, and timeline, and the board of directors or whoever has the authority to do so approves those items (a process that can take a full month), they are ready to begin recruiting the throng of volunteers that will ensure a successful event. If the event is well organized and the Master Committee has recruited enough volunteers, the process of working on the event will be fun, which will guarantee that at least some of the committee members will be willing to serve the following year.

This cadre of volunteers will be recruited to serve on one of the following seven committees.

Honorary Committee.   This group of people actually does very little. But they are well known to the members of the community you want to attract to the event, so they lend their names to give interest and credibility to your event. You can use their names on your invitation and possibly in soliciting gifts. Honorary Committee members also make a donation to the event (usually significant, such as buying a large ad or a table) and give the event committee names of people or businesses who should be invited to buy tickets or tables or to underwrite the event in some way. Sometimes members of the Honorary Committee don't come to the event, and their attendance should not be a requirement. They do need to make a donation, however.

Publicity Committee.   This small committee of two or three people is in charge of publicizing the event in all media. Media obviously include your Web site, radio, newspapers, and possibly TV, but this committee also needs to think about where your constituency gets information about what is going on in their community. Church bulletins; posters at every laundromat, supermarket, and post office; and announcements at service clubs or union meetings can often attract more people to the event than newspaper coverage.

Arrangements Committee. This committee is in charge of the many details that make or break an event: food, drink, flowers, valet parking, sound systems, child care, translation, and the like. They work with the Master Committee to identify what arrangements they are in charge of, and they should not be seen as a catchall committee to do whatever other people don't want to do.

Materials Committee. This committee is in charge of designing the invitation and any other materials required for the event, such as a program, posters, fliers, and so on. Having one committee take care of all materials ensures the materials have a uniform look and message.

Invitation Committee. This committee is responsible for getting all the lists for the invitation and getting it out in a timely way. They generally are not in charge of designing the invitation.

Sponsorship or Underwriting Committee. This committee is in charge of soliciting businesses, corporations, or even major donors to buy a table or pay a chunk of the event's cost in return for having their name prominently displayed at the event.

Cleanup Committee. This committee is responsible for bringing or locating garbage bags and trash and recycling receptacles after the event is over and knowing where the cleaning tools—brooms, mops, cloths—are kept or providing them. They are responsible for putting chairs and tables away; returning platters, vases, and the like to their rightful owners; and knowing what the rules of the venue are for adequate cleanup. Because there is generally a cleaning and security deposit involved, someone from the Master Committee will want to be on this committee.

In addition to all these tasks, the Master Committee may want another small group to handle all the logistics for the night of the event—decorations, registration, seating, problems.

Balancing having enough committees to get the work done with not having so many that they are impossible to keep tabs on is a constant struggle. Building in regular reporting times and deadlines helps a great deal, as does having the committees be as small as possible while still able to get the work done.

As your event grows, you will want to consider hiring an event planner to take the place of some of the volunteers and to coordinate others. A good event planner is well worth her or his fee, and it is a much better use of money to hire such a person than to rely on your already overworked staff to pick up any pieces the volunteers weren't able to or handle tasks they just did not do. Using staff on these kinds of events is a hidden cost, but a real one.

Get the Money Ahead of Time

The ideal event is paid for and the cash is in hand well before the night of the event. Sponsors have sent in checks, attendees have sent in money for tickets, adbook ads are paid for, and so on. Any money that is raised the night of the event is extra. That way, if something goes wrong the night of the event, such as an earthquake, hurricane, or chemical spill, you may be able to negotiate keeping most of the money you have raised even if you have to cancel or postpone the event. If something goes wrong at the event—the Master of Ceremonies is ill, the speaker can't be heard because the sound system is bad—you can apologize and continue with the event without worrying that people aren't going to pay.

The most important thing is to have a lot of decent-quality food and drink. If people have enough good food to eat, they will usually be satisfied.

The Day of the Event

On the day of the event, the Master Committee and a representative from each subcommittee meet together and review the Master Task List, which has now become the Master Checklist. These lists should be almost grimy because of how often they have been reviewed, added on to, and modified. The purpose of this meeting is to walk through the event one last time to make sure every detail has been thought of. From the point of view of someone attending, what does the event look like?

The person arrives at the venue. Parking is clearly marked or easy to find. When she enters the venue, there are signs pointing her to the event. She checks in at a table where four or five people keep the process brief and the lines to get in are short. The check-in sheet shows that she has paid and that she has asked to sit at the Morgan table. The check-in person welcomes her warmly, tells her where the Morgan table is, and invites her to go to the drink table and enjoy some hors d'oeuvres. Once she has her drink, she can stop by a literature table nearby where she can chat with a person staffing the table about what good work the group does and buy a T-shirt or a raffle ticket, if a raffle is part of the event. Once she and most people are seated, but before the dinner begins, board members circulate and greet people. They introduce themselves to people they don't know and thank them for coming. They point out the program books (which are also adbooks) at each place.

The master of ceremonies (MC) introduces himself or herself, welcomes people, gives a brief overview of the program, and tells people how they will get their food. Either people are served at their table or—more often and less expensive—they are served walking through a buffet line. Avoid having people serve themselves unless you have massive amounts of food. You don't want anyone who came in late or was at the end of the line to have too little to eat because the first people through took heaping helpings. The MC points out the buffet lines (of which there are at least four) and where to get drinks. With a really big crowd, it is best to call people up table by table.

The food is served efficiently, and the Morgan table is impressed. As they are finishing and their plates are being cleared, the program begins. Everyone who needs to use the microphone knows how to work with it, as they have been shown ahead of time. The program is entertaining, moving, and concise. There are no long gaps between the time someone's name is mentioned and when they arrive at the stage because a stage manager is constantly cueing people. A discreetly placed timekeeper sits at a front table and cues speakers with signs that say, "Five Minutes," "Two Minutes," and "Stop Now." None of the guests know that there is a "Stop Now" sign because no one has had to use it.

At the end of the program, the MC or other designated person gives a pitch for more money. Envelopes are on each table along with the adbooks, and people are encouraged to make an extra donation right then and there and turn it in to the people circulating with baskets. (Depending on the nature of the event and how much people have paid to get in, the pitch can raise an additional sum of a few hundred to a few thousand dollars.) At the end of the program, people are encouraged to get dessert from the buffet table and to stay and have fun. If there is a raffle drawing, that happens after dessert; if there is a silent auction, successful bidders are announced at the end of the program. Many people leave shortly after the program, but a critical mass stays for quite a while longer, talking and having fun. Finally, as all plates, food, tablecloths, and so on are cleared away, the last of the crowd leaves. The Cleanup Committee does whatever needs to be done and the event is over.

If the walk-through looked like that, you have thought of everything that can be thought of. If as you walked through you realized you had not built in a time for dessert to be served, or did not have a designated timekeeper, you have time to take care of those details.

The committee in charge of the event evening arrives at the site at least two hours early. They help with putting up decorations, placing programs and contribution envelopes on each table, and taking care of any other details that can only be taken care of right before the event.

If the committee is as prepared as I have recommended, even if something happens at the event that you have not prepared for, there are enough of you to figure out a plan. If you are running out of food, you will notice ahead of time and race out and buy some more. If you have a shortage of chairs, you will go around asking all board members and staff to give up their chairs, and you will try to borrow more chairs from a nearby place. You have close to two dozen people who have put a lot of time and effort into this event. They will help, as will people attending.

After the Event

Shortly after the event, write up a final report as recommended in Chapter Eight. Count your income and pay your bills. Write thank you notes to everyone who did anything to help, and take yourselves out for a nice meal to celebrate a job well done.

HOW TO DO A RAFFLE

A common, easy, and fun way to raise almost any amount of money is a raffle. Almost everyone is familiar with raffles; most have bought tickets for them and perhaps even won a prize in one.

Because raffles are so common, most people don't realize that they can be complicated; when you are organizing a raffle, you can make your life more difficult by not paying attention to the myriad details that a raffle involves.

The first fact to keep in mind is that raffles have to be organized carefully so that they don't violate gambling laws. Although laws against raffles are rarely enforced, it is important to organize your raffle so that you are within the bounds of the law. In addition to federal and state laws, you need to find out the laws in your own community. Don't think that because you are a nonprofit you are exempt. Sometimes you will need to register with the sheriff's department; in some towns, laws against raffles are strictly enforced and you simply will not be able to do one. This section discusses how to set up your raffle so that you will be within the laws of most states. Ironically, but perhaps not surprisingly, states with their own lottery tend to be more likely to stop a raffle from taking place than states without a lottery.

Raffles basically appeal to people's desire to get something for less than it is worth. Your organization gets some gifts donated, which are used as the prizes. These gifts can vary from straight cash to services such as child care for an evening or having your windows washed, to adventures such as trips or products such as microwaves, DVD players, and so forth. Generally, there are five to ten prizes, one of which is a Grand Prize. Tickets are sold for somewhere between $1.00 and $10.00 each. Many more tickets are sold than prizes available, so a person's chances of winning are small. At an appointed day and time, all the tickets are put into a barrel or other container and stirred up, and a neutral person (such as a small child) draws out the winning tickets. The organization makes money from the number of tickets sold. There is no other source of income in a raffle. The costs can be kept low; ideally, the only costs are printing the tickets and getting the prizes to the winners. As a result, most of the income is profit.

There are three parts to a successful raffle, each requiring three steps.

Organizing the Raffle

Step 1. Get the Prizes.　Bring together a small committee of two or three people to decide when the raffle will be held and what the prizes are going to be. It is helpful if the prizes have a theme, such as "vacations," "services," "household," or "restaurants." Make a list of all the vendors who might give you a prize, and list specifically what you want from them such as dinner for two, a weekend at a vacation cabin, and so on. Remember that people who own small businesses, particularly those in storefronts, frequently get asked to donate raffle prizes. They may have policies against doing it; they may donate to five charities and will not take on any more; they may be having a hard time in their business and not be inclined to give anything. Have three times as many places to seek prizes as the number of prizes needed.

The small committee then goes out and solicits the prizes. Be sure to stress to each merchant how many people will see the tickets, how much other publicity you are going to do, that you will not ask for another item this year, or whatever is true for you. Merchants must think about how giving your organization an item is good for their business, and you must help them in that thinking.

Once the prizes have been obtained, the small committee goes on to manage the rest of the details of the raffle.

Step 2. Get the Workers. While you are soliciting prizes, start calling your volunteers to ask how many tickets they are willing to handle. Some people hate raffles—don't push them into taking tickets; they will resent it, and probably won't sell their tickets. Recruit people who work in large office buildings or unions, or who have large families or large circles of friends. Offer a prize for the person who brings in the most money for the raffle.

Keep track of who said they would distribute tickets. Raffles are a good opportunity to get some peripheral people involved, so don't just go to your reliable volunteers who already do everything else. Ask each person if they know someone who would be good at selling tickets. People's spouses or lovers, neighbors, business partners, or other acquaintances can be recruited for this effort.

Step 3. Get the Tickets. Once they have the prizes, the committee decides which will be the grand prize, the second prize, and so on. They decide on the date of the raffle drawing. Raffles should go on for at least one month, and they can go on for up to six months without losing momentum. The ideal time for a raffle is two to three months.

Printing the tickets requires attention to detail (see the illustration that follows for the points discussed). First of all, it is with the tickets that groups usually run afoul with the law. This is because raffle tickets cannot actually be sold. We speak of "selling" tickets but technically what we should say is that the ticket is free, but a donation of $1.00 (or whatever the price is) is requested. In principle, someone can ask for a free ticket and not give you any money. If you were to turn down that request, it would be clear that you are selling the ticket, and that is against the law. In this chapter, I refer to selling the tickets, because that is the common shorthand; however, keep in mind that we are not truly selling anything.

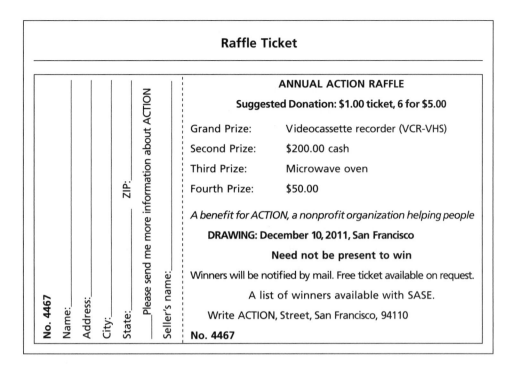

Raffle Ticket

No. 4467

Name:

Address:

City:

State:

ZIP:

Please send me more information about ACTION

Seller's name:

ANNUAL ACTION RAFFLE

Suggested Donation: $1.00 ticket, 6 for $5.00

Grand Prize: Videocassette recorder (VCR-VHS)

Second Prize: $200.00 cash

Third Prize: Microwave oven

Fourth Prize: $50.00

A benefit for ACTION, a nonprofit organization helping people

DRAWING: December 10, 2011, San Francisco

Need not be present to win

Winners will be notified by mail. Free ticket available on request.

A list of winners available with SASE.

Write ACTION, Street, San Francisco, 94110

No. 4467

You must print on the ticket how a person can get a free ticket and that a list of winners will be available, which helps ensure that the prizes are actually awarded. To increase sales, indicate that the donor doesn't have to be present to win.

The tickets must be numbered so that they are easy to keep track of. Although it costs more to have the printer number the tickets, it is worth it. Many organizations try to save money by not having numbered tickets or by numbering the tickets themselves. This is a foolish use of time. It is also critical that the ticket stub be perforated so it can be easily separated from the body of the ticket. Don't save money by printing cheap raffle tickets. Your volunteers will not distribute them as easily, and donors will be reluctant to give their money when the ticket does not appear properly done.

Not all printers can print raffle tickets. Find a printer who can, even if you cannot use your regular printer. Needless to say, seek to have the printing donated, but don't scrimp on printing. It should be your only cost.

Notice in the illustration that the seller is asked to sign his or her name on the ticket stub. This is another incentive that you can build in to your raffle: giving a prize to any person who sold winning tickets. You are obviously more likely to win such a prize if you have sold a lot of tickets.

To promote the organization, offer people a box to check to get more information about the organization sponsoring the raffle. If you do make such an offer, be sure you go through every ticket as they are turned in or after the drawing and send information to those who checked the box.

To know how many tickets to print, add up how many tickets the volunteer workers are willing to take, and note what your goal is for the raffle. Always print at least two hundred more tickets than your financial goal, because some tickets are bound to be lost or mutilated.

One final word concerning the law: sometimes organizations send raffle tickets to possible donors through the mail. This is against postal law and, if caught, your letters will be sent back. If you send the tickets by bulk mail, you risk having your bulk mail permit revoked.

In any case, raffles are not mail appeals. If you want to use the mail to raise money, do so, but do not combine raffle sales and mail appeals.

"Selling" Tickets

Step 4. Distribute and Keep Track of the Tickets.   Make a list of everyone selling tickets and the numbers of the tickets they take. Keep track of the tickets as they are returned. Have a date by which the tickets and the donations are to be turned in.

Step 5. Encourage the Workers.   E-mail or call your volunteers at least once a week to see how they are doing with their tickets. Remind them of the deadline and to send in their stubs and donations (rather than sending cash through the mail, they might want to substitute their own check and keep the cash). To encourage competition, tell them who is winning the "most sold" prize so far. The job of the small committee is not to sell tickets, but to keep other people selling them. A raffle works best when organized like a pyramid, with the most tickets being sold by a large number of workers, and the smaller number of workers distributing the tickets to others. Raffles fail when there are not enough people out selling tickets, or when the people who take tickets don't sell them. Be sure to have a lot of people selling tickets, and keep reminding them of due dates, praising those who are doing their job, and pressuring those who aren't. Every volunteer ought to be able to sell a minimum of twenty-five tickets. Most people who live in a town or city can sell fifty tickets in two or three weeks with no difficulty. Some people will be able to sell a hundred or more in one or two months.

Step 6. Set Up the Drawing.   Some organizations hold the raffle drawing as part of another event, such as a dance or auction. Using a raffle as a part of another event increases your profit, even though it involves organizing the other event as well. You don't need to have another event—it is fine to have a small party for all those who worked on the raffle and sold tickets and do the drawing there. The drawing is held on the date printed on the ticket. If you have good food and drink, the drawing is then a celebration and a reward for a job well done, as well as a way to ensure that all the sold tickets are turned in on time.

Wrapping Up the Raffle

Step 7. Round Up the Tickets.   Surprisingly, most people find the most difficult task in a raffle lies not in getting the prizes and not in getting the workers, but in getting the tickets and the cash back.

Some volunteers will be careless with their ticket stubs, or return stubs and promise cash later, or claim to have sold tickets when they really haven't. If you have encouraged people to turn in money and stubs as they go along, you will have less difficulty than if you wait until just before the drawing. Final submission of stubs and cash should be due at least three days, and preferably five days, before the drawing. That way, you can ensure that you have all the tickets accounted for well ahead of time. People should turn in unsold tickets as well so that all numbers are accounted for.

The problem with a raffle is that all the transactions are in small amounts of cash. Someone sells three tickets to a co-worker, puts the stubs and dollar bills into their wallet, then goes to lunch and uses that cash for lunch without thinking. Later, they turn in more stubs than cash, and, without a careful recordkeeping system, this error might not be caught.

Another advantage of getting ticket stubs in well ahead of time is that some people try to make their stub into the winning one by bending down a corner, sticking something on the back, or tearing it nearly in half and then taping it together. Workers will sometimes fold ticket stubs or spill stuff on them. These stubs cannot be used, and new stubs must be written. This is, in part, involves the use of the two hundred or so extra tickets. For the drawing to be fair, the stubs must be as uniform as possible.

Step 8. Hold the Drawing.   Get a big box or barrel for the ticket stubs. Be sure to mix and remix the stubs thoroughly after each prize is drawn. Start with the bottom prize and work up to the grand prize. Have a blindfolded adult or small child do the actual drawing to guarantee neutrality.

After the prizes are drawn, announce the prizes for top salespeople and award these. Many organizations give several prizes to their salespeople. In addition to the person who sold the most tickets, they award a prize to the person who got the most prizes donated, to the person who got the most other people to sell tickets, to the person who sold the most tickets in a week or to a single person, and so on. Having a lot of prizes for salespeople is a good motivator for those who are competitive during the selling process, and a nice reward at the end. After the drawing, sort through the tickets for people who checked that they were interested in getting more information about your organization. It can be labor intensive to sort through the ticket stubs, finding just the people who checked the box. However, this is an easy way to get a hot list and is worth the effort.

Step 9. Send Out the Prizes and Thank Yous, and Evaluate.   Arrange for the winners to get their prizes, either by picking them up at your office or receiving them in the mail.

Send thank you notes to each person who sold tickets and to all the merchants and others who donated prizes.

Count your money. Note how many tickets were unsold, where the problems were with the workers, the merchants, the tickets themselves, and so on. Make a file with all the information about the raffle, including a list of winners, a list of people donating items, and a list of volunteers, and add notes about timing and other issues. Next year, it will be much simpler to do the raffle if a committee can pull up a file and benefit from the previous year's experience.

ADBOOKS

An adbook provides a way for your organization to raise money from businesses and corporations by selling them advertising space in a booklet, program, menu, or other printed item. Even a nonprofit may buy an ad in another nonprofit's adbook to be supportive, but also to appear supportive to people looking at the adbook. Sometimes people buy ads to congratulate a friend or a family member who is being honored. The idea is that the people, businesses, and organizations buying ads would probably not give the money otherwise. The adbook is then distributed to people who are coming to an event and who will be likely to patronize the businesses that advertised there. Businesses whose owners may not care about the issues you represent may still buy an ad because they know your constituents use their business or want them to do so.

Adbooks are a superb fundraising strategy if they are done well and on a regular basis. Some organizations use this concept as a way to underwrite conventions, luncheons, concerts, or any special event where a program or printed agenda would be appropriate.

Adbooks are lucrative because the ad is sold for 200 to 1,000 percent more than it costs. Further, for businesses, the cost of an ad is a business expense, which is a better deduction than a tax deduction. An adbook can be as simple as a folded sheet of paper with ads on both sides, or as complex as a full-scale paperback booklet printed in color. An adbook can also include coupons.

One advantage of adbooks is that they train volunteers to ask for money face-to-face while giving the donors a concrete value for their money. Some volunteers who are reluctant to ask for outright monetary donations are willing to approach business people to buy ads. They know that business people want and need to advertise and that they are always looking for creative ways to reach more people. The advantage to the advertiser is that the cost of space in your adbook is always less than the cost of an ad of comparable size in a newspaper. Even though a newspaper reaches more people, if the advertiser's goods and services are particularly useful to your audience, your adbook reaches more targeted prospects. With fewer and fewer local papers, adbooks become an even better value for reaching niche audiences. Further, the publicity over the past two decades about corporate responsibility has created a large group of consumers who prefer to buy from businesses and corporations that are perceived to be involved in the community. Numerous studies show that a customer will choose a product made by a company that supports nonprofits over a similar product from a company where that information is not known. To appear in an adbook is good business, particularly if that adbook will be seen by a large number of people.

A word of caution: keep in mind that sometimes the IRS counts adbook income as "unrelated business income" and charges unrelated business income tax (UBIT). This is rare and probably won't happen unless your adbook is very lucrative and you do an adbook frequently. If it is that successful, paying tax on that income will not be a hardship. UBIT is much more common on ads that appear regularly in newsletters.

Distribution and Design

An adbook, like all fundraising strategies, requires careful advance planning. The first step is to plan the distribution of the adbook, what the book will look like, and the cost of the ads. If it is an adbook for a special event, the distribution will be simple: all those attending will receive one. However, if the adbook is to be distributed widely, you need to decide if you will send one to all your donors, put stacks of them in stores, hand them out in your neighborhood to people on the street, or use some other distribution strategy. To sell ads, you need to know what shape and size the adbook will be so you can determine the size of the ads and their price. The final number of pages will depend on the number of ads you sell.

Pricing Ads

There are no set formulas for determining how much ads should cost. Check with other nonprofits in your area that have done successful adbooks and see what they have charged. The price of the ads will depend in large part on how widely your adbook will distributed and how fancy it will be. If it is being given out to two hundred people, ads will be less expensive than if three thousand people will get one. If it is printed on glossy paper, for example, or in color, the ads will cost more than if it is simply printed in black and white. There should be some variation in price between ads on the inside cover of the adbook and those on inside pages. Cover-page ads (including the back cover and the two inside covers) are usually at least twice the price of ads within the book because the exposure is so much better. Some organizations charge more for ads in the centerfold as well, since they too will have more exposure.

The ads are sold either by dimension in inches ("display ad") or by the number of words ("classified ad"). A display ad is prepared by the advertiser and sent to you, either in hard copy or as a digital file, "camera ready," that is, ready to go to the printer. For a classified ad, the advertiser sends the ad copy and you have the message designed for inclusion in the book. Display ads can be sold in full-page, half-page, one-third page, quarter-page, and sometimes one-eighth page sizes (depending on how big one-eighth of a page would be). Some organizations choose only to have display ads so that they will not have to design classified sections. If you give people the option of sending you copy that you design in a display ad, then you can charge a design fee that covers your cost and gives you a small added profit.

It is a good idea to give businesses and individuals the option of buying a single line in your book and listing those advertisers as "friends" or "sponsors." These listings are less expensive—$25 to $50. They do not advertise a person or business but they do show that the person or business is supportive of your organization. People pay proportionately more for smaller ads than bigger ones because it is much less work for you to have two dozen big ads than fifty small ads. The price of an ad can include one or two free tickets to the event, or some other type of recognition at the event, such as a large poster on which all advertisers are listed.

Once you have the dimensions of your adbook and set prices for the ads, prepare sample pages to be given to volunteers selling the ads. A sample layout for an 8½" × 11" two-page spread is shown.

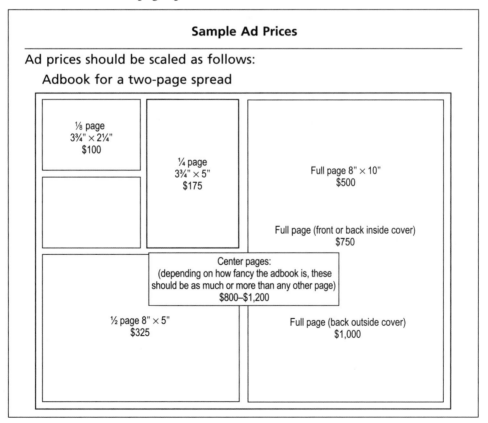

Sample Ad Prices

Ad prices should be scaled as follows:
Adbook for a two-page spread

⅛ page
3¾" × 2¼"
$100

¼ page
3¾" × 5"
$175

Full page 8" × 10"
$500

Full page (front or back inside cover)
$750

Center pages:
(depending on how fancy the adbook is, these should be as much or more than any other page)
$800–$1,200

½ page 8" × 5"
$325

Full page (back outside cover)
$1,000

Timeline

The next step is to set a timeline for ad sales. If the adbook is for an event, the event will be the distribution point. The deadline for final sales must be at least one month before the event to allow for design, layout, proofreading, and printing of the book.

Prepare the timeline in the same way as for a special event, with a master task list and a budget. A large adbook will require about an eight-week sales period. Two weeks before sales begin will be needed for planning and preparation of materials and training the salesforce. Four weeks at the end of the sales period will be needed for layout, proofreading, and printing. Thus, the total timeline will cover fourteen weeks.

Getting Ready to Sell

Make a list of businesses, other nonprofits, and individuals who might want ads. Ask all volunteers, board members, and staff to list all the businesses they patronize, companies they work for, companies their spouses and friends work for, and businesses that would serve a large cross-section of your donors. (For example, a women's organization would be sure to include women's clothing stores, beauty salons, and women's magazines.) To help people recall all the possible businesses they patronize, give them a list of suggestions, including banks, restaurants, vegetable stores, supermarkets, butchers, clothing stores, bakeries, liquor stores, and such people as your doctor, dentist, lawyer, mechanic, therapist, hairdresser, chiropractor, accountant, and plumber. Include in the final list all of the vendors your organization uses as well as other nonprofits with whom you have worked over the years, unions, friends and family of staff or board, politicians, and even major donors.

Set up a database with the name, address, phone, and a contact person for each potential advertiser. Include the name of the person who uses the business and any other information that will be helpful to the salesperson. (For example, Joe's Auto Supply, Joe Jones, owner, 512 Main St., 835-4692, joe@jauto.com. He is board president's brother-in-law; also, Sally buys everything for her motorcycle there.)

Print out a master list of prospects and have volunteers sign up for as many prospects as they feel comfortable taking. Don't skip this step because you want to make sure that one business isn't approached by two people, and that the best person makes the request for the ad. Most important, you need a master list to keep track of how the volunteers are doing. Ideally, you will be able to enter the name of the volunteer who will be asking into the database record of each business, then print out a list for each volunteer of their prospects. If you are a neighborhood or community group, you may also wish to have some volunteers simply approach every store on a square block of the neighborhood, in addition to any other businesses you may be approaching.

In addition to their prospect lists, the volunteers each need a supply of brochures describing the work of your organization, sample ad sheets with order forms to give each business, instructions for how camera-ready ads are to be sent, return envelopes in case the business owner wishes to mail in their ad or payment, and receipt books to record payments received at the time of sale.

Prepare the volunteers for difficult questions they may encounter, and provide possible answers including convincing arguments. Each volunteer should stress how many good prospects the adbook will reach, how inexpensive the ad is, and how much members of your organization enjoy the business, store, or service where the volunteer is selling.

Selling the Ads

Depending on the type of business you are soliciting and the general style of your community, volunteers may first want to call the business owner or manager and make an appointment. In soliciting ads from corporations or large firms, sending a letter or e-mail, and then following up with a phone call and visit will be imperative.

Two or three volunteers should act as "team leaders" for the rest of the salesforce. The team leaders play the same role as the planning committee for a special event. While they should sell ads, their main function is to encourage people on their team and to make sure that volunteers are making their calls. Volunteers must understand that they will be turned down more often than not. It will take from five to eight solicitations for every sale. As is the case when soliciting major gifts, you rarely know exactly why you were turned down. Don't spend a great deal of time thinking about it; simply go on to the next prospect.

As sales are made a progress chart should be posted at the office, and progress reports should be given to salespeople to encourage them. Once a week every salesperson should be given a list of the businesses that have already bought ads.

They can take this list with them on solicitations; business owners may be persuaded to buy an ad when they see the names of colleagues who have done so.

Thank businesses immediately after they send in their ads and their money. When the adbook is produced, send them a copy. Encourage your members to support the business they see in your adbook and to thank them for supporting your organization. Some businesses will not send payment until the adbook is published. Careful records will show which bills remain outstanding, and those businesses can be billed again after they receive a copy of the adbook. Because they have filled out and signed an agreement specifying the size and wording of the ad, it is extremely rare for businesspeople not to pay.

Producing the Adbook

After all the ads are in and the sales period is over, the book must be produced. Once the salesforce has done its task, a second set of volunteers handles the production and distribution details. A graphics designer or person with layout skills should be asked (or paid) to help ensure that the ads are laid out straight, that all the ads fit properly on each page, and that all the ads fit in the book. Layout can be done by hand, or using a graphics program on a computer. Attention should be paid to putting ads that look nice together on the same page and to having some "white space" on each page so that the ads don't look crowded. Great care should be taken to proofread all copy and to keep the display ads and all the copy clean.

Besides the ads, several pages are devoted to the group and the event, either throughout the adbook or in a specific section of it. These include the conference agenda or program notes of the event, information about your group, and a membership form. Many organizations also include a brief history of their organization, a page listing and thanking all their donors, and short biographies of board and staff. If the event you are doing the adbook for is a tribute or awards dinner, then include a profile of the persons, ideas, or groups being honored. High-quality, good-contrast pictures are very nice inclusions in an adbook.

When the book is ready for printing, someone who knows about paper stock and the printing process should help select the paper and ink and specify the printing process. Print enough copies to give one to everyone who comes to the event, everyone who gave to the event but did not come, all advertisers, and foundation funders; to have a supply to hand out over the course of the year; and to have enough for members of next year's salesforce to show the people they solicit.

The first year you produce an adbook is the most difficult. Businesses are taking a chance that you will do what you say in terms of quality and distribution of the book. If your adbook is successful and people patronize the businesses they have read about there, repeat sales will be easy to get. New businesses will be able to see exactly what they will get for their money. If they like what they see, they will be more inclined to buy.

Adbooks can be lucrative, both because the ads bring in much more money than the cost of printing them and because they are a repeatable commodity. They are good for training volunteers in fundraising techniques and for building community relations with businesses. They should only be done, however, when the group has the lead time, the number of volunteers required who can devote time to the adbook and are not also organizing the rest of the event, and access to the design and printing expertise required.

Using Direct Mail

For decades, direct mail has been the most common fundraising strategy in use. Although it is now being overtaken by online fundraising, it is still effective and an important strategy for almost any organization, particularly when used in combination with phoning and online strategies.

Simply described, direct mail involves sending a form letter seeking support for your nonprofit, and including a return envelope in which people can send back a donation. Direct mail appeals go to hundreds, thousands, or even millions of people by bulk mail. It is a strategy widely used in the United States, Canada, Australia, England, and many parts of Europe, but rarely used in countries where people don't use the mail for any financial transaction.

Some pundits have proclaimed that direct mail is a dying strategy and will soon be entirely replaced by online fundraising strategies. You may be tempted to skip this chapter if you think that your organization will not be using direct mail, but I would ask you not to. It is important to understand the psychology of direct mail, which can be useful in almost any communication you have with donors. Further, direct mail remains the only strategy that allows you to get something tangible (an envelope containing a request) into the hands of anyone served by the U.S. Postal Service for very small amounts of money per address. Used carefully, direct mail not only gives you new donors and eventually a solid income stream but also enables you to identify donors to whom you likely have no other access. Stories abound of donors recruited through direct mail whom no one in the organization had ever met but who sent $500 or $1,000 in response to a first appeal; other stories recount donors whom no one knew giving $25 for years and then leaving a large bequest.

I emphasize throughout this book that all strategies must be used in conjunction with each other. Direct mail, as you will see, is the most obvious example of this tenet.

A direct mail appeal is very simple: a letter describing the organization and its needs is put into an attractive envelope, along with a self-addressed return envelope and possibly a reply card that makes it easy for the donor to return a gift, and the identical letter is sent to hundreds or thousands of people. Appeals that are addressed to an individual—"Dear Mrs. Smith"—or letters sent by first-class mail are not technically considered direct mail pieces, although these more personalized letters may borrow from direct mail principles in their look or style of writing, and identical text may be going to dozens—or thousands—of recipients, with the only differences being the salutation. In the United States, direct mail appeals are sent in minimum quantities of two hundred, presorted by ZIP code for the post office; at the post office they receive bottom priority for processing in return for a deep discount in the postage rate.

Direct mail solicitation (often derisively called "junk mail") has been in wide use since World War II. In the 1970s and 1980s, direct mail fundraising was so popular that many organizations derived a large percentage of their income from it. Over time, the fundraising market became saturated with direct mail and its effectiveness has decreased. With the advent of online fundraising, many organizations have stopped using it and so, ironically, for many grassroots organizations direct mail has become more effective than ever. A major reason for the renewed or continued success of direct mail is that the volume of mail has decreased. People who do not wish to receive direct mail have registered with various agencies to have their names taken off of direct mail lists. Environmental concerns, along with big increases in the costs of printing and mailing, have caused many organizations to cut back or eliminate their direct mail programs. Many organizations have replaced personal snail mail with e-mail, online social networks, or even texting. Until the early part of this century, people who gave or bought by postal mail would report receiving fifty mail appeals and two dozen catalogs a week. Today, very few people receive that volume of snail mail, although e-mail has taken its place as a source of complaints.

The pundits who claim that direct mail is dying are augmented by those who claim that young people don't respond to it. There is a grain of truth in that statement. However, although Generation X and Millennials may not send in a check, mail appeals that offer an online option for giving will often generate a large online response.

Despite all the bad publicity it gets, however, direct mail remains the least expensive way to reach the most people with a message that they can hold in their hands and examine at their leisure. A well-designed and well-written direct mail piece sent to a good list can still yield a response that makes it worthwhile to develop and send: 0.5 to 1 percent on a first-time appeal, and 10 percent and often more from donors who have given before. Many organizations use direct mail letters beyond acquisition to communicate with current donors and to ask for additional gifts. Used properly, direct mail is one of the most powerful strategies a small nonprofit can have. After looking at how direct mail works for slightly larger organizations, I will show how even the tiniest grassroots group can make it work for them.

THREE FUNCTIONS OF DIRECT MAIL

Direct mail soliciting has three functions, which overlap with the strategies discussed in Chapter Three: acquisition, retention, and upgrading of donors. Along with special events, it is one of the most versatile methods for developing closer relationships with donors.

Acquisition: Get Someone to Give for the First Time

Donor acquisition is the main reason many organizations use direct mail. To see how it works, consider the experience of People for Good. People for Good trades the names of five thousand of their donors for an equal number of names of donors to another group, Friends of Progress.* People for Good merges the names from Friends of Progress with its own donor list to eliminate as many duplicate names as possible, eliminating three hundred names. To the rest of the

---

*Five thousand names is considered by many experts to be an appropriate test-sample size. The idea is that if you get a 0.75 percent or better response on five thousand names, you should send the appeal to the whole list that these names came from (assuming the whole list is larger). If the response is less than 0.75 percent, you can change the appeal to try to improve the response rate or abandon the list. To take advantage of direct mail's discounted postal rates, you only need two hundred names, but two hundred is not considered significant for predicting future response on that or a similar list. You can have slightly less reliable results using two thousand names for a test.

list from Friends of Progress, People for Good sends a direct mail appeal asking for a donation to its work. It gets just under 1 percent response, or forty gifts, most of them $40, the suggested donation, but others in the range of $25 to $500. Because the appeal also directed prospects to the group's Web site, it also gets ten new online donors, giving it a grand total of fifty new donors and $4,000 in income from a response of just over 1 percent. The cost was $1.50 for each piece of mail (including postage, printing, paper, and the use of a mail house for sorting and sending the mailing) sent to forty-seven hundred names for a total cost of $7,050.

The net cost for People for Good is $3,050, or about $61 for each of the fifty donors it acquired. This is called the "acquisition cost"—essentially the group paid $61 dollars to acquire one donor, which is a legitimate cost of doing business. These donors will now be moved to the next stage, retention. From this account, you can see right away that there is no point in starting a direct mail program unless you are willing to go all the way with it—trying to retain and upgrade these donors—because the first mailing usually loses money—sometimes a lot of money. Read on to see how that money not only will be recouped, but will grow.

Retention: Get Donors to Repeat Their Gift

Once a person becomes a donor, the organization tries to get that person to repeat his or her gift, then to give routinely. It starts by thanking donors within seventy-two hours of receiving their gifts and then asking the donors for additional gifts several times during the year. Small organizations should ask their current donors for additional donations at least two or three times a year, with a combination of mail, e-mail, phone solicitations, and special events. These requests should be interspersed with communication about what the organization is doing with the money. Asking frequently will not offend most people and keeps the name of your nonprofit in the donor's consciousness. It also enables you to take advantage of the ups and downs of each donor's cash flow situation, as donors may have money to make extra gifts at some times but not others. Every time you ask your donors for an extra gift by mail, you can expect that about 10 percent of them will respond. In this phase you make back the money you spent acquiring these people. Keep in mind that about 60 percent of people making a first gift will not make a second gift, but more people who make a second gift will make a third, and most people who make a third gift will make a fourth, and so on, assuming the organization continues to do good work and treats their donors properly.

People for Good follows this advice and, with a combination of e-mail and snail mail, solicits donations from this cohort of new donors three times a year. (Those who gave online are solicited online; those who gave by mail are solicited both with additional mailed appeals and online if the group has their email addresses to see if some of them will give entirely online, which is a far cheaper form of solicitation.) At the end of the year, People for Good has twenty more gifts from a cross-section of these fifty people. A few agree to give monthly, and one donor who gives $500 twice is moved into the organization's major donor portfolio for treatment as a major donor; over time, this donor becomes very important to the organization. In this second round, People for Good makes back most of the money it has invested in acquisition.

Upgrade: Ask Donors to Renew Their Gift

To be considered active (as opposed to lapsed), donors must make a contribution at least once a year, thus renewing their commitment to the organization. Most organizations have a renewal rate of about 66 percent—which is enough to generate a profit, including making back all the money invested in acquisition. Donors acquired through direct mail who show their commitment to the organization by renewing their gift are donors the organization might not have found otherwise. These donors can also be asked to volunteer, to give more money, to help with fundraising, to show up at demonstrations, and so on.

Large organizations that frequently send direct mail appeals often have a fund of $5,000 to $50,000 that they constantly reinvest in these appeals. Money coming in from one appeal is invested in the next until the fund is depleted. Organizations spending that kind of money often hire direct mail consultants to design their appeals and to handle all the details of writing, printing, and mailing them. It probably goes without saying that a mail appeal is a gamble—you might get 0.05 percent response or even no response at all. By carefully looking at the different types of lists, and by paying attention to what you send the donors and constantly fine-tuning the appeal package, you decrease—but do not eliminate—your risk. (Chapter Twelve describes the appeal package in detail.)

Direct Mail Acquisition: One Organization's Results

Income

10,000 pieces of mail × 1% response = 100 donors;
mode gift of $40, plus a number of other gifts received:

Income	$6,000

Three more mailings to those who gave asking for extra gifts:

10% response per mailing from 100 donors =
30 extra gifts

Income	$2,000

Three renewal mailings to these 100 donors;
66 renew at $50–$500

Income	$5,000
Total revenue	$13,000

Expenses

(Renting or exchanging lists, printing, postage, and other expenses)

10,000 pieces at $1.00 (higher volume will mean lower costs)

	$10,000

Further mailings to 100 donors

3 × 100 × $1.50

	$450

Renewal mailings (one to all 100 donors, a second to those who did not respond to the first, a third to those not responding to the first two)

200 letters × $1.50

	$300
Total expenses	$10,750
Net gain: 66 donors	$2,250
Net income per donor	$34

(*Note:* Costs of resolicitation and renewal will be less for donors who give online.)

USING DIRECT MAIL ON A SMALLER SCALE

By now, you are probably thinking, "Well, that counts us out. We don't have the money, we don't have the lists, and we can't wait a year or two for the repeat gifts and renewals to start making money."

Don't despair. There is a way for even small groups to use mail appeals effectively. They must decrease the risk by decreasing the amount of money spent on each mailing. At the same time, they must try to increase the response rate so that they at least break even on first-time mailings to a list and, with luck, make money.

These goals can be achieved in two ways: by mailing to more carefully selected lists and by mailing to fewer people at one time. In the example earlier, we used the conventional estimate of a 1 percent response from a new list; this estimate is useful for planning costs. However, direct mail expert Mal Warwick often cautions that there is so much variation in response from one organization to another and from one appeal to another that using this 1 percent figure as success can steer organizations onto the wrong path.

Factors such as attracting bigger donors, finding a whole new constituency of donors, testing messages, and so on are often as important as the percentage of response. Attracting a smaller response on the first mailing but a higher percentage of donors who renew year in and year out would make the mailing worth its costs. Despite this optimism, small organizations need some measurable gauge, and percentage of response will give you a way to budget money spent for money earned.

The next chart shows a direct mail scenario again but on a much smaller scale and with much more targeted lists.

As you can see, the average net income per donor from smaller mailings is much higher and the risk much lower than with larger mailings. However, neither set of income figures is particularly impressive given all the work involved. The costs examined here don't count the costs of staff time to acquire the mailing lists, produce the direct mail package, write thank you notes, record and deposit checks, and complete other fulfillment (such as producing and sending newsletters). Again, one wouldn't enter a direct mail program if this were the only kind of income you could expect.

An organization must be prepared to use the donors it has acquired to identify those who can give much more, and then ask them to do so. The organization must ask some of the new donors to volunteer and others to bring in other donors. Over the long term, some donors will include the organization in their will.

Direct Mail Acquisition: A Much Smaller Scale

Income

500 pieces of mail × 2% response = 10 donors;
mode gift of $40, plus a number of other gifts received

Income	$600

Three requests for extra gifts to the 10 new donors

10% response per mailing = 3 extra gifts, including one
gift of $200

Income	$300

Renewal letter with follow-up call to 10 people;
7 renewals

Income	$350
Total income	$1,250

Expenses

500 pieces of mail × $1.50	$750
30 letters asking for extra gifts × $1.50	$45
Renewal letter with phone follow-up to 10 people	$15
Total expenses	$810

Net gain: 6 donors	$450
Net income per donor	$75

(*Note:* If there is an option in your mail appeal for people to give online, you may not be able to track back an online donation to the mail appeal for record-keeping purposes. Nonetheless, every donation given online—and especially renewed online—will bring costs down.)

Direct mail illustrates more than any other strategy the fundraising principle of building relationships: if you are not willing to keep track of your success so that you know which lists work and which don't, if you are not willing to ask donors over and over, and if you are not willing to ask some donors for very large gifts, then you might as well not acquire them at all.

DEVELOPING LISTS FOR MAIL APPEALS

The cornerstone for the success of any mail appeal is the list of people who receive it. Compile or choose lists carefully. Make sure that each person's name is spelled correctly and that the address and ZIP code are correct. People tend to be miffed when their name is misspelled, and a wrong ZIP code will mean the letter won't be delivered.

Lists are divided into three categories of expectation, which describe the likelihood of people on that list making a donation. These categories are hot, warm, and cold.

Hot Lists. A hot list consists of people who have already made some kind of commitment to your organization. In order of decreasing heat, these people are your current donors, from whom can you expect a 10 percent response to any one mail appeal and of whom you can expect 66 percent to give a second time; lapsed donors from the past two years (expect a 3 to 7 percent response rate); volunteers and board members who are not yet donors (various response rates depending on the segment; however, the response rate should not be lower than 10 percent and could be as high as 95 percent with good follow-up); and the close friends and associates of all of the people above who are not yet donors (2 to 5 percent response rate).

Warm Lists. A warm list consists of people who have either used or heard of your services or your work, people who are donors to organizations similar to yours but probably have not heard of your organization, or people who have come to your special events. Although these lists may yield only a 1 percent response rate, they find you donors that you could not find otherwise.

Cold Lists. A cold list is any list that is more than a year old or any list of people about whom you know little or nothing. The phone book is an example of a cold list.

Hot Lists

The hottest list of people for any organization is its list of current donors. The second-hottest list includes friends of current donors, because most people's friends share their values and commitments. Therefore, to find new hot names to send appeals to, send current donors an annual mailing with a form on which to send the names and addresses of friends they think would be interested in your organization, as in the illustration.

Names of Friends Reply Form

Name and address: _____ E-mail:_____
__You may use my name __Do not use my name

1. Name, address, ZIP, e-mail: _____

2. _____

3. _____

4. _____

__I would rather not send in names, but I will distribute fundraising requests myself. Please send me ___ letters to send or give to friends.
__I will send this to my address book. Please e-mail me a PDF of the appeal with a hyperlink to the Donation button.
__I am willing to help with fundraising in other ways. Please contact me at: _____

Some people will send only one or two names, and most people will not send any, but others will send in dozens of names. Many organizations regularly remind their current donors to send in names of potential contributors by including a coupon in their newsletter and a request for names in other appeals. And of course all your donors should be encouraged to "like" your Facebook page so they can receive your regular updates on their Facebook home page or "join" your Facebook Group, which will enable them to receive direct messages from your organization via Facebook. They can also then promote your presence on Facebook to all of their "friends" on the site. (See facebook.com to learn how to accept donations directly through your organizations's Facebook page.)

Other versions of this are done very effectively online, with "tell-a-friend" or a form that can be filled out and sent in online.

Another source of hot prospects is your organization's board members, volunteers, and staff. On a yearly basis these people should also be asked to provide a list of names, which can be compared to the current mailing list; anyone who is not already a donor can be solicited. Of course, any board member, staff person, or volunteer who isn't already a donor is a hot prospect as well.

Warm Lists

People who buy any of your organization's products, such as booklets, educational materials, and T-shirts, are excellent prospects for a mail appeal because they are known buyers. Certainly, their names should be kept so you can advertise to them any new items you produce, and some of them will become members of your organization. The same is true of people who attend conferences, seminars, or public meetings that you sponsor. To keep mailing costs down, ask people who buy products or attend seminars you have sponsored for their e-mail address and advertise to them online (see also Chapter Fourteen for how to build your e-list and regularly solicit people using it).

People who attend special events who are not donors should receive an appeal soon after the event. Pass out a sign-up sheet or conduct a door prize drawing to get names, addresses, and e-mail addresses. People who previously gave your organization money but no longer do also constitute a warm list if you have correct addresses for them.

If your organization gives people advice, referrals, or other services by phone, by mail, or online, create a system to gather the names of people served, unless that information is confidential. This list is the least warm because not all the people using your organization donate to anything, you don't know if they were satisfied with what they got from you, and they may feel they deserve to get the information you are giving out for free. However, some will be grateful and want to help, and some will prefer to pay for the information rather than accept it for free.

Keep a log of these types of contacts in a database for later contact through mail or e-mail appeals. (If that seems too complicated, use the old-fashioned method of writing down names and addresses directly onto envelopes.) When people call, respond to their request and then ask if you can send them more information about your organization. Make sure you give people your Web address, and make sure your site also encourages giving. People who don't want an appeal will decline to give their address. Some of these people will go to your Web site later and become donors. Names from information requests that come through the mail can be transferred directly onto carrier envelopes; every time you have compiled two hundred envelopes you can send an appeal by bulk mail. Some organizations prefer to send appeals by first-class mail as the names come in. This ensures a hotter prospect, as people are more likely to open first-class mail, and they are receiving the mailing much closer to the time they have been in touch with you; but mailing first class is obviously more expensive than sending by bulk mail.

Renting and Trading Lists

The other kind of warm lists are lists of people who belong to organizations that are similar to yours. To get these names requires renting or trading mailing lists. No one actually buys a mailing list outright. By renting it, they acquire the right to use the list one time. Many organizations with large or specialized mailing lists rent their lists as an income stream. You may have noticed that if you give to one organization you will receive appeals from several similar organizations within a few weeks. Your name has been rented because you are a proven "buyer" through direct mail.

An organization rents mailing lists either from a mailing list broker or from another organization. Professional mailing list brokers have a wide variety of lists available, which are used by both nonprofit organizations and businesses. Ask larger organizations or direct mail consultants for the names of reputable list brokers, or simply search online for "Mailing list brokers for nonprofits." A quick glance through one Web site shows these possible offerings: season ticket holders to dance performances, donors who respond to natural disasters, liberal Democratic donors, donors to animal shelters, and so on. These lists come to you in ZIP-code order. The lists generally cost $75 to $125 per thousand names, with a minimum rental of two thousand to five thousand names. For a small additional fee, you can have lists crossed with each other, yielding the names, for example, of all donors to natural disasters who also give to animal shelters or liberal Democrats who are donors to the arts, and all of these in the ZIP codes you specify. A caution here: grassroots groups often assume that people in lucrative occupations (doctors, lawyers, stockbrokers) will be generous donors, so they seek lists of those names. However, the important variable is that they be donors. So if you rent lists, make sure you rent lists of donors: people who give away money, not just people who make money or have money. Be judicious in using rented lists.

Many low-budget organizations trade mailing lists with other organizations for a one-time use. Usually, lists are traded on a name-for-name basis: two hundred names for two hundred names and on up. An organization can also trade names for as many names as they have and rent the rest. If your organization has five hundred donors and you want another agency's list of two thousand donors, trade your five hundred and pay for the remaining fifteen hundred. Depending on your relationship with the other organization, it may rent the list to you simply for the cost of producing the list on labels or the cost of the labels plus handling, or it may seek to make some profit.

If you almost never rent your list, each of your names may be worth between two and five names of that of an organization that rents their list more often. If you have a mailing list of two hundred donor names that you have never rented out before, you may be able to trade for a list of one thousand.

Cold Lists

A cold list is a list of people about whom you know very little or a list that is six months old or more. Often, well-meaning volunteers will come in with a directory of the members of a club or the list of frequent customers from a store and suggest you use those names. Of course, they do not want their name associated with the mailing ("I don't want them to think I gave you these names"). Directories of people who belong to service clubs often state very clearly, "Do not use for direct mail" or "Do not sell, trade, or distribute." Obviously, we follow such requests. However, even without a proscription, we still wouldn't use these types of lists because we don't know whether the people on them give away money or if they are at all interested in our cause. The response from such a list will be minimal. The same is true for names and addresses that are six months old or more. People move frequently, and an old list will have old addresses, which will depress your response.

Stick with warm and hot lists. The response from direct mail is small enough as it is, and you don't want to be spending money mailing to people whom you really don't know anything about.

Dos and Don'ts of Sharing Lists

Organizations often feel reluctant to share their donor lists with other organizations. One fear is that their donors will prefer the other organization and stop giving or give less to their organization. Studies of donors show that this is not true. In fact, donor loyalty to the first group they give to in a series of organizations with related goals is increased as they learn of similar organizations. In other words, if a person gives to an environmental organization and then is solicited by several others, he or she may think, "I already support a group that does good work on the environment" or "I've been concerned about environmental degradation for a long time, and it's good that a lot of groups are working on it." Furthermore, most people who give to charity give to a number of them—usually between five and fifteen. Often, most of the charities are similar: they may all be arts organizations or environmental groups, or they may be civil rights and civil liberties causes, but there will be some similar theme in all the nonprofits. People change one or two NGOs each year, dropping one and taking on a new one. You are going to lose some donors every year (about one-third), but you will not lose donors simply by sharing your list.

To ensure that the names of donors who might take offense at being solicited by organizations other than yours are excluded from your rented lists, simply include a line in your newsletter or on your reply device that says, "From time to time we make our mailing list available to other organizations that we feel would be of interest to our donors. If you would rather we did not include your name, please drop us a line (or check here on the form) and we will make sure that you do not receive any of these mailings." You can publish this announcement in every issue of the newsletter and put it in the subscription form on your Web site to be sure that every donor sees it. Very few people will actually write in with this request, but it is worth it to keep those that do happy. Most people like to get mail, and although they grouse about how much direct mail they get, they also feel important and needed because of the volume of mail that comes to them, and they have too much going on their lives to spend a lot of time and energy being mad about a mail appeal.

Do not steal mailing lists or use mailing lists that are marked "members only" or "do not use for solicitation." Because mailing lists are fairly easy to compile and acquire, once you have the systems in place there is no need to be underhanded with others' lists. Further, your organization's reputation may suffer. Almost all mailing lists, particularly those rented from commercial firms, have a certain number of dummy names: names that are placed to identify the use of that list. The letter addressed to a dummy name goes to the source of the list.

Suppose you have liberated the list of members of a service club that has given your organization a donation. John Q. Jones is on that list, put there by the service club itself. ("Q" ensures that this is likely an unduplicated name.) When a letter arrives addressed to John Q. Jones, the service club knows it came from their list and will check out whether someone gave your organization permission to use the list. The situation can then become unpleasant and counterproductive to your fundraising efforts

Here is a final rule about list acquisition and development: do not save mailing lists. On a list that is more than three months old, 7 percent of the addresses will already be inaccurate. After you have used a list twice (if you have permission to do so), you have gotten 90 percent of the response you are going to get from that list. Concentrate your efforts on getting new names and refine your systems so that the names are as hot as possible. The quality of the list is pivotal to your direct mail success.

chapter TWELVE

The Logistics of Direct Mail

A direct mail appeal needs to be conceived of as a package rather than as simply a letter in an envelope sent to a bunch of people. The work of your organization is only one variable in determining the success of your appeal. The appeal is "wrapped" in a certain way to entice the donor to open the letter, then to read the letter, then to make a donation, either by sending a check in the return envelope or going online. This is a lot of pressure on a few pieces of paper with no power of their own.

This chapter discusses all the elements of putting together a direct mail package as well as a number of ways to use direct mail in seeking first-time, additional, and renewal gifts; what to do with the responses; and how to evaluate your direct mail programs.

THE DIRECT MAIL APPEAL PACKAGE

The standard package has four parts: the carrier or outside envelope, the letter itself, the reply device, and the return envelope.

Each part of the package is complementary to the others, and all the elements work as a unit to have the maximum effect on the person receiving the appeal. We will examine each element separately and then discuss putting the elements together.

The Carrier (Outside) Envelope

Many mail appeals fail because, although much attention has been spent writing an effective letter, it is enclosed in an envelope that no one opens.

First-class personal and business mail can be sent in an envelope simply with the recipient's address and a return address, and the sender can be reasonably certain that someone will open the letter. In the case of first-class mail, the envelope is simply a convenient way to deliver the letter. In a fundraising appeal sent by bulk mail, however, the outside envelope has an entirely different purpose. It must grab a prospect's attention and then intrigue them enough that they want to open it and see what's inside. The envelope in this case is like gift wrapping. Everyone wants to know what's inside a present. In fact, gift wrapping works so well that even when you may know what the gift is, there is still the thrill of discovery in removing the wrapping.

That thrill and that curiosity is what you should strive for with mail appeals. Make the prospect want to know what is inside the envelope.

Getting Personal. Think about how most of us look through our mail. We may have bills that we set aside and a magazine or other appeals that we glance at and either discard or put in a pile to read later. But if we find an envelope with our name handwritten on it, we will often put down the rest of the mail to open that envelope. If there are no such envelopes, we may open envelopes that promise interesting content in either words or pictures, or envelopes from organizations that we know and respect or from places we can't recognize just from the address. Maybe we see mailing labels inside, so we open that envelope. If an envelope offers us a way to save money, we open that one. If we are in a hurry, we throw away mail more quickly than if we are not. If we are procrastinating about doing something else, we may read something that on any other day we would discard immediately. Some marketing experts estimate that up to 70 percent of mail is thrown away unopened. So in designing your carrier envelope, use your own experience as to what you open first and what you are unlikely to ever open. However, don't rely on your experience alone. A fun conversation is to ask colleagues, neighbors, and friends to look at five appeal letters and tell you which one they would open first or which one they would throw away immediately. You will generate several different opinions, which is why you will never find one style of envelope that always works, with the exception of those that are hand addressed, which almost everyone will agree they will open.

If possible, then, write the addresses by hand. If you have a large volunteer pool or fewer than one thousand addresses, this is not too arduous a task if divided over several people. In addition to or instead of writing the addresses, you can make your letter look as though it was sent first class by using a precanceled bulk-mail stamp in place of the more common postal indicia. These stamps may be purchased at the post office where you send your bulk mail. The rules for sorting and handling the mail are the same as for any other bulk mailing.

Other Ways to Draw Attention.   Consider the rest of the envelope. If you are in a major metropolitan area where a lot of mail appeals originate, don't put your name and return address in the upper left-hand corner of the front of the envelope. Either use only your address without your organization's name in that spot or put your return address on the back flap of the envelope. In either case, the prospect asks, "Who is this from?" and opens the envelope to find out.

Use Common Sense.   Mission drives fundraising, and the truth of this tenet can be seen even in the design of carrier envelopes. Here are two examples:

A national organization advocating for the rights of GLBT (gay, lesbian, bisexual, and transgender) people is always careful to use its initials or an innocuous logo with its return address on mail appeals. It does not wish to endanger anyone who receives the appeal, even if this practice cuts into the response because some people throw away the appeal without recognizing who the group is.

An animal rights organization has compelling and disturbing photos of animals used in research. Although putting one of these photos on an envelope would certainly grab attention, the organization is conscious that children may see this letter, so uses no graphic photos in that way.

Timing and world events also play a role in designing carrier envelopes. Shortly after the attacks on the Pentagon and World Trade Center on September 11, 2001, a handful of envelopes addressed in childlike writing and containing military-grade anthrax were sent to Washington, D.C. Some postal employees were sickened; a few died. During that time, direct mail had a better chance of being opened if it looked impersonal.

If you are in a rural area, it is likely that the people receiving your appeal will open all letters that originate in their county or small town. In that case, you want your name and return address to be fairly prominent on the front of the envelope.

Most mail appeals are sent in standard business-size envelopes (called No. 10). Your appeal will stand out if it arrives in a smaller or odd-size envelope. Personal letters are not generally sent in business-size envelopes, so to make your appeal look more personal, send it in a No. 6-¾ or No. 7-¾, or in an invitation-style envelope. If you use smaller envelopes, make sure your return card and return envelope are smaller yet so that they will fit into the carrier envelope without needing to be folded. One caution: odd-size envelopes and letters can run up your printing costs, sometimes significantly, so check with your printer before making a final decision.

The least effective strategy is placing what's known as "teaser copy" on an envelope; however, it should not be totally disregarded. Teaser copy is a text, drawing, or photograph on the envelope that intrigues the reader or causes some emotional response meant to make them open the envelope.

Envelope color is another variable to experiment with, but in choosing colors, make sure that the type is still readable against the color of the envelope. Bright colors can grab attention, but readability is key.

You may wish to experiment with various styles of outside envelopes to find which methods work best for your organization. Save mail appeals that you receive and are moved to open, and figure out what about the envelope caused you to want to look inside. The more creative you can be in designing the outside envelope, the greater chance you will have of the prospect reading your appeal.

The Letter

Because of the cost and volume of direct mail, it has been studied very carefully for more than forty years. A few simple principles about writing a direct mail letter have emerged. In thinking about these principles, keep in mind that a direct mail appeal is not literature. Many otherwise good writers are not good writers of direct mail letters. The direct mail letter is not designed to be lasting or to be filed away or to be read several times with new insights emerging from each reading. It is disposable, part of a culture acclimated to disposable goods of all kinds—from diapers and coffee cups to contact lenses. The function of the fundraising letter is simply to catch the reader's attention and hold it long enough for the person to decide to give. The recipients of fundraising letters most often read these letters on their own time. It is not their job to read the letter, and if the letter has its intended result, they will wind up paying money for having read it.

Also keep in mind how adults respond to input: when reading, watching TV or a movie, listening to a lecture, or even, to a lesser extent, listening to someone they care about, they subconsciously go back and forth between two questions. The first question is, "So what?" If this question is answered satisfactorily, they move to the next question, which is, "Now what?" This seesaw is a strong screening device for filtering out trivia, boring details, and rhetoric. To be sure, what is trivial and boring to one person may be profound or lifesaving to another, so the answers to these questions will vary from person to person. However, details about when your organization was founded or the permutations of your organizational structure will not pass the "So what?" test, and the myriad problems that led to your current budget deficit will only bring on a fit of "Now what?" questioning.

As you write your letter, then, imagine the reader asking at the end of each sentence, "So what? What does this have to do with me, people I care about, or things I believe in?" If the sentence stands up under that scrutiny, then read the next sentence while asking, "Now what?" Does this sentence offer a solution, provide more information, or inspire confidence in the organization?

Using the "So what—now what?" spectrum as the foundation, build your letter on the following principles:

People Have Short Attention Spans.   A person should be able to read each sentence in your letter in six to eight seconds. Each sentence must be informative or provocative enough to merit devoting the next six to eight seconds to reading the next sentence.

People Love to Read About Themselves.   The reader of the letter wonders, "Do you know or care anything about me?" "Will giving your group money make me happier, give me status, or relieve my guilt?" "Did you notice that I helped before?" Therefore, the letter should refer to the reader at least twice as often and up to four times as often as it refers to the organization sending it. To do this requires drawing the reader into the cause with such phrases as, "You may have read . . . ," "I'm sure you join me in feeling . . . ," "If you are like me, you care deeply about . . ." When writing to solicit another gift or a renewal from someone who is already a donor, use even more references to what they have done: "You have helped us in the past," "Your gift of $50 meant a great deal last year," "I want you to know that we rely on people like you—you are the backbone of our organization." Using the word *You* makes your letter speak *to* the reader rather than *at* them.

People Must Find the Letter Easy to Look At. The page should contain a lot of white space, including wide margins, and be in a font that is clear and simple. Break up paragraphs so that each is no more than two or three sentences long, even if such breaks are not absolutely dictated by the content. Use contractions (won't, you're, can't, we're) to add to the informal style. This is a letter, not a term paper. Do not use jargon or long, complex words. Go on to a second or even third page in order to ensure that the letter is easy to understand.

People Read the Letter in a Certain Order, and They Rarely Read the Whole Letter. People often read the P.S. first. Then they read the salutation and the opening paragraph and, no matter how long the letter is, they read the closing paragraph. If they did not read the P.S. first, they read it now. Up to 60 percent of readers decide whether or not to give on the basis of these three paragraphs and will not read the rest of the letter. The other 40 percent will read selective parts of the rest of the letter, usually parts that are easy to look at, such as facts set off in bullets or phrases that are underlined. Only a small number of people will read the entire letter.

The Postscript. This is often the first—and sometimes the only—sentence people read. The P.S. is most commonly used to suggest action: "Don't put this letter aside. Every day new cases come our way and we need your help." Sometimes it offers an additional incentive for acting immediately: "Every gift we receive before April 15 will be matched by Nofreelunch Foundation," or "We have a limited supply of *Excellent Book* by Important Author. Send your gift of $50 or more as soon as possible to be sure that you get one." The P.S. can be used to tell a story:

> P.S. An independent study showed that the quality of our schools has improved because of Community Concern. It also showed that we have a long way to go. For the sake of the children, please make your donation today.

Or it can make the reader part of the story:

> P.S. You cared enough to come to our community meeting last week. We hope you will join us in our critical work by making a donation now.

The Opening Paragraph.   Use the opening paragraph to tell a story, either about someone your program has helped, some situation your organization has been instrumental in changing, or something about the reader of the letter. I have mentioned this saying before: "People buy with their hearts first and then their heads." Programs and outcomes need to be described in people terms (or animals, if that is your constituency). Remember that people have read a lot of stories in direct mail appeals and newspapers and have seen even more on the Internet and TV. They are used to being entertained by stories at the same time that they are skeptical of their authenticity, so make sure that your story is true (even if facts have been changed to protect someone) and that it is credible and typical. (You don't want someone saying, "What a sad story, but that could only happen once, so I'm not going to give.") Finally, have the story resolve positively because of the work of your organization. Here are some examples.

Someone Your Organization Has Helped

> Toni has been homeless for two years, moving in and out of shelters. Like half of the homeless people in our community, Toni works full time, but she has not been able to save the money she needs for the security deposit on an apartment. This week, because Homes Now has paid Toni's security deposit, she will be able to move into an apartment of her own.

The paragraph ends here. The body of the letter goes on to explain how many working people are homeless and how Homes Now helps homeless people with housing, job training, and child care. If this letter were being used with current or former donors to Homes Now, the opening paragraph would use this sentence in place of the third sentence: "However, this week, because of the help of donors like you, Homes Now paid Toni's security deposit for her and she has moved into an apartment of her own."

A Situation the Organization Helped to Change

> To some people it looked like a vacant lot, full of weeds, old tires, and paper trash. So when Dreck Development proposed paving it over for a parking lot, few people objected. After all, it is in a poor neighborhood and a parking lot would be useful to commuters who work in the industrial park a few blocks away. To Joe Camereno, the lot looked like a park.

He called Inner City Greenspace and asked us how to go about protecting this vacant lot. Today it is Commonwealth Park. How did this come about?

The opening ends here. The rest of the letter lets people know how Inner City Greenspace helps neighborhoods transform vacant lots, treeless streets, and abandoned buildings into more livable community spaces.

Where the Reader Is Part of the Story

As a resident of Rio del Vista, you were probably as shocked as I was to learn of the toxic waste dump proposed for Del Vista Lake last year. Working together, we were able to save the lake, but now a dump is proposed for Del Vista Canyon. We've got another fight on our hands.

The letter goes on to explain why Rio del Vista is often targeted for these projects and what can be done about it.

Any of these styles of opening can be effective. The one you use will depend on your list and the stories available or the role of the reader in the situation described.

The Length. There is has been much debate about the length of a direct mail letter. Many people claim that they never read a long letter and object to wasting trees to print them. Some direct mail consultants, on the other hand, advise their clients to send letters that are four to six pages. In fact, the evidence is overwhelming that longer letters are more successful: a two-page letter will get a better response than a one-page letter, and three to four pages will often get a better response than two pages. It is also true that consumers don't read these long letters—in fact, most of them only read the opening, the closing, and the postscript.

So why do longer letters work when people don't read them? Because a longer letter makes it look as though your organization has more to say and therefore has more substance to its work. It says to the reader, "We know you are not some slouch that will give to just anything, so we will explain ourselves." And it allows the organization to take the space it needs to make a case for itself without jamming words onto the page. For most small-budget organizations, two or three pages are effective. Remember that a letter can be printed on both sides of the paper.

The Closing Paragraph. The other paragraph people read, the last paragraph of the letter, suggests the action you want the reader to take. It is specific and straightforward:

> To make a difference right now, go online to HomesNow.org to make a secure donation, or place your gift of $35, $50, $75, or another amount in the enclosed envelope and mail it today.
>
> For your gift of $35 or more, you will receive our quarterly newsletter, *Chew on This.* Above all, you will know that your gift has provided free dental services to people who cannot afford to see a dentist.

If you are a membership organization with several different levels give only the simplest description in the letter. This last paragraph is a short paragraph. Explain the full details of benefits on the reply device.

The Rest of the Text. The rest of the letter tells more of your history, discusses your plans, tells more stories, gives statistics, and lists accomplishments. To break up the text, use devices other than straight paragraphs. These devices might include bulleted text, such as this:

Because of us:

- In 2003, a city ordinance banning the distribution of birth control to teenagers was repealed as unconstitutional.
- All teenagers in this community receive sex education as a part of their biology courses.
- We remain the only independent clinic providing referrals and birth control to anyone who needs it, regardless of their ability to pay.

Or underlining:

When it got up to <u>ten drive-by shootings</u> in one month, with <u>half of the victims children</u>, the neighborhood association had had enough!

Or adding a brief note that looks handwritten:

You can help!

Or:

Every gift makes a difference. Make yours today.

Who signs the letter is not critically important. If a famous person can be found to sign the letter, then the letter should be from that person. "I am happy to take time out of my busy movie schedule to tell you about Feisty Group." Otherwise, the chair of the board or the executive director can sign. The letter should be signed, however, and it should not be signed by more than two people or it begins to look like a petition. The person who signs the letter should have a readable, straightforward signature.

The Reply Device

The reply device is the mechanism by which people send a donation back to you in response to a direct mail appeal. The device can be a small card listing the benefits of donating and containing a place for the donor's name, address, and so on, and come with a self-addressed return envelope, or it can be a tear-off from the main letter, or a wallet-flap envelope.

The Psychology of the Reply Device.   In the letter, the organization refers to the reader using the word *You*. The reader reads about herself or himself. In the reply device, the reader responds to the organization while continuing to read about himself or herself. The reader is asked to respond by saying, "Count me in" or "I agree" or "I'm with you."

More and more, when people open mail from groups they have heard of or causes they believe in, they move right to the bottom line—how much will it cost to join? For this, they look to the reply device. If the reply device holds their attention, they may return to the letter or they may just give without referring to the letter at all.

The reply device may be the one piece of paper the donor keeps from the mail appeal, as happens when someone reads an appeal letter, decides to give, then puts the return envelope and reply device into their "bills to be paid" pile and throws the letter away. Two weeks later, the reply device must rekindle the excitement that the letter originally sparked, using a fraction of the space. For this reason, the design of the reply device is very important.

The reply device is usually printed on paper or card stock that fits easily with a check into the return envelope. Making the bottom portion of a letter the reply device or using a separate card or slip of paper allows you to change the reply device with every letter without incurring a great deal of cost.

Another option is the wallet-flap style of envelope; in that style the reply device is the back flap of the envelope itself. In general, these are more expensive to print so groups usually print them in quantity; once printed, no further customizing can be done, so if you use this style, be thoughtful about the content so that you can use it for some time, or use this style of envelope for big mailings. Further, a reply device that is separate from its envelope allows for one or the other to get lost without the person losing the address of your organization, and you can use the return envelopes for other things you may want people to return, such as postcard petitions or surveys.

The Design.   If possible, the reply device should display the logo of the organization and have a slogan or a short mission statement to remind prospects of what the organization believes in. Be sure to include your Web address and encourage people to go online to give.

Probably the trickiest part is wording the donor categories and benefits briefly. Many organizations use a simple series of boxes with differing amounts of money being suggested as donations, with the same benefits for any amount of money. (You'll find a discussion of benefits at the end of this chapter.) If you have more elaborate benefits of membership or incentives for giving, put the amount first, then describe the incentive. Here's an example:

> $35: Includes newsletter
>
> $50: Includes newsletter plus free hemp shopping bag
>
> Pledge ($10 per month minimum): Includes newsletter plus *Very Good Book* by our own Roberta P. Activist

Unless you have really clever names or particularly good incentives, naming your donor categories is not worth that much. "Patron," "Benefactor," "Friend," all have little or no meaning and inevitably reflect a hierarchy of giving that is just as well avoided.

The rest of the space must have room for the name, address, and phone number of the donor, or a place for a label. Make sure the response you want is obvious and easy to comply with: note on your reply device to whom to make the check payable and (in very small type) whether the contribution is tax-deductible.

People will read the suggested amounts until they find a number they are comfortable with or the amount that the letter has most emphasized. The following type of arrangement is fairly standard:

☐ $25   ☐ $35   ☐ $50   ☐ $100   ☐ other $_____

You may wonder whether to start with the highest suggested gifts or put a large number in that second slot. These strategies are not effective because people will not pay more than they can afford and you don't want to scare them off. An organization with the following sequence may wind up giving a message that small gifts are not encouraged:

☐ $500   ☐ $250   ☐ $100   ☐ other $_____

On the other hand, do not suggest an amount you would rather not receive, such as $5. If someone wants to or needs to send only that much, he or she can check "other." By suggesting it, you will get that amount from people who could have given a lot more.

When it comes time to evaluate your appeal, you will want to be able to distinguish one appeal's response from another's. You do this by coding the reply device for each appeal in some way. If you have access to inexpensive printing, you could print each reply device in a different color, add a number or date to a bottom corner, or change the device that goes with each mailing in some other way. If you don't have a way to have the reply devices printed differently, a cheap and easy method is to put a dot with a colored marker on each reply card and note which color you are using for which mailing.

The Return Envelope

Aside from the wallet-style envelope discussed earlier, there are two styles of return envelopes: business reply envelopes (called BREs) and plain, self-addressed envelopes. With a BRE, the organization pays the cost of the return postage; this amounts to about twice as much as a first-class stamp but is only paid on those envelopes that are returned. With a plain, self-addressed envelope, the donor affixes a stamp.

For small organizations, BREs are not necessary, and organizations have ceased using them as consumers have become aware of the cost. Unless you are working with a sizzling hot list of current donors, do not put a first-class stamp on the return envelope. Your response rate will be too small to justify this expense. On the other hand, do not try to save money by omitting an envelope altogether. Your percentage of response will decline significantly if you do not use a self-addressed envelope of some kind.

Other Enclosures

The letter, reply device, and return envelope are all that is necessary to make an excellent mail appeal. There are some additions you can use if you wish. Whether they will increase your response rate depends on many other variables, but they might.

The Lift Note.   A lift note is a small note equivalent to the notes in commercial direct mail packages that say, "Read this only if you have decided not to buy our tires." The note usually appears to be handwritten or at least printed in a different font from the text of the letter. It is from someone other than the signer of the letter and provides another compelling reason to give. For example, a letter signed by Judy Blacetti, director of an organization that helps seniors learn to use computers, had this lift note:

> I didn't want to learn to use a computer, but to please my son, I took a course at the Senior Center. This old dog has learned a lot of new tricks! I now teach other seniors how to use computers. It's fun, but also has a serious side, as people do research on medicine they have been prescribed or on their civil liberties or credit offers to see if they are legitimate. People can e-mail their kids and grandkids, and sometimes information found on the Internet saves money and may save lives. The courses are cheap because the teachers are all volunteers. Won't you help?—Lois Smith, age 82.

Of course, most people will read the lift note first, even though it reads as though you would read it after the letter. People's curiosity is aroused, and they now read about Lois Smith in the letter.

A Newspaper Article. If your organization has received positive press, reprint the article. If possible, reprint it on newspaper-quality paper so that it looks as though you cut the article out of the paper. People tend to think that if something was in the newspaper it is more true than if you say it yourself.

An Internal Memorandum. Similar in theory to a lift note, an internal memorandum gives readers the impression that they are learning something that they would not normally be privy to. For example, an organization working to feed refugees in Pakistan used this internal memo:

TO: Joe (the director, who signed the letter)

FR: Fred Smythe, Comptroller

RE: Recent food shipment

Joe, we can't continue to send this much food without a lot more money. I'm way over budget already and getting more and more requests from the field. There is no way we can send medical supplies as well. You have got to cut back.

Joe then scrawls the following note on the memo:

I received this memo just as I was about to send you this letter. Please help with as much as you can as soon as you can: if possible go to our Web site and give today. Every gift helps us save lives.

Fact Sheet. A well-designed, easy-to-read fact sheet highlighting exciting facts about your organization can take the place of one page of your letter. Many organizations now use a fact sheet with a two-page letter, and their results are as good as when they used a longer letter. Even though the number of pages is the same, a fact sheet is handy because the same one can be used with several different letters. A fact sheet should be on your organization's stationery. Among the "facts" should be that you depend on donations from individuals and what the minimum donation is for a person to become a member of your organization. This information reinforces the message of the letter, reaches those people who only read the fact sheet and not the letter, and allows you to use the fact sheet in other kinds of mailings or give it away at rallies, house parties, or other events. A PDF version of the fact sheet can be e-mailed to board members or posted on your Web site to be forwarded to others or downloaded for board members' own fundraising efforts.

Brochure.　Surprisingly, using a brochure in a direct mail appeal will almost always decrease your response. Brochures are more complicated to look at than fact sheets or newspaper articles and require more of the reader's attention. Because a brochure does not generally emphasize giving, it can wind up holding attention but not achieving the purpose of the mailing. Brochures are designed to be given away at special events or to people wanting more information, and to be sent with personal letters asking for money.

Putting the Package Together

Be sure that your letter and enclosures are free of typographical errors. One typo can change the meaning of a sentence or more often render it meaningless; moreover, typos give a bad impression of your organization's work, particularly the most common typos: pubic for public, or grunt for grant. Make sure that your Web site and return address are on everything: the reply device, the letter, and the return envelope. That way if someone loses the return envelope, she or he can still find you. Although the letter itself should be in a clean, readable font, the carrier envelope, reply device, and return envelope generally should be in a larger, bold font. Remember, the only impression that donors recruited by mail will have of your whole operation will be from what they get in the mail.

Be sure that the envelope color and the paper stock for your letter do not clash. Avoid strong colors, such as bright yellows or reds, and any dark-colored paper. People with vision problems have a difficult time reading type on dark-colored paper, and you don't want to lose a prospect because he or she couldn't read the letter. Use sharp contrast in your type and paper color so that the words are easy to read. Use recycled or tree-free paper and soy ink in the printing whenever possible; if you do, put the recycle graphic on your letter so that people will know you have paid attention to this detail. Similarly, if possible use a unionized printer and put their union "bug" (the insignia that signifies you have done business with a union shop) on the letter and envelope. Although response is not necessarily higher, those donors who do notice are pleased that you have not left your values behind to promote your cause by mail.

Do a spot check of all the printed materials before they are mailed; if you use a mailing house, ask them to do that. Sometimes a printer's mistake may leave the middle twenty-five letters smeared or blank. Although you can't look at every piece individually, you may be able to stop a mistake from being sent out.

Fold the letter so that the writing appears on the outside rather than on the inside, as with a normal letter. A person pulling the letter out from the envelope should be able to begin reading it without having to unfold it or turn it around.

Some states have laws that require that you to send a copy of each appeal to a government agency for approval before sending it out or to list your federal identification number on everything you send. Be sure to investigate and comply with these laws (your local AFP chapter or state nonprofit association should be able to help you find the laws for your state).

When to Send an Appeal

There is a saying among direct mail consultants that the best time of year to send an appeal is when it is ready. There is much truth in this saying, because there are no really bad times of year and no really excellent ones; the best time will always be when the appeal is fresh and exciting. Moreover, your mailing can be derailed by major natural disasters (droughts, hurricanes, earthquakes) at any time of year.

Every organization needs to adjust the timing of its direct mail appeals according to its constituency. Farmers have schedules that are different from those of schoolteachers. Your constituency's religion and how fervently they practice it will affect some timing. Elections will affect timing. Even the activities of other organizations your constituents belong to may have an impact. As such, you will want to mail over many months and keep track of what works best for your organization.

BENEFITS AND PREMIUMS

An organization that intends to have a large base of donors who repeatedly give small gifts must establish a workable benefits program. The purpose of a benefits program is to give donors something for their money that pleasantly reminds them of your organization or educates them further about your work so they feel even better about their previous gift and more inclined to make another one. Benefits are important for the simple reason that Americans are consumers. We are accustomed to getting things for our money, and even nonprofit organizations compete for the consumer dollar on this level. However, benefits don't have to be elaborate, and they don't really need to include anything beyond a well-done newsletter. Recent evidence, particularly by the researcher Penelope Burke, has indicated that donors don't want refrigerator magnets or a coffee mug as much as they want evidence that their money was well used and some minimal personal attention that shows their gift was appreciated.

In that vein, a thank you note is the first tangible "benefit." As mentioned before, it should go out within seventy-two hours of receipt of the gift. Information about the organization provided by a newsletter has proven to be enough of a benefit for many smaller organizations.

The newsletter regularly reminds donors of your work, encourages them to feel proud of their part in your accomplishments, and provides information not available elsewhere or a point of view not generally expressed in the mass media.

There are two guidelines for choosing benefits for donors. First, the fulfillment costs (that is, how much money it costs your organization to produce and send the item you promised) should never be more than one-fifth of the lowest membership category. Second, while you can always add benefits, it is far more difficult to take them away.

In deciding on a benefits package, then, start with small benefits that you know your organization can continue to afford and that you have the staff or volunteers to provide. The difference between a bimonthly newsletter and a quarterly one will not be nearly as important to the donor as it will be to your budget, staff, and volunteer time.

If you decide to have incentives for larger donations, try to find something that promotes your organization. A book about the work you do or that is related to a topic you address is good. Books can usually be purchased directly from the publisher in quantities of ten or more for 40 percent off the cover price. Paperback volumes are fine.

The problem with books or any other benefit, however, is that it may not be easy to find a new one every year, which is why many organizations offer premiums to encourage people to give but do not offer them as rewards for renewing or upgrading their gifts.

Premiums

Premiums are additional thank you gifts for donating within a specified time period. Announcement of a premium is often included in the mail appeal letter at the postscript, whose main purpose is to move the donor to act:

> P.S. Send your gift by December 1 and we will send you a special edition of a calendar created by a local artist for our group.

Or:

> P.S. We have a limited number of signed lithographs that we will send to the first fifty donors. Join today.

You don't want the renewing donor to put your appeal in the pile of bills to be paid later or to lose the appeal, so you offer a premium to encourage the donor to act promptly.

Premiums are particularly useful in securing upgraded gifts. The majority of these donors are probably going to give anyway; the premium simply encourages them to give sooner and more. For example, letters to people who gave $25 could entice a higher gift with a statement such as, "Gifts of $50 or more receive two free tickets to the spring concert."

The best premiums from your organization's point of view are ones that you already have. For example, suppose you are doing a concert and ticket sales are slow. Offer renewing donors a free ticket for renewing by a certain date. Or suppose you have had too many calendars printed and cannot possibly sell them all before the beginning of the new year. Offer them as a premium.

In using premiums for acquiring new donors, remember to add the cost of the premium when figuring the cost of the mail appeal. The cost of the premium will lower your net income, but if you gain even one or two percentage points in response, the cost will be offset.

You can also use premiums when you don't wish to commit yourself to a regular benefit—just send the premium item when you have it.

In weighing whether to offer benefits beyond the newsletter, and if so, what, try to imagine repurposing content you already have: for example, many people who are not in fundraising have no idea what a report to a foundation looks like. Take your most recent report, add "Not for distribution" on the top, and send it to your major donors. Or if an academic has published a monograph or paper on some aspect of the issue you work on that you have found interesting or useful, e-mail it to your donors (with permission of the author, if it is unpublished).

When weighing whether to give something as a benefit or a premium, go with the premium. People's lives are so busy that we want to create an incentive for acting now, before a hundred other demands have taken hold.

USING DIRECT MAIL TO SEEK RENEWAL GIFTS

The final use of direct mail is to renew gifts on an annual basis. There are many ways to set up renewal programs, but a simple, tiered renewal program based on size of gift works well. First, sort your donors according to their giving as small, midrange, and major donors. Small donors are people whose total giving is less than $100 in one year. Midrange donors are people giving between $100 and $249 annually, and major donors are people who annually give $250 or more. You can adjust these numbers to fit your constituency—the point is to create three categories of donors who are treated in somewhat different ways.

You could use direct mail to renew all your donors, with slightly different letters for each tier. However, it is better to use this system: at renewal time, all donors of small gifts receive a form letter asking them to renew their gift, all donors of midrange gifts receive a personalized letter, and all major donors receive a personal letter followed by a phone call and sometimes a visit. Although it is more work to segment your donor list in this way, your renewal rate will be higher and your chance of upgrading your donors is better. If you have a smaller donor base (fewer than five hundred donors), you should personalize as many renewal letters as you can. (For more on segmenting donor lists, see Chapter Nineteen.)

The list of small donors is further divided into four categories according to when the person gave—spring, summer, autumn, winter. Once each quarter, the names of donors needing to renew in that quarter are generated from the database, and they are sent a renewal letter with a reply device and return envelope. This is a much easier system than trying to write to people on the anniversary date of their gift, and it is much more effective in terms of renewal rates and cash flow than writing to everyone once a year regardless of when they gave.

The renewal letter follows the format of direct mail appeals. It starts with a sentence or two about the donor, affirming the importance of individual donors to the health and work of the organization. The letter goes on to list a few of the organization's accomplishments during the previous year and asks for a renewal gift, requesting that the donor increase his or her gift if possible. Although a renewal letter need be no longer than one page, do not jam the letter onto the page. Do not try to save space by saying so little that you wind up being cryptic or giving the impression that not much actually happened during the year. If you have more to say about your work than will fit nicely on one page, go on to a second page or the back of the page. Remember, for these donors especially, what they get from you in the mail is most or all of what they know about your work.

The reply device should be designed specifically for renewals, so the donor feels that he or she is a part of a group being asked to give again, rather than a new person being asked to give for the first time. In addition to the renewal, you can use the renewal reply device to ask the donor for other things, such as in the example shown here.

Here are the names of three people I think would be interested in____
(Name of Group):

_____

_____

____ You may use my name when writing to them.

____ I would like membership information to send to (#)___ friends. Please send me membership packets.

____ I would like information about legacy giving.

____ I would like to volunteer.

Don't put more than one or two of these other options on the reply device, and vary them over time. After six to eight weeks, generate a list of any donors who haven't renewed yet and send them a shorter and firmer letter:

> In your busy day, you may have forgotten to renew your commitment to Good Group. Please don't put this letter aside. Renew today.

Most organizations find it effective to send three renewal notices over a six- to eight-month period. They may then call the donors they have not heard from and ask them to renew. Donors who haven't responded after three renewal notices and a renewal call and who haven't given for the past fourteen months or more should be suppressed from getting a newsletter. Let them miss one or two newsletters before another notice is sent that says something like this:

> We miss you. We need you. I'd like to send you our next newsletter so you can keep up with all the important work people like you are making possible. Please use the enclosed form to send in a gift or let us know why you are not contributing at this time. Thanks.

A word of caution: there are many donors on your list who will respond to requests for extra funds and not to your renewal appeals. In their minds, they have given already this year. Any gift a person makes during a twelve-month period makes them a "current" donor. Sometimes organizations that have memberships get snippy with donors who have given but who haven't renewed their membership. Unless membership entitles you to something that your other gifts don't, this is silly and actually can alienate the donor. When you finally take someone off your list, make sure they really have not given for at least fourteen months.

Most social change organizations allow people to receive the newsletter or stay on the mailing list without paying if the person is interested in the cause but can't afford to join or to subscribe. This practice is certainly appropriate; however, you don't want to keep people on your list whom you never hear from. Many times these people do not read your newsletter or your appeals and don't even remember how they got on your list. Because I teach fundraising to hundreds of groups a year, I get a lot of newsletters and mailings. One organization, to which I have never and will never donate, has been sending me their newsletter since 1981! I have moved to three different states and had nine different addresses during this time. I have written asking to be taken off the list, I have called, I have sent the newsletter back marked "Return to sender." Keeping me on their list is a waste of resources; unfortunately, I know from speaking with other people that this kind of waste is not unusual.

We hear stories every so often of someone who was on an organization's list for ten years without giving a gift and then gave $100,000 or left the organization $20,000 in their estate. I am sure this happens from time to time (as in geologic time), and it is true you will miss these people, if, indeed you would ever have had them. However, the cost of keeping all the people on your list who don't give on the off chance that one will give is not sensible. Think of it this way: imagine one of your poorer donors who works at a low-wage job and sends $35, which may represent half a day's pay after taxes. He thinks you are going to do good work with the money he sends and probably would not be happy to know that some of his hard-earned money is being used to send newsletters to people you have not heard from in years.

Make this your general rule: to be considered active donors and stay on your mailing list, people must show their interest in a tangible way every twelve to sixteen months. They need to make a donation, indicate that they want to stay on the list even if they cannot donate, or volunteer. A quarterly renewal system for small donors will help you keep your mailing list clean and up to date and ensure that you are not spending money, paper, printing, and staff energy on people who are not going to respond.

In Chapter Ten I noted that a normal renewal rate is 66 percent—that is, 66 percent of people giving you a gift in one year can be expected to give you a gift the following year. The remaining 34 percent will not renew. No matter how often you appeal to people and how wonderful your organization is, many people will only give once and not again, or some will give two or three times and not again. Whether they renew probably has little to do with you and more to do with them changing jobs, marrying, divorcing, moving, getting sick, or changing their giving priorities because of one of these events. Therefore you must attract enough new donors every year to replace 34 percent of your donor base.

If your renewal rate is less than 66 percent, you are probably not doing enough to keep your donors. Examine your program to ensure that you are keeping up the following practices:

- Writing to donors more than once a year asking for money

- Thanking donors promptly with a personal note

- Sending at least three renewal notices

- Keeping records that are accurate and up to date

If your renewal rate is more than 66 percent, your organization does not have enough donors. Any organization can have an 80 percent to 90 percent renewal rate if they are only working with a handful of donors. A 66 percent renewal rate is a sign of health. It means you are bringing enough people into your system to ensure that you will have a decent number of major donors if you work with the other strategies in this book. The donor pyramid gets smaller as your donors move up from first time to habitual to major donors. There are fewer and fewer at each stage. To have an adequate number at the top, there must be an adequate number at the bottom.

APPEALING TO CURRENT DONORS

Once your organization has acquired donors, it should appeal to them several times a year. Too often, appeals to current donors are overlooked. Years of testing have proven that some donors will respond every time they are asked and others will give less automatically but more than once a year, and that donor renewal rates are higher for all donors (even those who do not respond to extra appeals) when they receive several appeals a year.

Many organizations have discovered that they can raise enough money from their current donors with repeated appeals to enable them to scale down their recruitment of new donors. Many large organizations appeal to their donors eight to twelve times a year, which tends to have a saturating, and in the case of many donors, alienating effect. Experience with hundreds of grassroots social change organizations shows that two to four appeals a year will raise significantly more money and increase renewal rates without irritating your donors. Since most people who give or buy by mail may get as many as twelve hundred pieces of bulk mail a year, two to four appeals a year from your nonprofit will barely make a ripple in the volume of mail most of your donors are receiving.

Repeated appeals are successful for a number of reasons. First, a person's cash flow can vary greatly from month to month. A person receiving an appeal from a group he or she supports may have just paid car insurance, so the appeal gets thrown away. If the organization were to ask again after two more months, the person might have more money available and make a donation.

Second, different people respond to different types of appeals. Sending only one or two appeals a year does not allow for the variety of choices donors want.

Organizations often discover that donors who regularly give $25 a year will give $50, $100, or more when appealed to for a special project. People who respond to specific project appeals are often called brick-and-mortar people. They "buy" things for an organization: media spots, food for someone for a week, a job training program, a new building.

We rarely know why people don't respond to appeals. Despite this lack of knowledge many people are willing to make the assumption that the donor doesn't want to give, when any of the following circumstances might be true:

- The donor has been on vacation and mail has piled up, so anything that is not a bill or a personal letter, including your appeal, gets tossed.

- The donor is having personal problems and cannot think of anything else right now, even though he or she might be quite committed to your group.

- The appeal is lost in the mail.

- The donor meant to give, but the appeal got lost or accidentally thrown away before it could be acted on.

Donors do not feel "dunned to death" by two to four appeals a year. On the contrary, they get a sense that a lot is happening in the organization. Their loyalty is developed when they know that their continuing donations are needed. Most important, they have an opportunity to express their own interests when a particular appeal matches their concerns.

WHAT TO APPEAL FOR

Once an organization has accepted the idea of sending appeals throughout the year, they often wonder what they are going to say in each one. Here are twelve ideas to help you choose some approaches. Some of these appeals are taken from or modeled on specific letters I know have worked well. Some will suit one organization better than another, but almost any organization should be able to find one or two ideas that they could modify and use for their group.

Seasonal Appeals

End of Year.   "As you close your books for this year, please remember (*organization*). We have many more clients this time of year, and your additional support can ensure uninterrupted service."

Beginning of Year. "One of my New Year's resolutions was to give more money this year to (*organization*). I realized that, like many of my resolutions, this one could fade if I didn't act now. So I sent an extra $35 on January 5. I imagine that many of our members made a similar resolution. Perhaps you did. If you are like me, time may pass without action. So join me, and send that extra donation now."

Holiday Appeals. *Lincoln's Birthday.* "President Lincoln was only one of the more famous people to be killed with a handgun. I know you want to end this senseless violence. An extra donation from you, sent today, will give us the extra funds we need to work on (*special program*) against handguns (*or* crime in the streets *or* to strengthen our community organization activities *or* to escort people who are alone across campus)."

Valentine's Day. "Do you often think of important people on Valentine's Day? Do you remember them with flowers, candy, or cards? I know I do. This year, I thought of other important people in my life—the people at (*organization*). They really depend on us, their members, for the financial support they need. Will you join me in sending an extra donation? You can send flowers or candy as well. Simply use the enclosed card."

Labor Day. "A time to take the day off. But what about all the people who want to work—people who are unemployed? For them Labor Day is another reminder of their joblessness. Our organization is providing training to thousands of people so that they can get good jobs in areas needing workers. Remember the unemployed this Labor Day with a gift to (*name of organization*)."

Columbus Day. "Columbus discovered America. This is one part of American history almost everyone knows. The problem is that this is only a half-truth: Columbus discovered America for white people. There were already people here—our people. We are Americans. Yet our history since Columbus has been one of genocide, displacements, and oppression. At the Indigenous People's Organizing Project, we are determined to reclaim Columbus Day. You have helped us in the past. Will you help us, on this holiday, to continue our vital work?"

Thanksgiving Day. "We would like to make Thanksgiving Day a little brighter for hundreds of people in our city who cannot afford to buy food. With your donation of $14.50, we will provide a family with a turkey and all the trimmings. Please give whatever you can."

Winter Holiday (Christmas, Hanukkah, Winter Solstice). "We are just $2,000 short of our goal to buy a new furnace for our runaway house (*or* send our staff person to the state capital to press for the bill we have been working so hard on *or* distribute thousands of leaflets telling seniors how to get their homes insulated for free). Can you help us meet our goal with a special end-of-year donation?"

Old Standbys

Anniversary. "Our organization is now entering its third (fifth, fiftieth) anniversary of service to the community. Celebrate with us by sending $1 (*or* $10 *or* $100) for each year of the important work we have done. For your gift, we will be pleased to send you a special anniversary parchment, suitable for framing. In addition, if you donate $1,000 or more, you will be invited to a special reception honoring Famous Person, who has been so helpful to our cause."

Famous Person. "I'm Handsome Famous Star. You may have seen me on television. In my personal life, I am very concerned about birth control (*or* tenants' rights *or* public education). I believe that Good Organization defends our rights in this area. Please join me in supporting them." (Famous person can be truly famous, such as a movie star, or someone well known only in your community and widely respected there.)

Another Member. "My name is _____ . I have been a member of Good Organization for five years. In that time, I have witnessed the continuing erosion of our rights and the seemingly malicious efforts of our leaders to take what little we have left. All that stands between them and us is Good Organization. In the past five years, our organization has succeeded in (*name program successes*). That's why I am giving a little extra this year. Thirty dollars is not a lot, but it really helps, and if everyone gave just $30, $50, or even $100, it would really add up. Will you join me?"

Urgent Need. "We have an urgent need to raise $5,000 to alert the public to the hazards of chemical dumping being proposed for the east side of town. This little-known bill, which has the support of our supervisors, will bring unwarranted health hazards to more than one thousand people. The town council is trying to slide this bill through without our knowledge. We must protest. Help us stop this outrage now with an extra donation of $25, $50, or whatever you can send."

HANDLING RESPONSES TO YOUR DIRECT MAIL APPEALS

There are few things as thrilling as receiving gifts from a successful mail appeal. When you go to your mailbox and pull out all the return envelopes that you know have gifts made by check or credit card, or when you get a report from your online provider with a list of donations, it is tempting to just deposit the money and go home early. But receiving the gifts brings on a whole new set of tasks.

All donors must be thanked, preferably within seventy-two hours of their gift arriving and certainly within seven days. Sometimes you will not be able to meet this time frame, so remember that a late thank you is always better than no thank you. (See also Chapter Eighteen, "The Thank You Note.")

The gift must also be recorded (for additional detail, see Chapter Thirty-One, "Managing Donor Data"). Use the following steps:

- Photocopy checks before cashing them. This step is a bookkeeping basic, but it also helps with fundraising, as a lot of information is on a check.

- Enter the gift in the database, noting what appeal it was responding to, and when the thank you note was sent out. Also enter new information such as a change of address.

- Cash the check or run the credit card as soon as possible. People wonder if an organization really needs money when their check is not deposited quickly or if their gift does not show up on their next credit card statement.

EVALUATING YOUR APPEAL

To know if your appeal has been effective and which of your appeals are the most effective and why, you must track and evaluate them. Without evaluation, all fundraising is simply shooting in the dark. To get maximum benefit from a mail appeal program, evaluation is essential. The process of tracking is simple: you want to note how many people responded to a particular appeal and how much money each appeal brought in.

Tally the responses as they come in from each appeal, using your database program or a spreadsheet. The heaviest response will come during the first four weeks after you could reasonably expect most people to have received the mailing (always send one to your organization in order to get a sense of how long it takes to arrive). Ninety-five percent of the responses will be in by the end of two months. Your tally might look like this:

Mail Appeal #1 Response		
Week	Number of Responses	Total Received That Week
1	42	$1,680
2	85	$4,675
3	122	$5,002
4	67	$2,345
5	40	$1,600
6	25	$1,000
7	18	$630
8	7	$280

After two months, add up the responses and the money earned and evaluate the appeal in these categories:

- Total number of gifts received and amount given
- Number of donors by category (less than $25, $25–$49, $50–$99, and so on)
- Percentage of response (divide the number of responses by the number of pieces mailed)
- The gift received most often (the mode gift, as described in Chapter Eleven, not the average gift)
- Cost of mailing
- Ratio of income to expense (divide the amount of money you received by the amount you spent)

- Any narrative comments, such as "Send earlier next time," or "Joe's Printing said he would do free printing next time."

The percentage of response and the mode gift are the most important aspects of the evaluation. The percentage of response tells you much more important information than the amount you earned from the mailing. For example, one organization's appeal to one thousand names generated only two responses (0.002 percent); one response was for $10 but the other was for $1,500! The board was told that the mail appeal had generated $1,510 but not the percentage of response, so they decided to do more mailings to similar lists. They quickly spent all their profit because the lists were virtually worthless and their original response (which was extremely poor) only appeared successful because of the chance response of one major gift.

After you finish your evaluation, place the mail appeal with all of its components and the evaluation in a file folder. If you decide to repeat the mailing, you will have all the information you need in one place.

After several mailings, pull out all the evaluation forms and see what they have in common. Do some types of lists seem to respond better than others? Did the mailing offering a special benefit do better than the one without? Does one set of facts or one particular story seem to stir more people to give?

Remember to test only one variable at a time. You cannot find out if more people respond to one benefit or another in a mailing that is also testing a lift-out note with a letter against a letter alone. Also, you must use portions of the same list to test responses to different variables. You cannot test one variable on a list to a service club and another on a list to a group of health activists.

If you have mailed fewer than two thousand pieces, the results of your evaluation will not be statistically significant. However, using your instinct and what information you are able to garner, you should be able to make some educated guesses about what is working well with your direct mail program and why.

Fundraising by Telephone

With the predictability of gravity, I always know that when I get to the part of a training or consultation where I recommend using the phone, I am going to get more pushback than with almost any other strategy. People invariably say, "I hate being phoned," "I always hang up right away," "I would never give to an organization that phoned me." But usually after four or five expostulations on the evils of phoning, someone will say, "I gave over the phone just the other night when the library called." "So did I," says someone else. At that point usually one of the people who "never gives by phone" says, "Well, that's different—that's the library. I gave to them also." We laugh and move on to explore the possibilities the telephone provides.

From about 1985 to 2003, telemarketing grew and grew, and although it was very unpopular, it did work with a large cross-section of the population. In the early part of this century, it was not unusual to get two or three calls in an evening, with paid callers selling anything from credit cards to rain gutters. In 2003, Congress passed one of the most popular pieces of legislation ever, the Do Not Call Register Act. You can now opt out of receiving telemarketing calls just by registering your phone number with a master Do Not Call list. Nonprofits are exempt from the Do Not Call list. Do Not Call has decreased the volume of calls so much that the environment is much more friendly to callers from nonprofits.

Phoning works. Telephone fundraising continues to result in a greater percentage of response than direct mail or online appeals, and it is an excellent way of reaching a large number of people with a (somewhat) personal message. With the advent of giving by text message, many organizations are exploring ways to use mobile technology for fundraising. In early January 2010, the Red Cross raised $22 million in five days for earthquake relief for Haiti, which led to a spate of calls into my office from tiny organizations thinking that at last they had found the magic fundraising wand. (Of interest, although giving by text is relatively new in the United States and Canada, it has been in wide use in Korea for some time.) However, successful fundraising by text relies on a visible event, high name recognition of the organization, and an infrastructure to handle the volume—all of which most nonprofits lack.

In this chapter I focus on the more traditional meaning of "dialing for dollars," which is available to any organization with any kind of telephone service or apparatus, and which does not require a natural disaster in order to be successful. As with direct mail, I will show you how a phone-a-thon can be modified for small organizations so you can raise money without offending donors and without much money in front costs. The two modifications small organizations make are to use very warm lists (such as lapsed and current donors; friends of board members, staff, and current donors; or lists of donors to similar organizations) and to use volunteers to do the calling. Even if a person is annoyed to be phoned during dinner, they will be less annoyed by a volunteer who is giving their time and doesn't sound as smooth as a professional telemarketer.

A basic fundraising axiom is that the closer you can get to the prospect, the more likely you are to get the gift. Phoning, as a telephone company ad used to say, is "The next best thing to being there."

BASIC TECHNIQUE OF THE PHONE-A-THON

In its simplest terms, a phone-a-thon involves a group of volunteers calling people to ask them to support your organization with a donation. A phone-a-thon is an excellent way to involve volunteers in fundraising because it teaches them how to ask for money in a way that they may find less intimidating than soliciting donations in face-to-face situations.

Phone-a-thons can be good moneymakers. They are usually inexpensive to produce and have a high rate of return. Between 5 and 10 percent of the people reached will contribute, possibly more when they are lapsed donors being called to renew their gifts and definitely more when they are current donors being called about a specific campaign. The costs involved include some long-distance charges; food and drinks for volunteers doing the calling; and some printing and postage to send more information to those people who request it, to send a reply envelope for people preferring to give by check, and, if you want, to send a letter to people who did not answer when you called. (The latter is more of a mail appeal but is a good way to follow up from a phone-a-thon.) For a phone-a-thon to be truly successful, you need to be able to accept donations by credit card on the phone, in addition to encouraging people to make gifts on your Web site.

A phone-a-thon can be organized by one or two people. It takes several hours of preparation followed by a five-hour block of time for the event. Several people are needed to make all the calls (for how to determine how many people, see the formula further on).

PREPARATION

To prepare for a phone-a-thon, the organizers take the following eight steps.

Step 1. Prepare the List.　Make a list of people who will be called. These potential donors are people who have either expressed an interest in your organization, benefited by something you have done for them, or are past or current supporters of your organization. The main criterion is that they would probably recognize the name of your organization and have positive feelings about your work. People attending community meetings you have organized, alumnae, and members of and donors to similar organizations are all prospects. A volunteer can create a master list of names and phone numbers. (If you can't find someone's phone number on the Internet, chances are this person does not want to be phoned. Do not spend a lot of time tracking down phone numbers. Just phone the people whose numbers are easy to find.) The list of prospects includes the names, phone numbers, codes indicating the person's relationship to the organization (L = lapsed donor, FB = former board member, E = attended an event), and any information it would be helpful for the telephone volunteer to have, as in the following illustration. The list will also have a column for recording whether the prospect made a donation and of what amount, which will be filled in after the calling is completed.

January Phone-a-Thon: People to Be Called					
Name	Phone	Code	Notes	Donation?	Amount

When you have a choice of calling a home or cell phone, use the home phone. Increasingly, however, people don't have land lines, which means you could reach them anywhere, and which makes it imperative to ask whether this is a good time to talk and, if not, be willing to call back or be called back.

Step 2. Create a Way to Record Results of Calls. Volunteers should have a printout of their prospect names, with columns to record the result of the call. After the calls have been made, you can use these printouts to check off the names and results on the master list and then enter into the database the names of people who made gifts or pledges.

The columns the phoners will fill in include

Donation made

Credit card information (train your volunteers to collect the data you need for the system you are using. Process these gifts within twenty-four hours, and preferably during or after the phone-a-thon.)

Address verified

E-mail

Thank you sent

Want more info (note whether sent)

Not home. Message left   ___Yes   ___No

Other data: (for example, "Lives in Florida all winter: use that address from Nov.-April," or "Wants to help with gala again: please call."

Step 3. Set a Date for the Phone-a-Thon. When looking for a date, pay attention to other events in your community. Don't call, for example, on an evening when everyone will be at a gala anniversary party or benefit auction for another organization similar to yours. Most people find that calling on a Tuesday, Wednesday, or Thursday night between 6 P.M. and 9 P.M. at the beginning of the month (near payday) works best.

Some organizations call on weekends with success, but calling on a sunny weekend afternoon may bring people racing in from their yard or interrupt them while entertaining and may irritate more people than necessary. No one is sitting in the sun on a Wednesday evening at 8:00 P.M.. Pay attention as well to what's on television: don't call during the Super Bowl, or the World Cup Finals, or on an election night, or during the Academy Awards.

Step 4. Write a Script. Generally, volunteers can ad lib after the second or third call, but initially a script of what to say gives them a feeling of security. The script should be brief and to the point, as in the following sample.

Sample Phone-a-Thon Script

Start the call with the point of reference you have for this person: why you think he or she will be interested in your organization. Speak slowly and pause for answer. "Hello, my name is Jill Activist, and I am a volunteer with Good Organization. May I speak with you for a minute?"

"Thank you. I am calling tonight as a part of a phone-a-thon. You came to our town hall meeting recently" or "You are a long-time member, and I want to thank you for your support, and also tell you about an exciting opportunity we have" or "Did you receive our recent appeal?" *(Pause for answer.)*

If the response indicates little familiarity with the organization's work, say: "We are a group of concerned people working on . . ." *and give a two-sentence or fifteen-second summary of your work. (Pause.)*

If calling a current donor, then remind the person of your work: "As you know, we are engaged in . . ."

If there is no reaction or a positive reaction from the person being called, continue: "We want to continue our important work on . . . and we need to raise $____ to do that. Our goal tonight is to raise $_____ . We are asking people to help us with a gift of $35 or more. So far, ___ *(number of)* people have pledged and we have $____ toward our goal. Can you help us with a donation?" *(Pause for answer.)*

If the answer is positive, continue: "Would you like to put that on a credit card? That way we can put the money right to work."

If the answer is yes, take that information and thank the person.

If the answer is "I don't give out my credit card on the phone" *or* "I don't have a credit card with me," *say,* "That's fine. How about if I send you an envelope and you can send a check?"

If yes, verify the person's address and say: "We are keeping track of how much we have in pledges tonight. Could you tell me how much you will be giving so I can add it in the total?" *(Pause for answer.)* "Thank you so much."

If the person says, "Can I just give online later?" *give him or her your Web address and again ask if they have an amount in mind. Asking this may seem awkward, but it tells prospects you are taking their commitment seriously, which makes it more likely they will follow through.*

Finally, ask if she or he uses e-mail and would like to hear from you by e-mail from time to time. Don't assume that someone has e-mail, even though most people do. Some of your best donors will not or will not want to use it in this way.

"Thank you again. Good night."

In addition to the script, write up a list of questions that volunteers may be asked, with suggested answers. Include questions and statements such as, "Why haven't I heard of you before?" or "I sent you guys money and never got anything" or "There are so many nonprofits in this town—do you work with any of them?"

Step 5. Prepare Three Letters and Appropriate Enclosures. Here are samples of each letter to be prepared.

A. *Letter for People Who Say Yes and Will Be Sending a Check.*

Dear _____,

Thank you so much for joining Good Organization with your gift of $____ this evening.

As you probably know, Good Organization primarily is supported by donations from people like you. Your gift will help us continue our work of _____ . *(Describe in two or three sentences.)* You will be pleased to know that, thanks to generous people like yourself, we made our goal tonight!

Please fill out and return the enclosed card in the envelope provided. You will begin receiving our newsletter in two weeks.

Sincerely,
Name of volunteer

Return Card Format

Name:_____

Address:_____

Enclosed is my pledge of $_____. Please charge my VISA/MC $___

Card #_____.

Expiration date:_____

Name as it appears on card:_____

Signature:_____

Sign me up for the e-newsletter. E-mail address: _____

Make checks payable to: Good Organization.

Mail to: Our address.

Web site: www.goodorganization.org

(Include a return envelope with a first-class stamp affixed.)

B. *"Sorry We Missed You" Letter to People Who Weren't Home.*

This is an optional step, but will bring in a few more donations and gives you some assurance that you have reached all the people on your list, either by phone or mail.

Dear _____,

Sorry we missed you this evening. We tried to call you because we wanted to ask you to join (or renew or tell you more about) Good Organization.

Good Organization is _____. *(Give a brief summary of not more than three to five short sentences.)* Our main program goal for this year is _____. *(The exact language of this paragraph will depend on whether you are asking for a renewal or a new gift.)*

I hope you will want to join us in our important work. For a gift of $_____, we will be pleased to send you our quarterly magazine, *The Right-On Times.* For a gift of $100 or more, made by the end of _____ (a month from the date the letter is sent), we will include a beautiful *(or important)* book *(or calendar or picture).*

Please take a moment to read the enclosed fact sheet, then fill out the membership form and send it with your donation or give online at www.goodgroup.org.

Sincerely,
Name of volunteer

C. *Letter to People with Questions About the Organization.*

Dear _____,

Thanks for talking with me this evening.

I am enclosing the information we discussed, which I hope will answer your questions. Please feel free to contact our office to discuss our organization further if you wish, and check out our Web site at www.goodgroup.org.

I hope that after reading this information you will decide to make a donation. I am sure that once you read about us you will agree that our work is very important. Please support us in whatever way you can.

An envelope and membership form are enclosed for your convenience, or you can give online at www.goodgroup.com. I look forward to hearing from you.

Sincerely,
Name of volunteer

Enclose with both the second and third types of letter a reply card or form that the donor will fill out (as discussed in Chapter Twelve, "The Logistics of Direct Mail"), a fact sheet or brochure about your organization, and a return envelope. It is not necessary to put a postage stamp on any of these envelopes.

To decide the quantity of each letter, count the number of people you will be calling and assume that you will reach one-third of them on the night of the phone-a-thon. Of this number, depending on how hot your list is, up to one-third of those people will say yes and need Letter A; another one-third of those reached will say, "Send me more information," and need Letter C; the rest will say no. The other two-thirds or more of people phoned—those not reached—will be sent Letter B. Much depends on how good your list is, but this formula should give you enough letters without having lots of them left over. With a small list and a fast printer, you could personalize each letter, or with a high-quality copier you could copy just the number you need.

If you are working with large lists and might have two hundred or more people who will receive either Letter B or Letter C, you can send those by bulk mail if each one is exactly the same. In that case, use the salutation "Dear Friend."

Step 6. Determine the Number of Phones and Volunteers You Will Need. To figure out the number of phones you will need, estimate that one person can make about forty phone calls in an hour (although she will talk to no more than fifteen people), and that people will call for no more than three hours. Therefore, one person can make about 120 calls in an evening (including calls to people who aren't home) and fill out the appropriate follow-up letters and mailing envelopes.

Since most people will not call for three hours straight, you will need one or two extra volunteers to make maximum use of the phones available.

Suppose you have six hundred names to call. If one person made all the calls it would take fifteen hours plus breaks (six hundred calls at forty calls per hour).

If each person has his or her own phone, five volunteers using four or five phones, along with one or two extra volunteers to spell people, will be able to get through the calls in one evening. In addition to the calling, allow two to three hours (or one or two extra volunteers) for getting everything ready that goes in the mail, processing credit card donations, recording information, and cleaning up.

You may wish to conduct the phone-a-thon over two nights. This has two advantages: you can call more people or use fewer volunteers, and you can call people on the second night who weren't home on the first night.

Step 7. Find a Place.   You will need one room or a suite of connected rooms with one or more telephones in each one. Depending on the number of telephones in your organization's office and the number of volunteers you have, you may have enough lines there. Real estate offices, travel agencies, law firms, large social service organizations, and the like are good candidates to let you borrow their telephones for the evening. You will be trusted not to disrupt or take anything, to clean up before you leave, and in most cases to pay for any long-distance calls. Some volunteers are willing to use their cell phones, but others will be reluctant to have their personal number show up on a stranger's phone, and some may not want to use their minutes that way.

Sometimes small organizations decide to conduct a phone-a-thon with volunteers working from their homes. Although there is nothing wrong with this method and just as many calls can be made, it is more fun and generates more momentum to have everyone in the same office. In addition, you will not be able to keep tabs on the volunteers and make sure that they are being assertive enough in their asking. In a group setting, successful calls or rude responses can elicit immediate praise or sympathy as appropriate. A group effort is also helpful in keeping track during the evening of how much is being pledged, and the people being called can hear a lot of action in the background, lending legitimacy and excitement to your effort. (If you have to use individual homes, have at least two people at each home.)

Step 8. Recruit Volunteers.   Use the phone-a-thon as an opportunity to bring in some new volunteers. People who have limited time or who cannot volunteer during the day can often be recruited to work one evening on a phone-a-thon. It is a straightforward commitment for a short time period and does not require preparation outside of a training session during the hour before phoning begins.

THE NIGHT OF THE PHONE-A-THON

The person or committee planning the phone-a-thon should arrive at the place where the phoning will take place thirty minutes before everyone else. Be sure that desktops or tabletops where volunteers are to sit are cleared off so that your papers do not get mixed up with the papers of the person who uses that desk during the day. On each desk, put a stack of the three different letters (if you are using all three letters and printing them ahead of time), their enclosures, the return envelopes, the mailing envelopes, and a couple of pens. Put a list of names to be called and a script by each phone.

Bring in juice, coffee, and snacks. Pizza, sandwiches, or other simple dinner food should be provided if volunteers are arriving at dinner time. The food should be kept in one part of the office, and volunteers should be discouraged from having food by their phones. Pay attention to details such as bringing in napkins, plates, and eating utensils. In a borrowed space take out your own trash. Do not serve alcohol.

After all volunteers have arrived, been introduced to each other, and had a chance to eat, go through the phoning process step by step. Review the script and make sure people understand and feel comfortable with it. Review difficult questions they might receive and simulate a few phone calls (one from each of the response categories: yes, maybe, no). Be sure people understand the different letters, know what to write on each, what enclosures go with them, and what information needs to be noted on the list of prospects.

Make people practice at least two times. Have them sit so they can't see each other (back-to-back works well) and go through the script, including ad libbing to questions their mock prospect asks. For a really good practice session, have people move to different rooms and call each other on their cell phones. This warming up is very important. It builds cohesion in the group and allows you, the coordinator, to make sure people are really going to ask. Take a few moments to get feedback on the exercise, which will probably have raised some additional questions beyond those you have already prepared people for.

You will need to decide whether volunteers are to leave a message on an answering machine or simply hang up. If you're going to send out a "Sorry we missed you" letter, you can instruct people to leave a brief message such as the following: "I wanted to talk with you about our work, but I'll send you some information instead. I hope you'll be able to help us." Be sure the message you leave is brief, since the only long messages people like to listen to are from new lovers or old friends.

After the orientation, each volunteer or phone team goes to a desk. The committee that has planned the phone-a-thon begins making calls immediately to set the tone and the pace. When a few people are on the phone, shy volunteers will feel better about beginning to call. Try to avoid a situation in which everyone in the room is listening to one person's phone call unless that person feels comfortable with that role.

A staff person or a phone-a-thon committee member acts as a "floater." He or she answers questions and fields difficult phone calls. The floater also continually tallies how much money has been pledged and records the changing total on a large board visible to the group. (If people are calling from different locations, updated information can be sent frequently by e-mail or instant message.) The volunteers then change their scripts to reflect new totals.

Each individual should be encouraged to take breaks as they need to, but the group as a whole does not take any breaks.

At 9:00 P.M. stop the phoning and begin wrapping up. The first steps in wrapping up are to finish addressing all envelopes or e-mailing donors who gave you their e-mail address and gather up the prospect lists, making sure all information has been recorded. Tally the final amount pledged and let the volunteers know how successful the evening has been. If the amount pledged is below your goal, explain that you set your goal too high. Do not let the volunteers leave feeling discouraged.

The callers should be able to leave by 9:30 P.M., leaving the planning committee to do any final cleanup.

AFTER THE PHONE-A-THON

Within two or three days, send all the volunteers a thank you note for their participation. If you borrowed a space to conduct the phone-a-thon, write the owner or manager a thank you note as well. Thank everyone for whatever they did to make the event a success.

If most people who donate give by credit card, you will have received most of your money right away. During the next two weeks you should collect about 90 percent of the pledges made. Obviously, everyone who gave should be thanked. Watch for an increase in online giving too—this may be related to the phone-a-thon. At the end of two weeks, go through your list and identify anyone who said they would give but has not yet sent in their money. Send them a gentle reminder, like the one shown here, accompanied by a return envelope and a reply form. Most organizations do not find it worth the time and cost to remind people of their pledge more than once. As I note elsewhere, the way some people say no is to say yes and then not pay.

Reminder Letter

Dear _____,

This is just a note to remind you of your pledge to Good Organization made on the night of _____. In case you misplaced our letter and return envelope we enclose another. Thanks again for your pledge of $ _____.

Sincerely,
Name of volunteer

Generally, about 7 percent of people who pledge do not send money. If you have a higher loss than 7 percent, it may be that your volunteers noted someone as yes who only said she would think about it. Make sure volunteers understand how important it is to be accurate and that they need to hear what the prospect said, which may be different from what the caller wants to hear.

Tally up the final amounts received and write an evaluation of the event. The evaluation should note how many people were called, how many people gave and how they gave, what percentage of pledges were received, how many volunteers participated, where the phone-a-thon was held, and who arranged for the space (if donated). Include copies of all the letters and return forms used. File all this away so that the next time you do a phone-a-thon you won't have to start from scratch.

GETTING PUBLICITY FOR YOUR PHONE-A-THON

A phone-a-thon may be a good time to generate some publicity for your group. Publicity can make the community more aware of your organization's work and can alert listeners or readers to the fact that many of them will be receiving phone calls from your organization on a specific day or evening. The organization's address, phone number, and Web site address can be included in all publicity so that people can make their donation ahead of the phone-a-thon and avoid being called.

Unless you are on very good terms with press people the phone-a-thon alone will not be a newsworthy event. It would be best, therefore, to use the occasion of the phone-a-thon to emphasize a new program, tell a human interest story, or have some other newsworthy reason to get press attention in which you mention the phone-a-thon.

All of your publicity should emphasize the need for community support. Stress that your organization relies on the community for the bulk of its support—or wants to rely on the community if you don't now. Talk about what a gift of $35, $50, or $100 will do for your programs so that people have a sense that a small gift can make a difference.

Use a Public Figure

One way groups have interested the press is by having one or two famous people participating in their phone-a-thon. "Famous people" include not only national celebrities but also people well known only in your community, such as the mayor, city council members, a well-respected community activist, the president of the community college, or a major corporate executive. The novelty that someone famous would help your organization lends credibility to your work. Also, almost everyone is flattered to be called by someone famous. If you decide to ask public figures to participate, be sure that they are well liked by your constituency.

Public figures can simply come for the first half-hour of your phone-a-thon and make a few calls without making an enormous time commitment to the event. It is an easy way for both you and them to gain goodwill while they show their support of nonprofit organizations and of the work of your organization in particular.

OTHER USES OF THE PHONE-A-THON

There are three more common uses of the phone-a-thon technique: using the phone only to get prospects, following a mail appeal with a phone-a-thon, and using a phone-a-thon to renew lapsed donors.

Phoning for Prospects

This takeoff on a sales technique means phoning a large number of people, giving basic information about your organization, and asking if the person would like to know more. If the person says yes, he or she turns into a prospect. There is no attempt to solicit a gift at the time of the phone call. The purpose of the call is to create a hot list for later fundraising appeals.

During the telephone conversation the caller determines the degree of interest by asking the prospect some open-ended questions about what he knows of the organization and whether he supports its work. When interest is present, the prospect will be sent more information about the organization and a list of ways that he can help, including giving money. Some organizations use this opportunity to seek new volunteers, get support for or against a piece of legislation, or ask for items that the program needs (for example, a shelter might ask for food or clothing). You can use these kinds of calls to get either an e-mail or snail mail address.

This strategy does not raise money per se. Instead it acquires donors. The costs of phoning and of any mail and follow-up may well be only slightly less than the total amount received as gifts. Nevertheless, the organization now has a group of new donors, many of whom will renew the following year and may give in response to appeals during the current year.

This strategy is best for new organizations that do not have an established constituency or for nonprofits that have little name recognition even if they have existed for some time. It also works well for political organizations seeking to familiarize people with their candidate or their election issue.

The script and the training of volunteers for calling are different for this method than with an ordinary phone-a-thon. The purpose of the call is only to determine interest and to get permission to send more information. Therefore, the script would be something like the example shown here.

Script to Determine Interest

"Hello, I am Jane Smith, a volunteer with the Guns to Butter Project. I would like to talk to you for a minute, and I will not be asking you for money. Is this a good time?" *(Pause.)* "Thank you. I'll be brief. Have you heard of our program?" *(Pause.)*

If the answer is "No" or "I don't know very much," continue: "Guns to Butter is an economic conversion program that believes that our community does not need a weapons manufacturer in order to have a healthy economy and lots of jobs. We are responsible for converting the shelling range east of town into a community agriculture project, which now provides nutritious vegetables and eggs to all the schools on that side of town.

"Have you seen anything about this project?" *(Pause)*

"What do you think about the idea of economic conversion?" *(Pause) If the response is positive, continue. More likely the person may say, "I don't know that much about it" and sometimes they may say, "I don't agree with you at all." For the latter, politely say, "I appreciate your honesty and thanks so much for your time." For the middle group, explain more about what you mean, including a little about your own story, as illustrated here. For someone who clearly agrees with you, move to the end of the call where you will ask for their address.*

"I had never even heard the phrase *economic conversion* until a few years ago. But what it means to me is that we can produce things people need, like food, instead of weapons, and still employ people. We want to convert the missile factory next, which is a huge effort.

"Let me just tell you the first two steps in that . . ." *(Talk for at most fifteen more seconds.)*

For all positive responses, end with: "I'm glad you feel that way. We rely on members of the community to get the word out about what we are doing, and I wonder if I could get an e-mail or street address and send you more information about what we are doing, including ways you can help."

If the answer is yes, then verify the name and address, thank the person for his or her time, and say good night.

Training volunteers for this type of phone work is more detailed than for a straight fundraising phone-a-thon, although some volunteers like doing this type of call better because it doesn't involve asking for money. Volunteers must be able to listen, deal with difficult questions, and know when to give up. Each call will take longer than calls in a fundraising phone-a-thon. Callers must be clear that they are calling only to determine interest, not to convert people.

Callers should practice handling difficult questions and responding to them in some depth, and they should familiarize themselves with many facts about the organization and the issues.

No list is needed for this phone-a-thon. You can call a random sample of any list of people to determine their interest. You can also use this strategy to determine the interest of people who give to an organization doing work in an entirely different arena from yours, but where there could be a connection. For example, an AIDS-related service organization traded its list for a list of donors from several arts organizations and called them to determine their interest in the service organization. Because the arts community has been hard hit by the AIDS epidemic, there was a high level of interest and the arts group gained many new donors.

You may want to consider using professional telemarketers for this type of phoning. Although you will pay them, they are used to dealing with objections and can be counted on not to take people's comments personally. There are many reputable telemarketing firms, some of which specialize in phoning for nonprofits. Your organization may be too small for them to consider taking you on as a client, but they may have freelance people you could hire. You may also want to consider asking someone from such a firm to provide the training to your volunteers.

Phoning After a Mail Appeal

This method is quite straightforward. A mail appeal is sent to a list of prospects. After two weeks, all the prospects who have not sent money are called. The purpose of this method is to increase the return from the mail appeal.

The script is the only part that is slightly different from a regular fundraising phone-a-thon, in that a sentence is added such as, "I am Terry Baca from the Greenbelt Project. We recently sent you a letter about our work. Did you have a chance to read it?" Depending on the answer, the rest of the script is the same as that described in the first section of this chapter. If the person has read the letter and seems in favor of your goals, skip right to the question, "Will you be able to help us with a gift of $____ ?"

You will not indicate in the original letter that the prospects will be called. You want as many people as possible to send in their gift without being called. Some organizations have successfully tried a variation on this method by telling prospects in a letter that they will be called unless the organization hears from them by a certain date prior to the phone-a-thon.

Phoning for Renewals

As discussed earlier, in average organizations about one-third of all members do not renew their donations from one year to the next. As a result, organizations spend most of their renewal budget trying to woo these recalcitrant members back into the fold. Usually, an organization will send the member two or three renewal letters one month apart, each notice firmer or more pleading than the one before.

The phone-a-thon can be used in place of either the second or third renewal notice. In addition to saving the cost of printing and postage, it provides a way to have much more personal contact with donors than is generally possible. Over time you will notice a cross-section of your donors who respond more to being phoned than to mail. For those people, you may not send any renewal letter, but instead call them each year. (See also Chapter Nineteen, "Segmenting Donors").

Many organizations have renewal phone-a-thons twice a year. They find that although the response to a second or third renewal letter is 2 to 5 percent and sometimes less, the response to phoning is often at 10 percent and can be as high as 20 percent. These organizations are cutting their member losses by 5 percent or more. This guarantees that the organization will have at least a 66 percent renewal rate, and it may be able to add another 5 percent onto that.

A renewal phone-a-thon is almost exactly like a regular fundraising phone-a-thon. First, identify from your mailing list all the people who have not donated in the last fourteen to sixteen months, not including those who have had less than a month to renew. (Unless your organization is in a terrible financial bind and you really need the money, a person will feel harassed if you call too soon after your first renewal notice is sent.)

Next, prepare the letters to thank people for renewing and to contact people who weren't home when you called, as discussed in the first section of this chapter. Both of these letters are brief. The point is to remind the member of his or her commitment to give; there is no need to convince the person of the worthiness of your organization. Each letter is accompanied by a return envelope and a return form (pledge card).

When volunteers call the lapsed donors, they will generally hear the following reasons for not renewing: out of work, forgot about it, thought she or he had renewed, didn't receive the renewal letter, or was just about to renew and is glad you called.

It is important to believe whatever the donor might say. A person who claims to have renewed although you have no record of receiving her renewal could be asked to produce a canceled check, but it is easier and more productive simply to take her word for it and reinstate her on the mailing list. Follow the adage, "The customer is always right."

When someone says that he no longer agrees with the course you are taking or that he has a disagreement about a particular issue, ask him to explain. It may shed light on how the public perceives something you have done or you may be able to clear up a misunderstanding.

At the end of the phone-a-thon, make sure you have carefully sorted all the names into those who have renewed, those who requested to be taken off the mailing list, and those who were not home. Deal with complaints that same evening with a letter such as the one shown here.

> Dear Mr. Upset,
>
> We are sorry you have not received your newsletter for the past two years. At your request, here are all the back copies you have missed. We will enter your name on our mailing list for the next year as a complimentary member. Your past support means a lot to us, and again, we apologize.

As you can see, grassroots organizations can take advantage of fundraising by telephone. In addition to raising money, finding prospects, increasing renewal rates, and allowing an organization to have more personal contact with its donors, fundraising by telephone has an added advantage of teaching volunteers how to ask for money. The skills volunteers learn through phone-a-thons can then be put to use in major donor campaigns.

Creating an Online Fundraising Program

Some of the most exciting new strategies in the fundraising playbook are those using Internet technology. Fundraising magazines, blogs, and newsletters detail amazing stories of organizations posting something on YouTube and raising thousands of dollars, or having an e-appeal go viral and bring in hundreds of donations. The ubiquity of handheld devices such as Blackberries, iPhones, and other Smartphones means that information about your organization can be viewed at any time and from anywhere. People whom your organization would never reach using other strategies can comment on your work, forward your URL, and donate online 24/7. Organizations that read these great fundraising stories rush to be on Facebook, "tweet" on Twitter, and blog and change their Web site as often as possible with as many bells and whistles as they can download quickly. Many wind up being very disappointed and as quickly as they rushed to use online tools, they abandon them.

What small organizations have to be clear about is that online fundraising is a set of strategies that work very well for some causes and less well for others, but that, as with any strategy, this is not the pot of gold at the end of the rainbow. That said, many small organizations are using online strategies to produce a reliable source of a few thousand dollars every year, with almost guaranteed growth if the organization continues to pay attention to its current online donors and to recruiting new ones.

Online fundraising must be part of any organization's plan, but it should not be the whole plan. Like all fundraising strategies, online strategies do not work instantly—it takes time to build an e-list, to drive traffic to a Web site, and to create an audience for a blog.

Online strategies are excellent for recruiting donors, but these donors have to be taken care of: thanked, sent more information, kept up to date, and so on. We need to take a page from direct mail fundraising, which was the online strategy of the 1980s and 1990s. Many organizations acquired thousands of donors using direct mail, but organizations that have continued to increase the income from their donor base, as well as continuing to acquire donors, were those that built relationships with their donors using more personalized mail, the phone, thank you notes, personal invitations, and personal solicitation. Strategies have to be integrated with each other and they need to complement each other. No strategy, even my personal favorite—face-to-face solicitation—should be seen as "the" strategy.

The advantages of online fundraising are many: first-time gifts given online tend to be higher than those given by mail or phone. You can build an e-list of thousands of people at a tiny fraction of the cost of keeping in touch with people by mail. You can take advantage of the fundraising opportunities presented by a current event within a day or two—unheard of with mail.

Many fundraising professionals think that within the next five years upward of 40 percent of all gifts of less than $1,000 will be made online.

Throughout this book, I have indicated the many ways that even a small organization must have an online presence. In this chapter, I look at some very specific uses of online technology that are available to small organizations. In doing so, I am going to take for granted the following:

- Your organization has a Web site, including its own domain name.
- You have high-speed or wireless Internet access.
- You use e-mail for a large percentage of your communications with colleagues, board members, and even your own staff.
- You are familiar with search engines, and you visit Web sites to get information, verify facts, and keep up to date on issues of concern to your organization. In other words, the Internet is part of your life, and you are as likely to look up a recipe or get directions by going online as by looking at a book or map.

For organizations working in very rural or very low-income communities, in which online access is either not available or not common among your constituents, use other strategies this book recommends until online strategies (particularly cell phone strategies) become more accessible to you.

THE AUDIENCE FOR ONLINE STRATEGIES

The biggest audience for online fundraising is among the Millennial Generation (born between 1977 and 1997). They are known as "technological natives": 90 percent of people under thirty use the Internet regularly compared to 71 percent of people over thirty. Millennials were surfing the Internet at the same time they were learning to ride a bike, and text messaging and social networking are integral aspects of their daily life. At almost 60 million here in the United States, there are almost as many Millennials as Baby Boomers (78 million). Insofar as you can generalize about an entire generation, Millennials are likely to vote and they are civically active. According to an article in *The American Freshman*, part of UCLA's Higher Education Research Institute, in 2005 an all-time high of 83 percent of first-year college students reported that they volunteered at least occasionally in their last year of high school and 71 percent reported volunteering weekly. This activism bodes well for them being donors, as almost all volunteers also give away money. Obviously, recruiting younger donors requires using "Web 2.0," a shorthand for online strategies that invite comments from users or even allow users to shape and define content: blogs, social networking sites, and wikis are some examples. Numerous Web sites, blogs, books, and consultants can be found on the Internet that give step-by-step directions and advice on how nonprofits can use social media to advance their goals. Many are designed for individuals who are completely new to the social media scene, while others share tips for more savvy users.

However, young people are not the only audience for online fundraising. If you work regularly with major donors and major donor prospects (who can be any age, but tend to be middle-aged and older), you will often hear them say, "I saw that on your Web site" or "I hadn't heard of your organization before so I went to your Web site." Many times in the past few years when I have called prospects to follow up on a letter or e-mail regarding an organization, they have said, "I am looking at the organization's Web site right now." Donors use the Web site to find names of board members, profiles of staff, and analysis of current events. If they like what they find there, they are likely to give. If they find outdated information, broken links, or incomplete information, they may infer that the organization is similarly poorly put together.

Finally, current donors of all ages and sizes of gifts will forward blog posts, note that your organization is their favorite on their social network profiles, and forward your e-appeals and activist alerts, if you have them. Senior citizens are the fastest-growing group of Internet users; as Baby Boomers become seniors, they may make up the biggest demographic using the Internet.

As you think about your online presence, keep in mind all the places that a donor might look for information about your organization or your cause and make sure you are present in any place they might go. Large institutions now have staff whose job it is to comment on, correct, or add to information about their organization anywhere it appears online, but few, if any, small organizations can keep up with all the possibilities the Internet offers. For fundraising, you will need to use those strategies that reach the most people with the message that your organization is raising money: your Web site and your e-mail.

WEB SITE

Imagine the amount of work you would do to get ready to have a hundred people visit your office for an Open House. You would clean and dust, hang up pictures, put away files, possibly buy some flowers or plants, and generally make your space one you could be proud of. You want the people coming to your Open House to think, "This organization looks like it gets a lot done and it welcomes visitors." Imagine the care you would spend on creating materials for twenty major donors interested in your work. You would have pictures, graphs, and fact sheets, and you would put them together in a logical order in a nice folder. Well, a Web site is all that kind of work and more. Potentially millions of people could visit your organization there, and you want as many of them as is humanly possible to easily find what they are looking for and to see an invitation to give as often as possible.

Don't try to save money by building a site cheaply or using someone to build the site who understands only the technology and not the marketing aspects. Hiring a Web designer is a good investment. What you pay for design can range enormously, but be prepared to spend at least $500 to get started and more as you add more pages and have more options. A really excellent Web presence and Web strategy can easily cost $5,000 even for a small organization, so this is a project you might want to approach your major donors to underwrite. Many sophisticated donors understand the need for a top-notch Web site and will help you with an extra gift. Dropping unprofitable fundraising strategies and freeing up the money to focus on your Web site is another way to pay for it. Many organizations have found the money for their site simply by eliminating people from their snail mail list who have never donated or haven't made a gift in several years. One organization with a mailing list of ten thousand and a donor base of two thousand dropped five thousand names from its list after figuring out that it was costing $2 per person per year to keep those nondonors on the list. The organization invested the $10,000 it saved into creating an entire online fundraising program with its Web site as the key element.

Of course, having a Web site is not like having a refrigerator or a painting, where the initial investment is almost all the money you are going to spend. A Web site is actually more like the laundry—the washer and dryer may be the big investment, but you have to do laundry quite frequently if you are going to have clean clothes. You catch up one week and are behind by the next. The site needs new content at least monthly, and it will need to be completely redesigned every few years. These are expenses you must plan for. Most small organizations find that having a talented freelance Webmaster is the best solution. Some organizations bring that person on staff to maintain the organization's Web presence as well as manage other communications and publications.

Your Web site must have a prominent "Donate Now" icon at least on the home page and preferably on every page. The "Donate Now" button should take users to a secure site where they can make a gift by credit card, or at least to a page that they download, fill out, and send in with a check. One way to be able to accept credit cards is through a service such as Network for Good or other so-called charity portals, which are nonprofits that exist to collect donations for other nonprofits and that can handle credit card donations and even pledges. Your bank may also be able to serve as a portal for accepting online donations. (There will be a charge for this service, and some services will also charge the donor a small fee.) If you anticipate a high enough volume or you sell products and services on your site as well as accept donations, you will want to explore having your own merchant system.

Your Web site's "look" must be the same as everything else you publish. A simple example, but surprisingly often not observed, is that the logo on your Web site should match the logo on your stationary and business cards. The content of your annual report should also appear on your site. And of course, you should collect names of visitors just as you would if people came to your office. Have an e-mail sign up that is easy to subscribe to—and easy to unsubscribe from.

The best way to learn about Web sites is to visit the sites of organizations with missions that are similar to yours, even if they are larger organizations than yours, and to visit the sites of organizations you know do well with online fundraising. Ask who designs their sites and contact those designers to see how much they would charge you. Many fine and talented online fundraising firms, which work with very large institutions, will work with much smaller organizations for little or nothing from time to time, as will online marketing firms. They enjoy the challenge of promoting an organization that is not well known, or perhaps your organization may better reflect their politics than the larger organizations that pay them better. You will never know until you ask.

Driving Traffic to Your Site

Part of the planning for your site is determining who would use it and how you are going to get these people to visit the site. This is called "driving traffic" to the site; it is the difference between a merely well-designed site and a successful one. There are literally billions of Web sites in the world, and some of the most interesting ones remain unknown and unvisited because no one thinks to look for them. Here are some simple and low-cost ways to drive traffic to your site.

Make sure your Web address is on everything you publish—your business cards, your e-mail signature, your letterhead, your newsletter (in several places, often as a footer on the bottom of each page)—and that it is part of your voice mail message and on any information you give out about your organization.

Register with all the key search engines: Yahoo, Google, and the like (find a list of current search engines at www.searchenginewatch.com). Further, ask your Webmaster to make sure that your "meta tag" and "title"—two items hidden at the top of the code for your site—have as many relevant words as possible so that search engines can index your site. Get help thinking through the two- or three-word description for your organization that will show up in a Web search that will encourage people to click your Web site. For example, if I type the three words related to your issue into Google or another search engine, your site should come up in the results, preferably in the top ten results. Ditto if I type in, for example, "Prison reform, Springfield, MO" and you are a prison reform organization serving southwest Missouri; your name should pop up right away. Make sure that any printed or online directories of nonprofits, service providers, chambers of commerce, and so on list your Web site along with your postal address.

Link to other organizations and make sure they link to you. Make a list of organizations you would see as allies or as offering complementary information to yours and make sure that people can go to their sites from yours and vice-versa. Every so often visit related sites and see what they say about you.

E-mail is one of the best ways to get people to visit your site. Gather as many e-mail addresses of donors as you can and send them an e-mail newsletter or e-mail alert monthly or quarterly. You can use this communication to announce new content on your site or to suggest action, with a hyperlink that brings them to the site for more details.

As with all fundraising strategies, never promise on the front end what you can't deliver on the back end. If you say your e-newsletter is quarterly, it has to come out quarterly and not twice a year! I have signed up for more than a dozen e-newsletters and never received any of them. On the other hand, I am on lists of e-newsletters that I never signed up for. It does not make sense to add someone to your list who hasn't asked to be on it, and it really doesn't make sense not to add people when they have used your Web site to sign up. Be sure that "fulfillment"—the cost in time and money to fulfill promises made—is built into all your planning.

E-MAIL

Building an e-list is critical to using e-mail for fundraising. Make sure you have sign-up sheets at any meeting or event your organization sponsors, and always include a line for e-mail address in any reply device or correspondence with donors and prospects. You can use your e-mail list in a number of ways, but most organizations will do well to use it in the following two ways.

To Send an E-Newsletter

An e-newsletter is not the same as your paper newsletter. It is much shorter, with lots of headlines and hyperlinks to the Web site for those wanting to read more. It can come out more often than a paper newsletter; most organizations find that a combination of a paper newsletter that arrives two or three times a year and a monthly e-newsletter works very well. The e-newsletter can also solicit advice or ask for comments, and thus invite more interaction from those reading it. Every e-newsletter should contain an invitation to give online.

E-NEWS MAY BE NO NEWS

Because I work with so many organizations and give money to quite a few, I used to get quite a pile of newsletters every month. Over the last few years, most organizations have asked their donors and readers to move from paper to e-newsletter formats. Generally, this is done with a fairly guilt-inducing appeal: "Would you like to save trees and help our organization use our money more wisely?" Well, of course I suppose I would prefer to save trees and not waste money. "So, please do not insist on getting the newsletter in the mail anymore, you self-absorbed old fossil" (of course, this is not how it is worded, simply how it comes across). So, with a sigh, I agree to receive the newsletter online.

While I feel good about myself, I also have mixed feelings, as I like paper newsletters. I stuff them in my briefcase to read on the subway or prop them up on my sugar bowl while eating breakfast. Now I get very few newsletters in the mail and dozens online. The problem is that I get so much e-mail and get so behind on e-mail that I delete all the e-newsletters without reading them, as they seem like so much clutter in my inbox. Whereas I used to read (or at least glance through) 80 percent of the newsletters I got in the mail, I now read at most 10 percent of those I receive online.

More critical from the point of view of the organization is the fact that I also delete their e-appeals, and in the last two years I have stopped giving to several organizations for no other reason than that I did not see their appeals. To be sure, when I want to know something about an organization, I can visit its Web site, and often find the newsletter there, so I am not completely out of the loop, but the impetus is on me to get there. In talking with other Baby Boomers, I have found I am not alone. We have joked about starting an online support group for those of us wanting to do the right thing with regard to trees, but still liking to get mail. Many organizations have also noted a lower-than-usual renewal rate in the years after trying to convert all their donors to e-mail. This is why I recommend that organizations use both paper and e-format for their newsletters and over time, using the segmenting strategies described in Chapter Nineteen, make sure they are not losing donors because they have converted them to e-mail.

E-Appeals

Once you have a list of people who have opted to be on your e-list, you can appeal to them for money. This list will include donors and nondonors. E-appeals work best when they are tied to a campaign and occur within a very tight time frame. The appeal is sent out, with a request to give online right now for an urgent cause. Three or four days later, all the people who haven't given are sent a second appeal. The second appeal highlights progress toward the goal mentioned in the first appeal in order to create some excitement that may push the initial nonresponders to give now. Three or four days later, a final appeal is sent to all those who still haven't given. This appeal notes that the campaign is coming to an end and invites people to be part of it so as to put the organization over its goal. It is important to do these appeals in this three-part format for maximum effectiveness.

Presented here is a sample of the three-part appeal from an organization working to stop a major corporation located in a poor neighborhood from continuing to pollute the air around its plant instead of installing scrubbers in its chimneys. This organization had conducted a large canvass to get people to sign a petition calling on the local health department to crack down on this corporation's air pollution activities; the canvass also gathered people's e-mail addresses. Many people on the list live in the neighborhood, but the majority live in the surrounding area. Note that every time the words "Join Us" or "Give Now" or "Sign Up" or any related phrase appears, the reader needs to be able to click through to the donation page without needing to read the rest of the appeal (just like reading the opening sentence of a direct mail appeal and then going right to the envelope). Generally those words are in a different color to indicate they are hyperlinks. Ditto with "read more"—this takes the reader to that page of the Web site, which also has a "Donate Now" icon.

First Appeal

Dear Friend of Clean Air,

Thank you for joining with more than eight thousand people to call for an end to air pollution by SteelWorks in the Morepark neighborhood. *Just by signing up* with Clean Air for All you have placed yourself with thousands of neighborhood residents and our allies who are increasing the pressure on the health department and other government agencies to enforce *existing laws* concerning pollution.

Now, we ask that you take one more step:

Become a member of Clean Air for All *(click here to join).*

Your membership donation of $35, $50, or whatever you can afford, ensures that you will be helping us keep the pressure on to stop air pollution and stave off more cases of asthma, bronchial infection, and other pulmonary diseases that are rampant in the Morepark area of our community.

Recently our members have:

- Demonstrated outside the house of the president of SteelWorks, who is famous for saying, "Poor people get all kinds of diseases, and I am tired of being blamed for it" *(read more . . .)*
- Joined with hundreds of people to demand hearings at City Hall as to why the Health Department continues to drags its feet on this issue *(read more . . .)*
- Educated schools, primary care clinics, and senior centers about the many problems associated with this type of pollution

Thanks to all this pressure and media attention, the prospects for forcing SteelWorks to stop polluting are high.

Membership amplifies your voice! JOIN NOW

Our goal is two hundred new members before the next City Council Meeting. We want to welcome you! And we promise you will see the fruits of your efforts.

Rachel Cardoza,
Membership Coordinator

A few days later, a second e-mail went to everyone who had not responded to the first letter.

Second Appeal

Dear Friend,

I am a card-carrying member of Clean Air for All because I believe those of us who live near the SteelWorks plant have a special role to play. We need to increase pressure on the health department to respond to the needs of the people concerning the air pollution coming from SteelWorks.

The authorities seem to believe that we will never stand up for ourselves, but I am here to say that this is NOT TRUE. We are standing up, and hundreds of other people in this town are standing with us.

Will you stand with us too? *Click here to join now.*

Because we live in this neighborhood, we must protest the way we have been overlooked for many years. Because what has happened to our neighborhood could happen to anyone, we ask everyone to join us TODAY.

You too can become a card-carrying member of Clean Air for All. We are well on the way to our goal of 200 new card-carrying members, with 123 so far! Please help us show the City Council how many people care about clean air.

Click here to donate with membership dues of $35, $50, or whatever feels right to you.

We will send you a downloadable file with a card that you can use as a signature on your e-mail, or make into stickers to put on envelopes or just print out and carry in your wallet.

On behalf of all of us who simply want to breathe clean air,

> Thank you,
> Marlon Board Member

Third Appeal

Dear Friends,

We only need thirty-seven more of you to join us by TOMORROW! Please take this last chance to join! Help us go into Thursday's City Council meeting with *two hundred new members*! Showing up at the Council meeting with such strong backing will bolster our case tremendously. *Click here to join now.*

We know you are with us in spirit. If you are one of the many people who have helped with petition drives, calls, and distributing materials, please help now with a donation. Become a member today!

We've been able to mobilize our campaign quickly because we rely on a broad base of individual donors for funding. Your support helps us stay independent and keeps our voice strong.

Take a moment now to go online and make a donation at www.cleanairforall.org or send a check. Your donation will be put right to work. If you have already given, thank you again!

Sally Crawford,
Treasurer, Clean Air for All

Each appeal linked to the Web site where donors could give online. The Web site home page featured the appeal as well, with the number of new members updated every two or three days. This kind of time-limited, goal-oriented appeal works very well in encouraging online giving. You could do an offline, snail mail appeal at the same time, but it could not be done in such a short time frame.

ON THE WEB

(See Premium Web Content: Institute for Conservation Leadership Report: *Reality Check: How Grassroots Environmental Groups Are (or Are Not) Raising Money On-Line,* by Andy Robinson; and *How Five Trends Will Reshape the Social Sector,* by La Piana and Associates, published for the James Irvine Foundation.)

chapter FIFTEEN

Establishing Voluntary Fees for Service

One More Chance is a thirteen-year-old program that believes we all need one more chance to get it right. It works with boys ten to thirteen years old from low-income homes who have had a brush with the law. These young people may have been accomplices in a robbery, been caught with marijuana, or been repeatedly truant from school. Their crimes are not violent and are often the result of poor judgment or peer pressure. One More Chance (OMC) runs free summer camps that aim to help the boys gain confidence and social skills, learn how to deal with peer pressure, and reflect on what kind of adults they want to become. Graduating from the program is rewarded with having police records expunged. The program is very successful and highly regarded. Three years ago, the organization's state funding was cut dramatically and, despite a valiant effort, it was not able to raise the money it needed from private sources.

Many times over the years, OMC had been approached by more affluent parents who wanted their sons to attend the camp. Because the organization's mission was to serve low-income boys, these requests had been declined. OMC now decided to change the policy and started a voluntary fee-for-service plan, asking all the parents to consider contributing to the program if they could. The organization explained that the true cost of the camp was $4,500 per camper, and parents were asked to give $50 or more. The camp also set a limit of seven boys from more affluent households for each group of twenty boys attending. OMC very quickly had to add an extra camp session to accommodate the additional requests for spots. Some parents paid much more than $4,500, and many paid $50 to $500. Every parent paid something, and many of the low-income parents paid $100 and $200. Further, these parents expressed delight in being able to pay as a way to set an example for their boys.

With this voluntary fee-for-service program in place, the camps developed more mixed-race and mixed-class groups of campers, with the behavioral results in the graduates even better than before. More parents became involved in the camps as volunteers, and students became more likely to brag about having graduated from an OMC camp. Best of all from a fundraising point of view, OMC has been operating in the black, with a diversity of funding, including some state funding that has been restored, fees for service, and some individual donors who are not involved with the camp.

The experience of this organization is repeated over and over as organizations reluctantly start some kind of fee for service, only to discover that many of the constituents prefer to pay and that others, who don't meet the means test to qualify for the free program, would happily pay. More and more organizations are realizing that giving services away perpetuates a somewhat patronizing system in which some people are seen as needy and others as those who meet needs. Further, when people pay what they can, they feel empowered to demand better services or to ask questions of their service provider. These reactions strengthen the organization providing the service, as they begin to get accurate feedback on their work. From a fundraising viewpoint, fees can also provide an income stream that helps keep an organization afloat.

Many nonprofit organizations have mandatory fees. They charge below the "market rate" for their services, but in order to get the services, one has to pay a fixed price or a fee determined by some criteria, such as income or reimbursement from insurance. Health clubs, counseling services, job training and placement services, public swimming pools and recreation areas, national and state parks—many of these have mandatory fees.

This chapter discusses how organizations that have traditionally provided free services and wish to charge voluntary fees can determine those fees and collect them.

WHAT TO CHARGE FOR

There are three questions to ask of your organization when thinking about creating a voluntary fee-for-service income stream.

1. Is there anything we do for free for one group of people that other people would be willing to pay for?

In the example earlier, many people had children who had had a brush with the law and needed the kind of camp One More Chance offered. Organizations that depend on more than one language in their work, such as those serving immigrants or working in a multi-ethnic city, have realized they can sell translation services to a variety of buyers—lawyers for depositions, conference presenters for simultaneous translation for workshops and keynotes, and even city governments for any number of services they may provide. With enough translation business, they can hire people to do this at profit to themselves and not take away from their core programming. In one instance, a local Humane Society contracted with a free health clinic with several staff who spoke Spanish to translate their brochures and adoption materials into Spanish and later to help Spanish-speaking families and individuals adopt pets or use the free spay and neuter service the Humane Society provided.

2. Is there anything we know how to do that other professionals would like to learn from us?

Many times, grassroots organizations have a much clearer sense of what potential clients want and need than do large social service agencies. The grassroots organization may not recognize this knowledge as potentially saleable, but it is. For example, a social service agency contacted an organization working with teenagers in a public housing project to help find out if the teens would use a basketball court if night lights were installed so they could play after dark. Their own social workers had not been able to get a definitive answer because the tenants of the public housing project distrusted the agency, thinking it was in league with the police. The grassroots organization was able to learn that the young people probably wouldn't use a basketball court after dark, but instead wanted a safe space with a bank of computers where they could do their homework and play computer games. This information led to a collaborative project to help residents of all ages learn how to apply for jobs and do research online, and how to use social media for community organizing in their neighborhood.

Take some time thinking about these questions and ask people in other nonprofits what skills and talents they think your group has to offer. You probably know far more than you think, and you would be surprised at the people who might pay you for your knowledge.

3. What evidence do you have that you cannot charge something, especially as a voluntary donation, for the services you are providing for free right now?

VOLUNTARY FEES

You can charge voluntary fees in one of two ways: you can still provide services for free but request money to help cover the cost, or you can ask that people pay an amount they choose for the service, with whatever they pay being acceptable.

Which system you use depends on the nature of the service you provide. Organizations serving homeless people will generally not require a contribution. Cultural organizations, agencies serving the working poor, mental health providers, and so on may opt to require some payment.

You can also mix the two methods. For example, one homeless shelter provides shelter, showers, and clothing for free and does not attempt to charge. But it has a suggested voluntary donation of $0.50 for meals and a mandatory processing fee of $10 for job placement (collected after the person has received his or her first paycheck). This agency now receives donations from clients for almost 70 percent of its meals served, with many people giving $1, and a collection rate of 80 percent on its job fee.

Museums, theaters, and other cultural facilities will often have a mandatory fee, but their schedule will also include a day or evening when admission is free or they may waive the fee to a resident of the city or someone under sixteen years old or a senior. Corporations will sometimes underwrite a day at an art museum or the botanical garden in exchange for good publicity. The organization then advertises that its facility is free to everyone on that day.

Staying Legal

Charging fees is perfectly legal, but if you are asking for donations rather than fees, it must be very clear that the donation is voluntary. No coercive measures can be used to collect voluntary fees. A coercive action would be one that makes a person feel the service was not really free, that he or she was the only one asking for free service, or some other method of seeming to intimidate a person into paying something or more than they want to. Behavior that is coercive can be a matter of perception, but any obviously coercive actions need to be avoided.

Here's an example: one free-meal program separated those who had given a donation from those who had not, with those who contributed placed at tables with tablecloths and given dessert. In another instance, admission to a class on how to prepare for job interviews was free, but the person registering people loudly announced each donation that was given so that someone sitting across from her could record it. Although thoughtless and probably unintentional, this practice caused some who had intended to take the course for free or even for a low price to pay more than they had wanted to; others simply left before reaching the registration table.

People tend to be embarrassed by any practice that makes them feel as though they don't have enough money. Any system that can embarrass someone may cause them to feel pressured to pay more than they want to or can afford; at that point the voluntary fee is no longer truly voluntary.

The second legal obligation is that your fee, whether voluntary or mandatory, be below what a for-profit business would charge for the same or a similar service.

Setting the Fees

There are several ways to set your fees. The least effective, judged by the amount of money raised, but least intrusive is to post a sign near a collection box that simply reads, "Donations" or "Donations welcome" or "Your gift ensures that we can continue to provide this service to others. Thank you." You will tend to get only people's spare change; however, you will never be accused of forcing someone to give, and this can be a good way to introduce the idea of giving to people who are used to receiving the service for free, and to any of your staff who are reluctant to charge a fee.

If all your services cost about the same amount, you may want to suggest a range for the voluntary contribution. You could post a sign that says, "The cost of providing our services ranges from $10 to $25. Any amount you can pay will ensure that we can continue to provide these services to all who need them. Thank you." If you want, you can add an explanation: "The budget for the services you are receiving was previously provided by the government (or United Way or foundations), but these funds have been cut back. To make sure that we can continue to help people, we are asking all our clients to give what they can. Thank you."

The most effective system is one similar to that used by the youth camp described in the beginning of this chapter. The true cost for each camper was announced and people were asked to pay something toward that cost. If you have a variety of services, another method is to suggest an amount for each one. Here is an example of the range of donations suggested for various services from an organization serving immigrants:

- Translation of a document: $.10–$5.00 per page
- Help getting a green card or other documentation: $50–$500
- Accompaniment to an appointment (social service, medical): $10–$30
- Help enrolling your children in school: $5–$25 per child

Just as when fundraising from individuals, asking for a specific amount rather than leaving the amount up to the prospect will result in more people giving something, so suggesting specific amounts for services rendered will bring more donations overall and will show that you are serious about raising money and know what you are doing.

Most service providers have someone who staffs a desk by the front door. This person should be trained to ask for money, particularly if any of the people using your services cannot read a posted sign. The front-desk person adds to whatever they would normally tell people, "The service is free, but if you want to make a donation, that helps us keep our doors open. The donation box is over there." Many people will ask if there is a charge, which makes it easier to explain. For people accustomed to getting the service for free, explain that you are still providing it for free but that you are asking people who can help to do so. If you hand out literature to your clients, include a card explaining your need and a return envelope. They can drop the envelope in the box provided or send it later. When introducing voluntary fees, err on the side of being too low key rather than too assertive. Over time, as people have a chance to think about it and talk to each other, they will start to give more money.

INTRODUCING THE PROCESS OF COLLECTING FEES

At first, volunteers and staff will be uncomfortable with the process of asking clients for money, regardless of what process you use. In discussing the move to asking for money, validate everybody's feelings: yes, it is difficult to ask for money, and it may be more difficult to ask people who have very little. It would be a much better world if people did not have to pay for things to which they are entitled—housing, health care, education, or food—and did not have to feel embarrassed about receiving these necessities. Next, place the new policy in context: your organization has to keep on providing services, and your costs are going up while your ability to get government (and possibly other) grants is probably going down. Your clients would much rather you exist than watch you go out of business. They will help if they can and will feel good about helping.

Once everyone has a few experiences of asking for money and seeing people feel good about giving, their initial discomfort will go away.

WHEN SERVICE IS PROVIDED BY PHONE OR E-MAIL

So far, we have concentrated on organizations that can collect fees at the door or at the time of service. But what if your way of providing service is by telephone or by mail or e-mail? Your organization has a harder task. Certainly, you cannot ask someone calling a crisis hotline for a donation, even once they are past the crisis that caused them to call. Voluntary contributions for service will not be possible in those cases. However, if your information is not crisis-related, after you are finished giving it, ask if the caller would like to receive more information about your organization and how it is supported. If you send something in the mail, include a letter asking for a donation and insert a return envelope. If you send something by e-mail, include a link to your Web site, where information about how to donate should be prominent.

If part of your service includes mailing information to people, include a card and return envelope. The card should tell how your group is supported and ask the person to return the envelope with a donation when they are able. A card is more effective than a letter because the letter may get put aside while the person is looking at the other information you sent. However, they will be inclined to put the card with the return envelope and respond once they have determined that your information is useful. You may also wish to use a wallet-style envelope, on which the outside flap serves as the reply card (see Chapter Twelve for more on reply devices).

Make sure your Web site has a "Donate Now" button on each page (see Chapter Fourteen for more on online fundraising). People visiting your Web site are not all going to be financially strapped and they may be happy to make a donation.

Setting up a voluntary system for collecting money from people you serve will create a steady income for you, and the amount may be greater than you think. Further, the system may inspire people who are former clients or people who appreciate your work to give. Many times, even volunteers who work with your organization are just as uninformed about how it is supported as anyone else. Once educated, volunteers often give regularly. Finally, asking people to pay a nominal fee for service may even generate more clients who feel better paying a little than getting a service for free, which will serve your broader mission.

Canvassing

Canvassing is a technique that involves a team of people from your organization going door to door or standing on the street requesting contributions for your organization's work. The canvassing technique is most successfully used either by well-known state or national nonprofits (or their local chapters) or by local organizations working on an issue likely to be familiar to the people being canvassed. Canvassing is primarily an organizing strategy; no organization should undertake a canvass simply to raise money. Canvasses work best when the organization is doing work that directly affects the people being canvassed. Canvassing is often used in relation to political campaigns to get out the vote or to drum up support for a candidate or issue. Used in the context of organizing, canvassing can be an excellent strategy for acquiring new donors; by returning to neighborhoods, it can also be used for retaining donors.

There are two kinds of canvass: a door-to-door canvass and the increasingly common street canvass. (Many of the techniques discussed in this chapter can be applied to a phone canvass, which can be conducted using the principles of a phone-a-thon described in Chapter Thirteen.) Door-to-door canvasses and street canvasses are similar both in terms of advantages and disadvantages and in terms of organization. This chapter primarily focuses on door-to-door canvassing because it has the greater potential to acquire donors who can then be renewed and upgraded.

Although part-time or temporary canvasses can be run with volunteers, most canvassing is a full-time operation involving salaried or commissioned employees who work forty hours a week and solicit in commercial districts or residential neighborhoods on a regular, revolving basis. Well-run canvasses can bring in from

233

$50,000 to $500,000 or more in gross income annually. However, they are labor-intensive and generate high overhead costs that, for most canvasses, absorb between 60 percent and 80 percent of the gross earnings. Street canvassing, which is often done by a for-profit firm on behalf of a nonprofit organization, takes even more of a bite. Like all fundraising strategies, canvassing only works if the organization has both the commitment and the ability to continue to work with the donors acquired through the canvass.

ADVANTAGES AND DISADVANTAGES

There are three main advantages to canvassing as a fundraising strategy. First, an established, well-run canvass can provide a reliable source of income for your organization. Second, the volume of personal interaction from the canvassers' face-to-face contact with dozens of people each day can bring as many or more new members as direct mail. Third, canvassers bring back to the organization the public's opinions and perceptions of what the organization is doing. When a canvass is used primarily for organizing rather than fundraising, the money the canvass brings in becomes only one of several goals; other goals can include getting petitions signed, encouraging people to vote, educating people about local issues, and reaching people who may not respond to (or even receive) direct mail or online appeals, such as people who have very low incomes or low literacy skills or who are recent immigrants.

There are also disadvantages to a canvass. If it is done on a full-time basis, it requires separate staff and office space as well as extensive bookkeeping and supervision of the canvassers. As with a small business, canvass income can be unreliable if the supervising staff is not well organized or not good at managing staff people or if too many canvasses are operating in an area. The canvassers themselves can give the organization a bad reputation if they are unkempt, rude, or unpleasant to the people being canvassed, or, again, if too many canvasses are operating in an area and donors get tired of them. (In England, street canvassers are so ubiquitous that they have been nicknamed "chuggers," short for "charity muggers.")

The biggest disadvantage is that when donors find out how little of their money is actually going to the work of the organization, they are often angry and unlikely to renew.

ELEMENTS NEEDED TO RUN A CANVASS

Four elements must be present for an organization to operate an effective canvass. First and most important, the organization must work on issues most people will recognize and be sympathetic to and that have solutions which are easy to explain. The work of your organization can have national impact and your organization might be a branch of a national group, but especially in door-to-door canvassing, you must explain how this issue affects the resident directly. (Broader issues, such as saving whales or working on human rights work well with street canvassing but are less effective in door-to-door canvasses. No one entirely knows why this is: perhaps people in their own homes are more conscious of threats or opportunities for their neighborhood than when they are out and about. People who stop for a street canvasser are less likely to have already supported the organization the canvasser represents (which is why they stopped), but door-to-door canvassers can't screen in quite that way.

Second, people must feel that even a small donation will make a difference. Many people make a cash donation to a canvass, but even those who give with a check or credit card will rarely give more than $100. People must feel that their small donation is needed and will be well used.

Third, people must feel confident about your organization. Their confidence will be inspired by your organization's accomplishments, which must be clear and easy to discuss. Newspaper articles about your work are a major boon to canvassing. A specific plan of action that can be explained simply and quickly and that sounds effective is essential. Some organizations' work lends itself naturally to canvassing because it is on issues of general importance and interest to the majority of people, such as health care for all, lower utility rates, or fixing up public parks. Canvassing on behalf of litigation can work if the suit is easy to understand and if there is a clear "good guy" (represented by your organization) and "bad guy." Complex regulatory reform or issues requiring historical background, legal knowledge, or patience in listening to a long explanation do not lend themselves to canvassing.

Finally, you must be able to distinguish your organization from any other organization doing similar work without implying any disrespect for the other organization. In some communities where there are not only two or more organizations working on similar issues but also several organizations canvassing, potential donors get confused and then angry that they are being solicited so often for issues that seem interrelated. People will explain to your canvassers that they just gave to your nonprofit last week, that someone from your organization was just there. No amount of protest from you will change their minds. The only thing that will help is to distinguish what you do from what others do.

All these requirements for a successful canvass, except the focus on local work, are also necessary for many other fundraising strategies, particularly mail appeals and phone-a-thons, when the object is to get the donor's attention quickly and hold it long enough to get the gift.

SETTING UP A CANVASS

First, check state and local laws and ordinances concerning canvassing. If canvassing is heavily regulated in your community, it may not be worth the time involved to comply with the regulations. Some communities have tried to stop canvassing operations altogether by enacting ordinances governing what you can say when soliciting door-to-door and establishing strict qualifications for canvassers, including expensive licensing. Being able to canvass on a busy street may be regulated differently from a door-to-door canvass. If your canvass violates even a minor subregulation, city or state authorities could force it to cease operation and the episode may bring bad press for your organization. Many of these ordinances have been challenged in court and found unconstitutional, but most organizations have too much work to do to take on costly and lengthy legal battles in this area.

You can find out about state laws governing canvassing from your state attorney general's office, which is usually the office that monitors all rules related to charitable solicitation. Many states publish handbooks on canvassing regulations.

Local ordinances are sometimes more difficult to discover, as several city departments may have jurisdiction over different parts of the canvassing operation. Contact the police department and ask for notification and application procedures for a canvass. Be sure to write down whatever the person tells you and get his or her name so that if you get a different story from another police official you can refer to the initial phone call.

Contact the city attorney's office for information regarding solicitation of money for charity. Sometimes the mayor's office has some jurisdiction over these matters. In general, informing as many people in official capacities as possible about your canvassing operation will ensure the least amount of interference later.

Study the Demographics

After making sure that you can comply with the law, you must determine if your community is a good candidate for a canvass. Gather demographic data on your area: for various neighborhoods, find out the population density, the property values, how many of the people are homeowners, what type of work most people do, what the income levels are, and so forth. This information is available from various sources, including the census, items in the newspaper, volunteers and board members who have lived in the area, and the chamber of commerce, and from developing your own sense from driving around the neighborhoods.

Remember one important point in assessing demographic data: a canvass rarely does well in an affluent neighborhood, and canvassers sometimes conclude that "rich people" are unfeeling tightwads. It's true that affluent people generally do not make contributions at the door. Their charitable giving is usually done in response to major gift solicitation, personal mail appeals, or special events. Canvassing operations do best in middle- and lower-income neighborhoods, where giving at the door is more common.

Another demographic item you need to evaluate is whether the population is dense enough per square mile to make it worthwhile to canvass. Canvassers need to be able to reach eighty to one hundred homes per night (assuming a high number of people are not home). This means that there must be enough people in the area and that the terrain must be flat enough to allow canvassers to walk quickly from house to house. It is much harder to run a successful canvass in a rural area simply because of the distance between houses and the lack of people.

Finally, you need to evaluate whether the area is safe for canvassers. A good canvasser may be carrying $500 or more by the end of the evening, much of that in cash. Canvasses in high-crime areas (which still can be successful) sometimes send their canvassers in pairs, but this doubles the labor cost. Others have a roving car to check in on canvassers and to pick up their cash.

Street canvassing only works in places where there is a lot of foot traffic: busy downtown areas, malls, busy subway or train stations, farmers' markets, and the like. In that case, the demographic you are looking for is lots of people out shopping, going to restaurants, or heading to and from work. Few people will stop, so the canvasser has to be willing to move quickly from person to person until someone agrees to talk.

Hire Staff

If you determine that your area can support a canvass, you are ready to hire canvass staff and prepare materials for them. The staff of a canvass varies from place to place but typically includes several individuals and the following roles.

Canvass Director.   This person supervises the entire canvass operation, including hiring and firing canvassers, researching areas to be canvassed and mapping out the revolving canvass for the area over the course of a year, keeping the organization in compliance with the law, keeping up to date on new laws, and planning and updating materials.

Field Manager(s).   Each of these staff people transports and supervises a team of five to seven canvassers. Each field manager assigns their team to various parts of the neighborhood, collects the money at the end of the evening, and trains new canvassers on the team. This person also participates as a canvasser at the site.

Support Person.   The support person serves as secretary, receptionist, bookkeeper, and office manager. She or he keeps records of money earned by each canvasser, replaces canvass materials as needed, schedules interviews with prospective canvassers for the canvass director, answers the phone, and generally acts as backup person for the canvass operation. This person does not canvass.

Canvassers.   These are the people actually carrying out the canvass. Canvassers work from 2 P.M. to 10 P.M. five days a week. They usually have a quota—that is, an amount of money they must raise every day or every week. Their pay is either a percentage of what they raise (commission); a straight salary; or, most commonly, a base salary plus commission.

Canvassers must represent the organization accurately and be respectable ambassadors for it. The individual canvasser is often the only person from the organization whom donors will see and may well be the only face a donor will ever associate with your group.

Because the pay is low and the hours long and arduous, there is a high turnover in canvass staff. In the summer, college students help expand canvassing staff. In the winter months, recruiting canvassers is more difficult. High unemployment will lead to more people willing to be canvassers, but in general canvassing is seen as a fairly thankless task that involves lots of rejection for low pay. I have never met or heard of a career canvasser.

Develop Materials

Canvassers must be equipped with various materials. These include any identification badges or licenses required by the city or state, clipboards to carry the materials to be given away—brochures about the organization, return envelopes, and newspaper clippings about the work of the organization—and a receipt book.

Many canvassers use a petition to get the attention of the person being canvassed. The canvasser asks, "Would you sign a petition for . . . " and briefly explains the cause. While the person is signing, the canvasser asks for a donation as well.

Canvassers should try to get the gift right at the door. However, for people who need to think about whether to give or discuss it with a partner or spouse, the canvasser can leave a brochure and a return envelope. A brochure should also be given to people making a donation because some of them will send an additional donation after reading it. Your Web site should also highlight the same project the canvassers are talking about. To learn more and to ensure that the canvasser represents a real organization, people interested in the cause will go to the Web site and may give online. Canvassers should not assume when people say they need to think about your request that they mean they are not going to give. This is a common mistake. Many people do not make decisions on the spur of the moment, and people who need to think about what their gift will be to your organization may well become major donors.

Petitions, brochures, and any license are displayed on a clipboard, which lends a degree of authority to the canvasser. People are more likely to open their doors to someone who looks like he or she has a good reason to be there.

THE CANVASSER'S WORK DAY

At the beginning of the canvassers' work day, their field manager describes the neighborhood they will be canvassing and relates any new information or special emphasis on issues that they should present to this neighborhood. The crew has a late lunch or early dinner, and the field manager drives them to the canvass site. They begin canvassing around 4 P.M. and end at 9 P.M., when they are picked up by their field manager and taken back to the office. They turn in their money, make their reports, and finish around 10 P.M.

Because canvassing is hard work, essentially involving daily face-to-face solicitation with a "cold" list, it is critical that the rest of the organization's staff and its board members see the canvass staff as colleagues and as integral to the total operation of the organization. To help build this support, many organizations require noncanvass staff to canvass for an evening every couple of months. Further, because many people who don't give at the door may later give online, organizations that note an upward blip in giving after a canvass has been through a neighborhood may want to give each canvasser some kind of bonus, or consider paying skilled canvassers a higher hourly rate as an acknowledgment that they may well have raised more money than the amount they return with in any given evening.

Second only to quality of canvass staff in ensuring the success of a canvass is efficient data management. After each neighborhood is canvassed, an evaluation of the neighborhood should be filed along with the demographic data on that neighborhood that led to its being chosen as a canvass site. These data can then be reevaluated in light of the canvassers' experience. Any special considerations, such as "no street lights," can also be noted in the evaluation.

Many people worry that theft by the canvassers will be a problem. Theft occurs no more often by canvass workers than by any others. Careless bookkeeping, however, can cost money and can give the impression that money has disappeared. At the end of the evening, both the canvasser and the field manager should count each canvasser's money brought in. The field manager enters the amounts under each canvasser's name on a "Daily Summary Sheet." The money and the summary sheet are then placed in a locked safe, and the secretary or bookkeeper will count the total again in the morning and make a daily deposit to the bank. At the end of the week, the bookkeeper tallies the total receipts of each canvasser and prepares the payroll. Donor names are entered into the database, with the source of gift noted as "canvass."

RETAINING DONORS ACQUIRED THROUGH A CANVASS

Donors recruited through a canvass should be treated the same way all other new donors are treated: they need to be thanked, added to the newsletter list, and kept informed about the organization.

After two or three months of their first gift, and every two or three months after that for a year, they need to receive a solicitation either by mail or e-mail, thanking them for their support and asking them for an additional gift. The organization is seeking to move the person from giving to a canvasser to giving directly to the organization. If the donor does not respond to these requests, he or she should be phoned, or, if the organization is able to do this, the donor could be recanvassed at home.

There is always the option of renewing a gift given at the door, but it is impossible for a street canvasser to renew donations.

ALWAYS BUILD RELATIONSHIPS

One of my first fundraising jobs was door-to-door canvassing for nursing home reform in the late 1980s. I did it for about two weeks, and it was one of the hardest jobs I have ever had. As such, I have a soft spot for canvassers and when they come to my door, I am polite and I always talk to them briefly. There is one canvasser who comes to see me three or four times a year, and has done so for about five years. She is in her mid-fifties (my age), and she always starts her pitch by saying, "We're making progress—we haven't won yet, but we will." She works for an environmental justice organization. She does a lot of things right: she asks if she is interrupting anything, she pats my dog, she says she will be brief. She hands me a short report on what the organization has been up to, and she cuts to the chase quickly. "Can you give $50—it would really help." There is one thing I wish she would improve on: she never uses my name or refers to any previous donations I have made, which gives the impression she doesn't remember that I just gave $50 three months ago. If I say, "I think I gave not too long ago," she says, "Yes, you just gave in March as a matter of fact." I know and like the organization she canvasses for, and if she were to be conscious of building a relationship with me, she would get much more money. For a canvass to really work, the canvassers have to see their work as finding donors, not just donations, a classic lesson that applies to all kinds of fundraising.

Canvassers who fail to bring in their quota for more than a week must be retrained or fired. Strict discipline is important in a successful canvass; keeping performance records will help to maintain a good canvass team.

Canvassing is an excellent strategy for community organizing; if done properly it can be a good way to mobilize members and make money. However, there are many pitfalls, and it is neither a simple nor a low-cost strategy. Canvassing changes the nature of the organization. It doubles or triples staff size and requires office space and additional equipment. Only organizations that have thoroughly researched the pros and cons of canvassing should consider using this fundraising method.

chapter SEVENTEEN

Opportunistic Fundraising

Recently I gave a workshop at a conference on the topic of opportunistic fundraising: how to recognize a time when you are with someone (or hundreds of people) doing something not related to fundraising, and suddenly asking for money would be exactly the right thing to do.

I asked if anyone could think of such opportunities. One participant said she had been tweeting from a fundraising event she was attending. Her tweets were very positive about the group and she was sharing some information the speaker was giving. She said, "I could suggest that people give money and have a link to the group's Web site." An appreciative murmur filled the audience. (One could assume that someone even tweeted this suggestion to people not at the workshop.) Another participant said that at his family reunion many people congratulated him on doing such fine work, which they knew about because of his blog. In his next blogpost, he mentioned donating money to a specific organization, and by the next week, several people in his family had given. Another even more appreciative murmur . . .

Then someone said that she and other people in her organization led workshops for teachers and coaches, and that the workshops are very popular and always get rave reviews. She suggested that her organization send a mail appeal to the people coming to the workshop after the workshop is over. I like to encourage almost any fundraising effort, so I said, "Great idea. Or, even faster and possibly more effective, would be for you to figure out a low-key way to ask for money at the end of the workshop and to provide envelopes for people if they want to give right there."

Her face fell, despite yet another appreciative murmur from the audience. "But that would mean I would have to do it," she noted, stating the obvious.

The fact is that every day we have opportunities to ask for money but we don't take them. This omission is called "leaving money on the table." People are ready to give, but the moment passes and they move on to the rest of their lives and forget about that impulse. The first step is recognizing those moments, the second is figuring out how to use them.

To do those steps, you need to do a thorough inventory of all the work you do now and see how fundraising could easily be built into it. This is called "opportunistic fundraising," which simply means taking advantage of a situation you are in anyway. This kind of fundraising doesn't take extra time and doesn't require a lot of advance planning. But it does require an awareness and sensitivity to the opportunities that present themselves.

Let's look at a couple of weeks in the life of an advocacy organization working on reproductive rights.

Sunday. Volunteers from the advocacy organization are stationed at various locations around a community: outside of five grocery stores, near the doors of three liberal Protestant churches, and near a coffee shop in the middle of a large shopping mall. Their intent is to inform people that the local school board has eliminated sex education in the schools, and the only mention of sex will be in the context of abstinence. Their literature contains information about the poor results of "abstinence-only" education elsewhere, with evidence of higher rates of teen pregnancy and sexually transmitted disease than before the policy was implemented. They ask people to sign up for an e-alert for more information and to come to school board meetings when the issue is being discussed. They also suggest that parents or teachers bring the issue up in their local PTA, and they show people samples of a kit with fact sheets and suggested actions to get the school board to reverse this decision and give people a card with a Web site address where they can download a copy of the kit. They have placed themselves in ZIP codes where the vast majority of people will agree with them. They want to focus on education, not fundraising, so they don't ask people to become members of the advocacy organization and they don't have a jar out at any of their locations to collect money.

Here is what they find: most of the people coming out of the grocery store and churches either don't have children or have grown children, and many of those at the mall are teenagers. But the volunteers are still able to enlist a lot of these people to sign up for the e-alert, and enough of them are either parents or teachers that they make their goal. Most interesting, however, is that over and over they hear this refrain: "I'd be happy to contribute some money" or "How can I become a member of your organization?" or "Is there anything I can do if I don't have kids in the school system?" The teenagers have a different refrain: "This policy is so messed up" and "My mom says it's stupid." One suggests to her friends, "Maybe we could do a car wash or something to help raise money."

Monday.   Talking over the experience from Sunday's efforts, the volunteers conclude that although they met their goals for talking to parents and teachers, they missed a great opportunity to involve a lot of other people, particularly those whose involvement would mean making a donation. They decide to revise their tactics for the following weekend.

The Next Sunday.   Once again the organization's volunteers spread out around the community with the same literature, but today they also have membership forms, a jar for collecting donations, and business-size cards that give people their Web and Facebook addresses and information about membership. The mall volunteers, using the wireless capacity of the coffee shop, set up two laptop computers so that people can look at their Web site and, if they want, join online. They also prepare a special handout for teenagers.

This Sunday, they sign up thirty members at $35 each, are given two checks for $100 each, and later download the names of ten new people who joined online. In addition, their jars have collected nearly $200. With only slightly more work, they continued their educational and advocacy push, but this week they also raised more than $1,500.

Tuesday.   The executive director of the reproductive rights group attends a lunch meeting of the chamber of commerce. She has joined the chamber to take advantage of some of the educational opportunities they provide and to give her organization more visibility in the small-business community. At lunch, the owner of an office supply store comes over and wishes her luck in all the important work her organization is doing. He hands her his card and says, "If there is any way I can help you, let me know." She calls him later that day and asks two things: "Can our volunteers set up their information station in front of your store this Wednesday, and would you consider donating or deeply discounting office supplies for us?" She adds the second half of the question on the basis of her experience on Sunday. Yes to both, he says. A 50 percent discount on office supplies for a year saves the organization more than $4,000.

Thursday. The public policy director of the reproductive rights group meets with staff from a number of other organizations concerned in one way or another with reproductive rights issues. Some work in social service agencies, some work in education, and many are involved in advocacy. The purpose of the meeting is to prepare a joint statement to the press on the school board issue and to compare notes on their other work.

All the organizations are feeling stressed about money. "Is there anything we can do together to help all our fundraising that won't take much time?" someone asks. Ideas are bandied about, but the simplest one is for each organization to make sure their Web site has a link to all the other organizations' sites. There is no clear income from this action, but each organization now has heightened visibility for very little work.

Friday Night. The development director meets friends for dinner and a movie. One friend says her mother saw the volunteers from this organization outside of her church but didn't have time to stop. Does the development director have anything with her she could give her mother? Of course she does: she has the business cards created for last Sunday's work, and she hands one to each of her friends. By the following Tuesday she has a check from her friend's mother for $500.

FIND YOUR OWN OPPORTUNITIES

It is true that organizations working on immediate and hot-button issues will be able to generate cash in the moment, but every organization has opportunities for fundraising every day that they fail to take advantage of. Doing an audit of your day will reveal these opportunities.

Review the opportunities that might arise for your group in each of the following typical daily events.

Communicating with People

People in organizations communicate with dozens of people on the phone, in person, or by e-mail every day. Certainly, most conversations cannot include a fundraising component, but many more could than presently do.

In Person.   Any board member, staff, or volunteer talking with people about your nonprofit can hand them a generic business card about your organization that would contain a giving option on the back. (The front would have only the group's name, address, phone, and Web site, but no one person's name.) The back of the card would look like the example shown here.

I want to help. Here is my gift of

☐ $45   ☐ $100   ☐ $____other

Make checks payable to Good Group and send to the address on the front of this card, or donate online at www.goodgroup.org.

Make sure everyone in your organization has some of these cards. Board members and volunteers can write their own names on the card. People should be encouraged to hand them out like candy.

Most staff have a "signature" on their outgoing e-mail. Where appropriate, add a line that says, "You can help—donate now at www.ourgroup.org." Board members can add to their personal e-mail signature: "Visit my favorite nonprofit at nomoretoxicwaste.org."

Everyone who is on Facebook or uses social media generally has some kind of profile. Encourage everyone in your organization to add your organization to their profile.

Voice Mail.   If you have voice mail, be sure that one choice is, "If you wish to make a donation, or speak with the development director . . . " or "For information about how to donate, visit our Web site, www.goodgroup.org, or leave your address at the tone and we will send you free information."

In other words, make fundraising part of your message—these soft asks will offend no one and will help raise money.

Publications.   Many organizations produce brochures, reports, booklets, and even books. All of these should contain information about how and why to give.

This information should be placed where a person would be likely to see it, usually at the front or back of the publication. Where appropriate, include return envelopes. Make sure it is easy to order these materials online, and if you have your own online gift store, add a donation line on the checkout page.

Other Opportunities

Let people know that money is one way they can help if they want to.

When people e-mail with questions, answer the question and include a hyperlink to your Web site.

When people write to you for a publication, include fundraising materials in your response.

When you visit your major donors, ask them for names of people they think would be interested in giving.

When giving a speech, tell people how they can help, and be sure to mention making a gift and telling others about giving.

Use birthdays, weddings, Christmas or Hanukkah, or other holiday times to suggest that people make a gift to your organization in lieu of a present. Many people feel that they have enough stuff and are happy for a chance to give something meaningful.

Make sure all program staff, organizers, administrators—all nonfundraising staff—are helped to figure out when and where adding a fundraising pitch would be appropriate. Conduct an inventory of their days, and show them when fundraising might be included.

During staff meetings, ask people to report how they included fundraising in something they did or why they decided not to include it. Learning that there are far more opportunities to ask for money than we have realized also goes hand-in-hand with learning when a fundraising pitch would be out of line. By sharing information like this, you will also learn where fundraising pitches simply are not worth the time or the money, and where they really pay off.

Here are some more examples from a variety of organizations.

• A theater sells sweets, coffee, tea, wine, and soda before every play and during intermission. Near the cash register sits a jar with a notice that change dropped in will go to one of the theater's programs. Every night, people drop in between $30 and $50 extra.

- A program serving homeless people has an art program. Some of the homeless people who participate create attractive works. From time to time, local galleries have displayed and sometimes sold the art. Several people have asked if the art pieces are available on note cards or T-shirts they could buy. In response, the organization creates a series of note cards using some of the images from these artworks. Boxes of cards sell out quickly, so the program reprints them and offers them on its Web site. These cards become a small but reliable income stream and a further source of visibility, which leads to other donations.

- A garden store donates most of the plants, seeds, and compost for a youth program's organic garden. The organic garden is located in a well-trafficked area and displays a small board thanking the store for its support and telling more about the garden. As a result of this notice, the store owner is often praised by his customers for his support of the garden. He decides to mobilize that praise by putting the youth program's brochures in his store, with return envelopes, and by having the phrase, "Looking for a great cause? Go to www.youngsprouts.org" printed on the bottom of his receipts. The envelopes used in his store are marked so the group knows the origin of the donation. The organization receives three or four donations a month in these envelopes, including an occasional large gift.

By doing an opportunity inventory, almost any organization can raise more money with only a small amount of extra effort.

The Thank You Note

Early on in my fundraising career I learned a valuable lesson about thank you notes. I had gone to work for an advocacy group working on women's health issues. The organization was run collectively by two utterly overworked staff people and forty volunteers. The organization had won recognition for its work to expose and eventually remove from the market a dangerous birth-control device and for championing reproductive rights issues. Several months before I began working there, a woman who had read about the group's victories in the newspaper sent $25. She did not receive a thank you note. She did, however, receive the organization's newsletter, and she heard about it from time to time. A year after making her gift she received a form letter requesting a renewal. She threw it away.

Some time later, this woman learned that a friend of hers was a volunteer in the collective. "That group sounds good," she told her friend, "but they don't even have it together enough to send thank you notes for gifts. I can't imagine that they are really fiscally sound or that they use money properly."

Her friend defended the organization: "We do really good work. We don't send thank you notes because we are too busy doing other stuff. It is not fair to conclude that we don't use your money properly just because you don't get an acknowledgment."

The one-time donor replied, "It is fair. It is my only contact with them. They claim to want a broad base of support, yet they show no regard for their supporters. But since you vouch for them, I'll give them something." She sent $15. (As stressed throughout this book, please note the power of personal asking as demonstrated here.)

I was hired during the year between this donor's $25 gift and her $15 one. I had been brought up in the school of thank you notes, from thanking my grandmother for birthday gifts when I could barely hold a pencil to writing thank you notes for every gift that came into the seminary where I had my first fundraising job. So without much thought, in response to this $15 gift, I sent this woman a scrawled three-line thank you note: "Thanks for your gift of $15. It's a help financially and also a great morale boost. We'll keep in touch."

Two weeks later, this woman sent $100. Again, I scrawled a thank you note, with an extra line about her generosity. A few months later, she sent $1,500. I wrote another thank you note and asked if I could come and see her. She turned out to be both quite wealthy and very supportive of women's rights. She told me that she usually gave relatively small initial donations to organizations to see how they would respond. She wanted to see how much regard they had for people giving small gifts. She said, "If I send $500 or $1,000, almost any organization will thank me. Many grassroots groups talk a good line about not making class distinctions and everyone being welcomed, but the only people they really care about are the program officers of foundations and wealthy donors." She had decided to give money only to community-based organizations that had proven that they valued all gifts. I was flabbergasted that a sign of proof could be a sloppy three-line thank you note, but for her it was better proof than a longer form letter with her name typed in and certainly far better than no acknowledgment at all.

Since then I have seen over and over that a simple handwritten note or computer-generated thank you letter with a personal note as a postscript can do more to build donor loyalty than almost any other form of recognition. Of all the things you send donors, the thank you note is the *one* thing you can almost be certain the donor will read. Smart organizations use the thank you note to describe briefly a program they are proud of or some recognition or victory they have achieved, and they add a personal element. The idea is to thank the donor, and to give that person an easy anecdote or interesting factoid that they might share with a friend or neighbor.

Unfortunately, thank you notes tend to be one thing that organizations are sloppy or even thoughtless about. They either don't send them, send them weeks late, or send a preprinted card or note with no personal note added. These practices are unjustifiable. Sending thank you notes easily falls far too low on people's work priority lists. It has to be placed at the top. We have a saying in fundraising: "Thank before you bank."

PEOPLE LIKE TO BE APPRECIATED

Beleaguered development directors often ask me why people like thank you notes so much. Why don't they like the newsletter or the Web site even more? There is far more content in those places, and a lot more money has been spent on those and other communication vehicles. Probably, reasons vary. Like the wealthy, testing donor I mentioned earlier, some see thank you notes as a sign that the organization really does value all gifts. Others may just like to know that their gift has been received. But most often, people like to feel appreciated, and while some highly enlightened types might be able to get by with the warm feeling that comes from doing the right thing, the majority of us lesser mortals want someone else to have noticed our good deeds. Thank you notes are polite and gracious and, most of all, they are the right thing to do. (Moreover, for gifts greater than $250, an acknowledgment is required by law.)

Whatever the reasons, for fundraisers it is enough to know that donors value being thanked. Doing what donors like—as long as we stay inside the mission and goals of the organization—builds donor loyalty. A loyal donor is a giving donor and is likely to talk about the organization to his or her friends and colleagues. Donors who give are more likely to increase their gifts, as they can, as the years pass.

DON'T DO AS I SAY

What about the donor who claims not to want a thank you note, or the one who even more strongly states that thank yous are a waste of time and money?

The donor who claims not to want a thank you note should nevertheless get an e-mail or a thank you call. Again, if the donor has given more than $250, you can explain that the acknowledgment is a legal requirement and one you are happy to comply with because you truly appreciate the gift. People who say they don't want to be thanked are usually genuinely trying to save the organization time and money. You will have greater loyalty if you thank them anyway, using a different method from a written note sent by snail mail. When these donors say, "You shouldn't have done that" or "That's really not necessary," they often mean, "Thank you for taking the time. I can't believe someone would bother to notice me."

If the person is very close to your organization—perhaps a volunteer, board member, or someone who used to work there—you can combine your thank you call with another function, such as to remind them of a meeting: "I called to thank you for your gift of $50. We put it right to work! You are so generous with all your resources. And speaking of which, I hope you can still come to the finance meeting this Wednesday at 7 P.M. at Marge's."

Overall, experience shows that, all else being equal, when you thank donors you are more likely to keep them and when you don't, you are more likely to lose them. Of course, there will be exceptions to this rule, but it is almost impossible to figure out who is really an exception and who is just pretending to be, so thank everyone and save yourself from worrying about it.

DO IT NOW

How can you most efficiently thank your donors, and who should do it? Perhaps the most important rule about thanking donors is that no matter who is doing it—from the board chair to an office volunteer—gifts should be acknowledged promptly—ideally within three days of receipt, and certainly within a week in any circumstance. The official thank you note coming from the office does not need to be signed by the person who knows the donor, but that person should be informed of the gift so that he or she can thank the donor personally. (Another note is not necessary—a call or e-mail will suffice.) If you are fundraising properly, you will also have dozens of donations coming in from people you don't know. Volunteers and board members can send thank you notes to these donors, under your supervision. Writing or personalizing computer-generated thank you notes is actually a good way to involve board members who are resistant to asking for money in doing fundraising, and this activity counts toward their obligation to help raise money.

LOGISTICS AND CONTENT

There are three methods to use in creating thank you notes to send in the mail. The first two are equally fine, and the third is not as good but is far better than nothing.

Handwritten Thank You Notes

Have some note cards or half sheets of paper printed with your organization's logo on the front, and its mission statement at the bottom or on the back. There is only a small amount of space to fill on a note card, so you can take up the whole space with a few short sentences. That is much better than a three-line thank you on a full sheet of stationary.

People should come to the office to write the notes, and only the most loyal, trustworthy people should ever be allowed to write notes at home. It is just too tempting to put them aside at home. Also, information about a person's gift, while not secret, is not something you want sitting around someone's living room.

The only requirement for handwritten thank yous is legible handwriting. The format is simple.

> Thank you for your gift of $____. We will put it right to work on *(name your program or most recent issue).* Gifts like yours are critical to our success, and we thank you very much.
>
> Sincerely,
> *(Your name)*
> Board member

If the writer knows the person, he or she follows the same format but adds something more personal: "Hope your cat, Fluffy, has recovered from her spaying."

Not Handwritten Thank You Notes

It may be that handwriting thank you notes or handwriting all of them is impossible, especially when you get a lot of contributions, such as at the end of the year, when volunteers aren't as available, or after a successful direct mail appeal, when you are swamped for a few days with responses. Then you just send handwritten notes to people close to the organization, and you use a computer-generated letter for people you don't know. This letter should be on the organization's stationary and needs to be a little longer. Your donor database can be programmed to merge the donor's name and salutation, along with the specific gift, into a more general letter. If you use this method for most thank yous, change the content of the letter every two months to be current. Then your volunteers can add a personal note at the top or bottom of the letter.

Start the text several lines down the page and use wide margins.

Dear Freda,

Thank you so much for your gift of $100. We have put it right to work! As it turned out, your gift came at a particularly crucial moment, as the coffeemaker in our community room (where all our AA and NA meetings are held) had just given its last gasp. We were able to buy a new, heavy-duty coffeemaker on sale, which wouldn't have been possible without your gift.

I am hoping you will be able to come to our art auction next month. We'll be selling the works of some well-known local artists and featuring paintings and sculptures by some of the residents of our treatment program. The works are quite excellent to have made it into this juried event.

Again, thank you so much! I look forward to staying in touch.

You will notice that the letter refers to a recent event (the coffeemaker giving out). This gives a sense of immediacy to the gift. If the organization had incurred a much greater cost, they could still have referred to the gift in this way:

Your gift came the same day we found out our toilet and pipes leading to the toilet have to be entirely replaced. I would have been really discouraged, but your contribution cheered me up. (Some plumbers from the union shop next door said they would replace the whole thing just for the cost of materials, so it is not going to be that expensive at all!)

The letter also invited the donor to an event. You do not need to be having an event: the point is to refer to things happening in your office. Give your donors some sense of your daily work. Even things that seem routine to you can be made to sound interesting. Here's an example:

Dear Ricardo,

I was taking a break from writing a report and decided to sort through the mail. There were a few bills, some newsletters, and then, your gift of $50! Thank you! $50 really goes a long way in this organization, and we are grateful for your support.

I just finished talking with a woman who gave our brochure and Web site information to her son. She said she had expected a miracle, and though of course that didn't happen, maybe something more lasting did. Her son called the HelpLine. It's a start, and that's what we provide for people.

Please feel free to drop by sometime. Though we are usually busy, we can always take a few minutes to say hello and show you around. I'll keep you posted on our progress.

Or:

Dear Annie Mae,

I just came from an eviction hearing for one of our clients. I feel really good because we won and we got some damages to boot! Then, going through the mail, I came to your gift of $25. Thanks! I feel like you are a part of this victory.

Or:

You wouldn't believe how many people came to our community meeting last night—more than fifty! People are hopping mad about this incinerator proposal, and I am feeling confident that we may be able to defeat it and finally get the recycling bill passed. Your gift of $50 will go a long way in helping with community outreach. Thanks for thinking of us at this time. You don't know what a great morale boost it is to receive gifts from supporters like you.

If you have a matching campaign or a goal for an annual campaign, then refer to that:

Your gift of $100 will be matched dollar for dollar. Your gift brought us to nearly $2,000 raised in just two months!

Or:

Your gift of $75 took us over the $1,000 mark in our goal of $3,000. Thanks!

If you are a volunteer, mention that in your thank you:

Giving time to this organization is one of the high points of my week. I know we are making a difference, and we can't do it without money! Your donation really helps!

The Friendly Form Letter

The least effective option for thank you notes, but one you sometimes have to resort to, is the form letter. If you use a form letter, acknowledge that it is impersonal, but give some sense of the excitement that would lead you to use such a method. Here's an example:

Thank you for your recent gift. Please excuse the impersonal nature of this thank you—we are no less enthusiastic about your gift for not being able to write to each of our donors personally. The response to our call for help with sending medical supplies to Ghana was both gratifying and overwhelming. We will send you a full report about this effort in a few weeks. Right now, we are packing up boxes of supplies—supplies you helped pay for. Thanks again!

A thank you note will double as a receipt if you name the specific amount of money the donor gave. Also, all thank you notes need to say, "No goods or services were received in exchange for this gift." You can have that statement preprinted on your thank you cards along with the logo and mission statement of the organization.

THANK YOU CALLS

Donors you are very close to or who give you more than $500 in one gift should be called as soon as their money comes in and thanked personally. Generally, this will not take much time, as you will reach voice mail or an assistant. When leaving a message, do not say the amount of the gift—just say, "We got your donation today and just wanted to thank you so much! You'll get a formal thank you letter soon. Hope all is well." If you reach the donor, don't talk long: the message can be fairly similar to the one you would leave on voice mail. Some donors may be in the mood to talk, so call when you have a few minutes and can have a conversation. This is sometimes a nice way to get to know your donors without having a request for money as the motivation.

You can also call donors to thank them if you need to use the form thank you letter mentioned above. The calls should be made by volunteers, who can generally call fifty donors in a hour. Even when they reach someone, they can say, "I don't want to take too much of your time, but just wanted to thank you personally for your gift. You'll be getting an acknowledgment in the mail as well." A thank you phone call allows you to skip writing personal notes on your form thank yous and is fairly effective.

COMMON QUESTIONS

There are four common questions remaining about thank you notes.

Can We Thank People by E-mail? If you regularly correspond with someone by e-mail, then it is acceptable to thank them this way. However, don't use e-mail as a general practice. Someday e-mail (or whatever it becomes) may well replace all paper correspondence, but we are not there yet. As snail mail becomes less common, people actually value it more, so for the time being, use regular mail. (For gifts of more than $250, even if you are in regular contact by e-mail with the donor, you should send a thank you by snail mail to keep a paper trail.)

How Do We Thank People Who Give by Credit Card Through the Internet? Donations made by credit card must also receive a thank you note; however, for donations that come through the Internet, you may be able to do it electronically. If you use a charity portal to handle your credit card donations, that service will have an automatic trigger response back to the donor indicating that the donation has been received. For most of these portals, you can change the wording of that trigger receipt, and you should do so every couple of months to keep the information current. If you are able to personalize that receipt, it will not be necessary to send another thank you note by mail.

How Do You Address People You Don't Know? The choices for salutation to people you don't know are by first name only, by first and last names (Dear Robert Park), or by title (Dear Mr. Park). There is no clear right or wrong answer on this point and no way to avoid possibly offending someone. You will probably offend the least number of people by using titles: "Dear Mr. Fernandez" or "Dear Ms. Crawford." (Certainly, you could write to the person according to how they write to you. A letter signed, "Mrs. Alphonse Primavera" should be answered in kind. Ditto with people who use "Dr." or "Rev.") If there is ambiguity about whether the donor is a man or woman, you can write "Dear Friend." If you live in a fairly casual community, you can use a first name, "Dear Terry" or "Dear Lynn."

Don't waste a lot of time worrying about the salutation. Having received many thank yous that say, "Dear Mr. Klein," I know how off-putting it can be, but it does not cause me to stop giving to the organization. Anyone who will stop giving you money because you (or anyone else) cannot tell from their name whether they are male or female, or whether they prefer to be called by their first name, last name, Mr., Ms., or Mrs., is probably not going to become a regular donor anyway. Far more important is to make sure donors' names are spelled correctly. People are far more attached to their name than to their honorific.

Do All Donors Get a Thank You?   The answer is always yes. You have no idea how much a gift of $25 or $5 or $500 means to someone. You need to act as though you would like to get that amount or more again. You also don't know whether people use getting a thank you note to judge whether to continue giving to your organization. Why take a chance?

Keep up with thank you notes as gifts come in. Each thank you is a link to the donor and, in addition to it being the right and gracious thing to do, you should see it as paving the way for the next gift.

PART THREE

Strategies for Upgrading Donors

Part Three and Part Four focus on strategies that will help organizations solicit and receive major gifts from their donors. The goal of any organization that gains the support of a broad base of individual donors is to become the favorite organization of a cross-section of its donors. The financial payoff in building a base of donors is twofold: first, having a large number of small donors will yield a profit, and those donors will bring in other donors; and second, a subset of donors will give larger and larger gifts. Undoubtedly, the most money in fundraising is from people who give big gifts over the course of their lifetimes or as part of their estates, or both.

By building relationships with donors, your organization is in a position to ask people who are giving donations regularly to consider giving bigger gifts, and you are likely to receive a positive response from some of them. You want your donors to think, "This is my favorite nonprofit" or "That is an organization I would do a lot for." The strategies described in this section will help you raise bigger gifts annually. I start with a discussion of segmenting your donors—identifying which cohort of donors responds to which strategies so you can use the strategies appropriate to that subset and stop using strategies with donors who won't respond to them. I then discuss how to set up and maintain two key programs—a monthly donor program and a legacy program—and how to move from a major donor program to a major donor campaign. The principles for conducting a major gifts campaign can be applied to other strategies as well, and I encourage you to look at all your strategies through the campaign lens.

The process of getting current donors to give more money is called *upgrading*: donors who respond to these strategies have become the *thoughtful* donors described in Chapter Three, "Matching Fundraising Strategies with Financial Needs."

It is highly unusual for people to start their giving to an organization with the largest gift they can afford, so almost all thoughtful donors will come out of the donor base that is built using the strategies described in Section Two. The only time someone's first gift might be the largest gift they can give is when they or someone close to them has been deeply affected by the issue the organization addresses or the service it provides.

Thoughtful gifts are most often gifts of more than $250; a thoughtful annual gift may be thousands of dollars, and a capital or endowment gift will be even larger. In this section, I use $250 to describe the minimum thoughtful gift and then discuss much larger gifts. It is important to note, though, that if your organization's donor base has a large number of low-income or poor people, there will be people giving less than $250 who are nevertheless giving your organization the biggest gift they can afford. For this reason, some organizations will set $100 as the minimum major gift. On the other side are people giving $1,000 for whom that is not a particularly big gift and who easily could give more if you asked them.

When you identify donors who are giving what is a thoughtful or significant gift for them, even if it is a smaller amount of money, treat them with the same respect with which you treat thoughtful donors who give larger gifts.

In fundraising, we spend a lot of time working with the people who can give large amounts of money. All donors expect that bigger donors would get more attention and would think it odd and not a good use of resources for an organization to do otherwise.

But we don't overlook other kinds of giving and the significance of their gifts to any donor. First, that is the right thing to do. Second, there is a practical angle: someone who gives $10 monthly through a monthly donor program may get a better job or a less expensive apartment and change his gift to $25 each month. When he gets promoted, the gift may increase to $50 each month. Or a person may give a small amount for years, then leave her estate to the organization. In fact, research shows that longtime, loyal donors making small gifts are most often the ones who leave an organization a gift through a bequest.

Through the process of identifying prospects described in Chapter Seven, "The Logistics of Personal Solicitation," and by being very thorough and careful with donor data, we can keep track of all our thoughtful donors, not just the ones who are able to give large amounts of money.

The strategies that were described in Section Two, which are primarily used to acquire and retain donors, can also be used to some extent to upgrade donors. Similarly, many of the strategies described in this section could be used for acquisition or retention. However, used to their best advantage, the strategies in this section are really about fund *raising*, and are the logical sequence to the strategies described before.

chapter NINETEEN

Segmenting Donors

I hope it is obvious by now that having a donor is not like having a pillowcase or a table. Donors take maintenance. They are living, breathing beings with feelings and attitudes, and they are being sought by more than 1.8 million other nonprofits. Certainly, they gravitate to organizations they believe in, but if they have a choice between two organizations they believe in and one pays attention to them and the other doesn't, it is not hard to guess where they will send their money. Segmenting donors basically means figuring out how various cross-sections of your donor base like to be asked for money and avoiding using strategies that they don't like or don't respond to.

If one donor says she or he hates to be phoned or wants to receive no more than one appeal a year, we tend to think that a huge number of our donors think exactly like this one. I have known organizations that stopped sending multiple appeals because one donor complained, even though fifty donors might have sent in an extra gift! Donors are not all alike. Some dislike being phoned, but others give only by phone. Some will delete an e-newsletter but read any paper you send; others will do the opposite.

Because people have individual likes and dislikes, we should accommodate these preferences when we can. For example, if someone sends your organization $35 with a note that says, "I only give once a year, so please only ask me once a year," code this donor to suppress his name for any other mailing during the following twelve months. That person will not be invited to an event or get the spring appeal. Similarly, someone who writes on her reply card, "Absolutely no phone calls" should never be phoned, and that information should be in her donor record. In fact, even if you know the phone number (for example, it is on their check), don't enter it into your database. If it is not part of your data, you will not be able to make a mistake and call.

Most donors don't tell us directly what they want. They may still have desires, however, and they indicate their preferences by their behavior. Our goal is to make an informed guess about their behavior before they decide not to give us any more money. Segmenting, which means dividing your donor lists into smaller batches according to various criteria, allows you to take their preferences into account and saves your organization time and money because you are not using strategies with people who have never responded to them.

The first set of segments is very simple. Donors should be sorted by how long they have been giving your organization money (longevity), how big their gift is (size), and how often in the same year they make a gift (frequency). Let's look at each of these criteria.

Longevity

In many ways, the most important donors are the ones who have given you money for at least three years, regardless of the size of their gift. Create a category for those people. If your organization has been around for a while and your records are good, you may want to create categories for donors who have given for five or even ten or more years.

Size

Determine what amount of money is more than most people in your constituency can give, and create a list of donors who give that much or more. In some organizations, this may be $100, but for most it will probably be $250 and up.

Frequency

Although there are many donors who give only once a year, there are many others who give every time they are asked. Create a category for people who give two or more times a year.

Once you have segmented your donors according to longevity, size, and frequency, sort your donors as follows:

- People who have given $250 or more at a time more than once a year for three or more years

- People who have given $250 or more once a year for three or more years
- People who have given between $100 and $249 once or more than once for three or more years

In descending order, these donors are your best prospects for upgrading and are often good people to consider for volunteer opportunities. Your personal solicitation efforts should be directed to these segments. They care about you and have shown that caring for several years. These donors are signaling that they like your organization. Chances are they will respond favorably to personal attention.

Share this list with board members, trusted volunteers, and people who know your community and who have some discretion. Ask if they know whether any of the people on these lists are capable of giving a lot more. Perhaps Jane Smith gives you $250 twice a year and has done so for three years. A volunteer knows that Jane Smith gives $1,000 to an organization similar to yours and says that Jane always speaks highly of both organizations. Because as a general rule donors should be asked to upgrade their gift every third year, Jane is a little overdue. Your next solicitation to her can ask her to consider making a gift of $1,000.

Donors who only give once a year should only be asked once or twice a year, whereas you can send an extra appeal during the year to people who give every time they are asked; these are also people who should be asked to join a monthly donor program. People who always renew by phone should no longer get three renewal letters before being phoned; instead, send them one renewal letter and then call them. People who only give online can be taken off all snail mail lists.

By observing patterns among your donors, you can save yourself a lot of time and money and increase your fundraising income with little extra work on your part.

In addition to categorizing by size, longevity, and frequency, note which donors only come to events or perhaps only come to one event. These donors should not get regular appeal letters unless you have evidence that they respond by giving to those as well. If a donor only gives when she comes to your signature event, does so for three years or more, and does not give to any other appeals, that is a sign that she does not need to get the other appeal letters. If one year that donor does not come to the event, then you could send her a letter after the event telling her how well the event did and how she was missed and asking for a contribution.

Note which donors only give to appeals for specific things (playgrounds, scholarships, capital projects) but who never send money in response to general appeals. If you have a specific need, these are the donors to approach more personally for that need. These are often your best prospects for capital campaigns as well.

Identify the people who give several times a year and either send them one more appeal or ask them to become members of a pledge club to see if you can convert them to monthly donors. All donors should be offered the chance to become monthly donors on all your reply devices and as a suggestion in renewal letters, but donors who give frequently should be offered that option in a special letter about the advantages of pledging. (For more on setting up a monthly donor program, see Chapter Twenty.)

Your goal in looking closely at how donors give to your organization is threefold:

• You give donors the kind of attention they want.

• You save the organization from phone calls or letters from frustrated donors saying, "You send too much mail" or "I can't stand being phoned" or "You are using all the money I gave you to ask me for more money."

• You are able to focus your primary fundraising energy on donors who are loyal to the organization, as opposed to donors who are loyal to a person in the organization or to an event.

STAYING IN TOUCH WITH DONORS

In times of economic downturn or world instability, loyal donors are not only the bread and butter but also the lifeblood, to mix metaphors, of an organization. Whatever work you can do to build their identification with your organization is critical. Matching strategies of asking with types of donors, as described in this chapter, is one way to help build loyalty.

Of course asking for money, even in a way the donor responds to, cannot be the only way you are in touch with donors. You need to make sure you are telling the donors what you do and helping them be ambassadors of your work with their friends. Examine all the ways you are in touch with your donors and put yourself in the donor's shoes. If all you knew about an organization was what donors receive, would you as a donor feel proud to be a member of this group? Puzzled? Excited? Would you have a sense of the consistency of your organization's work or would it seem scattered?

For example, for three months in a row an e-newsletter from an organization that works with students in the public schools has featured pictures of young people in political demonstrations. The captions require knowledge that is not provided in the newsletter: "Elkmont High School Students Protest HR 2233," "Lakeshore Middle School Students Protest Harris Firing," and "Monument Parents Upset Over Locker Room Decision." One has the impression that this organization works primarily through protests and walkouts around issues that are not common knowledge. Moreover, its thank you notes are generated by computer and merely state, "Thank you so much for your gift of $___. It helps us do our important work improving public education." Although a handful of major donors are sent additional information, mostly because they are also serving in some volunteer capacity, what donors read in the e-newsletter is all most of them know about the organization's work. When it conducts a small survey of donors, the organization is surprised that no one knows about its tutoring program, or that it is sending ten students to internships in Washington, D.C. These are also exciting program activities that lend themselves to photographs and show much more of the range of the organization's work.

The organization rethinks its communications so that each e-newsletter features an in-depth story on one program area and smaller updates on other programs. The thank you notes are changed so that they also contain a one-paragraph description of one aspect of the work. Not surprisingly, more donations flow in and donors add notes to their reply devices, such as, "Great story about the interns—what a wonderful opportunity for those students."

Read a year's worth of communication sent to your donors and see what you would know and not know about your work if that was all you got. You will quickly spot problems and be able to fix them. Further, see if you can add any personalization to your thank you notes or contact donors with an occasional letter or phone call to show more personal appreciation of their efforts. A letter that begins, "This is the fifth year you have helped us. Let me tell you some things your gifts have helped make possible over the past five years" is a relatively easy letter to create when seeking renewals.

We appreciate all gifts and all motives for giving. But our best chance of getting a donation year in and year out is by building a relationship with the donor—a relationship that goes beyond any of the people in the organization. Segmenting, then deciding how to treat each segment of the donor list, is an easy and important step in building and keeping a broad donor base.

chapter TWENTY

Setting Up and Maintaining Monthly Donor Pledge Programs

Getting donors to make a gift large enough that they need to divide the payments over a period of time in order to fulfill it, or to commit to giving a certain amount of money frequently, is probably the oldest and most institutionalized form of thoughtful giving, and is traditionally called "pledging." Pledging is found in almost every religious tradition in the practice of tithing, in which a person pledges a certain amount of income, usually 10 percent, to his or her house of worship. Since few can afford to give the entire 10 percent at once (if they could, they should be giving more), most donors give the amount promised over some period of time. In an annual giving program, they give it over the course of a year, usually in monthly or quarterly payments; in a capital campaign, a pledge may stretch over as many as five years.

In fundraising, the word *pledging* has come to have two different meanings, which creates some confusion. People solicit pledges from friends and family for participating in "thons": a certain amount pledged for every mile they will walk, bike, or run, for example, or every book they will read or bird they will sight. In that meaning, the person seeking the "pledge" will be getting one-time donations from as many people as possible. Public radio and television stations also hold "pledge week" drives in which they exhort listeners to become members, which is really another form of a membership drive.

For clarity, then, this chapter refers to a strategy of an organization seeking to convert a number of current donors to giving on a regular basis—monthly or quarterly, or seeking to have some donors start their giving with a monthly pledge. Monthly giving is very popular in Canada and Australia; some of the most creative pledge campaigns come from those countries. Online giving and the option of giving by credit card or direct debit have made monthly donor programs easier and cheaper to initiate and maintain than when pledges were both sought and had to be collected by mail. A monthly donor program allows an organization to have a steady cash flow, and many organizations seek to have their core operating costs covered by the income from such a program.

A pledge is a legally binding contract in which a donor commits a certain amount of money and then fulfills the commitment with regular payments. Although few organizations would sue a donor who did not fulfill her or his pledge, it is important for donors to understand that this is a serious commitment and, under accounting law, the organization must count pledges as accounts receivable.

To summarize, there are two great advantages of a pledge program to an organization: first, by spreading payments over time, donors giving from income (which are most donors) can give more than they could give all at once, and second, a well-run pledge program means reliable monthly income.

There are also clear advantages for the donor. People who are committed to an organization can express that commitment with a bigger gift by pledging than they could with a one-time donation. Many working people who could not give $300 all at once could afford $25 a month. Further, people who give $100, $500, or even $1,000 in one-time gifts may be able to repeat that gift four times a year or even every month. Certainly, donors can't make this kind of commitment to every organization, but they can and will make it to their favorite organization if the mechanism is in place for that organization to ask them.

Converting people from making one or two gifts a year to giving monthly is the simplest strategy with which to start the upgrading process. You will have the pleasant surprise of seeing some people increase their giving by 400 percent—or even 1,200 percent—as they go from giving $25 a year to giving that much every quarter or every month. Further, renewal rates for people who pledge are higher than for regular donors, particularly if those pledging are giving by credit card or direct debit, which will continue until the card expires or the donor instructs the bank to stop the payments. Finally, donors who pledge are more likely to include your organization in their will; in fact, introducing a pledge program is often the first step in introducing a legacy giving program.

INTRODUCING A MONTHLY DONOR PROGRAM

Once an organization decides to institute a monthly donor program, it needs to introduce it in all its fundraising materials. First, send a special appeal to your current donors asking them to consider becoming a monthly donor. In the appeal letter, explain that the reader is a valuable supporter and that your organization wants to give him or her an opportunity to give more in a way that is comfortable for them. Explain how helpful it is to your organization to have a known amount of money coming in every month and what kind of work you can do with these extra funds.

Second, use a small amount of space in your newsletter to discuss your monthly donor program. Third, include monthly donor information on all your return forms as one of the choices. Fourth, consider doing an e-mail campaign, as discussed in Chapter Fourteen, with the focus on monthly pledging.

Make it as easy as possible for people to pledge by allowing them to put their pledge on a credit card or to fulfill it through direct debit from their bank account. Make it possible for them to sign up for a pledge program while making a donation online. Your organization will have between 90 and 95 percent collection success with these methods, and, to stop giving, the donor has to take action. This is what makes monthly donor programs successful: unlike other kinds of appeals in which the donor has to choose each time to give, with credit card or direct debit payments, the donor has to choose not to give.

Organizations sometimes find it helpful to provide incentives for becoming a monthly donor by creating a special category for these donors, such as a "Sustainer Council" or "Stability Club." People who pledge can also be given a benefit not available to other donors and can be listed in a special category in newsletters and annual reports.

MARKETING A MONTHLY DONOR PROGRAM

A catchy name for your pledge program is fine, but donors respond mostly to the needs your organization is set up to meet. As with other giving appeals, allowing donors to see exactly where their donations go can spur them to sign up. For example:

$25 a month provides food and water to 40 refugees.

$50 a month provides ten students with free tutoring to help them meet their goal of graduating from high school.

Describing what you do in terms of small amounts of money spent each month also educates your donors in a different way about your programs.

In addition to having information about your pledge program in all your materials, talk about it once or twice a year in your organization's blog and profile a monthly donor from time to time in your newsletter and on your Web site donation page.

The people most likely to respond to an invitation to become monthly donors are donors who are now giving in the $100–$1,000 range and who have done so for a few years. These are people who clearly like what you do. Write a personal letter to each of them asking if they would consider giving monthly and follow up with a phone call. The letter might look something like the sample shown here.

Dear Nora,

You have been helping us for the past five years with $50 sent several times a year. I hope you know how much we appreciate your generosity. Your gifts have made possible such recent accomplishments as the following:

- *Accomplishment*

- *Another accomplishment*

However, even though we know our program is effective, we also know that the need for what we do is growing daily and we are not able to keep up. So we are asking all longtime loyal donors like you to consider stretching their giving by signing up for our "Say Yes to Everyone" circle.

Here's how it works: you make a monthly commitment to our organization, such as $50 or $100 or whatever feels good to you. This amount then becomes an ongoing charge on your credit or debit card or it can be taken directly from your bank account each month. If you would rather pay by check, we can send you monthly reminders with return envelopes.

If 200 of our longtime donors become monthly donors, we will be able to raise an additional $100,000 annually. That amount of money would allow us to say yes to everyone who needs our services.

I realize that signing up to become a monthly donor would represent a much larger gift for you, and I don't expect you to decide on the basis of this letter alone. I will call you in a few days to discuss it further.

I look forward to speaking with you.

Thank you for all you do for our organization,

Constance Volunteer

Just as in a major donor campaign, the letter is followed by a phone call to discuss the gift further. Be clear in your call that you know some donors will be able to say yes to this request and that others are already giving as much as they can. You do not want to give the impression that a $100 or $200 a year gift is not enough!

Another way to advertise your monthly donor program is by putting the letter in the form of a testimonial. While the letter is very much the same, the voice is more personal: "In thinking about my own giving to Good Works Organization, I realized I could not afford to give $1,200 a year all at once. But with a little planning and fewer double espressos at the coffee bar, I realized I could give $100 a month. I am really pleased that I have been able to stretch my giving in this way, as I know it makes a huge difference in the work Good Group is able to accomplish. Will you join me? Here is how it works:" and so on.

COLLECTING MONTHLY DONATIONS

Many sustainer programs have failed because the organization did not put time into collecting the pledged amounts or did not have a system in place to keep track of payments. Credit cards expire after a few years, or people cancel them if they have had problems with identify theft. In establishing a new card, the donor may forget that he or she had a recurring gift to your organization, and you will need to call and ask for a new number.

If you also have a paper system for collecting pledges (an option I recommend offering for donors who would prefer to give by check), you must have good systems in place. I have pledged to more than a dozen organizations over the years; with some of them I made one or two payments, then forgot about my pledge. Most of those organizations failed to remind me of my pledge or reminded me in such a sporadic way that my pledge was paid sporadically. In one case, after being asked to pledge $25 a month to an organization that I found appealing but knew little about, and after making payments for a few months, I received a letter from the organization asking if I could either transfer my pledge to a credit card or pay the rest of my pledge in one payment because they "found the process of depositing so many checks every month too time consuming." Since the reason I had committed to give a certain amount every month was to be able to make a larger gift than I could at one time, I found their request lacking in an understanding of the purposes of a pledge program. Further, I found my feelings a little hurt by the implication that losers like me were taking up so much of the organization's valuable time with our endless donations. As a result, I stopped giving altogether. Perhaps not surprising, I never heard from the organization again.

KEEPING TRACK OF PLEDGES

It is easy to keep track of pledges in your fundraising database. Most databases have fields built in to record pledges and to make sending reminders simple, or you can buy a module specifically designed for managing a monthly donor program. If your database does not have this feature already or you do not want to add another component to your computer systems, set up fields in your existing database to record pledges and the payment due dates. As payments are made, record them. For people paying by check, send a reminder each month or quarter so that it arrives right before the first of the month, when most people are paid. If people are billed regularly on this timetable, you will have the smallest number of dropouts. Send a form such as the one shown here, sized to fit the stamped return envelope that accompanies it. The forms can be generated right from the database or they can be filled in by hand. Make sure to note how much has been paid and how much is still owing.

Sample Pledge Reminder Form

Organization Name and Address

Date

Dear *Donor Name,*

Your monthly (quarterly) pledge of $_____ is now due.

Please remit in the enclosed envelope. We are very grateful for your ongoing support and for your commitment to our work.

Director or other
staff name

Total amount pledged $_____
Total amount paid to date $_____
Make checks payable to: Your organization, address
Your gift is tax deductible to the full extent of the law.

Most nonprofits find that they collect between 80 and 85 percent of pledges that require the kind of billing described here. If a person has been reminded three times without paying, assume that he or she is not going to fulfill the pledge. Some nonprofits have found it helpful to call the donor to see if there is a problem that the organization can rectify. Usually it has nothing to do with the organization, but instead that the donor's financial situation has changed for the worse or that the donor didn't realize what a difficult commitment his pledge would be for him. Don't hound people for payment. Simply roll them back into the regular donor program.

At the end of the year, send a personal letter with the final pledge note asking the donor to renew his or her pledge. Include a renewal form. The letter can be simple and straightforward, such as the example here.

Dear_____,

This is the last payment on your pledge of $250. Your ongoing support has been tremendously important to us this past year. We have been able to use the extra funds provided by our Sustainer Council to do _____ and _____. Thank you very much for your commitment.

I hope that you will renew your pledge. We will continue to send you reminders, and you will receive *(name a benefit here)*, available only to people who pledge. I enclose a form for you to fill out. Thank you again for all your support.

Sincerely,
Director or Board Chair

TWO DON'TS OF PLEDGE PROGRAMS

There are two warnings to heed in setting up a monthly donor program.

First, don't set up any pledge program unless you are confident that your record-keeping and accounting systems are adequate to handle it. You want to be particularly thorough in handling direct debit and credit card collections, as banks have long and unforgiving memories. Ask board members and other volunteers to be the first to give using a credit card or direct debit so you can work out any glitches in your system, then move on to your donor base. Organizations often find that they upgrade their own infrastructure as they upgrade their systems to handle more sophisticated ways of interacting with donors. In that way, they not only raise more money but also run more efficiently and effectively overall.

Second, be sure to keep in touch with your monthly donors just as you do with your major donors. I have heard many monthly donors complain that once they signed up, they never heard from the organization again. Thank you notes, personal notes, and calls are very important to this segment of donors. Don't take these people for granted—they can be your bread and butter and are often your most stable and loyal donors.

Building Major Gifts Programs

The financial payoff for all fundraising is receiving large gifts from some of your donors. To build a major donor program, no matter the size of the organization, a majority of staff, board, and volunteers must feel comfortable asking people for money in person (see Chapter Six, "Getting Comfortable with Asking for Money"). For many people, that comfort starts with being able to ask someone for $20 for a ticket to a benefit event such as a dance or for $35 to become a member.

Some people never move past that level of comfort, but if an organization is to grow and thrive, a critical mass of board, volunteers, and staff must be able to ask for much larger gifts—$500, $5,000, $50,000, and even more.

A person doesn't have to like asking for money to be able to do it. Some of the most successful fundraisers I have known have confessed that they always feel anxious when asking for money. But they do it anyway, and sometimes their nervousness makes them prepare more thoroughly for the solicitation and feel even better about themselves and their group after they complete it.

Once an organization is in the habit of asking for large gifts, it quickly moves to needing a more systematic plan for soliciting such gifts. That system is a major gifts program. Some groups prefer to do their major donor fundraising in the form of a campaign; major gifts campaigns are discussed in Chapter Twenty-Three.

Before beginning a major gifts program, your organization must make a number of decisions: how much money it wishes to raise from large gifts, the minimum amount that will constitute a major gift (in this book it is $250), how many gifts of what size are needed. In addition, you must decide what, if any, tangible benefits donors will receive for their gifts and what materials will be needed for the solicitors. Finally, a core group of volunteers must be trained to ask for the gifts.

GETTING OVER MY OWN FEAR OF ASKING

Over the thirty-five years I have been in fundraising, I have been privileged to ask a few thousand people for gifts of all sizes, including three requests for $1,000,000. (Of those three, one person gave the whole amount, one gave $300,000, and one told me she would rather fall face first in her own vomit than give our organization money, but that's a long story.) My feelings about asking have evolved from "Do I have to?" to "This is exciting." To this day, sometimes I think, "Do I have to?" or "Can't someone else take a turn?"

Even though I tell people not to take rejection personally, I have to admit that on bad days I sometimes do take it personally, and I have to work to let it go. In my experience, no one ever arrives at a place of total peace with asking, but with familiarity, we have more of those peaceful times and fewer times of anxiety, frustration, and maybe even resentment at having to do this work.

Often my feelings of peace are enhanced by euphoria at being told, "Yes, I'll do it" or gratitude at someone's extraordinary generosity or pride in the accomplishments of the organization. Some donors make it easy to ask because they are so moved by the work or are warm, caring people. Sometimes I am just flooded with relief—the donor said yes right away, or the donor wasn't at work when I called!

Feelings are not facts. They come and go, and they are often not very logical. I have found the best way to be the most comfortable with asking is to feel confident that I have made a significant gift, not just of my time but also of my own money, before asking for a major gift. When I know I am asking a prospect to join me by making his or her own gift, I stand on firm ground.

SETTING A GOAL

The first step in seeking major gifts is to decide how much money you want to raise from major donors. This amount will be related to the overall amount you want to raise from all your individual donors and can be partly determined on the basis of the following information. (For more on goal setting, see Chapter Thirty-Nine, "Creating a Fundraising Plan.")

Over the years fundraisers have observed the following pattern of how gifts come into organizations:

- About 60 percent of the income comes from 10 percent of the donors.
- About 20 percent of the income comes from 20 percent of the donors.
- About 20 percent of the income comes from 70 percent of the donors.

In other words, the majority of your gifts will be small, but the bulk of your income will come from a few large donations. Given that pattern, it is possible to project for any fundraising goal how many gifts of each size you should seek and how many prospects you will need to ask to get each gift.

For example, if your organization must raise $50,000 from grassroots fundraising, you should plan to raise $30,000 (60 percent) from major gifts, mostly solicited personally; $10,000 (20 percent) from habitual donors, mostly solicited through phone, mail or e-mail, and regular special events; and $10,000 from people giving for the first or second time, solicited from mail and online appeals, speaking engagements, special events, product sales, and the like.

If you have 500 donors, then, expect that about 50 of them will be major donors, 100-plus of them will be habitual donors, and about 350 will be first- or second-time donors or donors who only give to your special event or in response to a friend who is on staff and for whom your organization is not a high priority. The lowest major gift you request should be an amount that is higher than most of your donors give but one that most employed people can afford, especially if allowed to pledge. Even many low-income people can afford $20–25 a month, which brings being a major donor into the realm of possibility for all people close to your group.

Some organizations try to avoid setting goals. Their feeling is that they will raise as much as they can from as many people as they can. This doesn't work. Prospects are going to ask how much you need; if this answer is, "As much as we can get," your agency will not sound very well run. If prospects think you will simply spend whatever they give you, they will give less than they can afford or nothing. Further, without a goal there is no way to measure how well the organization is doing compared to its plans. Just as you wouldn't instruct a builder to build a house that will be "as big as it needs to be" or "as big as we can afford," you can't build a donor base with vague or meaningless assertions.

APPORTIONMENT OF GIFTS

It would be great if you could say, "Well, we need $40,000 from 10 percent of our donors, so that will mean two hundred people giving $200 each." But two hundred people will not all behave the same way—some will give more, most will give less. Given this reality, fundraisers have made a second observation: for the money needed annually from individual donors, you need one gift equal to 10 percent or more of the goal, two gifts equal to 10 percent (5 percent each) or more of the goal, and four to six gifts providing the next 10 percent of the goal. The remaining gifts needed are determined in decreasing size of gift with increasing numbers of gifts. Using this formula, you can create what is called a Gift Range Chart or a Gift Pyramid.

Gift Range Chart			
Goal: $100,000			
	Number of Gifts	**Size of Gifts**	**Total**
Major gifts	1	$10,000	$10,000
	2	$5,000	$10,000
	5	$2,500	$12,500
	10	$1,000	$10,000
	20	$500	$10,000
	30	$250	$7,500
Total	68 gifts	$250–$10,000	$60,000 (60 percent of total)
Other gifts	100	$100	$10,000
	150	$50–$75	10,000
Total	250 gifts	$50–$100	$20,000 (20 percent of total)
Remaining gifts	Many	$5–$99	$20,000 (20 percent of total)

Let's imagine an organization that needs to raise $100,000 from a wide variety of individual donor strategies. Using the pattern just outlined, $60,000 will be raised from major gifts. Their gift range chart will look something like the example shown here.

The most important and useful part of the chart is the top part, which plots sizes and number of major gifts, but the chart should not be seen as a blueprint. If an organization has one donor who can give 15 percent of the goal, then ask for that; in that case you will need fewer gifts at the lower end of the chart. An organization in a rural community may not be able to generate the number of gifts needed, so it will have to get fewer gifts at larger sizes.

The chart serves as a guideline and a reality check. For example, if your goal is to raise $100,000, but the biggest gift you can imagine getting is $500, then you will probably have to lower your goal. The chart is also helpful for board members and other volunteer solicitors who may have difficulty imagining raising $100,000 but can imagine thirty people giving $250 each.

HOW MANY PEOPLE TO ASK

Every fundraising strategy, presuming it is done properly, has an expected rate of response. For major gifts, the expected response rate is that 50 percent of prospects will say yes to making a gift when the gift is requested by someone who knows the potential donor, knows that that prospect believes in the cause, and feels reasonably certain that the prospect could give the amount of money being asked. However, if the prospect does say yes, there is a further 50 percent chance that he or she will give less than the amount requested.

With this understanding, for every gift you seek through personal solicitation, particularly at the upper reaches of the chart, you will need at least four prospects—two will say yes and two will say no. Of the two who say yes, one will give a lesser amount than requested. Because the prospects for higher gifts who say yes, but give less than asked for, help fill in the number of gifts needed in the middle and bottom ranges of the chart, you will need only two or three new prospects for every gift needed in those ranges. Overall, look for about three times as many prospects as gifts needed. For the $100,000 goal, then, the top portion of the chart would be expanded to include numbers of prospects, as in the following chart.

Major Donor Gift Range Chart and Prospects				
Goal: $60,000				
	Number of Gifts	**Size of Gifts**	**Total**	**Number of Prospects**
Major gifts	1	$10,000	$10,000	4
	2	$5,000	$10,000	(X4) 8
	5	$2,500	$12,500	(X4) 20
	10	$1,000	$10,000	(X4) 40
	20	$500	$10,000	(X3) 60
	30	$250	$7,500	(X3) 90
Total	68		$60,000	About 222

In other words, when your group asks four qualified people for $10,000, two will say no, one will give $10,000, and one will give less than $10,000. As you go down the pyramid, you are filling in the next layer with the smaller gifts from the higher layer, so you don't need to identify quite as many prospects for the gifts you need in the lower layers of the chart and you don't need four times as many actual prospects as donors.

MATERIALS FOR MAJOR GIFT SOLICITATION

In addition to the gift range chart and a list of prospects, three more elements need to be in place before your organization can begin to solicit major gifts: what, if any, benefits you will give to major donors that are not available to other donors; materials that describe your work and how to make donations; and people to solicit the gifts.

Benefits

While helping the organization is the main satisfaction for the donor, an added incentive, particularly one that doesn't actually cost you very much such as free tickets to a special event your organization is hosting, a mug, or a book related to your work, will show that you appreciate the extra effort the donor is making and will remind the donor of his or her gift to your organization.

There is no evidence that one kind of benefit works better than another, and there is some evidence that donors prefer more personal attention and more information about your organization than tangible benefits (see also the discussion of benefits in Chapter Eleven). Certainly, the benefit should not be very expensive. Under IRS law, any value of a benefit that exceeds the vague criterion of "token" is not eligible for the same tax deduction as the rest of the gift. For example, if someone gives $500 to an organization and receives an etching worth $50, the donor can only claim $450 of this gift on their tax return because $50 is more than a token amount. If the same group gave a T-shirt or tote bag worth little or nothing on the open market, the donor could claim the whole $500 as a tax deduction. The IRS is increasingly questioning expensive benefits for donors.

The benefit should be easy to deliver, which is why many groups use T-shirts or books as benefits. Because of the number of items people can commonly get for their gifts to public television, public radio, or major national organizations, a small organization should probably offer something that is related to its programs. For example, an organization working for stricter controls on and alternatives to the commercial use of pesticides sends its major donors a short booklet on alternatives to pesticides for home gardens and indoor plants. An after-school program for inner-city children aged eight to eleven asked the teachers to save drawings the children made that they didn't want to take home. The organization sent the best of that art along with its thank you notes to donors. This benefit is truly of token value, but it is very popular with donors. Now the organization has one day on which the children are asked to make "thank you" drawings. A public policy think tank has a once-a-month "briefing call" that donors can call in to. The policy director gives a short update on the policy issues the organization is working on, discusses pros and cons of different positions, and invites questions and comments. This is popular with some major donors and also gives the staff an early sign of what questions and comments a friendly audience might have about a particular policy position.

A major donor program can be run successfully without giving any benefits beyond what are offered to all donors, such as the newsletter. This approach will only work if the donors are thanked personally and promptly and if the organization keeps in touch with them using the ways recommended in the section on renewing major gifts later in this chapter. Personal attention and information on what work the organization was able to do as a result of the donor's gift will always be the most effective benefits for maintaining and upgrading your donors' giving.

Descriptive Materials

Materials that describe your program are the second element needed for soliciting major donations. An organization should have a well-designed, easy-to-understand brochure. It does not have to be elaborate or printed in several colors, but it should be professionally laid out, well written, and free of grammatical and typographical errors. It should contain information that is similar to that found on your Web site. Because this pamphlet will be used primarily in personal solicitation, it should focus on ways to make thoughtful gifts. For example, tell people how they can give online, how to make a monthly pledge, how to give by credit card, whether you are seeking gifts of stocks and bonds, and so on. The brochure does not need to explain everything—it can refer donors to your Web site or give them the option to request more information.

The brochure is essentially a published, though perhaps condensed, version of the information contained in your case statement (see Chapter Four). It also helps volunteer solicitors by giving them something to leave with a donor and to refer to if they forget some information they meant to impart. Return envelopes and return cards must be included with the brochure. This packet can be augmented by a sheet of frequently asked questions or one-page descriptions of specific programs. In all your materials, whether you leave them with the donor or encourage the donor to visit you online, make sure that information about how to give and choices about giving are completely clear.

Solicitors

Finally, you need to have a core group of people willing to do the soliciting. Some of these people should be members of the board of directors, but the board's work can be augmented by a group of volunteers. These people should be trained in the process of asking for money (see Chapters Six and Seven). They do not have to have previous experience in asking for major gifts, nor do they need to know many prospects personally. But they must be donors—ideally, major donors—themselves.

KEEPING IN TOUCH WITH MAJOR DONORS

One of the most frequent complaints from major donors is that organizations treat them like ATM machines—they punch in the amount they want and then walk away until they need money again. To keep donors interested in your group requires showing some interest in the donor, particularly some interest in why the donor is interested in your group. To give major donors this extra attention takes work, but it is work worth doing for several reasons: first, because it is courteous; second, because it brings donors closer to the work of your group, making them potential activists or advocates; and third, because it will bring in more money.

In addition to the time when you ask major donors to renew their gifts, you should be in contact with them two or three times a year. You will want to be in touch with some donors more often than that, depending partly on the size of their gift and mostly on their personality and expressed level of interest. Remember that major donors are a good source of feedback, advice, and volunteer energy, as well as a source of other major donors.

There are several easy ways to keep in touch that make major donors feel personally appreciated and that do not cost the organization much in time or money. You can choose from the suggestions here or develop your own system, but be sure to get a system in place.

Send a Holiday Card During December. The card should wish the donor happy holidays and be signed by the chair of the board, a board member with a personal relationship to the donor, or a staff person. If possible, write a brief note on the card. The card goes alone—no return envelope, no appeal letter. (You may also send major donors a year-end appeal in a separate mailing.) Unless your organization is religiously identified, make sure the card has no religious over-tones, including cultural Christian overtones such as Santa Claus, elves, or Christmas trees. The same applies to the postage stamp you choose.

Attach a Personal Note to Your Annual Report. All donors should receive a copy of your annual report. Those going to major donors should have a personal note attached. The note can be on a Post-It and does not have to be long. It says something like, "Thought you'd be interested in seeing this year's report since you have been so important to our success" or "I hope you are as proud of our work as we are—your gift helped make it possible." It doesn't matter if you don't know the donor—a personal note shows that they are appreciated. If you know that something in your report will be of particular interest, note that: "Paul, that program you asked about is featured on page five" or "Fran, check out the photo on the back inside cover." Staff usually write these notes, but again, board members with relationships to these donors can write them as well.

For smaller donors, it is acceptable to send a PDF of the annual report to them by e-mail. Note in your e-mail that a paper copy can be requested from the office. Note in your paper report that if someone wants a PDF version sent by e-mail, they can request that. If your report is interesting and easy to download, people will forward it to friends and colleagues. The paper copy may well grace the coffee table or magazine rack in the waiting room of an office. The annual report is a very important piece of communication. Even the smallest nonprofit should budget some money so that the report looks attractive, has some photos, and is well written and laid out.

Report Successes During the Year.   If you have positive press coverage, if you win a victory in your organizing or litigation efforts, if you are commended by a community group, service club, or politician, take the opportunity to send a special letter to major donors telling them of the event. If possible, include a copy of the article or commendation. This letter does not have to be personalized.

Note a Donor's Accomplishments.   If you learn that someone graduated from college, won an award, or had a baby, send a card. Don't spend a lot of time trying to learn this kind of information, but pay attention and respond when the information comes your way. Although not an accomplishment, if you know a donor's birthday, you can send a card then, too. If you have your donor's e-mail address (and you should), you can send e-cards to save postage.

Include Brief Personal Notes with All Mailings.   You can include a brief note with anything major donors will be getting anyway, such as invitations to special events or announcements of meetings.

Include Major Donors in Some General Mailings.   Although you will not send major donors all the requests for extra gifts that are sent to the rest of your donor base, when a mail appeal is particularly timely or concerns a specific issue that will be interesting to them, include major donors in the mailing. You can always put a Post-It on the mailing that says, "This is just FYI." Ditto for e-appeals: the subject line for major donors can be "Just FYI."

Send a Quick E-Mail.   You will be in touch with many of your major donors by e-mail, particularly if you have an e-newsletter. From time to time, drop them a brief e-mail note or forward something that you think they will be interested in seeing.

By keeping in touch with your major donors, you will lay the groundwork necessary to approach them for a renewal of their gift in the second year they give and a request to increase the size of their gift the third year of their giving. Even if no one in your organization has ever met this major donor and their gift came unsolicited, through personal notes and letters you will begin to build a rapport that will enhance the interaction when you meet the person in the future.

RENEWING MAJOR DONOR GIFTS

The process for approaching major donors to renew their gifts will vary depending on the amount they have given. This section describes how to ask for renewals of various size gifts.

Gifts of $250 to $499

Near the anniversary of the donor's gift, send a letter asking him to give again. The letter should be personalized, with a handwritten note added as a postscript. In the letter, describe the highlights of the year just passed and attribute some of that success to the donor's gift. Wherever possible, use stories to illustrate your work rather than simply narrating one dry fact after another. One paragraph should be devoted to the needs of the coming year. The next paragraph asks the donor to renew his gift. The letter should ask for the same size gift as the donor gave the previous year, which both reminds the donor of the amount of his last gift and shows that your organization keeps careful records. Include a reply card and a stamped return envelope marked to the attention of the person signing the letter. The reply card always notes that giving online is an option and carries the organization's Web site URL.

An alternative to the letter is a personal e-mail, but only use e-mail if you know the donor prefers it. Most people feel they get too much e-mail, and it is harder to personalize e-mail than snail mail.

Gifts of $500 to $999

Use the format for gifts up to $500, but follow your letter or e-mail with a phone call within ten days. In the letter, let the donor know you are going to call.

The phone call will go something like this:

"May, this is June calling to follow up on my letter."

"Yes, June. It's lovely of you to call. I've already sent in my check—and congratulations on your good work."

June can then thank May for renewing her gift and ask if she has any other questions or tell her something that wasn't in the letter (but be brief!). The whole interaction will not take more than five minutes unless May has some questions. June will very likely get May's voice mail, and her message will be essentially the same, "May, this is June calling to follow up on my e-mail. I just wanted to thank you again for your support last year, and ask you to consider giving again this year. I will try you again on Wednesday."

After two attempts, return to e-mail and say, "Dear May, Would love to talk with you about our work, but I know you are really busy. Do you have any ten-minute windows in the next day or two?"

Many times these interactions will be completed by e-mail, with May responding, "I am drowning in work, but want to help. Remind me in a month." If used well, e-mail is a great boon to donor solicitation.

Gifts of $1,000 or More

Send a much briefer letter telling the donor you would like to visit with him or her and that you will phone to set up a time. If you are simply asking for a renewal, the telephone request for a meeting will often go like this:

"Frank, this is Earnest. Did you get my letter?"

"Yes, it came yesterday."

"Great. Can we get together sometime to talk about the possibility of you renewing your gift?"

"You don't need to visit me for that. I'll be happy to renew."

In this exchange, even though he is planning to renew his gift, Frank may still feel pleased that he was given this attention; again, the interaction is very brief. If Frank does want to meet, he will be drawn even closer to the organization and you will have a chance to see how your group appears to someone who is thoughtful about how much money to give you.

Some major donors, particularly those who live far away from the organization, are willing to accept and even prefer e-mail to phone follow-up. You will still send a letter the old-fashioned way and offer to call or call and meet, but you can add a note to your letter that says, "Feel free to e-mail me at jill@goodgroup.org if that is easier for you." Be sure to note the content of your e-mail correspondence in your database and note on the donor's record if he likes to use e-mail.

When to Ask for More

Two questions often arise: How many times should you ask donors to renew their gift at the same amount before asking for an upgrade? And similarly, once the gift is upgraded, what is the appropriate amount of time to wait before asking for another upgrade? The answer to both questions is simple: know your donor. The sooner you meet the donor and learn more about her, the sooner you will have a sense of whether she likes to be visited, whether she is giving to her capacity and cannot give more right now, whether she would rather make up her own mind about when and how to increase her gift, and so on.

Of course, you can't know all your major donors right away, and some you may never meet. When you don't know, follow this formula: get the gift, the following year ask for a renewal, the third year ask for an upgrade. If you receive a larger gift after asking for an upgrade, ask for a renewal of that gift the following year and the next year ask for a gift that is larger by one-third. Then repeat the cycle: for a couple of years ask for a renewal and then another upgrade, and so on. If the donor stays at the same level, keep asking for more unless you get information that the donor is giving as much as he or she can afford.

In addition to this formula, use common sense. If someone gives you $5,000, you may need to ask for a renewal for several years before asking for more. If someone gives you $250, then ask them to double their gift. On the other hand, think twice before asking someone giving $10,000 to double. You can always add the phrase "or more" onto any request you make if you really don't know how much more to ask for.

Of course, your organization must be able to justify needing more money, and that need must be expressed to the donor in a compelling way by putting it into programmatic terms. Hiring another staff person, for example, is not compelling; serving twenty more children (what the additional staff person is needed for) is.

THE HARDEST YEAR

In planning to add a major gifts component to your fundraising, keep in mind that the first year of recruiting major donors may be the hardest. Do not set your goals too high; you don't want volunteers to be demoralized by failing to reach an unrealistic goal. Major gifts solicitation can be done in the form of a campaign— that is, with a formal beginning and ending time, specific materials, and a special committee, as described in Chapter Twenty-Three, or it can be an ongoing program, with different volunteers helping at different times.

The most important step to take in a major gifts program is to start. Even if you have only one prospect, ask that prospect. If the largest gift you can imagine someone giving is $250, start by asking for $250. A major gifts program builds on itself; simply establishing the groundwork for the program will begin the process of getting major gifts.

Legacy Giving

The term *legacy giving* (also called *planned giving*) refers to arrangements made for a nonprofit to receive contributions from the estate of a donor. These gifts in general are made by longtime donors who believe the work the organization does must continue after their own lives are over, and, more important, who have faith that the organization will continue to do a good job for years and years to come. These are not necessarily major donors; many bequests come from donors who have given small amounts to an organization for a long time. When I look around at board meetings I attend, I often reflect that in fifty years (which is really very little time), people who aren't even born yet will be running the organization. I will be deceased. What would I need to know about this organization to trust that it will continue to attract people to its board and staff (people who don't exist yet) who will continue to do good and needed work? Whatever information creates that confidence is fundamental to getting donors to consider legacy gifts.

Some organizations use legacy gifts for annual expenses, but because the gift is not repeatable, this practice is unwise. A more appropriate use is for capital improvements. Most nonprofits use legacy gifts to build endowments. An endowment is a permanently restricted fund invested to generate interest. The principal, or corpus, is never spent but is added to as more legacy gifts come in. The interest income can be used as the organization wishes, unless the donor has created terms restricting how the gift can be used. Interest income is usually used to offset general operating costs, as these are the most difficult to raise money for. In Chapter Twenty-Four, I discuss endowments in more detail.

GETTING READY FOR A LEGACY GIVING PROGRAM

Many organizations think that getting ready for a legacy giving program involves going to seminars and memorizing complicated financial planning language, then identifying the organization's oldest donors, explaining to them what you have learned, and watching them sign on the dotted line before they totter off into the sunset. In fact, before anyone in the organization begins learning about legacy gifts, a number of things have to be in place.

First, it is critical that your organization discusses and agrees on the need to exist far into the future and comes to grips with what that means for your overall mission. Second, in addition to deciding how far into the future your organization needs to exist, you need to look at whether people trust you to do your work now and whether, in general, they understand your need for money. Does your nonprofit have a good reputation—not just for work accomplished, but for stewarding resources, handling money responsibly, and raising money with integrity? Although many grassroots organizations could answer yes to all these questions, they may be surprised at the extent to which their donors have no sense of how their group deals with money. If you never have an audit, if you don't include financial information on your Web site, if you don't publish the names of your donors from time to time, and if you don't regularly talk about how you raise money, your donors may have never thought much about your financial needs. For example, if someone asks where the local humane society or college or symphony orchestra gets its money, many people would answer that these institutions get a lot of money from individuals and bequests. Because of that, as people write their wills, many think of leaving some of their estate to the humane society or their alma mater or local arts organization. You can start a legacy giving program without people being aware of how your organization raises and spends money, but it will not go very far until that information is more commonly known.

Third, and closely related to the previous point, you need a donor base that includes people who have given your organization money for several years and who think of your organization as one they will support as long as they can. Many organizations need to develop their donor base before they begin a legacy giving program—not just in terms of numbers of donors, but also in terms of donors giving year after year.

If one or more of these elements are not in place, skip this chapter and re-read the preceding chapters. Do what is recommended in those chapters and you will be ready to come back to legacy giving in a year or two.

PREPARING TO TALK ABOUT LEGACY GIVING

Many organizations that have the donor base in place to start a legacy giving program hesitate to do so because of the almost universal taboo about talking about death: not only do people feel awkward talking to anyone about their death, they feel doubly awkward raising the subjects of money and death at the same time. Such a discussion may seem not only in bad taste but intrusive. However, it is important to remember that in the United States, bequests, which are the most common form of legacy giving, account for nearly 10 percent of all the money given to nonprofits. In fact, the money given from bequests in most years is equal to the money given by foundations and always surpasses the money given by corporations. (An old joke in fundraising is that dead people give away more money than corporations.) If you want people to think of your organization when they are drawing up their estate plans, you will have to ask them in one way or another.

When you ask someone for a bequest you are not asking them to die—as inevitable as that will be for us all. You are instead making a statement about your organization and its need, complimenting the donor on her or his commitment to your cause, and giving her or him another opportunity to act on that commitment.

THE IMPORTANCE OF A WILL

To give you a sense of the market, more than half of all people in the United States die without a will. Of those who make wills, only about 7 percent include gifts to nonprofits in their last wishes. Even among very wealthy people, for whom a gift from their estate would lower the estate tax for their inheritors, only 18 percent include any gifts to nonprofits. Nonetheless, the vast majority of legacy gifts, regardless of size, are bequests. Fully four out of five planned gifts are made this way, so for many organizations, particularly grassroots ones, establishing a solid bequest program is as far into legacy giving as they will ever need to go.

The terms of almost all legacy gifts, even very complicated ones, are laid out in a will.

Everyone should have a will because no one knows when they are going to die and because everything you own (and owe) during your lifetime you also own (and owe) after your death. You have the authority to direct what happens to your property after you have died, but if you choose not to make a will the state will make that direction for you. Introducing your donors to legacy giving is thus a service to them because it causes them to think about making or updating their wills. Your nonprofit may get some money as a result, but the main service is that making a will protects the donor's family and other interests.

If a person dies without a will (called "dying intestate"), the law specifies who will receive the estate, as follows:

- If the person is survived by a spouse and not survived by a child or parent, the spouse receives all their property.

- If a person is survived by a spouse and a parent and not a child, the spouse and parent share the property.

- If a person is survived by a spouse, child, and a parent, the spouse and child share the property; the parent receives nothing.

- If a person is not survived by a spouse or a child or a parent, then the person's brothers and sisters and the children of any deceased brothers and sisters share the person's property.

MOTIVATING DONORS TO MAKE A WILL

In most grassroots organizations that have middle-class, working-class, and low-income donors, the first step in a legacy giving program is motivating donors to make a will. The second step will then be to encourage them to name the organization as one of their beneficiaries. A few case studies about what happens to people who don't have wills motivates most donors to create one. Names have been changed in the two examples presented here, but they are true stories.

Most people underestimate the worth of their estate and overestimate the time or cost involved in setting up a will. They do not realize that when there is no will, whoever ends up dealing with someone's estate can be in for a tremendous amount of work. Finally, aside from the distribution of property, a will can carry

THE IMPORTANCE OF A WILL

Mary Springhill, age fifty, died of breast cancer. She had no children and her parents were deceased. She was separated but not divorced from her husband. Mary was a fairly successful artist, and her estate, including a house, a new car, and some savings, was worth a little more than $400,000. Mary had never gotten around to writing a will; during the time she had cancer, she was too sick to think about preparing one. Mary had left her husband three years prior to her death, after enduring his physical and emotional abuse for fifteen years. Now, as the surviving spouse and sole heir, he is the beneficiary of her entire estate.

Fay and Marianna were lovers for five years. Fay had inherited an apartment building and a handsome stock portfolio from her father. She and Marianna lived in a home Fay had bought before they got together. They were planning to add Marianna's name to the title of the house, as well as to create wills, when Fay was killed in an auto accident with a drunk driver. Because Fay had no will, her parents became her legal heirs. They had never approved of Fay's relationship with Marianna. After Fay's death, they evicted Marianna from her house and told her that she would receive nothing from Fay's estate.

wishes about how the person wants to be buried, whom he or she wants looking after children or pets, and any other legal or other obligations the deceased wishes heirs to assume.

A warning before proceeding further: nonprofits cannot be involved in the creation of someone's will. They can encourage people to create a will, offer workshops about wills led by attorneys or estate planners, and discuss what they know about wills with donors and in written materials, but they must not get involved in giving legal advice or in helping people to write their wills. The only advice anyone in a nonprofit should give current or potential donors is that donors consult their own attorney or financial planner. The reason for all these cautions is that people who work for nonprofits are subject to being accused of "exerting undue influence," thus opening the way to legal challenge of a will.

THE BEQUEST

The simplest form of legacy giving to a nonprofit—and the most common—is the bequest. People note in their wills what property they wish your organization to have: cash, stocks, bonds, art—anything of value. People who already have wills and don't want to change them substantially can add a "codicil" or amendment to their will to specify gifts to your organization.

One of the most famous and earliest bequests was given by Ben Franklin in 1790. He left the equivalent of $4,000 to be divided between the people of the state of Pennsylvania (76 percent) and the City of Philadelphia (24 percent) on the condition that it not be touched for two hundred years. (Franklin had great faith in the future of his state and city!) In 1990, when the two hundred years were up, Franklin's bequest was worth $2.3 million. A group of Franklin scholars given authority to recommend the best use of the money decided that the city's money should be kept in a permanent endowment at the Philadelphia Foundation and the state's money should be shared between the Franklin Institute and a consortium of community foundations around the state.

HOW SOMEONE MAKES A BEQUEST

Anyone can make a bequest. All that is required is that they are alive and of sound mind when they make their will and that they own something they can't take with them. Many people think bequests are only for wealthy people, but in fact, if all someone owns is a late-model Ford, he can leave that car to a nonprofit, which can then keep whatever amount it can sell the car for.

All bequests are revocable during the life of the donor—a will can be changed any number of times. Your organization may be included in one will and left out of a later version. Thus unrealized bequests (bequests promised to you by donors who are still alive) cannot ethically be counted toward a fundraising goal.

Wording of Bequests

Although nonprofits cannot direct people in the wording to be included in their wills, they can, in any published information about the organization, let donors know the appropriate wording for various types of bequests they may wish to leave to your group.

The General Bequest.   The general bequest is the simplest bequest, whereby a donor gives a stated amount to the nonprofit without attaching any conditions. The bequest reads as follows:

> I give and bequeath to *(exact legal name and address of organization)* the sum of $____ *(or a specific piece of property)* to be used as the board of directors directs.

To be absolutely certain there is no confusion about which nonprofit organization the donor meant, it is a good idea to include the address of the group.

Similar to the general bequest in language and intent are two other types of bequests.

Bequest of a Percentage.   With this type of bequest, the donor makes the following type of statement:

> I give and bequeath ___ percent *(a specific percentage)* of the total value of my estate to *(exact legal name and address of organization)* to be used as the board of directors directs.

Bequest of Residue.   A bequest of residue is a provision that all wills should have. It leaves the remainder of a person's estate to an organization or a person after all other bequests are fulfilled. These bequests are often the largest ones; they read as follows:

> The rest, residue, and remainder of my estate, both real and personal, wherever situated, I give and bequeath to *(exact legal name and address of organization)* to be used as the board of directors directs.

The remaining three types of bequests have more strings attached or only come into play under certain circumstances.

Contingent Bequest.   A contingent bequest leaves a bequest to the nonprofit if any of the other beneficiaries are unable to receive their bequests because of death or other circumstances. Everyone should have a contingent bequest in their will in case circumstances have changed since it was drawn up.

> Should *(name of heir)* predecease me, the portion of my estate going to *(name of heir)* I give and bequeath to *(exact legal name and address of organization)*.

Income Only to Be Used.   This type of bequest carries the following wording:

> I give and bequeath to *(legal name and address of organization)* the sum of $____ to be invested or reinvested so that the income only may be used as the board of directors directs.

Designated Bequest.   This type of gift provides a sum of money for a specific or designated project or program.

> I give and bequeath to *(legal name and address of organization)* the sum of $___ *(or the property or percentage)* to be used for *(specific description of program, scholarship, building, and so on)*.

Ideally, a designated bequest has some kind of contingency, such as the following:

> Should this program no longer be needed, or be fully funded from another source, the bequest may be used as the board of directors directs.

The most flexible bequests are those that are best for the nonprofit; it is the wording of those that you will wish to advertise.

You can see from these various types of bequests how a donor might change his or her will over time to make your organization more of a direct beneficiary. Some donors start with a contingency bequest, basically saying that if one or more unlikely things happen, your organization will benefit. They may move to a percentage or an actual amount for your organization. Later, they may change their bequest to a residue bequest—anything they have forgotten about is yours. The fact that bequests are revocable works in favor of nonprofits as well as donors and should not be seen as a disadvantage.

GIFTS FROM INSURANCE AND RETIREMENT FUNDS

Any time a person owns an asset, such as an insurance policy or investment in a retirement fund, he or she will be asked to name a beneficiary. That beneficiary can be a nonprofit organization, or the person can name an heir and then a nonprofit in the case that the heir dies first. Here are a couple of common examples.

Existing Life Insurance Policies

People generally buy life insurance to protect their survivors if sufficient assets have not been accumulated. The value of the life insurance policy may cover mortgage debt or protect a business. As a person gets older, she or he may not need that protection and can change the beneficiary of their insurance to a charity of their choice. With certain kinds of policies, the older the life insurance policy, the more cash value it has built up; that value can be given outright during the policyholder's lifetime. (This, of course, is not as much money as it would have paid as a death benefit.)

Buying Life Insurance to Fund a Gift

For people wanting to make a gift to an organization that is far greater than they imagine they would ever be able to give from accumulated assets, buying a life insurance policy and making the charity a beneficiary may be a way to go. The premiums on such a policy may be tax deductible.

From an organizational viewpoint, this kind of insurance is problematic because it means the donor is paying out money to help your organization, but you will not see the results of this money until the death of the donor, perhaps far in the future. If the donor stops paying his or her premiums, the nonprofit has neither the insurance nor the donor.

IRAs or Other Retirement Plans

Many Americans are eligible to participate in some kind of tax-deferred retirement plan. You can encourage your donors to make your organization the primary, secondary, or final beneficiary of their plan or to name your organization as a recipient of a percentage of the proceeds. This money may come to you if the person dies before retirement or before they have used all the money in the plan.

The types of legacy giving I have described are the vast majority of planned gifts and will keep the average small nonprofit quite busy.

INTRODUCING YOUR LEGACY GIVING PROGRAM

You have probably thought, as I often have, "I don't know how I would bring up the idea of leaving a bequest with anyone; even if I did, they would be completely shocked. If they weren't upset, it would be because somebody else probably asked them already and I am too late."

These feelings are totally normal. I have known donors who had a favorite grassroots organization to which they made significant donations and for which they volunteered, only to make legacy gifts to their university or another much larger institution. They made this decision because they could not be sure the grassroots organization would last long enough to benefit from a bequest or because they did not trust that the organization could manage an endowment. This is a vicious cycle, and people in fundraising roles in small organizations need to break it by making this option known to all their donors and convincing some of their bolder donors to take the leap with them. Once a few do it, others will follow.

The best way to introduce a legacy giving program is also the easiest and most low-key: begin to include the topic in all the places you already publish information about ways to give. Discuss your endowment and your vision for the future, and ask donors to think of you when they are making their estate plans. For example, you can put a short article about bequests in your newsletter that refers people who want more information to your Web site, where among the menu items under the "Ways to Give" tab, "Types of Bequests" leads to a detailed description and perhaps a sample codicil that people can download.

Once a year, send a mailing specifically focused on bequests to your whole donor list, or if you want to segment, to donors who have given for three or more years in a row. You may wish to use a brochure explaining bequests and send it with the mailing. Leave a Legacy is a public service campaign to encourage people to make wills, and the campaign's Web site, LeaveaLegacy.com, has all the language you need to use in your materials. It also has wonderful donor stories illustrating the importance of making plans for the disposition of your estate. Gaywill.com is a similar service for the LGBTQ community.

In every newsletter and on your Web site, include a notice (like a classified ad) that your organization is receiving bequests and ask people making up their wills to remember you. Here is sample language for such ads:

> As you are making out your will, remember us with a bequest. Our full legal name and address are _____. For more information about bequest language, call or write: *(phone number, postal and e-mail addresses)*.

Or:

If you have provided for *(name of your group)* in your estate plans, please let us know.

Givers can also be reminded that they can name your organization as the first, second, or final beneficiary for part or all of the proceeds from IRAs, insurance policies, wills, or any other estate-planning documents.

Present this information frequently and people will begin to notice. Once they begin to notice, they will remember your organization when they are making out their wills. It generally takes about three to five years for a legacy giving program to begin to produce results (that is, that you actually begin receiving bequests or you know that some of your donors have provided for your organization in their wills), so it is certainly not a quick fix to an immediate financial crisis.

Create a Legacy Giving Mailing List

As you do more mailings about legacy giving and as people contact you for more information, you will develop a list of people who have identified themselves as wanting information about legacy giving. This list includes some serious prospects who want to help your organization and may consider doing so with a legacy gift. It also includes people doing fundraising for other groups who want to see your material and people who love to get mail and write away for everything. You will have to sort out the serious prospects from the others in order to focus any personal attention you want to give to genuine planned giving prospects.

Many organizations create a "legacy society"—a named group of people who have included your organization in their wills. This segment of people gets special mailings from time to time, some of which can describe your organization's legacy giving options in more detail, using examples and stories. People in such groups can be invited to receptions or lectures designed for them. These groups turn out to be of a nice cross-class makeup because to be part of such a group, a person simply notifies the organization that he or she has left it a bequest, which could be of any size.

People interested in legacy giving can also be encouraged to sign up for information sent by e-mail. Any e-mail notices you develop should also be posted on your Web site and reached through an icon, "Making a Bequest" or "Ensuring Our Future." Look at the Web sites of large organizations to get ideas for how to promote legacy giving using the Web.

Hold a Seminar

A good community service that can also generate some legacy gifts is a seminar on estate planning. Invite people who have indicated an interest in legacy giving and announce your seminar to the broader community, if you like. Have an estate planner there and plenty of materials both about your organization and about estate planning strategies. If you can, have someone there who will discuss how he made up his estate plans to include your organization.

The purpose of the seminar is to help people think through what they are going to do with their estates, so you don't want to spend a lot of time talking about your organization. However, you will need to mention yourselves a few times to drive the point home that if a person includes a nonprofit in their will, you hope it will be yours.

A seminar lets you meet people, making follow-up easier. One follow-up technique is for your seminar to be the impetus for forming groups of people who want to discuss estate planning or legacy giving options with the help of an expert. Each month or so, your organization (or a coalition of similar organizations) provides an expert for these prospects to meet with who presents one topic in depth. (The group can also discuss related personal issues, such as when children should have access to their inheritance, the kindest thing to do with pets at the death of an owner, living wills, and so on.)

Work Collaboratively

Many organizations have found success in cosponsoring seminars such as those described previously. More people attend, and it is clear that no one charity is being emphasized.

Beyond bequests, there are other legacy giving strategies, some of which can benefit donors during their lifetime by paying dividends on money put in trust for the nonprofit after the donor's death. Some organizations have had good luck working with their local community foundation to hold and manage trusts such as these and related types of funds. Since community foundations are set up to handle complicated giving arrangements, they have the language and the knowledge of how to do so as part of their program. A foundation may also impart to donors a sense of solidity and stability that reassures them that their investment will be well managed. Your organization receives the interest, just as you would if you were managing the asset, but without any of the headache. You will pay a fee for this service, and you do not own this asset, but the money is also pooled with other investments, giving you more—and more reliable—income than if you tried to manage the trust on your own.

Once you are able to move past your anxiety and awkwardness about talking about legacy giving, you will see that a legacy gift is probably the most mutually beneficial gift a donor can make. In any gift, the organization benefits from the donation and the donor benefits by knowing that work he or she believes needs to be done will continue. The bigger the gift, the more assurance the donor needs to have that this will be the case. An organization expresses its gratitude to these donors for moving the work forward through thank you notes, special events, and other kinds of attention.

An organization that wants a working legacy giving program will have to have in place all that is required for any successful fundraising program: a desire to work with donors, the capacity to gather and sort data about donors, people willing to ask, plans and goals for the future, and a belief in the enduring value of the work.

Launching Major Gifts Campaigns

Once an organization understands and has implemented the process of identifying prospects for major gifts and asking them for money, and has developed a working major gifts program, it should consider moving to a more formal major gifts campaign. The main differences between an ongoing major gifts program and a major gifts campaign are that a campaign is time-limited—it begins and ends on specific dates; the goal of the campaign is made public; and markers toward achieving the goal are announced frequently, as in thermometers showing how far the organization has come toward its goal, e-blasts announcing progress toward the goal, and whatever other communication method works well for the organization. Reaching or surpassing the goal in the time frame that is set becomes part of the excitement. Although a major gifts *program* has a goal that is part of an organization's overall fundraising plan, the program is in place all year and progress toward the goal is not necessarily being tracked by anyone except staff and one or two board members. You have a full fiscal year to reach the goal, and achieving it is part of the accomplishment of meeting your income goals. Because a major gifts campaign, on the other hand, is time-limited and public, you can use it to generate publicity about the overall needs of the organization.

During the time of the major gifts campaign, a few volunteers devote themselves intensively to meeting a specific financial goal, giving amounts of time and effort to the campaign that would be difficult to maintain beyond a short commitment.

A major gifts campaign requires nine steps, some of which are the same as for any major gifts program. The steps are listed below, then discussed in detail.

1. Set a goal

2. Prepare supporting materials

3. Identify and train solicitors

4. Identify prospects

5. Assign prospects and solicit gifts

6. Kick off the campaign with a special event (optional)

7. Hold regular reporting meetings

8. Celebrate the end of a successful campaign with a special event (also optional, though it can attract media and recognize donors)

9. Recognize donors and incorporate them into ongoing fundraising efforts

THE STEPS IN DETAIL

Step 1: Set a Goal

The first step in a major gifts campaign is to decide how long the campaign will last and how much money will be raised. For small organizations, a campaign of six to eight weeks is ideal because volunteers and overworked staff can maintain momentum and excitement for that much time fairly easily and a lot of money can be raised in this short period of time. (See Premium Web Content: "How to Raise $50,000 in Six Weeks," by Kim Klein, *Grassroots Fundraising Journal.*)

To determine a fundraising goal, first calculate how many prospects could be asked in that length of time. Generally, a volunteer can ask about one to three people a week for six to eight weeks without undue strain. A committee of five volunteers, then, could ask between 40 and 120 people during an eight-week campaign. Assuming the usual 50 percent rate of success, your organization would have from 20 to 60 new major donors after such a campaign.

If you have a shortage of volunteers, you can ask each volunteer to solicit more people per week, but only volunteers with a lot of time and comfort with the process of asking will be able to do more than twelve asks in one month. Your better bet will be to lower the goal so that the major gifts campaign is something volunteers will want to do again, not something they give their all to and burn out doing.

Knowing how many gifts you can get, now plot how many gifts of specific amounts you will need in order to reach your goal, using the following method.

Select the lowest amount that will be solicited in face-to-face meetings. Most groups choose $500 as the minimum request for which they will seek a meeting; others start in-person solicitations for gifts of $250. Rarely would it be worth the time to make face-to-face solicitations for less than $100. Next, make a rough determination as to the biggest gift you might get from the prospects you have and consider that gift 10 percent of the total goal. With the largest and lowest gifts decided on, you can now chart the size of gifts you will ask for and how many of each you will need to meet the goal. (See Chapter Twenty-One for how to create a Gift Range Chart and sample charts.)

With your gift range chart complete, you can figure out how many workers you will need to carry out the campaign. Divide the number of prospects by the number of weeks, and divide that number by the number of requests each solicitor will be asked to make in one week, and the resulting number is the number of volunteers you need. For example, let's say your goal is $30,000 and you decide you need 120 prospects. Your campaign will last six weeks, so 120/6 = 20 prospects per week/2 per person per week = 10 volunteers. Remember that all the people working on the campaign need to make their own gift first, so the first gifts are pretty easy.

Don't get bogged down in making your chart. Basically, it should have fewer people in the top part and more at the bottom. The point of the chart is to recognize that not everyone will give the same amount and to set a limit on the number of people needing to be solicited. Share this chart with prospects and donors; it lets them know that your organization has planned the campaign and allows them to think about how they might like to fit into it.

If you are doing a major donor campaign for the first time, set your overall goal slightly lower than you think is achievable with good solid effort so that you are almost bound to make it. This will give an early sense of accomplishment and provide momentum to future campaigns. A good campaign goal feels like a stretch, but one that will be accomplished if the majority of workers do their share.

Step 2: Prepare Supporting Materials

A campaign needs a number of materials for solicitors to use, some of which will already exist in your organization and some of which will need to be created for the campaign. The supporting materials are of two types: materials that solicitors will give to donors, and materials that are for the solicitors' use only or that relate to the campaign committee.

For the solicitor to use with donors you will need the following materials: a campaign case statement; a pledge card; and stationery, envelopes, and return envelopes.

A Campaign Case Statement.   The case statement can be in the form of a report or a brochure. It should be simple and inexpensively produced. It can be designed in-house and printed with a laser printer, then copied on a high-quality photocopy machine. The case statement spells out the goal of the campaign, the gifts that are needed, what the money will be used for, and a brief history of the organization. It invites donors to a celebration at the end of the campaign (if you are having one) and tells them what special benefits they get for their money (if anything). Whether to go to the trouble of having a special benefit will depend on your organizational culture, what benefits you have access to, and how the solicitors feel about the need for them. (See also Chapter Eleven for a longer discussion of benefits and premiums.)

A Pledge Card.   This is a reply device designed for major donors. On it, either the donor or the solicitor writes down the donor's name, what he or she has agreed to give, and the method of payment. Once the solicitation is complete and the card filled out, it is returned to the office, and the data from it is entered into the database.

Stationery, Envelopes, and Return Envelopes.   Have enough of these stationery items printed for all the prospects, with a few extras for mistakes. These materials are used for both initial letters and thank you notes. It is not necessary or useful to create special stationery or envelopes for a major donor campaign.

For the solicitors' or committee's use only, the following materials will be needed:

- A timeline of the campaign steps
- A complete description of the campaign and some soliciting tips
- The organization's overall budget
- A list of difficult and commonly asked questions about the organization and possible answers
- A list of the other solicitors and whom to contact for more information

All of these materials should be put together in a _____
which can be as simple as a manila folder but which loo_____
the campaigner on it, and seems official. You should also s_____
e-mail so volunteers can download what they need and ____
something or if they want to give a prospect a copy of t_____
should be encouraged to e-mail or call with questions or cor____

Step 3: Identify and Train Solicitors

Invite people to be on the campaign committee as solicitors. Look____
believe in the mission of your organization, who are well respected_____
munity, and who you know have a sense of discretion, as much of the ____rmation
that will be exchanged in the committee will be of a confidential nature. Ideally,
invite one or two more people than the number of people you need to meet your
goals. That way, if a solicitor has an emergency, or if two solicitors want to work
together, or if someone just flakes out, you have backup. Committee members
should fulfill two simple commitments, with a third commitment optional. First,
all members should themselves be giving a gift that is significant to them; the
number of committee members and the total amount of their gifts are counted
toward the goal and are an encouraging way to begin the campaign. Second, each
member must agree to solicit a certain number of prospects each week for a
certain number of weeks. Third, and optional, members of the committee
can provide names of prospects for the master list. If your committee does not
provide these names, you will need another way to get them.

Some organizations have found that getting people to agree to be on the major
gifts committee is the biggest hurdle to starting their major gifts campaign. People
they approach may be afraid they won't be good at asking for money, or they feel
they don't know anyone to ask or they don't have time, or they put forth any
number of other objections. To get people to consider serving on the committee,
first ask them to come to a training session where they will learn what is involved
and what their commitment would be. Tell them (and mean it) that there is no
obligation to serve on the committee after the training, but that you would like
them to be open-minded. If the training is fun, the food is good, and the other
people who might be on the committee are friendly, in general you will have no
trouble getting the majority of people to agree to serve. Reassure them that they
will not be asked to do more than their time allows and that if they don't already

...one they feel comfortable asking, they will be provided with names of ...pects. Be sure to emphasize that what is required for successful major donor work is commitment to the mission of the organization.

Once enough people have agreed to consider serving on the committee, set a meeting for the training at which they are briefed in more depth about the campaign and taught how to ask for money. After the training, ask who wants to be on the committee and have them stay longer at the meeting for prospect assignment. After the first one or two campaigns, you will have a core of people who like being on the major gifts campaign, so recruiting for the campaign will get easier.

The meeting will last about three hours, with the following agenda:

- Introductions of the committee members to each other (10 minutes)
- A review of the campaign and the organization's need for money (20 minutes)
- Training in how to ask for money, including practice solicitation (1.5 hours)
- Assigning prospect names and giving out supporting materials (30 minutes)
- Review of campaign goal, whom to call with questions, final questions of committee members, and maybe a little snack (30 minutes)

End the meeting on time or early for maximum morale.

The staff or fundraising committee of the board should conduct the meeting, but many organizations find it helpful to have an outside trainer lead the training in how to ask for money (see also Chapters Six and Seven). It is imperative that every person on the committee be at this training even if they have participated in fundraising solicitations before. The experience of people who know how to ask for money will be of great benefit to those who are feeling unsure. This initial meeting helps the committee develop a sense of itself as a team and should encourage a strong camaraderie from the very beginning.

Step 4: Identify Prospects

Review Chapter Seven, "The Logistics of Personal Solicitation," for the basics on prospect identification. Review your list of current donors to identify the following types of people: those who have given a major gift, those who have the ability to give a major gift, and those who should be asked to give more this year. For example, anyone on your list who has given the same large donation for two or more years ought to be asked to increase their gift; this campaign provides an excellent way for this upgrade to happen. Staff, board members, and the committee members can be asked for names of prospects to ensure a big enough list. Unlike an informal, ongoing major gifts program, in a campaign ideally all, but certainly most, of the prospects must be identified before the campaign can begin.

Prepare a master list of all the prospects on a spreadsheet as shown here.

Major Donor Campaign Prospect Tracking Form				
Prospect Name	Amount Asked For	Solicitor	Outcome	Thank You Sent

Everyone on the committee should receive a copy of this spreadsheet, sorted alphabetically. Once the assignments are made, the spreadsheet can be sorted by solicitor name to keep track of how well each solicitor is doing. No one should be solicited who is not on this master list to ensure that no one is asked by two people. All of this information is highly confidential.

Step 5: Assign Prospects and Solicit Gifts

At the meeting, after the solicitors are trained and familiar with the materials and the campaign, they are each given a copy of the master prospect list. Each member of the committee should read through the list quietly and note who they might be willing to solicit. Then the committee chair or facilitator should read each name out loud, with committee members identifying whom they can ask. Should two solicitors be willing to ask the same person, they briefly discuss and decide right there which of them is going to do it. (They also have the option of going together to see the prospect.) As the names are read aloud and assigned, committee members should decide how much each prospect will be asked for and where they fit on the gift range chart. By the end of the meeting, everyone should have a list of prospects and the chair or the development director should be confident that no one prospect will be solicited twice. Doing this process out loud also helps to ensure that prospects are being asked for the right amount and that the right person is doing the asking. Solicitation can now begin.

Step 6: Kick Off the Campaign with a Special Event (Optional)

A kick-off event is not a gala affair, but all the prospects and all the solicitors should be invited, along with staff and board who are not serving on the committee. Serve drinks and hors d'oeuvres. Someone from the committee should give an enthusiastic but brief speech about the campaign, including its goals and what the organization will be able to do with the money raised. The event also provides a time for people to see who else is involved and who is being asked to give—this peer identification adds an important element to the desire to give. The speech ends with, "We will be contacting all of you individually in the next few weeks to see what questions you have and whether you can help in this important endeavor."

These kinds of events work best when the prospects know the organization, when they may already be donors or volunteers, and when the money from the campaign will be going to something specific and interesting. Make sure you will have a good turnout of prospects by calling people to invite them, and by asking for RSVPs.

Step 7: Hold Regular Reporting Meetings

Regular reporting meetings (or conference calls, if you are geographically spread out) to discuss progress and boost the morale of campaign volunteers should take place every two weeks during the campaign. The meetings need last only thirty minutes; many organizations hold them over breakfast at 7:30 A.M. so people can attend them before work. Between the check-in meetings, send e-mail every two or three days (and toward the end of the campaign, every day) noting progress toward the goal. You can put the amount raised so far in the subject line of the e-mail so people don't even need to open it to see what is happening. "Now at $15,500" "Now at $18,000" "Crossed over $20,000." The e-mail is brief: "Eric brought in two gifts!" "Mary has completed all her solicitations." Don't say anything about people who haven't done much—the absence of their name will be evident to all. The purpose of the meetings or calls is to give everyone a chance to report their progress, which forces everyone to have made some progress between meetings. They can share frustrations, fears, and successes.

Although solicitors will complain that the meetings are taking valuable time, you will notice a direct correlation between the number of meetings (or phone calls) attended and the number of solicitations made. A handful of people can be relied on to do their work without checking in—may your committee be entirely made up of them—but these people are so rare they could be a category on the Endangered Species List. Make the committee members check in. If someone is really not doing their job, the chair of the campaign will need to call him or her privately and see what is going on. That person's prospects may have to be assigned to someone else, which is why it is good to have more volunteers than you absolutely need.

Step 8: Celebrate the End of the Campaign with a Special Event (Optional)

Though holding an event to close the campaign is optional, it is an excellent way to recognize and reward the committee as well as the donors. A simple reception with drinks, fruit, and cheese from 5:00 to 7:00 in the evening, with a speech announcing the successful conclusion of the campaign, is fine. Some groups have formal dinners—or in the case of capital campaigns, ground-breaking ceremonies—but it is not necessary to be elaborate. This event is largely for the solicitors, and something simple but gracious will help ensure that they will be willing to do it all over again next year.

Step 9: Recognize Donors and Incorporate Them into Ongoing Fundraising Efforts

Aside from raising money, a major donor campaign strengthens donor loyalty, brings in new donors, and upgrades current donors. As mentioned many times in this book, you need to be in regular touch with all these donors through a newsletter and occasional personal correspondence. Because major donors may not get the regular mail appeals that other donors get, they must be kept abreast of the organization's work in other ways. Like all donors, major donors must be thanked promptly when their gifts arrive, and the solicitor should be informed as her or his prospects send in money. All donors to the campaign should receive another thank you note at the successful end of the campaign, telling them the organization was able to reach its goal and stressing again the work you will be able to do with this money.

Major gifts campaigns must be done right to succeed. Don't try to take short-cuts or launch the campaign without proper preparation. A major gifts campaign should be both fun and lucrative, and its success will be a reward for good planning and good organizing.

PART FOUR

Large-Scale Fundraising

In the following chapters, I look at needs that can only be met with large gifts, and I discuss the strategies that raise that kind of money. In Part Three, I introduced the idea of moving from a major donor program to a major donor campaign. In this part, we look at two more strategies that can be done as campaigns: raising money for capital needs, which is almost always done as a campaign, and raising money for an endowment, which can be done either as an ongoing program or as a campaign.

The last chapter in this section looks at feasibility studies: how to evaluate whether a big campaign may be successful; how and when to do such a campaign; and, very important, when not to.

Sometimes organizations feel that they must be more sophisticated than they are or have more infrastructure in place than they do in order to conduct a capital or endowment campaign. I find that actually starting these large-scale fundraising efforts is a great way to get sophisticated in a hurry and to see clearly what needs to be quickly put in place. Campaigns in particular are fun; they bring out the latent competitiveness in many of us, and there is excitement and creative tension built into racing to meet the goal. Capital and endowment campaigns often stimulate volunteers far more than an ongoing (and from the volunteer viewpoint, never-ending) annual needs effort.

Large-scale fundraising strategies are loaded with details, and like special events, many details build on others, so there is not much room for mistakes or carelessness. Further, you don't want to open an endowment and then never mention it again, or start a capital campaign but then stop when you get discouraged. As with all fundraising (and I may have mentioned this before), persistence, attention to detail, and a willingness to take some risks are key to success.

Setting Up an Endowment

During boom years, even the smallest NGO can be found putting money away into an endowment, a reserve fund, or just a savings account. This money is invested in mutual funds or certificates of deposit and, with a little tending, the principal grows, sometimes dramatically. Endowment income can be a reliable part of an organization's annual needs, and for organizations with large endowments, the endowment gains can be a major part of income. During bust years and dramatic stock market downturns, putting money aside is less popular and thought to be less possible.

Just as a family or an individual saves for retirement or hard times, any organization that possibly can should put some money aside. Institutions that should be permanent fixtures in the nonprofit landscape need to start endowments. There are ways to invest the principal in an endowment safely and to ensure both long-term growth and some income.

ENDOWMENT DEFINED

An endowment is a permanent savings account for an institution. Money is put aside as principal and a small percentage of that principal (traditionally 5 percent) is used for the annual needs of the institution. In years when the principal increases more than 5 percent, the value of the overall endowment increases accordingly, which then increases the amount the organization can use while still staying at the 5 percent figure. In years when the principal does not increase by 5 percent, the organization can still take out 5 percent of the asset without truly eroding the original principal. During huge market downturns, however, even the original principal may lose value; taking out any of it for operating expenses is not as useful at those times, as doing so further lowers the endowment's value.

Using a mix of investments, an endowment generally can weather market instability and still be productive. Like any source of money, an endowment can lose value or even disappear, which is why organizations have to have diversified income streams so that the investment income from an endowment is not critical to survival.

BENEFITS OF ENDOWMENTS

Though the advantages of endowments may seem obvious, let's review them:

- Just like a savings account, an endowment provides a measure of financial security and takes some of the anxiety out of annual fundraising.

- An endowment allows, indeed forces, an organization to think in terms of long-range planning, because an endowment implies a commitment to exist in perpetuity.

- An endowment provides a vehicle for people to make larger gifts to an organization than might be appropriate as an annual gift, and an endowment allows people to make one-time-only gifts with the assurance that the gift won't be spent right away.

- An endowment gives people a way to express their commitment to an organization through their wills; few people will leave money to an organization that does not have some kind of permanent fund. (See Chapter Twenty-Two for more on wills.)

- An endowment attracts donors who perceive it to be a sign of good planning and long-range thinking in an organization.

- Principal from an endowment can be used for capital expenses (such as a building purchase) and as collateral for loans, if ever needed. In extreme circumstances, the endowment can be used to keep the organization afloat until it can generate other income. (While what's called "invading principal" is something organizations try not to do, there are circumstances in which it might be the best or only recourse, and it is nice to know you have that possibility.)

DISADVANTAGES OF ENDOWMENTS

Endowments have some serious drawbacks.

- If an endowment is big enough, it allows an organization that should have gone out of business, or at least changed the way it works, to exist permanently and to stay the same.

- The income from a large endowment can allow organizations to become unresponsive to their constituency.

- As we have seen in the first decade of this century, endowments can provide a false sense of security. Interest rates vary, stock markets crash, and, of course, money can always be invested badly.

- The existence of an endowment may discourage some donors from giving who prefer to support organizations that they perceive to need the money more. However, some donors may choose to give to an endowment rather than to annual operating costs.

- As with any large source of money earmarked for a specific program, endowments that are linked to certain programs can cause the work of the organization to become driven by the donor's stipulations rather than by its own mission. Moreover, by the time it is clear that the program needs to be changed or abandoned, the donor is usually deceased and the terms for changing how the funds are spent may not be in place. If the endowment is large enough, lengthy and expensive court cases may result.

- Managing an endowment is an additional piece of work for board and staff. This management time can become the tail that wags the dog, particularly if there are problems with the investments or disagreement about how to use the income.

There are also some philosophical concerns for social justice organizations about endowments. Money that is in an endowment has been diverted from the tax stream but is not being used directly for tax-exempt activities. Organizations that are troubled by decreasing support from government funding and increasing privatization of services they believe the government should be providing with tax dollars will need to grapple with this dilemma. An organization that believes it is doing work that the government should be using tax money for (such as social services, support of the arts, support of school programs, libraries, and so on) is essentially "privatizing" that work by raising private "nest egg" funds. (A historic footnote on this point: in 1791, as part of the French Revolution, the revolutionaries seized and sold off all endowments belonging to church or private institutions, reflecting the Jacobins' belief that the state should provide what its citizens need for quality of life and that using private intermediaries, particularly "the long arm of the dead donor," did not promote a healthy society. A law was subsequently passed that essentially curtailed the creation of foundations, and this remained in effect in France until 1987.)

CONSIDERING AN ENDOWMENT OR RESERVE FUND

It is obvious that only organizations with strong annual campaigns are really in a position to start endowments. When thinking of starting an endowment, organizations often focus on the money: how much to raise, how to raise it, whom to ask for it. But there are two critical questions that must be answered before even one dollar is invested in your endowment.

Does Everyone in the Organization Agree That Your Organization Should Exist Permanently? Most nonprofits involved in social change are formed with the idea that if their work is successful, they will put themselves out of business. The founders generally do not think of the group becoming permanent, and everyone may be surprised at how long it is taking to solve the problem the organization was created to address. Arts groups, independent schools, historic preservation societies, parks and wildlands conservation groups, and some social services are clearly permanent, with their work always needed or wanted. In contrast, environmental, feminist, liberation, and advocacy groups, if they are successful, will cease to exist.

Sometimes the most interesting part of the endowment process is discussion of this question at the beginning: Should we always be here? "Permanence" in terms of endowment has shades of meaning. It can take its traditional meaning of "always and forever" or it can take the meaning of "fifty years from now." But endowments do imply existing well past the lifetime of anyone in the organization, and they require the leadership of the organization to imagine the day when people who are not yet born are sitting on the board of directors and working as staff. Will your work be needed then? What is the evidence of that need?

It is important to make sure that everyone among board, staff, key volunteers, and donors agrees that permanence is a value. When people don't agree on that condition, the fundamental reason to have an endowment and the driving force of endowment fundraising are already in trouble.

What Will Endowment Income Be Used For? Just as couples may have differing ideas about how and when to use savings, so may board and staff differ about using endowment income. Some will see the income stream as a relief from constant fundraising and will not expect the group's annual budget to grow substantially. Others will see the endowment income as paying for particular programs or doing things the group has not been able to do before.

What you use the income for is related to how big you want your endowment to be. An organization with a $250,000 budget simply looking for a little financial relief along with some financial security will be happy to start with a $100,000 endowment that yields both $5,000 a year and the knowledge that there is principal that can be borrowed against or added to. This money can be used to increase staff health care benefits, buy better equipment, or fix up the office. It is not enough money to change the direction of the group in any way, but it is enough to make life easier. A group looking for enough endowment income to open a satellite office or explore new program directions will need an endowment of $1 million or more from which they can safely draw $50,000 a year.

Once these two questions are resolved (which can take as much as a year of discussion), you are ready to begin the initial logistical steps. These steps involve authorizing the endowment, determining what gifts will be accepted, and deciding on investment policies.

THE AUTHORIZATION

First, the board agrees to create an endowment fund and to hold this money in perpetuity. This fund will be reflected in all financial reports as a separate line item. Once this decision has been made, the group should consider and decide on a series of policies about the endowment money.

Use Policy

Policies detailing how the interest income from the endowment will be used can be couched as broad statements, but they should not be so broad that they are subject to a variety of opposing interpretations. For example, one organization's policies stated, "Endowment income is to be used for operating costs." Later, that group opened a second office and added new programs. Some board members thought the endowment income should be spread to include all operating costs for all programs; others felt the income was limited to operation of programs in place at the time the policy was created and that new programs were therefore on their own to raise all the money they needed.

Invasion Policy

Are there any circumstances under which the organization would use (invade) the endowment principal? There are no right or wrong answers to this question, but in most cases endowment principal is only invaded under the most dire circumstance or when the endowment is going to be used to pay for another long-term asset, for example, as the down payment for a building.

The organization will need to decide on the categories of dire. Most board policies establish that endowment principal can only be used if the organization itself is in danger of closing and that the amount taken from the principal must be paid back within a given time period. Some boards rule that the principal cannot be touched even if drastic cuts are required, whereas others decide that the principal can be used to balance the budget, but not for more than two years in a row.

Although no organization can think of every contingency, and certainly you don't want to spend hundreds of hours on your policies, you do need to spell out in the authorization the most common things that could happen. There have been several instances in which a board of directors and staff worked hard to build an endowment then years later, after all those people were gone, another board with too much latitude to invade voted to use endowment principal to balance the budget, gradually burning through the whole corpus.

A related question is, Who will have the authority to decide whether to use endowment principal? Most boards rule that the whole board would have to approve of such a use. Others stipulate that up to a percentage of the principal can be used on the vote of the executive committee; beyond that percentage, the decision must go to the whole board. At the full board meeting, some boards require unanimous agreement; others deem that a simple majority is sufficient. Some of these procedures will be determined by how the organization makes decisions on other matters.

Gift Acceptance Policy

Another broad category of decisions involves determining what types of gifts you will accept, who has the authority to accept them, who will draw up contracts with donors about them, and under what circumstances the organization will accept or decline a gift. (Most organizations should have some gift acceptance policy in place even if you don't have or never intend to have an endowment. As you can see from the examples that follow, any kind of fundraising effort could raise these types of questions.)

For example, will you accept the gift of a house? "Well, why not?" you ask brashly. One NGO discovered that it was given a house because the owner could not sell it, even at a huge loss. Another accepted a house with a lien on it. Another accepted a duplex with tenants, intending to convert the building into an office. When they sought to evict the tenants, they faced a public relations nightmare, including this headline: "Single mothers evicted for 'social justice.'"

Will you take jewelry, art, or antiques? You have to think about what you will do with this stuff. How will you sell it? Do you have access to appraisers and buyers of fine art? These items may be worth a lot of money, but you may not be able to sell them. You can spend hours of staff and volunteer time trying to get a fair price for these items; at the end of the day they have cost you more than they were worth.

Will you accept stock from companies that make weapons, degrade the environment, or use sweatshop labor? (Because stock should be sold immediately, most organizations can accept stock from companies they disagree with without feeling that they are supporting the company.)

Will you accept endowment gifts that are restricted in use? For example, if someone wants to endow your children's program forever, will you accept that restriction? If they want to create a new program and endow it, will you consider that?

To keep things simple, at the beginning most grassroots organizations should accept only cash, appreciated securities (stocks and bonds), and life insurance—all with few or no use restrictions. Others kinds of assets can be negotiated on a case-by-case basis.

Your published gift acceptance policy can be quite simple: "The board of directors of People for All Things Good reserves the right to turn down any gift that it believes will not be in the best interest of our mission or that we cannot handle appropriately." What you publish is not as important as having this conversation with your board and staff and everyone understanding what you are getting into. The tendency of most organizations is to accept all gifts ("Don't look a gift horse in the mouth"), but without spending an inordinate amount of time on it, you need to be clear that some gifts can be burdensome beyond their value.

If you have questions about the types of gifts you should accept and what is involved, hire a consultant with experience in creating endowment policies to help you. This may save you money and time later.

Investment Policies

Finally, your organization needs an investment policy. Will you invest entirely for income, or will you have a mix of investments that allow for growth of the principal and income? Will you require socially responsible investing and if so, what screens will be put in place? For example, some nonprofits specify that they will not invest in certain kinds of products or businesses, such as tobacco, box stores, or logging. Others require evidence that the company does not engage in union busting, has a racially diverse staff and board, or offers health and other benefits for domestic partners. If you do social screening, you need to set priorities. If you try to screen out everything bad, you will have few places in which to invest.

Once the organization begins receiving endowment funds, the board will need to create an investment committee. This committee can include people who are not on the board. Friendly bankers, your biggest donors, and program officers at foundations can help with recommendations for candidates for this committee and sometimes may serve themselves. For many grassroots board members, their biggest investment is a new car; investing endowment funds requires learning a number of new concepts. Even if the board delegates responsibility for investment decisions to others, it must still educate itself in order to monitor the management of the endowment. It is not always easy to tell what is a good or bad investment, nor is it always easy to tell if someone is using your lack of investment knowledge to their (and not your organization's) financial advantage. Although you may want to hire an investment professional, don't ever trust your investment decisions to just one person or a group of people who are all friends with each other.

Here is a checklist to help you determine if you are ready to start an endowment.

Is Your Group Ready for an Endowment?

We currently have a strong individual donor program in place. We regularly meet with our major donors, and a majority of our staff and board feel comfortable asking for money in person. Further, our annual income from individuals has been growing for the past three years, both in amount of money and in number of donors.	☐ Yes ☐ No
The entire board, staff, and key volunteers (hereinafter referred to as "We") agree that our organization needs to exist at least fifty more years.	☐ Yes ☐ No
We have considered the drawbacks of having an endowment and have decided the advantages to our organization merit the risks.	☐ Yes ☐ No
We have decided on the use of the income from our endowment.	☐ Yes ☐ No
We have decided on an approximate ideal size for the endowment (understanding that this may take several years to achieve).	☐ Yes ☐ No
Authorization to open an endowment has been given by the board and is reflected in the board minutes.	☐ Yes ☐ No
The board, in discussion with all appropriate parties, has created the following policies: a use policy, an invasion policy, a gift acceptance policy, and an investment policy.	☐ Yes ☐ No
We have a plan for creating an investment committee once we begin receiving endowment funds.	☐ Yes ☐ No
We are excited about moving into this next phase in our organizational development.	☐ Yes ☐ No

Do not short-circuit these steps in creating an endowment. They do not have to be monumentally time consuming, but they allow you to have some in-depth discussions about the future of your organization that you should be having anyway. Once you have agreed on a case for needing to exist far into the future and you have in place the policies you need, you can announce your endowment and encourage people to contribute to it as an ongoing part of your fundraising. You can direct your bequests and other legacy gifts to it, and then, if you want, you can conduct an endowment campaign, as discussed in Chapter Twenty-Five.

Endowment Campaigns

An endowment campaign has the same structure as an annual fund campaign, a major donor campaign, or a capital campaign in that it has a financial goal for which a gift range chart and timeline have been developed to help the organization meet that goal. Many organizations conduct a feasibility study to determine what the goal of the campaign should be or even whether to commit to the campaign at all (see Chapter Twenty-Seven for a discussion of feasibility studies).

As with a capital campaign, the tasks for launching an endowment campaign include forming a committee of solicitors, compiling a list of prospects, and developing creative materials that describe the campaign and its benefits. Once these tasks have been done, the prospects are prioritized and solicitation begins. Unlike other types of campaigns, an endowment remains open for new gifts even after the campaign has ended. The gifts sought during the campaign are from donors who will give over the next few years; gifts through estates are not the focus of the campaign itself, but are the focus of an ongoing endowment.

For all their similarities, there are subtle and not-so-subtle differences between the steps of endowment campaigns, described in the following, and those of other kinds of campaigns.

STEP 1: SET A GOAL

To determine a goal for your endowment campaign, you need to decide how much interest income you want and what amount of principal will be likely to generate that amount of interest. A financial adviser will be able to help you with projections. In general, an organization can safely assume that it can take the equivalent of 5 percent of the principal out every year and the principal will continue to grow.

To generate $50,000 a year in interest income, then, will require an endowment of about $1 million; to generate $200,000 a year will require an endowment of $4 million. An endowment is not a quick fix to a cash flow problem! The principal of your endowment is not guaranteed to grow: it can fall behind both in inflationary times and, more obviously, with market crashes and economic instability. Organizations will have years when they cannot draw the amount of money they need from their endowment without eroding the principal.

There are two ways to get to your goal: one is to conduct a campaign for that goal. If you need $1 million, your campaign goal is $1 million. However, if that sum seems out of your reach right now but you think you could get to, say, $250,000, you can conduct a campaign to "seed" your endowment fund. With this type of campaign, you raise a decent amount of money and do not draw anything out of the account until it gets to the initial goal you have set. Once the campaign is ended, you keep raising endowment funds as part of your fundraising work, but without the intensity of a campaign. Having some money raised will help donors feel more assured that their endowment gift is joining existing money. The problem with the "seeding" approach, however, is that too often the endowment levels off at the small amount raised by the campaign. The endowment principal is too much money for the organization to spend, but not enough to generate the kind of interest that will really help with the annual fundraising crunch. If you decide to seed an endowment with a campaign, then be sure that you have a plan in place for having the endowment grow after the campaign is over.

Sometimes groups just want "something to take the edge off"—the stiff drink approach to endowments. They want a pot of money that generates between $5,000 and $10,000 a year, so they only need between $100,000 and $250,000. An endowment campaign is not the best vehicle to raise this small amount of money. For any need of less than $25,000, an organization should consider increasing its annual fundraising goal, perhaps by diversifying to a new strategy or being more aggressive with current donors, or just opening a savings account. Generally it is not worth the effort of starting an actual endowment campaign if your goal is to raise less than $500,000.

Of course, however much money you decide to raise in your campaign, you should always be seeking and accepting additional endowment gifts. But get your endowment moving by setting a large enough goal to be meaningful. (See Chapter Twenty-Four, "Setting Up an Endowment.")

STEP 2: CREATE THE GIFT RANGE CHART

Once you have a goal, you need to create a Gift Range Chart (see Chapter Twenty-Six, "Capital Campaigns," for more guidance on structuring a gift range chart). A chart for a goal of $1 million is shown here. As with capital campaigns, discussed in the next chapter, an endowment campaign differs from an annual major donor campaign in that it seeks a lead gift equal to 20 percent of the goal instead of 10 percent, and all the gifts are fairly large. The chart calls for one gift equal to 20 percent of the goal, two gifts that equal 10 percent of the goal, and three to five gifts that make up the next 10 percent of the goal. Six to eight donors, then, contribute 50 percent or more of the total goal.

	Number of Gifts	Gift Size
Endowment Campaign Gift Range Chart		
Goal: $1 Million		
	1	$200,000
	2	$100,000
	4	$50,000
	5	$25,000
	10	$10,000
	20	$5,000
	20	$2,500
	25	$1,000
Total gifts	87	

In general, gifts of less than $1,000 are not sought (although all gifts are gratefully accepted). Because donors have several years to pay off these gifts, $1,000 is affordable even for lower-income people. For example, a pledge of $27 per month, which is relatively affordable, carried out for three years totals $1,000.

Organizations with a donor base of very-low-income people, however, need to think twice before launching an endowment. Even if such an effort could be successful, it means the organization will have a kind of financial security that few, if any, of its supporters have. This can exacerbate a danger present in all endowments: a perception on the part of donors that the organization doesn't need annual gifts and that, in fact, the organization has lost touch with its base. A further danger is that donors will give to the endowment instead of to the annual fund. As the saying goes, you will have robbed Peter to pay Paul.

STEP 3: CREATE THE TIMELINE

The timeline for an endowment campaign is generally not less than two years and definitely not more than five years. The timeline for the campaign does not include all the discussion involved in deciding to do a campaign or the feasibility study, but it does include the preparation time in terms of prospect research and materials. It usually takes the best part of a year just to solicit the lead gifts (because many of the lead donors will have to be talked with several times) and to create appropriate materials, and it may take another year to solicit all the other gifts. Three years allows for the unforeseen to be dealt with and the maximum number of donors to be solicited. Five years is the outside maximum amount of time an organization can sustain interest and passion for a campaign while maintaining annual fundraising. Usually two to three years is the ideal amount of time to conduct a campaign. A fourth year can be used as a "wind-down" period, and pledges can be paid over five or more years even if the solicitation phase of the campaign is completed in two years.

STEP 4: FORM A SOLICITATION TEAM

Traditionally, endowments are funded by gifts from estates. This is why traditional endowments are not generally funded using a campaign strategy; rather, they grow as donors leave money to them and as the investment grows. In other words, a person may pledge to give a bequest from his or her estate, but the receipt of the gift usually depends on the death of the donor as well as the time it takes to settle the estate (which can be years). Some organizations have counted the unrealized value of bequests as part of their endowment campaign goal, but this is both foolish and unethical. Bequests can be changed anytime before the donor's death, so even when a donor has promised you a bequest, it may not come to you if the donor has a change of heart or circumstance. Only irrevocable legacy gifts (such as trusts) can be counted toward a goal.

In conducting an endowment campaign, organizations are asking donors for assets that will be given in the next few years. Although gifts made from a donor's annual income are certainly welcome, they will never be as large as asset or estate gifts, because even the wealthiest donors reserve the bulk of their income for their own needs.

In forming a committee, then, you are looking for people who are comfortable asking donors for assets; usually, these are people who have made an asset gift themselves. The people on the solicitation team include members of the board and people who have made large gifts to the endowment. Although this is the ideal committee makeup for any campaign, for an endowment it is imperative that those who are asking know what it feels like to decide to give a gift that they cannot give very often, and maybe only once in their lifetime. The role of volunteers in these campaigns cannot be overstated. Staff can ask, and they do, but even then a staff person will need to have made an endowment gift in addition to their annual gift.

To form the solicitation team, first identify the people closest to your organization who believe in endowments and can make the largest gifts. A team consisting of a board member and a staff member asks each of these potential solicitors for their own gift, then asks them to be on the team. Some members of the solicitation team are usually identified during the discussion about whether to have an endowment. They are the ones who argue in favor of it and say that they will give to such a campaign.

Conventional financial planning dictates that one should "never touch principal." Yet principal is what you are asking for. In a sense, you are asking people to transfer some of their "endowment" to your endowment. This is a process that requires thought, commitment, and careful consideration. All the solicitors must be people whom the donors trust to have gone through this process. Moreover, there is something very convincing when a person can say, "My husband and I have accumulated a nest egg of $1,000,000 over many years of saving. It is for our retirement and for emergencies. But the threat to the environment (or our children, or world peace) is bigger than our need for a nest egg. We want to make sure that Important Group is able to do its work well into the future and maintain its economic stability. So we are giving 10 percent of what we have invested in our nest egg—$100,000—to the endowment as our investment in our community's future."

Even someone with no real assets can make a good solicitor, as long as he or she has given a significant gift. In one organization, a board member postponed buying a new car. He described his gift this way: "My old car can be coaxed into a couple more years of use. In the meantime I am going to give the equivalent of a car payment on a new car for two years to the endowment campaign. That will bring my gift to $5,000. I don't have any real assets, but I can give by postponing getting an asset, and my gift will have far more permanence than a new car." In another instance, a solicitor described her gift this way: "I put some money aside every month and once a year I go away for two weeks. This year, I vacationed at home. I saw friends, I planted a garden, I read books, I went to free events at my library, and I gave the money I saved to the endowment. I had a great time, so although my gift was significant for me, it was not painful."

The solicitation team can be formed slowly. It can start with two or three endowment donors and, as more donations are received, new donors can be asked to join the team.

STEP 5: COMPILE AND ORGANIZE THE LIST OF PROSPECTS

In all campaigns, the rule of "top down, inside out" is the way to organize your prospects. Ben Franklin, who was one of America's earliest and best fundraisers, advised, "Apply to all those whom you know will give something; next, to those whom you are uncertain whether they will give anything or not, and show them the list of those who have given; and lastly, do not neglect those who you are sure will give nothing, for in some of them you will be mistaken."

Franklin's advice is what we mean by "inside out." Start with the people closest to the organization. Those will be board members (if they are not the closest people to the organization, then reconsider doing an endowment campaign), other major donors, volunteers, former board members and volunteers (assuming no ill will accompanied their becoming "former"), staff, and so on. Then, start from the top of that list and work your way down. The first gift should be solicited from the person closest to the organization who can give the biggest gift. This may not be the biggest gift you need, but it should be the biggest one you can get right now.

Sometimes it is hard to figure out which of the people who are closest you should approach first. Think through who on the list can give the biggest gifts. This exercise should narrow your list somewhat. Now think about who is most excited about the endowment. Remember there are going to be major donors who love your organization's work but who are not going to support the endowment. There will be some who simply don't agree that a grassroots organization should have an endowment. There will be some who have given to other endowments only to see the endowment funds spent on annual needs by a careless board. And there will be others who wish your endowment effort well but are only interested in funding more immediate needs. Finding donors who agree with all three premises of the case for an endowment—that the organization currently needs some financial stability, needs to exist indefinitely into the future, and is mature enough or sophisticated enough to handle this kind of money—and who also have the capacity to give is not simple.

Use common sense in identifying these prospects. Think about what else you know about the people on your list. For example, a person giving $50 every quarter might be close to the group, but she is probably far from the biggest donor. However, if her $50 gifts are derived from income earned from investments, then she definitely goes to the top of the list because perhaps she would give you the asset that is yielding that $50 each quarter. Someone who gave you $1,000 that he won in the lottery, whose gift prior to that was $25, and who actually ekes out a living as an artist, is not going to be high on the list, but he may be an excellent solicitor because he actually gave an asset that he could have used himself.

Many people will say that they have no idea what assets their donors have. If you really have no idea, then you are going to have to find out more about your donors before you begin asking them for gifts to your endowment. However, a general easy rule to follow in soliciting capital or endowment gifts is to ask for a gift that is ten times the amount of the donor's annual gift. You want to make it clear that this gift is in addition to their annual gift. You don't want your annual income to decline while you are doing the campaign. When you tell donors that you are asking everyone for the same thing—ten times their annual gift—people are not offended, even if the size of the gift is absolutely out of their range. The real risk you take in following this formula without other knowledge is that you would ask someone for too little.

The final step in compiling a prospect list is to be sure you have enough prospects. A prospect for an endowment gift is someone who has demonstrated a commitment to your nonprofit, usually by giving over several years and often through other than just financial involvement; someone who has the money; and someone whom you know or you have access to.

As with capital campaigns, you need about four times as many prospects as the number of gifts you seek because 50 percent of your prospects will say no and 50 percent of the group that says yes will give you less than what you ask for.

In our $1 million gift range chart shown earlier, you would need about 348 prospects (87×4) to be certain that you could complete this goal. You don't need to have all the prospects right at the start, but you do need at least some of the prospects for the biggest gifts right from the beginning. You would be ill advised to launch a million-dollar endowment campaign with fewer than one hundred prospects for the gifts of $2,500 or more. Far worse than no endowment at all is an endowment campaign that splutters and moves slowly. The energy of the campaign is part of what makes it successful or not. A report that "Our campaign is going so well" makes people want to give. The news that "Our campaign is getting off to a slow start," or "We asked a bunch of people who said no" is not as appealing.

STEP 6: SOLICIT THE GIFTS

For a full description of the process of soliciting large gifts, please see Chapters Twenty-One, Twenty-Three, and Twenty-Six on major gifts programs, major gift campaigns, and capital campaigns, respectively.

The primary differences between major gifts or capital campaigns and endowment campaigns is in the case. A person being asked for a major gift needs to be convinced that there is a pressing, immediate need that your organization can meet and that this need must be addressed with, among other things, some very large gifts. A capital campaign makes the case that the pressing needs of the organization cannot be met adequately in the facility you are in or with the equipment you currently have or without some other large investment. The case for the endowment goes one step further, explaining that the organization needs stability currently and into the future. It tells donors that their commitment to your current programs is so important that you hope they want to help make your work a permanent feature of your community.

Even the most progressive people can become fiscal conservatives when asked for capital or endowment gifts. They may well believe that your organization does wonderful things toward ending racism or providing creative learning opportunities for kids with disabilities or advocating for more just tax policies. But do these same donors believe you will be able to manage investing large amounts of money or be good at managing a building? Donors will have these questions, and organizations must be able to respond to them. When an organization wants to start an endowment, there will be an added question that no one can really answer: "What will happen when everyone who is currently involved in this organization is gone?" Taking seriously the right (and indeed, the obligation) of donors to raise these questions and doubts and preparing thoughtful and reasonable answers are the marks of organizations ready for capital and endowment projects.

Capital Campaigns

A capital campaign is an intensive, time-limited effort to raise money for a project that presents a one-time need over and above the annual budget. Capital campaigns traditionally are used to finance buying, constructing, or refurbishing a building, including making the space accessible to people with disabilities; increasingly, they are being used to make office space "green" (that is, using more environmentally sustainable materials or systems). Sometimes a capital campaign is used to begin an endowment.

The financial goal of a capital campaign is often at least as large as the organization's annual budget and often many times larger. Most capital campaigns last two to three years; some go on as long as five years. Capital campaigns allow donors to pledge a large amount and take as many as five years (and for very large pledges, ten years) to pay it off. Donors are asked to give to the capital campaign in addition to their regular annual donations, and they are explicitly asked not to decrease their annual gift in order to make a capital gift. Capital gifts are usually so large that donors cannot finance the gift from their income and must donate cash from savings or other assets (stocks, bonds, real estate).

In understanding a capital campaign, it is helpful to review the fundraising context, first presented in Chapter Three, in which a capital campaign would be the strategy chosen.

THE ORGANIZATION AND ITS FINANCIAL NEEDS

Organizations have three types of financial needs.

Annual Funding. Annual funding is the money the organization needs every year. For most grassroots groups, raising this money consumes all their fundraising time.

Capital Funding.   From time to time, organizations need something that they don't need every year. For this kind of need, additional money has to be raised beyond the annual budget. For small capital needs (new computers, ergonomic office furniture), an organization may just add money to its annual budget and raise it with an extra appeal, or it may submit a proposal to a foundation or an appeal to a generous major donor. When the capital improvement involves buying, retrofitting, or renovating a building, the organization usually needs to conduct some kind of campaign to raise the money from a number of sources.

Endowment Funding.   As discussed in Chapter Twenty-Two, organizations that think they will be needed forever, or at least as far into the future as they can project, will want to invest some of their money and use only the interest from the investment as part of their annual income. The principal that is set aside to be invested is usually referred to as an endowment.

   Donors can provide income for these various funding needs through a few different vehicles.

Gifts of Income.   The majority of people earn money every year from a job, investments, a pension, or some combination of these sources. About seven out of every ten people give some of their earned income away. These gifts generally provide for the annual needs of the organizations they donate to. In other words, some of my income as a donor becomes some of your income as an organization.

Gifts of Assets.   In addition to their income, many people have savings or an inheritance invested in various forms of assets: stock, real estate, bonds, art, insurance policies, and so on. A donor can also give these assets to an organization, which generally uses them for capital. In other words, I give some of my savings— or my capital—to increase the capital of an organization.

Gifts from Estates.   Everyone eventually dies, but as described in Chapter Twenty-Two, they control what they own even in death through the terms of their will. Through a will, a trust, or other estate-planning mechanism, donors can arrange for nonprofit organizations to receive some or all of their estate.

These gifts are most often used for endowment. In other words, the last gifts I will give, which form my legacy, are used for the nonprofit to exist long after I am gone.

Unless restricted by the donor, organizations can, of course, use gifts of assets and estates for their annual needs. In the case of very small gifts or when donors regularly give stock as their annual gift, this may be appropriate. But for the most part, using assets and estate gifts for annual purposes is unwise because these gifts will not recur.

Similarly, but probably less obviously, using gifts made from a donor's income for capital or endowment purposes is also ill-advised. First, you don't want to raid your annual income for funds to pay for capital costs (a practice that, unfortunately, many organizations have done and lived to regret), and second, if a person can afford to give a certain amount from income, he or she should be encouraged to give that amount every year and not just for a one-time event such as a capital or endowment campaign. I hope that it goes without saying (but I will say it anyway, just in case) that if a person wishes to give a gift from his or her income to a capital or endowment effort, a group should not turn that gift away; they should accept it and thank the donor appropriately.

When contemplating a capital campaign, many organizations will say, "Our donors don't earn that kind of money." However, your donors' earnings are less important than their savings. I have seen nonprofits mount successful capital campaigns with lead gifts from older donors living on fixed incomes who have some highly appreciated stock or a piece of property they are willing to give. Because the donor can deduct the fair-market value of his gift and avoid the capital gains tax on that asset, he is able to make a much greater gift than he might have thought he could.

Keep in mind, then, that with a capital campaign you are not asking donors to make extra gifts from their income; you are asking them to go to a whole new level with your organization—giving assets and often paying their gift as a pledge over a period of several years. Some organizations elect to conduct a feasibility study before embarking on a capital campaign. Such a study will look at, among other things, whether your donors have the ability and willingness to access assets. (See Chapter Twenty-Seven for more information on feasibility studies.)

BEST USE OF CAPITAL CAMPAIGNS

Some grassroots organizations have conducted what they called capital campaigns to raise money to move to a new office space or send staff to conferences, which meant their goal was $5,000 or less, their time frame was a few weeks, and people were simply asked to put in a few extra dollars. However, capital campaigns are best used to seek gifts of assets from a wide pool of people and institutions, not just to seek "something extra" from the annual incomes of current donors. Capital campaigns should be seeking people in your donor base who may own property or securities and who would not help you in this way every year, but might give you a big gift once in a while. For this to be your intention, your capital campaign goal needs to be at least $100,000. If you need to raise less than $100,000, consider structuring your campaign as a major gifts campaign as described in Chapter Twenty-Three and run the campaign for a short time during one year, or seek two or three foundation or corporate grants to meet the goal and don't run a campaign at all.

Although your most loyal annual donors will also give to a capital campaign if they can, there are many other types of people who give to capital campaigns who are not regular annual donors. For example, three years ago a local attorney helped a small community organization in Alabama file a lawsuit against its city. The attorney admired the group's feistiness and its willingness to take risks. She was impressed that the sole staff person would work for a low salary and that the volunteers put in many hours at the organization beyond their own jobs elsewhere. She did not charge for her assistance with the lawsuit, and she donated $100 after it was over. Because she did not wish to become a regular donor to this group, she did not respond to subsequent annual appeals. However, she did have lunch with the executive director from time to time, and she continued to provide legal advice when asked. She bought a table at the organization's annual event for $1,000 for two years in a row, and she gave the group $2,000 when asked to help send a number of its constituents to the World Social Forum. When, a few years later, the organization decided to buy a building to house its organization, it asked her for a lead gift of $20,000. The work she had done pro bono on the lawsuit had been worth about that much, and the staff figured she still admired them. She did, and she admired their boldness in asking her. She gave $10,000 outright and pledged an additional $10,000 as a challenge to be met by other lawyers.

Universities and private schools often have the experience of receiving a one-time gift to a capital campaign from an alumnus or alumna who had been a minimal donor prior to the campaign. Some people like the idea of contributing to something as substantial as a building.

To ask donors to stretch their own giving and to seek donations outside of the immediate "donor family" means having a goal that implies stretching will be required to meet it. It must seem to a prospect—including a corporation, government agency, foundation, or religious institution that might not support your annual program work—that the organization cannot get this money simply by asking a few people or writing a single grant proposal.

BEGINNING A CAPITAL CAMPAIGN

A capital campaign begins when the organization has identified a large one-time need. The board of directors must fully concur with this need and must support the idea of conducting a capital campaign, which is a lot of extra work for everyone and may require an initial outlay of money to hire extra staff and develop materials.

Key volunteers who are not on the board along with longtime major donors should also be consulted about doing a capital campaign. Everyone who is important to an organization should have an opportunity to voice his or her concerns and feel part of the decision. There are dozens of buildings in the United States that are underutilized because key people in the organization were divided about the idea of constructing a new building and the people opposed to the capital campaign were outvoted. The organization may have had a few donors or funders who paid for the building, but without a lot of community support, the building is more albatross than asset. Sometimes the organization has enough money for the building, but exhausts all its donors in the capital campaign and doesn't have the money to run all its programs or sometimes even to finish furnishing the building. So the building becomes underutilized. In other instances, campaigns have had to be called off halfway through the process because so many volunteers and donors had left the organization to protest doing the campaign in the first place. A capital campaign is a highly visible enterprise; it needs widespread support within the organization.

Estimating Costs

After all the parties have been consulted and there is general agreement on the need, a goal needs to be set. Similar to the understanding that in a fancy restaurant the eventual cost of the meal will be double the entree (with drinks, dessert, and tip), the true cost of a campaign is far more than the cost of the project itself. One agency learned this fact the hard way. It needed larger office space and decided that buying a building would, in the long run, be less expensive than continually paying rent. The agency's managers found a building that suited them priced at $250,000. They launched their campaign for $250,000, forgetting that there would also be closing costs, insurance, furnishings, the cost of the campaign, and so on. In the end, the true cost of the building was $310,000. The organization spent two years climbing out of a $60,000 deficit caused by their lack of understanding of the full financial implications of the building purchase.

The following items need to be added in to the actual cost of whatever you are buying or doing with the money you are raising.

Fundraising Materials.   Materials to be used for the campaign include at least some of the following: a case statement, brochures, pledge cards, background information for solicitors, pictures, architect's renderings, a special newsletter to capital campaign donors to keep them informed of progress, and a prospectus (see further on).

Cost of Staff Time.   Someone has to handle pledges, write thank you notes, report to the board, work with the contractor, decide who has to approve paint color or carpet choices, know what to do when someone donates stocks, and handle emergencies.

Accounting Systems.   The organization's books need to be set up to keep the campaign's income and expenses separate from the annual budget, and there need to be reminder systems for collecting pledges (which may extend well past the end of the campaign). If you plan to use current staff for that task, then you will have to figure out how the work they are currently doing will get done. In a multiyear campaign, it is unlikely that an organization could get by without hiring extra staff.

Office Extras.   You may need to put in extra phone lines or buy more computers. If you hire staff, that person will need to sit somewhere, so you may need another desk and chair.

For the Building Project Itself. Someone with expertise in this area will need to help you list costs related to the building, such as construction insurance, building permits, design costs, disaster preparedness, fire extinguishers, landscaping, plumbing, and wiring, and help you with how much to estimate for cost overruns or unforeseen delays.

Furnishings for the Building. What are you going to bring from your current office and what else will you need? What will these items cost?

Debt Service on a Bridge Loan. You will probably have to pay bills before pledges are fully paid, and you may have to borrow money to cover the gap between pledged income and received income. The interest on that debt needs to be factored into the goal of the campaign. Banks will lend money with pledges as collateral, but you have to pay interest on the loan.

Additional Costs. Add 15 percent for people who pledge but cannot finish paying or decide not to pay. Add another 5 to 10 percent onto the grand total and you can feel reasonably safe that this will be the cost of the campaign.

In any fundraising endeavor, but particularly in campaigns with big-ticket items such as buildings, follow the adage: plan expenses high and income low.

Preparing a Case Statement

Once the need is established and the costs are known and provisionally approved by the board, the next step is to write up a case statement for the campaign. This case statement is separate from the organization's overall case statement, although certainly it borrows from it. The capital campaign case focuses solely on the goal of the campaign and shows how this goal will help the organization meet all its other goals. The case statement implies or overtly states that the work of the group will be greatly enhanced by the addition of whatever the campaign is proposing to achieve and will be significantly slowed down or impaired by the lack of whatever is being proposed. The final page of the case statement is the financial goal displayed as a gift range chart.

The Gift Range Chart

The pyramid that is constructed by a Capital Campaign Gift Range Chart is much shorter and narrower than that of an annual major gifts campaign (see Chapter

Twenty-Three). In a capital campaign, the lead gift equals between 15 and 20 percent of the total goal, and 80 percent of the money comes from about 10 percent of the donors.

The Gift Range Chart follows this pattern:

One gift = 15 to 20 percent or more of the goal

Two gifts = 10 percent each or more

Four to five gifts = 5 percent each or more

So, 50 percent to 70 percent of the goal will come from about seven or eight gifts.

After these largest gifts, increase the number of gifts and decrease the gift size as makes sense for your group and number of prospects until the goal is reached. An example is shown here.

Capital Campaign Gift Range Chart		
Goal: $1,000,000		
Number of Gifts	**Gift Size**	**Cumulative total**
1	$150,000	$150,000
2	$100,000	$350,000
4	$50,000	$550,000
8	$25,000	$750,000
10	$10,000	$850,000
15	$5,000	$925,000
20	$2,500	$975,000
25	$1,000	$1,000,000

In this example, eighty-five gifts will be required. Whereas in an annual major gifts campaign we assume that about three prospects will be needed for every gift that is given, except in the higher reaches of the chart, with a capital campaign we look for four times as many prospects as donors in each gift range in order to give the group a little padding for those people who give less than $1,000. In this example, then, the organization will need to identify 340 prospects (85 × 4). All of these people will have to be asked in person, and some of them may have to be visited more than once. If any of these gift amounts are to be sought from foundations or corporations, proposals will have to be written.

Sometimes grassroots organizations feel that seeking only gifts of $1,000 or more will exclude too many people who may want to be part of the campaign. However, when they realize how many people it will take to reach their goal and how many people will have to be asked, they usually see the logic of focusing the capital campaign largely on people who can give big gifts. Further, by offering people the opportunity to pay their pledge over two or three years, a $1,000 gift becomes doable for many middle- and lower-income people.

Timing

The final decision the organization must make is about the timing of the campaign. Try to find out what other organizations will be having capital or intensive fundraising campaigns during the time you wish to run your campaign and assess whether any of your prospects will be key prospects for those groups. It's best to launch your campaign during years when you expect your annual campaign to be doing well and to make sure you do not anticipate any shortfalls in annual income. Because during the capital campaign your annual income will probably not rise, do not plan major new programs outside of the capital project.

Final Approval

Once you have prepared the case statement, with costs, gift range chart, and timing, bring the whole package back to the board, key volunteers, and staff for reapproval. While these people may have approved the concept of the campaign, when faced with the realities of the money and time involved, they may wish to change their minds. Without full board and staff ownership, the campaign will fail. Taking the time to make sure that everyone understands the implications of the campaign is imperative because once the campaign is launched publicly, it must be seen through to the end.

FOUR PHASES OF THE CAMPAIGN

A capital campaign is conducted in four parts. The first phase is the "quiet" phase: it starts when the case statement is ready and approved. The second phase is the "launch," when the campaign is publicly announced and begins to seek support beyond the inner circle of donors. The third phase is often called the "public" phase; this is the most intensive and continues for the longest time. This is the phase when solicitors are visiting prospects and gathering commitments. When the campaign has reached between 85 and 95 percent of its goal, the "wind-up" phase or "topping off" phase begins.

The Quiet (or Pre-Campaign) Phase

Have you ever noticed how an organization will have an event to announce its capital campaign and declare, "We are proud to launch our $3 million building campaign today, and we are pleased to report that we already have $2.3 million pledged"? Do you wonder how it could have raised all that money in just one day? Of course, that money was not raised in a day; in fact, it may have been raised over a period of months or even years. The purpose of the quiet phase is twofold: to test the concept of the campaign on people who could actually meet its goals and to give a feeling of momentum at the public launch. Everyone may feel good about the case and the need for this campaign, but the true test of its possibility for success is whether people feel good enough about it to give a big gift. Some campaigns have to be abandoned or seriously rethought at this phase if not enough people step up with early gifts, but no real harm is done at that point because the campaign has not been made public. Once the campaign is made public, you want people to say, "Wow, that's great they have raised so much money already. My gift can move them forward."

The goal of the quiet phase is to get 30 to 50 percent of the campaign's total from the top three to five donors. Most fundraisers feel that if you can get the largest gifts first you will be able to find all the remaining gifts needed. (The largest gifts are called the "lead" gifts, though they may not truly be the very first gifts, as those should come from board members.) The power of the lead gifts may sound like a superstition, but there is much anecdotal evidence to support it. Lead gifts provide momentum, instill confidence in the campaign, and inspire other big donors. Smaller gifts seem more helpful when they are put toward a goal already partly reached.

Conversely, starting a capital campaign without lead gifts is dangerous because the momentum lags. Furthermore, if an organization doesn't know possible lead donors at the beginning of the campaign, where does it think it will meet them later? It is worth postponing a campaign for months or even years in order to ensure that the first gifts given are also the largest. At the risk of redundancy, let me repeat: an organization does not need to know all of its prospects ahead of time, but it must know those that are capable of making the lead gifts, and it must have a sense that it will ultimately know about as many donors as it needs for the whole campaign.

The Prospectus.   To solicit lead gifts, you will need to design a document called the prospectus, which is a brochure, a booklet, or sometimes a PowerPoint or video incorporating information from the case statement in a shorter and more artistic format. The prospectus will be given to all prospects, and it must look good. The prospectus shows the prospect that you know what you are doing and that your organization is able to handle large amounts of money and manage this large capital project. The prospectus should also be posted on your Web site, along with regular updates on the progress of your campaign, your gift range chart, and how donors can contribute. Few, if any, gifts will come from the Web site, but it is good for visibility and consistency of message.

The Lead Gifts.   The lead donor must not only be able to give a big gift, he or she must also be a person who likes to set the pace, to set an example, and to take a leadership role. These first large gifts come from people who will gamble with you that the campaign will succeed and who actually pride themselves on being risk takers. Obviously, they must care very much about your cause and be committed to the capital project. Frequently (and ideally), the lead gifts come from a few people who were involved in the planning and approval of the campaign. If those people are not able to give the biggest gifts, they need to know people or institutions that can.

Approaching the Lead Prospects.   The process of approaching people who could make lead gifts is the same as approaching any major donor—a letter, followed by phone call and request to meet, followed by a meeting at which the gift is requested—with one slight change. With requests for capital gifts, an answer almost never comes at the meeting; often the prospect wants more information that must be sent or brought to a subsequent meeting.

When prospects seem to be stalling or wanting more information, see it as a good sign. In fact, many fundraisers believe that if a person says, "I need to think about it" in response to a request for a large gift, they have asked that person for just the right amount. The amount was not one she could give easily at the meeting, nor was it an amount that was patently out of her range, but it was an amount she could give, albeit not very often. A person who says yes to a request for $10,000 in one meeting may be someone who has thought a great deal about the campaign and made her decision, but it also may be someone for whom $10,000 is not a stretch gift. Don't be discouraged by prospects wanting more information or needing additional meetings; making a capital gift is a big decision. Most people will make, at most, a handful of capital gifts in their lifetimes. Even very wealthy people can't afford to give capital gifts very often, and they want to make sure their gift will be well used.

These gifts should be solicited by teams of two people—usually a board member and a staff person or two board members. The board members must be giving what is a stretch gift for them and should be willing to share information about their gift with the prospect. For example, the board member might say, "I am giving ten times my annual gift to this campaign and paying my pledge over five years" or "My partner and I decided this endeavor was as important as our car, so we are giving the same amount as our car payment over the next two years." If the solicitor feels comfortable, he may also share the actual amount of his gift. The point to make clear to the prospect is that the people asking are giving as much as they can possibly afford and that their gift has been made after a lot of thought. They are hoping the prospect will make a similar commitment.

The prospectus should be shared with the lead donors; once they have agreed to a gift, they should be asked if they would be willing to help solicit other gifts. Some people find it flattering and sometimes emotionally moving to be asked for a gift by someone who has given the biggest gift.

Once the very top of the pyramid has been filled in with donors, the organization is ready to move to the second stage.

The Launch

The launch of a capital campaign should be marked with a special event. The press, donors, volunteers, and foundation and corporate staff should be invited. The press should receive a press release ahead of time with background information on the group and the campaign or they should be given one at the event. The invitation to the launch should be attractive because it is the first impression most prospects will have of your capital campaign. The event itself doesn't need to last very long. If you want to make it into a regular special event, you can add a dance or speaker, but this is not necessary. Large graphics on display should describe the overall goal of the campaign and show the gift range chart and how much money has been raised. A board member should describe to the gathered crowd how important the campaign is and invite everyone to celebrate the donations that have come in so far. Drinks (including champagne) and hors d'oeuvres may be served.

The Public Phase

Immediately after the launch the public phase begins. During this time teams of two people are visiting prospects with as much speed as that process will allow. Most prospects are visited at least once during this time, and this phase is the longest. As each gift is received, the total still needed is revised and publicized, at least to staff, board members, and solicitors, so there is a constant sense of movement toward the goal. During this stage, the three most important elements are maintaining accurate information on donors and prospects, keeping track of where the organization is in the solicitation process with each prospect (often called "moves management"), and keeping in touch with volunteer solicitors. Thank you notes must go out promptly. When people pledge to pay over the course of several years, they must sign a pledge agreement. It can be very simple, as in the example shown here.

Sample Pledge Agreement

I, *(name)*, pledge the sum of $_____ *(amount)* to be paid in monthly *(or quarterly)* installments of $____ for the next ___ years.

This document constitutes a legally binding agreement, and I know that plans are being made and money is being spent based on the expectation that I will pay this pledge in the way I have described. A copy of this pledge agreement has been placed with my will.

Signed:

_____

Solicitors must be notified of new gifts as they come in; they should be in touch weekly and meet every month or two to report on their progress. Any problems they run into must be dealt with promptly. One such problem is conditional gifts. Prospects often will offer to make a gift on certain conditions: "I'll give if three other people match my gift" or "I'll give if the conference room can be named for my mother" or "I'll give if I can have a seat on the board." Conditional gifts, regardless of how benign the condition proposed, must go through an approval process, preferably at the board level. Solicitors can say to such prospects, "That's a very kind offer. Let me see what we can do about it. I don't have the authority to make those promises." Then the organization decides if it wishes to accept the condition or not. An organization should never take money on conditions that it doesn't wish to meet. People should not be able to "buy" board seats, for example.

The Wind-Up Phase

When more than four-fifths of the money has been pledged, the organization goes into a wind-up phase. At this point you look for one or two people who can put the goal over the top: "Mr. Jones, we are $10,000 short of our goal—would you finish this campaign with a gift of that amount?" To find people who can close the campaign in this way, go back to your original prospect list for lead gifts and see if any of the people on that list were not asked because solicitors felt that they would not take a risk on being the lead gift, or see if any of them said, "Come back to me when you are further along." The wind-up phase is also a good time to ask for a lot of small gifts, because at this stage gifts of $1,000 are clearly helping to move the organization toward its goal.

The end of the wind-up phase is a large celebratory special event. If you are purchasing or constructing a building, this is often a ribbon-cutting or ceremonial groundbreaking event, if that hasn't happened already.

POST-CAMPAIGN

Volunteer solicitors should be given their own party, such as dinner at a fancy restaurant, and should be presented with gifts of appreciation. These are often plaques. Though nice, the gifts should not be expensive. Staff should also be rewarded at this party, possibly with a certificate for a weekend away at a bed-and-breakfast or a gift certificate to a store they would like.

Staff and solicitors should review all the donor records for the campaign to make sure they are accurate and that all needed documentation is in place. A special report should be sent to all donors and funders describing the successful conclusion of the campaign and reiterating what wonderful work the group will be able to do in its new building.

Soon after the end of the capital campaign, you will need to increase the amount of money you are raising annually, since you will not have had an increase in two or three years while the campaign was active. A good capital campaign usually has the effect of helping increase annual income, as donors feel closer to the organization and realize they can afford to give more than they thought. Further, the high visibility of a capital campaign will often attract new annual donors.

As you can see, a capital campaign is a time-consuming project and one that requires keeping track of a lot of details. Only organizations with a strong working board of directors, a loyal donor base, and a well-designed major gifts program should undertake such a campaign.

Conducting Feasibility Studies

Afeasibility study is a survey of people whose agreement and support you would need in order to succeed at a particular project. Usually, prospective donors, board members, community leaders, and program officers at foundations and corporations who might be approached to contribute to a project are asked to state anonymously what they think about your capital or endowment project and what level of support they or their organization might provide. Generally, the survey is done in two or three parts: a written survey sent to all the prospects who will be asked for major gifts, a phone survey to a smaller number of donors who will probably be asked for lead gifts, and optional in-person interviews or a focus group with handful of key leaders. (See Premium Web Content for sample feasibility study surveys (capital and endowment), a sample feasibility study report, and a case study of the use of a feasibility study.)

WHO CONDUCTS THE FEASIBILITY STUDY

Most organizations hire a consultant to carry out their feasibility study. The reason for this is straightforward: for the prospects to feel that they can be as honest and candid as they want, their answers have to be truly anonymous. Maximum anonymity is ensured when they are asked by a consultant whom they don't know to fill out a form sent by mail that does not call for them to include their name and address and that they return to the consultant, not the organization. Although some people might be willing to say whatever they want to say to anyone, human nature is such that to spare someone's feelings or to avoid a confrontation, many people will not be as direct if they know that what they say is going to get back to someone they know.

The written survey consists mostly of structured questions presented in a multiple-choice format so that the survey is easy to complete and the results can be easily tabulated. A few open-ended questions can also be included, which ask such things as whether prospects have confidence in the leadership of the organization and what they think about the organization's program directions. Use the open-ended questions to find out prospects' opinions on anything the organization may have done or said that was at all controversial. Once the results of the survey are in, the consultant looks for any pattern of response and for issues that need to be clarified. The results of the written survey form the basis of the questions in the phone survey. On the phone, the surveyor can probe a little more, record anecdotes and examples, and even query respondents about whether they agree or disagree with some of the opinions or findings that came from the written survey. Many studies don't include in-person interviews. They are helpful if there is a need to clarify the case or probe further about any anomalies found in the phone or written surveys, but otherwise you might have enough information to go on without them.

A feasibility study is complicated and time consuming to conduct, which make it expensive. The least-expensive study conducted by a professional will likely cost $5,000; many studies run as high as $50,000. The size of the income that can be expected from the campaign resulting from the feasibility study will not correlate directly to the cost of the study, because a campaign with a low goal will not necessarily involve fewer surveys or fewer phone calls. Because of the costs involved, these studies are usually reserved for large campaigns.

WHETHER TO DO A STUDY

There is no need to do a feasibility study in the following situations:

- If you intend to do the campaign no matter what the study shows. I have known half a dozen organizations that spent money on a study only to conclude that the results showing lack of support were wrong. They proceeded with their campaigns—some succeeded and some failed.

- If you are going to use the study simply to find out whether or not you can make your goal. You will discover easily enough whether you can raise the amount of money you need by asking for lead gifts from qualified prospects before the campaign is announced publicly. If they all say no or give much lower gifts than you needed, don't announce your campaign, and go back to the drawing board.

- If your goal is less than $2 million, the cost of a full-scale study is not justified. You can decide to do only a written survey or a limited phone survey if you have some specific questions, but what you really want is to go to the lead prospects and see what they say.

You will need to do a study under the following circumstances:

- The key leadership in your organization has a mixed reputation. I conducted a study for a capital campaign for an organization whose executive director had been there thirteen years. She was well liked, but as one key prospect said, "The organization has gotten too big for her, and neither she nor her board can handle the responsibility of a building." The study showed that unless the organization made significant changes in staffing, such as hiring an associate director who could handle a lot of the administrative and human resource issues the executive director was not good at, few were likely to contribute.

- Your building project may be controversial in some way. A proposed homeless shelter discovered that it would face major neighborhood opposition if it expanded in the way it envisioned. By slowing the process down, the shelter was able to address neighborhood concerns with public education programs. Once that was done, the campaign proceeded successfully.

- You want to raise more than $2 million and you have never raised that amount of money before.

- You want to know exactly what the capacity of the people closest to the organization is before you ask them. The results of your study will not show you what any individual donor can give, but you will learn whether there are people in your sphere who have the capacity and willingness to give large amounts. You will need to figure out who those people are.

A feasibility study gives you an added measure of assurance and will help you define and counter big problems. When you are raising large amounts of money, a feasibility study will allow you to discover the capacity of your donors in a way that would otherwise be difficult, given our society's strong taboo about talking about how much money a person actually has.

In my experience, grassroots organizations that are able to raise the first third of their goal from five to ten people will be able to raise the rest of the money to get to their goal. I advise groups to use that guideline as the most reliable indicator of whether their campaign will succeed.

If you want more assurance without having to buy a feasibility study, you can talk to the people who would have to take the lead for your campaign to succeed. Tell them about the possibility of the campaign and ask what they think about it. Tell them you are "testing the waters," or "getting feedback on this idea." Make the conversation very casual, but pay close attention to what they say.

WHAT FEASIBILITY STUDIES TELL YOU

Feasibility studies often predict that a campaign will bring in a lower amount than it actually raises in the end. Some consultants prefer to err on the side of underestimating the amount that can be raised, but the main reason campaigns exceed their goals is that it is impossible to factor in the effect of the excitement generated by the campaign on the prospects. It is one thing for prospects to talk on the phone about what they might, theoretically, do for a campaign should it be launched, but quite another for them to be asked in person to give to a campaign by someone they admire. On the phone, a person is sober and serious and not wanting to mislead the questioner. He names an amount that is perhaps a stretch for him but that he feels confident he would be able to pay. Later, during the real campaign, when a friend or colleague comes with a staff person to ask for his gift, he is likely to become excited by the enthusiasm of the askers and end up giving more than he told the interviewer he might during the phone survey. Perhaps on the phone a prospect said she would be unlikely to give, but faced with the reality of the campaign she may not want to be left out. Her objections, which seemed so big during the phone call, can fade in the light of the campaign. This does not mean you should add on a few hundred thousand to whatever the study suggests you can raise, but it does mean that you can be confident that a well-done study will present an amount that is at or below what you can really bring in.

ACHIEVING SUCCESS

Of course, there is no assurance that any plan will succeed. But you have a better chance of succeeding if you have a plan than if you don't. Moreover, evaluating your success will be easier if you have a plan—in fact a plan is what makes evaluation possible.

Another requirement for success is to make sure your board of directors is on board. If a board of directors does not want to work on the campaign, the campaign is going to go nowhere. People look to the board for leadership. Your board may well be made up of people who cannot make big gifts to a capital or endowment campaign. That's fine. But they need to make some gift, and they need to be involved in planning the campaign.

The best way to know if you are going to succeed is to take the time to plan properly, as discussed in the chapters on capital and endowment campaigns, then implement the quiet phase of your plan. The requests made during the quiet phase give you the most accurate information with the least amount of public risk.

PART FIVE

Fundraising Management

The next five chapters explore what an organization needs to have in place, and what fundraising staff need to do (and not do) in order to have a manageable job. I find that fundraising programs fall apart in one or more of the following ways:

- The organization doesn't have a clear case or loses sight of its mission and goals in its search for funding.
- Strategies are not used properly and so are rendered ineffective and then abandoned.
- The fundraising function is not managed properly: data entry is sloppy, the fundraising staff have far bigger jobs than anyone could do, and the organization is not good at using volunteers to augment its paid staff.

Part One helped you avoid the first pitfall, Part Two addressed the second problem, and this part addresses the third situation. I start with a brief description of the physical setup a development function needs. In Chapter Twenty-Nine, I describe how to sort through the massive amounts of information that are available to you to identify the information you actually need and will put to use. These two tasks alone require excellent time management, the subject of Chapter Thirty. Aside from understanding fundraising, using good time management practices is the most important element of having a manageable job with a successful fundraising program. Chapter Thirty-One looks at the information you

361

need to have about your donors, and Chapter Thirty-Two describes when and how you should use volunteers.

The procedures described in this entire section are sometimes referred to as "back-office functions." Little of what goes on in fundraising management is seen by the public or, in some ways, even by the board and other staff. Nevertheless, these tasks and skills provide a foundation to the work you do; without a solid understanding of them, your fundraising will be chaotic and unsuccessful.

The Fundraising Office

Few offices of small organizations are adequate in size, equipment, or support staff, but there are some basic office requirements without which fundraising staff and volunteers will be unable to carry out an effective program. Some of the requirements detailed here cost money, but because they will pay for themselves, these costs should be seen as front money. In the case of equipment such as desks and computers, local corporations may be able to provide these for free. Other requirements cost time, which also must be seen as a front-end cost.

First and perhaps most important, there must be a separate space in the office for fundraising staff, preferably a room or at least a partitioned area. This space must be quiet and include a desk of adequate size with drawers, a chair, a filing cabinet with at least three drawers, a bookshelf, a telephone, and a computer that is not more than two years old, with a flat-screen monitor and a computer desk. (If there is more than one person working on fundraising, each person will need their own space, desk, computer, and so on.) The computer can be a laptop plugged into a docking station, but resist the idea of having a staff person use his or her own laptop as the official fundraising computer. This computer must have a backup system that backs up data automatically every day or every other day. The space must have proper lighting and ventilation, and it should not be used by people other than fundraising staff and volunteers—too much of the information here is confidential. Moreover, files, reports, letters, and the like need to be kept in order and should not be handled by anyone who is not dealing with them. Donor data should be protected with database passwords. (Most organizations have one password to get to the names and addresses of the donors, another to get to their giving history, and a third that gives access to everything. Only two or three people should know all three passwords.

The organization must take the fundraising process seriously. Both paid and volunteer fundraising staff should be seen as professionals needing certain tools to carry out their jobs. A computer, a decent database program, a desk, a phone, and separate space are the tools of a fundraiser in the same way, and with the same importance, as hammers, saws, levels, and the like are the tools of a carpenter. Just as you can't build a building without construction equipment, you can't build a donor base without fundraising equipment.

Obviously, fundraising staff should not have a nicer office space or fancier equipment than everyone else in the office. The whole organization should examine its working conditions from time to time and make it a priority to improve them if needed. It is ironic that many social change or social service groups will work in conditions that include too much noise, dim light, ergonomically horrible chairs, and inadequate equipment when they would be outraged to read about such conditions for other workers. Good working conditions cost time and money, but poor working conditions cost more: lower productivity, emotional stress, repetitive stress injuries, burnout, loss of creativity, loss of information, and, finally, loss of income to keep the organization going.

Managing Your Information

A major part of fundraising involves sifting through and using information—information about people, about sources of money, about timing, and about strategies. Internet search engines give us the capacity to gather far more information than we can possibly use, and it is easy to spend hours following one link to another, reading fundraising blogs and e-newsletters, participating in free or low-cost fundraising Webinars, or doing prospect research. But successful fundraising means knowing what you need to know and putting together what you know so you cam implement your fundraising plan: specifically, asking the right person at the right time for the right amount; scheduling the right event and inviting the people most likely to be interested in attending; inviting as many people as possible to join your organization as donors and keeping up with those donors; and using volunteers to the best of their abilities.

Managing and distilling information is now a far more challenging task than finding it. Too often what I find in a fundraising office are piles of papers and CDs on the floor, a desk strewn with to-do lists, Post-Its stuck all around the computer monitor, the occasional package of cashews or candy, and a cup of coffee perched precariously atop an overflowing in-basket. Whatever "order" this system has is thrown off when a cell phone, buried by mail and financial reports, rings, and the staff person must dislodge the heap in order to answer it.

Too often we mistake the message that such an office sends—the inability to get and stay organized—with being overworked. Since having too much work is often a major component of many fundraisers' lives, one problem compounds the other. A fundraiser confided to me recently that she was freaked out but also secretly relieved when her office flooded. Now she had an excuse for not getting work done she wouldn't have gotten to anyway.

365

People in fundraising must always be clear about what they need to do and what they don't. This chapter will help you deal with the overload of information.

INFORMATION YOU NEED FOR FUNDRAISING

To know what to keep, what to throw out, what to enter or what to delete, what to put in order, and what to ignore, you must make a list of priorities about your job. What information do you need to be on top of, what do you need to have access to from time to time, and what doesn't matter at all? Although the answers to these questions will vary from person to person, most fundraisers must keep track of the following information, which will be the most important to their work:

- Information pertaining to current donors
- Information pertaining to prospects
- Information about the organization that will be used to get more donors and prospects
- Information about past fundraising activities
- Useful how-to information (such as this book)

Any papers that come across your desk or e-mail that appear in your inbox that do not pertain to the categories listed here need to be deleted, recycled, or at least put out of sight. Among other items that will get deleted or tossed are these: newsletters from organizations whose work is unrelated to the work of your nonprofit, advertisements for seminars and classes you will not be attending, catalogs, annual reports of foundations your organization will not be applying to, old to-do lists, and reports on all causes unrelated to your organization's work. Similarly, delete any files that are not related to current or prospective donors, past donors, past fundraising efforts, or other income streams that you are in charge of, and ancillary information about any of those deleted items. In your physical filing cabinet, use the bottom file drawer for reference material about your organization. Put in that drawer one copy each of your past newsletters, proposals funded, evaluations of direct mail appeals, reports on special events, board minutes and reports, and financial statements.

Every piece of paper and every file in your computer should be held up to this test: Will this item help us raise money or get something else we really need from someone? If yes, who and how? Then put it in the appropriate place: the prospect's file or the reference drawer. If the answer for any piece of paper or computer document is no, throw it out or delete it or forward it to another staff person whose work it will help.

KEEPING TRACK

Once you learn those simple rules about what to keep and what to get rid of, keeping track of information will actually not be that difficult.

First, review the basics: What is your job? What do you have to know? What would people reasonably expect you to be able to lay your hands on quickly? Even if you are the only paid staff person, you still have a limit to your job. These are the types of information you must have and have easy access to:

- Minutes of official meetings of the organization and reports offered to the board, the public, or the IRS about the organization. Keep one (at most two) copies of board minutes, audits, 990s, newsletters, direct mail appeals, annual reports, and so on.

- Data about donors: their names, addresses, and gift history, as well as information that would help you or someone else ask them for more money or for some other type of involvement. Some of this information may be on paper (physical letters from donors, for example) but almost all of it will be on your database and backed up every day or two. A Web-based backup system gives you the most assurance that the data will never be lost.

There are other items you probably should have if you are a one-person shop—you decide. But do you really need dozens of samples of invitations or annual reports? (Pick the best ten and throw the rest away.) Do you need the latest reports from the most prolific think tanks on every subject from ozone depletion to police brutality, from campaign reform to the role of women in rural Hindu communities? No. What is your organization trying to accomplish? You will be kept busy enough keeping up with what pertains to you. Moreover, if you really need it, you can probably find it online.

Having set priorities on the kinds of information you need—and limit yourself to five priorities at the most—sort all your papers and computer files into those categories and throw away or delete anything that doesn't fall into them. Especially get rid of the masses of information you now keep that you feel you "should" read: the stuff that you bring home but never quite get to, the stuff you downloaded to read in the airport but always manage to ignore in favor of something else you have found. If you feel that you "should" read it, you won't. Lighten up. It's all right not to read everything; it's even all right not to read most things.

The final guideline about what to throw out or delete is that if you haven't looked at it in six months and it is not needed for the IRS or as an archive copy, trash it.

YOUR FILING SYSTEM

Next, think through your physical and electronic filing systems. Create broad categories, then file within those categories. Categories might include board, donors, prospects, foundations, finances, programs, and publications. You may want to keep some of these items in files for each year. Within some of those categories you may want subcategories. For example, the board section might have the following subcategories: board members—current, past, potential; board reimbursements; board minutes; and staff reports to the board.

To test your filing system, ask a friend or another staff person to come into your office and start naming things for you to find. It should not take you more than two minutes to find any piece of information—physical or virtual—you are in charge of. If you can't do that, reassess your system. Once your system passes this test, see how well it works for someone else. Suppose you were hit by a train—how obvious is your information setup? If it takes someone else more than five minutes to figure out where something is, your system is too mysterious.

Many otherwise neat people have sloppy virtual files, so give this problem extra attention. I know, because I am one of these people. Virtual files fool you because you don't often notice how much room these are taking up—the "clutter" is invisible, so it is easy to let the information on your hard drive get out of control. I, who rarely handle a piece of paper more than once, will spend an hour scrolling through my files with the intensity of a mad scientist—did I save it under "November" because it happened in November, or under "Special Events-Ideas-Fall Plans" or in "Docs-Fundraising-Special Events-November"? Why would I even have a filing system like that?

The same standards apply to computer files as to paper files: Will you need it again? How can you name the file and the subfile so their contents are obvious?

Again, apply the standard, "If I were hit by a train, could someone else find this?" Give it a name that makes some sense.

For many people, their "sent" e-mail box is another "filing system." Looking for mail you've sent might work well for correspondence, but the sent box quickly and easily gets overloaded. Again, consider what would happen if that computer crashed, taking your sent file—which is probably not backed up—with it. Relying on your e-mail records also requires you to rely a lot on your memory, which, as you and I both know, is not reliable.

STICKING WITH IT

To help you stay on top of your papers and computer files once you get organized, write on a Post-It the one, two, or three things that will most help you stay focused on what to keep. Here is one person's Post-It:

Is it a donor?

Is it a prospect?

Could it lead to a donor or a prospect?

Another has this:

When in doubt, throw it out.

After all, what is the worst thing that can happen?

Another's says:

If this were my last day at work and I was sorting through my stuff, would I give it to the person succeeding me?

In our business, information is like food: we eat it, we serve it to others, we save it for a few days, but we don't keep it permanently. It is useful for what it does for us, but is not really useful beyond being converted to energy, enjoyment, or, in this case, donors and donations. Seeing information in that light will let you be in control of it so that you can use it to do your work.

Managing Your Time

E ffective time management often marks the difference between a good fund-raiser and someone who is never going to make it in this field. First, remember that the fundraising job is never done and you are never caught up on your work. Also, according to Parkinson's Second Law, expenses rise to meet income. The more successful the fundraising plans are, the more plans the organization will make to spend that money. Consequently, no amount of money raised is ever enough. Fundraising staff (paid and unpaid) must set their own limits because no matter how supportive the organization may be of your work, it is still relentless in its need for more money.

Here are some guidelines for using your time to best advantage.

GUIDELINES

There are certain tasks that must be completed either every day or every week.

Every Day

Reserve Time When You Cannot Be Interrupted.   For at least one (and sometimes two or three) hours each day, let someone else or your voice mail answer the phone. Do not talk to other staff, turn off your cell phone, and do not reply to e-mail. Use that time for planning, writing, analysis of your fundraising results so far—anything that requires being uninterrupted.

Create To-Do Lists at the End of Each Day.   Spend fifteen to thirty minutes at the end of the day creating your to-do list for the next day. At the beginning of the day, review your to-do list. Unless something comes up that really can't wait, do only those tasks already on your to-do list. Put new things on tomorrow's

371

list. Don't plan to do more than can be done in about half to three-quarters of the day. The rest of the time will be taken up with stuff you must deal with that you did not plan. If you plan eight hours of work in an eight-hour day, you will wind up working twelve hours. Plan four to five hours of work, and you will be able to leave after eight or nine hours.

Make Sure Thank You Notes Are Getting Sent.   Ideally, a board member or volunteer is coming into the office to write or personalize thank you notes on a regular basis, or the executive director is adding a personal note to thank you notes going to major donors. You must stay on top of this process.

Update Your Database Daily or at Least Every Other Day.   It's easy to do backup after you have entered the information that will enable you to generate a thank you note, but don't get behind on it.

Every Week

Review Your Fundraising Plan for the Month.   Go over your plan to make sure you are on target. Don't put off tasks such as getting a letter to the printer, calling a foundation, or setting up meetings of the major gifts committee or the special events committee. Do these tasks on time.

Watch for Time Sinks.   How many times have we looked up at a clock and in total disbelief said, "How could it be four o'clock?" or "Where did the day go?" Sometimes this is a sign that we have been absorbed in important work, but sometimes it is a sign that we have used up our time doing a lot of stuff that seemed important but wasn't, or that is important but could have been handled in a fraction of the time. Here are the most common time sinks.

E-Mail.   A great time saver, to be sure, e-mail also has become one of the biggest time sinks ever.

This is not just because of spam and her sister, the spam filter, although that is part of it. It is also because it is easy to spend a lot of time reading e-newsletters following links to (and then reading) blogs, and taking a short break to look at your friend's dog video, which leads you to the animal shelter's Web site, and so on. You can limit the amount of incoming e-mail a great deal. Unsubscribe from anything you don't read and is not useful to your work. Have personal e-mail sent to your personal e-mail account and don't use work e-mail for personal stuff (and don't check personal e-mail more than once a day). Delete without reading anything that has been forwarded to you that you know is simply a list of jokes or a petition. Don't feel obligated to answer every e-mail, particularly if you get e-mail from people who are not and are never going to be important to your organization or who would never have paid the money to call you.

Although a great deal of your work will take place on e-mail, you need to impose limits on how you use it. Check your e-mail only three or four times a day—first thing in the morning, at the end of the morning, in mid-afternoon, and right before you go home. Limit yourself to thirty minutes per session unless there is some reason to go longer. Even at that limit, you are using up to two hours of your workday on e-mail. Don't check your work e-mail in the evening, and limit how much time you spend with it on the weekend. E-mail allows people to work all the time, but e-mail is not in charge of us: we are in charge of it.

The Telephone. You can limit the length of your calls by standing up while you are on the phone. If you know the telephone is a big temptation for you, move it off your desk so that you actually have to move to answer it or to make a phone call. Because you know that for most of the calls you make you will get voice mail, spend a few seconds before you call thinking about the exact message you are going to leave. We all hate to get rambling or disjointed messages, yet many of us leave them. This wastes our time and the time of the person we are phoning. Although friendliness and warmth are wonderful, limit yourself to one expression of either of these: "Hope your day is going well" does not have to be followed by, "And I hope your weekend was fabulous" or "And I hope you are feeling good and having time to enjoy this wonderful weather." Ditto with "OK, take care. Look forward to talking with you. Great to hear your voice." Pick one of those, prefer-ably a short one. Cell phones are another time trap. Unless you have some reason that your cell phone needs to be on all the time, turn it off when you are at work. If your work often takes you out of your office, be judicious about who has that number and don't feel obligated to answer calls that are not relevant to work during working hours. Think, too, of how you use social media in relation to your work and keep your work use of Facebook, Twitter, and the like confined to work areas during the workday.

Chatty Co-Workers. Learn to sort out what kinds of conversations are important for maintaining morale and showing interest in other people, and what conversations simply occur because you or your co-worker are procrastinating getting work done. Schedule social time with co-workers you like so that you will not have to steal time away from work. When you spend time talking with someone when you know you should be working, you are neither really enjoying the conversation nor, obviously, getting your work done.

People Who Drop By. If someone comes by whom you don't need to talk with and you don't have time to talk, try the following tactics: tell them that you will call or e-mail later, or set a lunch date right then, or stand up and remain standing while talking to them (they will not sit down if you are standing). Another tactic is, at a moment when you are the one speaking, look at your watch or your calendar. This will remind your visitor of time without you being rude. You never need to act hurried or rushed with spontaneous visitors so long as you don't get panicked about how you are going to get rid of them.

CALENDARS AND ACTION PLANS

The understanding that information is time-related is integral to running an efficient office. Once you have organized your office, paper, computer files, and desk in a way that allows you easy and quick access to the information you need and provides a sensible system that someone else can follow, assign a time by which you will have used or acted on the information you are keeping track of so effectively. There are two principal methods: calendars and action plans.

Calendars

Create a "year-at-a-glance" calendar and a separate appointment (or daily) calendar using your electronic calendar or by buying paper versions.

Although you can certainly invest lots of money in fancy calendar applications that allow you to record your expenses, keep birthday reminders, car mileage, meeting notes, priority to-do lists, meeting agenda items, tax information, and the like, I have yet to meet anyone who actually used all those systems.

You also want to have a system that allows you to indicate the days you are not going to work. I like a "year-at-a-glance" calendar posted on the office wall because everyone can see what days you will work and what days you won't. It also helps you to see what days no one is going to work. Here are some of the days for which you should not plan any work:

- Major holidays and one or two days before and after those holidays
- Your vacation
- Your birthday (don't work on your birthday)
- The day (or two, if you wish) after any work meeting or conference that you know will be grueling or for which you have to travel a long distance

What you have left is close to the true number of days you could get work done.

Now note the dates of board meetings, the annual meeting, special events, proposal deadlines, newsletter deadlines, and any other meetings or deadlines that you can anticipate. Indicate how many days it will take you to prepare for any of these events, so you don't schedule long meetings or big projects during that time.

If you do this on paper, you will have a clear visual picture that allows you to assess quickly, "Can I take on this commitment?" "Does it make sense for me to attend this conference when I will be exhausted from our annual retreat?" "Should we conduct our major donor campaign during our audit?"

Remember also that some of the days of the year will be used up by illness (yours, your partner's, your children's, and so on), by goofing off or not working efficiently, and by work emergencies that take precedence.

Finally, synchronize your to-do list and your calendar. Enter your major to-do's on the calendar you are using, such as "send thank you notes," "update database," "newsletter copy due," "proofread annual report," and so on. This calendar does not take the place of a to-do list. However, most people do not keep the relationship between their to-do list and their calendar clear enough. For example, someone calls and asks for an appointment. You look at your appointment calendar and, seeing a clear day, make the appointment, only to realize later that the day was kept clear because of the approaching deadlines covered by the to-do list. Whenever possible, set your meetings, appointments, lunch dates, and so on by referring to your whole calendar. A day does not stand alone. Do you really want to have a 7 A.M. breakfast meeting with a major donor the morning after a board meeting that will run until 10 P.M.?

Finally, make appointments with yourself. My friend Bill, who has a hard time saying no to anything, assigns meeting times to HH in his calendar. Then, when someone trying to set up a meeting with him leans over to peer at Bill's calendar and says, "Bill, looks like you have an open afternoon," Bill will have protected a hard day of work, even though it involves no appointments, by making a long appointment with HH (HH stands for "ha-ha"). These fake appointments jar him into not saying yes. He can say, "I have a meeting," which for him, as for most people, is easier than saying, "I have to write the campaign brochure." It also spares him the frustration of having to respond when someone says, "This will only take twenty minutes—it will be good for you to have a break from your writing."

Following are some things to avoid in using calendars and scheduling your time.

Avoid Having a Home Calendar and a Work Calendar.   People who maintain two paper calendars (one for work and one for social appointments) almost always miss their Monday morning appointments (because they don't have their work calendar with them) and are constantly trying to recall whether they can make an evening meeting on Thursday, because they think that's the night of their daughter's soccer match—or is that Wednesday? Have only one daily calendar—whether paper or electronic—that shows your whole day, from home to work and back home. Put your important home-life appointments and activities in that single calendar.

Avoid Bemoaning Your Busy Life.   When you say to yourself or others, "I am so busy" or "I don't know how I'll get everything done," you tend to set up a self-fulfilling prophecy. Further, comments such as these don't accomplish anything except to use up time. Most people are busy and few people get everything done. Tell yourself instead, "I can get this done. I have enough time."

Skip Unnecessary Meetings or Conferences. Conferences, trainings, Webinars, workshops, and seminars are the order of the day. They are both expensive and time consuming and rarely worth either the time or expense. Choose the events where you will really learn something or see people you truly want or need to see. Then go and be there. Too often we decide to attend a conference half-heartedly and spend most of the time during the plenaries and workshops checking e-mail or sending text messages, or slipping out to answer our cell phones. If you choose to attend a conference or seminar, either be at the event or don't be there.

Avoid Scheduling Too Many Meetings.   Although we have work to do in meetings and, admittedly, a certain amount of the work we do at meetings is socializing and building camaraderie, many meetings are not essential, and almost every meeting lasts too long. Question every meeting: Is this meeting necessary? If it is, do I need to be there? Can I be there for part of it and not all of it? If you have any say in what will go on at the meeting, make sure there is an agenda with times beside each item. People tend to talk for the amount of time that is listed. If needed, they can negotiate the need for extra time as it comes up.

Action Plans

One of the difficult things about working with individual donors is that this work has no externally determined deadlines, so you have to create your own. Once you have your calendars set up, you are ready for the next step in organizing your fundraising office: creating action plans.

Whenever you work with a donor or a prospect, make a note in that person's record of what you intend to do next. This is called your "action plan" or more simply, the "next step." This information should be recorded in a separate field related to their name in your database. An action plan is brief, such as, "Invite to Marian's house party" or "Call with outcome of organizing effort in Roane County" or "Send report on toxic waste dumping as soon as available." Then add a date by which you plan to take the action. Put this date in your calendar. Note the donor's last name or some identifying phrase that will remind you to check what you were going to do on that date. Contact-management software is very helpful for keeping up with these plans, but the calendar and task functions in most PDAs also do a great job, and simple paper and pen have worked well for decades. Find a system that works for you and use it.

If you are systematic about your donors, for each major donor or major donor prospect you will have a date on which you are going to do something to move along the process of building her or his relationship with the organization. By spreading these dates out over the year, you can give more personal attention to donors and not get jammed with unrelated donor meetings during a campaign or at the end of the year. If you have thousands of donors, you obviously will have to decide which ones you want to work with personally, but the action plan concept can be used for group activity also, such as, "Oct. 1: All $50–$249 donors receive news alert mail appeal."

A fundraiser's job is often compared to that of the circus performer who balances plates on sticks by keeping the plates twirling and runs from stick to stick to keep the spinning going. If she misses, a plate falls and may break. The calendar is the stick, and the action plans are the plates. This is how you keep your plates spinning and not falling. The overall idea is to have as little to remember as possible. You shouldn't have things in your memory that you could record somewhere. This system frees you to use your mind to be creative or to learn new details about new people and write those down later.

The wide variety of tasks involved in fundraising is both exciting and one of the many difficulties of the job. You can minimize some of the difficulties by relatively simple procedures to keep your office running efficiently. A calendar and action plan system allows you to use the information you accumulate to raise maximum dollars for your organization.

Managing Donor Data

Accurate, up-to-date, and thorough records that are easy to access are a basic necessity for an ongoing fundraising program. Without such data, you have little capability to ask donors for more money, target projects to specific donor interests, track response to appeals, set goals, or evaluate your progress against your plan. It will also be difficult to do any of the other activities required for maintaining and increasing the number and income from a broad base of individual donors or evaluating any of your other fundraising strategies.

Obviously, the most important thing to keep track of is information about your donors. When you are first starting out, you can do this on an Excel spreadsheet, but you are going to want to move to a fundraising database pretty quickly. You can augment your database with paper files on donors, which is often easier than trying to enter all that you might know about someone. (At the risk of appearing anti-technology, I would stress that a paper system that works is preferable to a database that doesn't. People raised billions of dollars before there were even memory typewriters, let alone computers. However, a database that works well for you gives you a lot more options than any paper system and allows you to sort information in many useful ways, so one of your earliest investments should be in a good database.)

Your database needs to be able to do at least the following six functions:

- Hold a lot of names

- Hold a lot of information in many fields about each name

- Sort fields quickly and easily

- Produce reports by compiling information (such as total number of gifts from the summer appeal, amount pledged versus amount received, difference in direct mail costs and income between this year and last year)

- Be able to interface with your e-mail system for sending e-newsletters, action alerts, and e-appeals
- Merge with a word processing program for individualizing letters and formatting labels of different sizes for mailings

PURCHASING A DATABASE PROGRAM

Although some off-the-shelf database programs can be customized to meet all of the requirements listed here and more, I strongly recommend getting a program designed for fundraising. All computer programs will have bugs that have to be fixed, and all people using computer programs will run up against the limitations of their own ability to understand a function and the inability of the manual to explain it. When you purchase a program designed for fundraising, there should be a technical support person you can call. If you have a customized database program, on the other hand, you have to hope that the person who customized it is available. Just in the past few years, people have told me the following sad stories about using their customized database programs: "We can't get that database to do a mail merge for our major donor campaign and John, who designed it, is in Nepal for six months." "The database has freaked out! It won't sort anything and it freezes every five minutes. Mary, who customized it for us, is mad at us and won't help." "Fred, the guy who put this program together, decided that we need all new computers and refuses to fix this until we agree to buy them. Meanwhile, it seems to have lost all current information. I know it's in there, but I can't figure out how to restore it."

Your database should be as useful as having another staff person. A big myth about computer programs for fundraising is that they are all terribly expensive. You can pay a lot if you want, but there are some very effective programs that are priced at well under $2,000, and there are even some open source programs that can work quite well. Several commercial database vendors will let you pay over time with low or no interest, and several have versions you can "grow into"—that is, you buy a program that has fewer functions or holds fewer names, and as you grow and need more sophistication, you apply the cost of your previous program to an expanded version that serves you better. The final reason to buy a database program designed for fundraising is that you will get upgrades to the program, usually for free. (For help buying a database program to suit your needs, ask other similar-sized organizations what they use and what they like and don't like about their programs, create a list of what you need a database to do, and visit techsoup .org for software comparison charts.)

Before you buy a fundraising database program, try it out—most reputable products have demonstration versions available for download. This preview will show you what the program can do and give you a sense of how user friendly it is. Before buying anything, be sure all your questions have been answered and that you understand the answers. Don't be afraid to ask elementary questions and don't let salespeople make you feel stupid or old-fashioned. Finally, find out what kind of support the company provides once you purchase its program: Is there a toll-free telephone number? Can you call as often as you need to? How difficult is it to get through to a tech support person? How are charges for this support figured? What kinds of training programs does the company have to help you understand the program, where are they held, and what do they cost? Remember that sometimes inexpensive programs have very expensive tech support, and often free programs have no tech support, which can make trying to use them very frustrating. Think of tech support as equivalent to the cost of maintaining a car—over and above the cost of buying it, but really part of the overall cost that has to be factored in.

Think through what information you will want to keep up to date so that you have consistent information on each donor. You don't need to know as much about someone who gives your group $25 as about someone who gives $25,000. You will want to know more about someone who has given you money several times a year for ten years than about someone who gave one gift and then didn't give again.

Databases designed for fundraising will have a number of built-in categories to help you think through what you need to keep track of, and you will be able to add fields for your particular situation. For all donors, however, you need to know the following information.

Name, Addresses (Home, Work, E-mail), and Phone Number(s).   Get the correct spelling of the donor's name from his or her check or online order.

People are offended when their name is misspelled, and they don't take into account that their handwriting on their reply device may have made their name impossible to read. Always seek an e-mail address in any snail mail communication.

Form of Salutation.   If you don't know whether your donor wants to be referred to by first name or using an honorific, use a formal salutation that is not sexist: "Dear Ms. Smith" is preferable to "Dear Mrs. Smith." For couples, try "Dear Friends" (see also Chapter Eighteen, "The Thank You Note").

Gift History.   Keep track of date of gift, size of gift, and what the gift was in response to (board member request, spring appeal, pitch at gala, and so on).

Renewal Date.   In many cases the renewal date will be in the "Gift History."

Correspondence Record.   Note "thank you sent" with the date, and make a note of any other correspondence you have. Actual copies of letters will probably be in a paper file; e-mail correspondence can be copied into the donor file.

Other Information.   This field may remain empty if you have no other information, but it can be used to note anything you know about this person that is pertinent to him or her being a donor or a prospect for a bigger gift. For example, "Sister of board president" would go here. Or suppose a gift of $30 comes in from Joe Cumberland, but his check says, "Joe Cumberland; Janice Ruark, MD." First, you can check to see if Janice Ruark is also a donor. If she is not, make a note: "Check was in both his name and Janice Ruark, MD." This information may be useful or it may never lead anywhere. Sometimes a reply card will carry the name of a person, such as "Lydia S. Turner," but the check says, "Sampson Family Foundation." An Internet search shows that Lydia Sampson Turner is on the board of the Sampson Family Foundation. Enter that. (Later you will figure out if you can ask this foundation for more money.)

Special Requests.   If you trade mailing lists with other organizations, be sure to give all donors a way to opt out of having their names traded; this information should be coded in a field in your database. People who indicate they only want to be asked once a year or who never want to be phoned will have that information entered also, for use in sorting donors for different uses. (In other words, Sally Vesey notes on her reply device that she only gives in the fall and does not want to be asked more frequently. When sorting for the spring appeal, her name will not show up on that list.)

This is all the information you keep on people who have given only once so far or who have given less than $100 for fewer than three years and whom you don't know anything else about. For people who give more than $100 or have given some amount for more than three years, or for people who give several times a year or whose gift does not reflect how much they could give considering how much they seem to care about your cause, start keeping the information on prospect identification outlined in Chapter Seven.

In addition to the standard pieces of information you want to have for all donors, there are two useful categories that can be easily added to your database fields: "Missing Information" and "Next Step." It often happens that you know some details about a donor but not enough to include her in the upper ranges of your Gift Range Chart, for example, or to ask her to give an extra gift for a capital improvement. It is helpful to focus on what you would need to know to feel comfortable asking the donor for more money or extra money. Possibly you need to know more about her friendship with a board member. Are they very close or simply acquaintances? Perhaps you need to know what other charitable commitments the donor has made. Maybe you need to know more about what the donor thinks about a particular issue that your group is working on. Or maybe it is something simpler, such as her phone number. Make a note of whatever you need to learn under "Missing Information." Once every month or so, pull up that category, which will give you a complete list of what you need to find out about particular donors.

The other useful category is "Next Step." Obviously, one logical next step may be to find the missing information, but this category can be used more proactively. The next step is often not to ask for more money but to be sure to send some article of interest that you promised the donor. Maybe Nancy, your board member who lives down the road from this donor, needs to invite the donor to a house party or a meeting. Maybe this donor has a lot of contacts, and you want to ask him to give you a list of them right before the spring major donor drive. Note what the next step is and a date by which it should be done. Then you can sort by dates and give yourself a current to-do list for next steps with donors.

THE IMPORTANCE OF DONOR RECORDS

People sometimes feel that gathering this information so systematically is an invasion of the donor's privacy and seems nosy and manipulative. They fear they will begin to see other people only in terms of money. To gain some perspective on the reasons for keeping donor records, keep the following three facts in mind.

If You Don't Record This Information, You Will Forget It. Without this information, you will not be able to raise money as effectively as you could with it. Many people have "birthday books" in which they write down all the dates of the birthdays they want to remember. No one thinks this is an invasion of privacy—in fact, they are pleased to get a card on their birthday. (Proof that people are happy to share a lot of personal information is seen in the popularity of social media such as Facebook and LinkedIn, where one can share information quite widely, even to the whole world if you want.) You are trying to use donor resources to the best advantage, which is what donors want and deserve. There is no point in asking someone for money several times a year who only gives once a year, but it is a shame not to ask someone who likes your organization and would gladly give more often if asked. Further, how will the organization know that your longtime loyal donor, Tania Lopez, hates to be called at work if someone doesn't record that fact? Or that Steve, who owns the deli, said he would cater your annual meeting for free if you get back to him by March? Finally, you are obligated by law to keep a record of gifts of more than $250 so that if a donor is audited by the IRS, you can provide verification that he gave the amount he said he had given to your organization.

Don't Record Anything You Don't Need to Know. Your goal is to get every donor to be as loyal to your organization as possible and to give you as much money as they can afford because of their loyalty, which is increased by their knowledge about the organization and their feeling of being appreciated by the organization. Everything you record about a donor should be information that helps you toward that goal. So, no matter how interesting it might be that Max was once lovers with Fred, don't record it. If a donor who is also a friend confides to you that she spent time in prison and is having trouble with the parole board, don't write it down. Think of this: If a donor asked to see his or her record, would you be embarrassed to show it? Why? What's in there that shouldn't be? You should be recording only information that is easily obtainable or that people would not object to your knowing, such as how many children they have or where they work.

This Information Is Highly Confidential.   Only a few people, such as the executive director, the development director, the treasurer of the board, and sometimes the bookkeeper or administrator, should have access to all the information in your database. Protect your information with passwords. Doing so will also give you some control over who can change a donor record and ensure that people working on the database can't mess it up or delete information by accident. Donor information that is not protected by passwords, such as paper files, should be in a locked filing cabinet with access limited to a few people. People who can see this information must understand its delicate nature and use the same discretion in revealing it as is used in recording it.

KEEPING YOUR LIST IN SHAPE

Update your donor records on a regular basis. Don't let more than ten names go unrecorded, or you will get careless with numbers and spelling. Many small, understaffed agencies put off updating their databases until the night before they need their mailing lists for the newsletter mailing. Then a staff member and a volunteer frantically try to get everything in order. That kind of list is inevitably full of errors.

Watch for duplicate entries, particularly when you are going to use the list for a mailing. Donors dislike getting more than one copy of your newsletter or mail appeal. A database program will not know that J. P. Miller and John Miller are the same person, or that Susan Jones doesn't live at 22 South Street anymore but is now Susan Moondaughter on 44 North Street. Every so often, print out your whole mailing list and go through it looking for duplicates, spelling errors, incomplete addresses, and so on. (If it is very large, print it out in sections by alphabet or number of records. Going through this is something that a detail-oriented volunteer can do.)

Don't keep people on your mailing list who have never given and whom no one knows. I have known many organizations that have mailings list of 4,000 but donor lists of 700. When I ask what the other 3,300 people are doing on their list, they will say, "This is our outreach program." But most groups have no evidence that they gain donors from this outreach, or even that all of these people are alive or at the addresses on their records. Considering that it costs from $3 to $10 per entry every year to keep someone on a mailing list—presuming you send at least two newsletters and at least one appeal—you could be spending hundreds or even thousands of dollars keeping people on your mailing list about whom you know nothing. That same money could be invested in mounting a true outreach or direct mail program to drive traffic to your Web site and using an electronic newsletter for outreach. (For what to do with names on your list that are not productive, see Chapter Eleven, "Using Direct Mail.")

Because as many as one-third of the people on a list move in a year, it's important to know when the address you have is no longer accurate. You can get address corrections from the post office by printing "Address Correction Requested" on all your bulk mail. You pay a certain amount for each piece returned to you, but the returns will have any forwarding address on them, which helps keep your list clean. Request address corrections at least once a year.

SAFETY FIRST

As I have mentioned before, you need to have a backup system that backs up your data daily or every other day. There are inexpensive and efficient backup systems that are Web based, and that means fires, floods, or earthquakes cannot destroy your data. Important paper documents need to be either scanned or copied and stored off-site or in a fireproof safe.

For many fundraisers, thorough data entry and retrieval is the bane of their existence. But keeping records takes less time if you do it regularly and don't get far behind than if you wait until the last minute and do it badly. Then you have to spend time cleaning up your mess. Keeping donor data current and accurate needs to be seen as being as necessary and habitual as brushing your teeth.

Working with Volunteers

Recently, a dear friend of mine who is also a professor recommended one of his students to me. She had just graduated from college and wanted to explore working in the nonprofit sector. She was willing to volunteer almost full time in order to get some experience and also to see if this was a career path she might want to pursue. I knew that if he recommended her, she would be excellent, so I sent e-mails to various understaffed organizations that do good work, asking if they could use someone like this. No one could. "It is a great offer, but I don't know what I would have her do," was the common theme. I thought it was a sad day in nonprofit history when more than a dozen social justice leaders could not take the time to imagine what a recent college graduate willing to work for free might be enlisted to do. The story ends happily, as the young woman found two places to volunteer that she likes, including one where she happens to be working with me on a project.

From about 1985 to 2005, many organizations found it had become more difficult to recruit and retain volunteers. There were far fewer traditional volunteers (people who didn't need to work for pay, as their spouse or partner earned enough for the entire family), and many more people were holding down more than one job and had no "free" time to offer. Since 2005, the situation has changed. The euphemistically named "economic downturn" has thrown hundreds of thousands of people out of work; many of them are volunteering while they look for jobs. Of course, as the economy improves, that cohort will shrink, but for the next couple of decades, there will nonetheless be millions of available volunteers as the Baby Boom generation retires and wants to keep active in the sector. In fact, I think there have always been far more people who would be willing to volunteer their time than a lot of organizations were able to take advantage of.

I believe that many organizations' fundraising programs rely too heavily on staff. In very large organizations, the solution to fundraising problems is often to "staff up." But you cannot "staff up" to the extent needed to have a truly effective fundraising program, and even if you had the money to hire enough staff, that is not an appropriate use of donations. If you need help managing volunteers, the solution is not to get rid of the volunteers but possibly to hire a volunteer director, or for the development director to make that part of his or her skill set. Using your time to mobilize volunteers is far more useful than using your time to do everything yourself, which you can't do in any case.

There are grassroots organizations that have twenty, thirty, and even one hundred regular volunteers. They have volunteers who have full-time jobs, children, and other volunteer commitments. They have volunteers who are on welfare, who are single parents, who travel extensively for work, who are elderly and not able to come to meetings at night, and so on. In other words, we can recruit and keep volunteers. What we need to do is focus on how, rather than how hard it is, to have a successful volunteer program.

 There are many fine books on volunteering; some are listed in Resource E in the Premium Web Content and will be helpful for you to consult. Put briefly, there are six things you need to do to get volunteers productively involved in fundraising.

Invite People to Participate in Fundraising.   Many development directors lament that no one volunteers to do fundraising. They conclude that no one wants to, but this is often not the case. Many fundraising volunteers have told me that prior to being on the fundraising committee or involved in some fundraising activity, they thought fundraising was either all about writing proposals, about which they knew nothing, or asking their own friends for money. Their friends, they would explain, couldn't give thousands of dollars, so they concluded there was no way for them to be usefully involved in fundraising.

As with any volunteer participation, organizations need to invite people to be involved in specific fundraising tasks that have a goal and are time-limited, and they need to promise appropriate guidance. Major gift campaigns, house party programs, and special events are all examples of such activities. Further, there are dozens of behind-the-scenes tasks that volunteers can do. Every time you are doing something that a reasonably intelligent person could do with a little bit of training, you need to stop and think, "Who could I ask to do this?"

Above all else, most volunteers want to feel useful, and there is no more useful place than fundraising.

Take the Time Necessary to Orient Volunteers to Your Fundraising Program. A two-hour in-service program in which you go over your budget, your fundraising goals, and your progress to date will set a good example of transparency and allow people to ask any questions they have or voice concerns. Such an in-service meeting can also set the context in which your fundraising plan is developed, as described in Chapter One, including how many nonprofits there are, where money for nonprofits comes from, who gives that money away, and so on. Use this in-service meeting especially to focus on your case statement; have volunteers practice describing your organization to each other and answering questions about it.

Volunteers need to feel "in the know," and they need to feel competent with regard to describing the mission, goals, and objectives of the organization. We often think a volunteer is unwilling to ask for money when in fact he or she may feel insecure about discussing the organization. I have often had volunteers say, "I didn't ask for the money because I thought I might do more harm than good in trying to explain what the organization is doing."

Help Each Volunteer Choose the Fundraising Strategies He or She Will Feel Most Comfortable Doing. In this way, you play to volunteers' strengths. In *The Accidental Fundraiser,* Stephanie Roth and Mimi Ho describe three broad categories of activities that volunteers will prefer, depending on their personality and confidence. Some prefer to raise money by entertaining. They happily host house parties, and they are good at organizing other special events. They know how to make people feel welcomed, and they are good at thinking through what would be fun or interesting for a group of people. These volunteers often like to work in groups; they are the ones you will find on special event committees.

The second type are people who prefer to sell things: these volunteers are good at selling products or events. They are excellent people to staff a booth selling T-shirts, mugs, books, and so on that your organization produces or distributes. They will sell products to friends, neighbors, and family, and they can be relied on to sell tickets to events. However, they are less willing to ask for money directly, which brings us to the third and smallest group. These are people who prefer direct asking to doing other fundraising tasks. People in this group are likely to have a little more experience with fundraising; they know that if you ask enough people you will get the money you need. Many of these people are or have been in sales or real estate and have overcome their own psychological barriers to asking. Some of them come from countries where taboos about money are not as strong as in the United States. Both the sellers and the direct askers have stopped taking rejection personally.

Of course, some people are good at all three approaches, whereas a minority of volunteers are not comfortable with any strategy that requires talking to people about money. This latter group can be put to work generating thank you notes, entering data, following media reports on your issue and blogging or tweeting about it to drive traffic to your organization's Web site, researching foundation funders—anything that you need in fundraising that does not require talking to people about money directly.

Paid staff should as much as possible focus on doing things that an organization really could not expect a volunteer to do. Tasks that require technical knowledge, that are tremendously time consuming, or that involve a lot of sequencing should take up the bulk of a staff person's time.

Remember That Good Enough Is Good Enough.   Staff-volunteer tension can come about when a staff person wants the job done perfectly—according to her or his own definition of perfect. For example, in a small nonprofit, two volunteers took on the task of writing and sending the e-newsletter, scheduled to go out on the third Tuesday of each month. Over six months, three newsletters went out on time and three went out two days late. Some of the newsletters had a few typos. These lapses were too much for the staff person, and she took the job back from the volunteers. Obviously, if the volunteers had usually been a week late with the newsletter and if it were riddled with typos, her action would be justified. But these volunteers were for the most part both reliable and thorough. Far too often in dealing with volunteers, the best becomes the enemy of the good.

Show Genuine and Frequent Appreciation.   Remember Cesar Chavez's dictum for organizing: "People are far more appreciative of what they do for you than of what you do for them." Thank them often. Thank you notes, thank you calls, and brief mentions at meetings go a long way. Flowers, plaques, and ribbons are fine, but they are not as important as the occasional grateful word.

Give Volunteers Time Off. People need time off for good behavior. Many volunteer fundraisers have found that their reward for doing their work well is more work. "Ruby, you did such a great job with the auction. You are a natural! Once you catch your breath, do you think you could chair the membership drive?" Such a comment is a sure way to guarantee that Ruby will run, not walk, away from your organization as soon as she can.

Make sure that, unless the volunteer insists otherwise, volunteers have at least two or three months between intense fundraising activities and that they are encouraged to get involved in other aspects of the organization as well.

Keep in mind, then, that what is most efficient for getting a job done thoroughly and quickly—excellent staff people doing every piece of work to their satisfaction—is rarely most effective for building an organization and developing new leadership. As you work on managing your volunteers, remember that you are ultimately trying to ensure that the organization will be able to continue even as key people move on to other things. By keeping your eye on the prize of longevity and stability of the organization, you will structure your volunteer management efforts much differently and will find that there are plenty of people who want to be active, engaged volunteers.

PART SIX

You the Fundraiser

For most of the years I have been in fundraising, study after study has shown that the average tenure in a fundraising job is less than two years. While some development directors are promoted to executive director and others (like me) leave to be consultants, most people leave one development job for another. Sadly, some very talented people leave the profession altogether. The cost of replacing a development staff person—including searching for, interviewing, selecting, and then training a new employee—is estimated by Cygnus Research to be, on the high end, 65 to 70 percent of the salary of that person and on the low end, 10 to 15 percent. It would seem that most organizations would do whatever they can to make the job attractive and sustainable.

Many theories are put forward about why there is such high turnover, including salaries not being high enough, the development staff not having enough involvement in program work, too much pressure on the job, and so on.

These may well be reasons that some people leave their fundraising jobs, but they are not the two main reasons people leave development jobs:

- Development is a job of great responsibility and little authority.
- There is a lack of understanding on the part of everyone involved as to exactly what the job of a development director is.

This section seeks to address and proactively prevent the second of these reasons. Many grassroots organizations have hired enthusiastic but inexperienced first-time development directors, and neither the organization nor the new staff person really has a clear idea of what the job involves. High expectations followed by huge disappointment either generate some badly needed clarification, possibly saving the person and the position, or in less functional organizations (unfortunately, the majority), result in the person leaving.

This section reviews the job of the development director, and the different ways organizations can seek help, from consulting to coaching to training, as well as some suggestions for dealing with the anxiety that seems to hang over many development directors. It also addresses the two things that even experienced development directors often find difficult to deal with: working with their executive director and some of the ethical dilemmas that present themselves in fundraising.

Hiring a Development Director

As small organizations grow, they grapple with the ongoing need to raise more and more money as well as manage the infrastructure (databases, volunteers, Web site, research, communication, reporting, and the like) required to do so. Inevitably, they must consider hiring someone to take charge of the fundraising function. This is a difficult decision. An organization is gambling that the investment of salary—money they often barely have—is going to generate much more money than they are currently raising. The gamble will pay off if the person they hire is effective, the board already accepts its role in fundraising, and the organization has its basic infrastructure in place—that is, adequate data management and a fundraising plan with clear goals and objectives. However, there is little margin for error. What if the person isn't skilled enough or isn't a good worker? What if everything is in place, but the fundraising program takes longer than planned to bring in the needed funds—how will the organization support itself in the meantime? And what if the organization doesn't have the infrastructure in place yet and needs to hire someone with the skills to make it happen?

To avoid these problems, three issues need to be clarified before your organization decides to hire a staff person to manage fundraising: the role of the fundraiser or development director, the tasks this person will carry out, and whether hiring a development director will actually solve the problems you have. Let's consider each of these issues in more detail.

THE ROLE OF A FUNDRAISER OR DEVELOPMENT DIRECTOR

First and foremost, everyone must understand that the person whose primary responsibility is fundraising does not run around bringing in money. Instead, a development director's job is to work with the board and staff to develop fundraising goals and sensible, easily understood plans to meet the goals. This person spells out the strategies that will be used and helps everyone figure out their tasks and stay on task. In addition to creating workable fundraising plans, the development director either does or supervises the following activities:

- Maintains accurate and accessible donor and prospect information
- Sends out thank you notes
- Writes reports, such as the annual report and reports to foundations or large donors on specific projects
- Conducts prospect research
- Coordinates all appeals, whether for acquisition or retention, and coordinates all upgrade efforts, such as campaigns
- Helps with special events and other income streams
- Helps with all social media
- Goes on major donor visits as needed and oversees maintenance of those relationships

Of central importance, the development director works closely with the board, helping board members make and then fulfill their fundraising commitments. The development director may also research the grantmaking programs of foundations and corporations and write grant proposals, if that is a part of the organization's plan, and there may be other fundraising strategies that he or she must oversee or implement.

The development director primarily works behind the scenes establishing a structure for effective fundraising by volunteers and ensuring that when volunteers do solicit donors, the volunteer is confident that the donor will be thanked promptly, names will be spelled properly, and information will be entered into the database accurately.

Many board members and paid staff imagine that hiring a development director will save them from further fundraising tasks. "Let's pay someone to do this so we can do the real work" is a common and potentially fatal suggestion. First it must be remembered that fundraising is real work, and it is work that should be integrated into the day-to-day functioning of your program and organizing efforts. Second, while the paid fundraising staff obviously relieves the load of other staff and may relieve the board of some tasks, everyone's consciousness of fundraising and their involvement in it must stay the same or increase for the expanded fundraising program to be successful.

THE TASKS OF THE FUNDRAISER

Many people wonder why the task of fundraising has so many different job titles attached to it, such as "fundraiser," "fundraising coordinator," "development director," or "resource developer." In many smaller organizations, the person is called the fundraising coordinator. In other, usually larger, organizations, this position is called the director of development or sometimes an even more exalted title, "Chief Development Officer." Some very lucky organizations have more than one staff person in their development department, but this chapter is geared to organizations moving to having their first development person.

Beyond the terminology, there are actually important differences between fundraising and development. Fundraising is the process of bringing in the amount of money an organization needs in order to carry out its programs from year to year. Development, in addition to coordinating the raising of an operating budget, includes most of the following activities:

- Creating a strategic plan (augmenting the case statement) and updating it on a yearly basis
- Instituting a public relations program
- Working with the executive director and appropriate board person to develop and then maintain a successful process for bringing on new board members
- Providing fundraising training for board, staff, and volunteers
- Planning and evaluating the financial needs and fundraising plans for the organization's future
- Developing the organization's capability to create other income streams, especially planned giving programs

One development director characterized the difference between fundraising and development this way: "In fundraising you make do with what you have. You keep the organization going and out of debt. In development, you start with what you have and you help it grow."

SOLVING YOUR PROBLEMS

Before you hire anyone, analyze your situation to see whether your problems actually lie in fundraising or whether it just looks as though they do. All problems in an organization show up in their money, and often they show up there first. However, fundraising may only be a symptom of other problems, in which case hiring someone to do fundraising will not solve the problem and may in fact make it worse.

To begin this analysis, answer the following questions:

- Is your board or some other group of volunteers active in fundraising?

- Does almost every board member participate in fundraising in some way, whether organizing special events, opening doors for you to other people, asking for money face-to-face, or helping in more behind-the-scenes but still useful ways?

- Does it sometimes seem that the board and perhaps the staff spend more time planning for fundraising than actually raising money?

- Do board members and other volunteers involved in fundraising seem to suffer from a lack of knowledge of what to do rather than a lack of enthusiasm?

- Is the executive director or other staff constantly pulled away from program development and organizing to do fundraising?

- Do the staff feel torn about setting priorities for use of their time?

- Is your budget more than $250,000 or do you need to raise more than $100,000 from sources other than government or foundations?

If your organization answers yes to three or more of these questions, you should seriously consider hiring a development director. This person would direct and kindle the fundraising energies of the board, plan for fundraising, train others in fundraising tasks, and enable program staff to get on with program work.

If, on the other hand, you need a better and more involved board, then you should strengthen your board and provide some motivational training for its members before you hire a development director.

If what you need is help with data entry, compiling financial reports, answering the phone, dealing with the mail, handling checks, processing credit cards, sending thank you notes, and the like, then you should consider hiring support staff, such as a secretary or office manager. If you need help compiling and writing reports, consider hiring a freelance writer on a project-by-project basis.

If what you want is someone to help you plan and carry out a time-limited fundraising project, such as a large event or a major gifts campaign, consider hiring a consultant.

PAYING THE DEVELOPMENT DIRECTOR

Imagine this scenario: an organization is debating whether to hire a development director. It has little money for such a position, and worries about both finding the right person and meeting a salary. As if in answer to a prayer, a handsome stranger shows up and offers to raise $250,000 (the organization's budget) plus a 20 percent commission. He will take his commission only from money he raises, he explains, so if he raises nothing, the organization pays nothing; for whatever he does raise, he will be paid 20 percent of the total. He predicts he can raise the full budget, plus his commission, in six months; if successful, he will earn $50,000, then the organization can re-up his contract if they want, or he will go on his merry way.

There are several reasons why no organization should accept such a deal (whether the stranger is handsome or not). First, no one else in the organization is paid on commission. People are paid a salary in recognition that their work is part of a process; they may be very good at their job without showing a lot of immediate progress toward ending racism, advancing Middle East peace, or whatever the organization is working on.

Second, a commission tends to distort salaries. In this case, this fundraiser would be earning the same salary in the course of six months that the executive director makes in nine months.

Third, this person will not bring his own list of contacts, nor do you want him to because you won't want him taking your donor list to the next job. He will be working with the organization's donors. Further, his whole livelihood depends on donors saying yes to his requests. Even a totally honest fundraiser working under these conditions would be tempted to distort information, seeing his groceries in the eyes of each prospect. In addition, this fundraiser may be willing to settle for a smaller gift gotten quickly rather than take the time to carry out proper cultivation for the size gift a donor is capable of making.

Fourth, what will the donors think if and when they find out that 20 percent of their gift went to this staff person? Few things make donors angrier than learning that a significant part of their gift was used for inappropriate fundraising expenses.

Fifth, as was stressed earlier, one person should not be in charge of actually raising money for an entire campaign or organization. Even if he is both honest and successful, the group will be $250,000 richer, to be sure, but no wiser in regard to fundraising.

Finally, the person coordinating the fundraising should absolutely believe in the cause and be a part of the team of people putting the campaign together. A "gun for hire" is unlikely to have a deep belief in the mission of the organization.

For these reasons, paying on commission is highly frowned on in fundraising. All the trade associations for fundraisers, including the Association of Fundraising Professionals, the National Association of Hospital Developers, and the Council for the Advancement and Support of Education, have issued statements advising organizations against commission-based fundraising. The only recognized exception to this policy is with canvassing (see Chapter Sixteen), where people are often paid a base salary and a commission. However, the nature of canvassing means the canvassers rarely deal with soliciting major gifts. Even so, the commission-based nature of canvassing has presented some of the problems discussed previously and is a gray area in fundraising.

Rather than being based on commission, the development director's salary should be based on other staff salaries. If you have a collective salary structure, then that person's salary would be the same as everyone else's. If there are pay differentials, then the development director's salary would be less than the executive director's but more than the office manager's. In a hierarchical structure, the development director is a management staff person, usually reporting directly to the executive director.

Organizations often think they have to pay a high salary to attract a capable development person. This is not true. A good person for your organization is someone who, first and foremost, believes in your work and wants to be part of it. This person will express his or her belief through fundraising, just as someone else is expressing their belief by doing direct service, organizing, or policy development. If someone who meets the criteria of believing strongly in your work has fundraising skills but can't afford to work at the salary you are offering, you may need to reevaluate everyone's salary. Chances are you are losing out on good staff people for other positions as well.

HOW TO FIND A CAPABLE DEVELOPMENT DIRECTOR

Once you have decided that you need a development director, the first step in hiring one is to create a fair and accurate job description. Many job descriptions fail to attract candidates because the job has been structured to encompass too many responsibilities. Avoid the temptation to add components to the job that are not related to fundraising or public relations. It is fair to ask the development director to edit and oversee the publication of the newsletter; it is unwise to ask that person to be the accountant as well.

You should be able to describe the job in one to two pages (see example). Think about what skills are essential, as opposed to those that are desirable but not imperative. Ask applicants to send a writing sample, since writing will be a large part of almost any fundraiser's job.

In addition to posting a job announcement on Craigslist, advertise on Web sites and in publications geared to nonprofits, such as *Idealist,* GIFT (grassrootsfundraising.org), and the *Chronicle of Philanthropy,* and with statewide nonprofit job banks and large-capacity builders' e-newsletters. Send the announcement to other nonprofits and ask them to forward it to people they think would be interested. Call directors and development directors you know and tell them the job is available. Don't rely only on e-mail to get the word out.

Don't get bogged down in trying to find someone with all the "right" qualifications and experience. If you find such a person, of course hire her or him immediately. But if you don't find such a person, look for other sorts of qualifications that are evidence of experience related to fundraising, such as running a small business, teaching, or managing personnel. Any job that required that a person be a self-starter and that called for planning, working with diverse groups of people, and good organizational skills is a good background for fundraising.

Look closely at volunteer experience and encourage applicants to describe their work as volunteers. Many people know more than they realize about fundraising from having volunteered. People with little or no volunteer experience are not good candidates because they will have little idea of how to work with volunteers.

In addition to broadening your criteria in hiring someone, it might be easier to imagine a capable but untrained person in the job if you are willing to hire a consultant for a few hours a month for the first few months to help your new staff person get a running start on her job, or to consider sending the new development director to some of the many classes and courses that are offered on fundraising. Even though they take a lot of work to implement, the theories and how-tos of fundraising are not particularly difficult to understand. Getting someone who is underqualified but bright, committed, and eager to do a good job is almost as good as getting an experienced person with the same attributes.

SAMPLE JOB DESCRIPTION— DEVELOPMENT DIRECTOR

The Peace Consortium is a twenty-year-old organization that supports the creation of a just society through training in nonviolence, developing public policy, and organizing on issues of peace and war in local communities. The Peace Consortium works in three states to strengthen grassroots efforts in the broad-based movement for progressive, systemic social change. It is offering a full-time development director position (1.0 FTE), reporting to the executive director.

Organizational Structure

There are currently four full-time employees: executive director, program director, IT manager, and office manager. Current annual budget is $750,000. Board and staff—particularly the executive director—are highly engaged in the organization's fundraising.

Function Summary

The development director will work closely with the executive director, fundraising committee, board, and ad hoc committees to coordinate a comprehensive resource development program that includes the annual membership campaign, expanding the number of major donors, and enhancing public relations outreach to increase the visibility of the Peace Consortium and its work. The job is full time; some weekend and evening work is required as well as occasional travel within the region.

Responsibilities

Management and administration: Work with board and executive director to develop overall strategies, goals, and outcomes and to track progress toward goals

Major Gifts Campaign

- Implement overall major gifts strategy

- Oversee cultivation, solicitation, and stewardship of all major donors

- Identify and implement strategies to attract new major donor prospects

Donor Acquisition and Renewal

- Develop and implement a plan for activities to attract new donors (working with the marketing committee), particularly expanding our online fundraising

- Monitor and refine annual renewal fund

Events

- Work with staff to bring in major donors through house parties, annual fundraising dinner, and other fundraising events as needed

Skills, Talents, and Experience Needed

- Minimum three years of fundraising experience with a nonprofit organization

- Experience in managing individual donors, events, cultivation, and major gifts work

- Ability to create, build, and maintain strong relationships with major donors

- Ability to plan and implement successful fundraising strategies and programs with major donors

- Knowledge of the basic components that make up successful fundraising strategies and programs

- Broad knowledge of progressive issues and organizations both locally and nationally

- Strong organizational and management skills, including program planning, budgeting, facilitation, time management, team building, training, and supervising

- Excellent written and oral communication skills

- Ability to work with diverse populations, including people of color, immigrants, women, lesbian, gay, bisexual, and transgender communities, people with disabilities, low-income people, people in rural communities, and people with wealth

- Strong demonstrated commitment to working to undo systems of oppression, including racism, sexism, classism, and heterosexism

- Ability to work flexible hours, including some weekends and evenings

- Ability to travel throughout the region

Salary

DOE; benefits package includes health care, vacation, and sabbatical after five years

How to Apply

E-mail your resume and an explanation of why you want to work for the Peace Consortium, along with a writing sample and three references, to Constancia Hernandez, Executive Director, at ch@peaceconsortium.org.

The Peace Consortium is an Equal Opportunity and Affirmative Action Employer.

Using a Consultant, Coach, Mentor, or Trainer

There are times in the life of almost every person or organization when hiring an outside person to help you think through or get through a certain time or situation can be very helpful. For a nonprofit organization's fundraising program, these times are characterized by one or more of the following situations:

- Your organization needs advice on how to improve its overall fundraising or some particular aspect of fundraising. You need someone with skill and knowledge who cares about the issues your organization is concerned with but is far enough removed to be able to "see the forest."

- You need help deciding on a course of action: Can you really launch a capital campaign now? Would a legacy giving program be a good strategy to explore? Should you create a separate 501(c)(4) organization so you can do more direct lobbying?

- You need someone to do a time-limited piece of work: run a special event, train the board in fundraising, plan a major gifts campaign, redesign your Web site, research funding sources, or write a proposal.

- You need someone to provide guidance and answer questions in designing the fundraising staff's work plan, especially when a bright and energetic but inexperienced staff person needs help getting up to speed.

- You need someone to run the development function of your organization temporarily until staff can be replaced.

- You need help with fundraising as you make a transition from a founder to a new executive director, or during a major change in direction, goals, and structure, or during a name change.

405

- Your organization has relied on government or foundation funding sources, and you need help getting out of the funding crisis that cutbacks in these funds have created.

The skills of consulting, coaching, mentoring, or training are all similar; sometimes one person is able to perform all of these functions. However, knowing the differences among them may help you decide which you need, and as we say in consulting, knowing what you need puts you 90 percent closer to being able to get it. Here is how these helping functions apply to fundraising.

Consultant.   A consultant works in partnership with an organization (usually working closely with one or two people in the organization) on a specific, time-limited project. How much that person does, as opposed to what he or she advises you to do, will depend on the consultant and on the project, but the job of a consultant is generally to get out of the organization as quickly as possible without the organization becoming reliant on him or her. A consultant is an expert who dispenses advice and has answers. Consultants are hired primarily for their knowledge and their ability to impart that knowledge. They focus on what will improve effectiveness and increase success.

Trainer.   A trainer provides a workshop, seminar, or in-service presentation that can last from twenty minutes to several days to a group of people who all need to know the same thing and, ideally, are about to embark together on a fundraising task. Trainers often will provide training to boards, major donor committees, or other subsets of an organization. Trainers also will work with many organizations at once. (Most trainers are also consultants, although many consultants are not trainers.)

Mentor.   A mentor works with one person and serves as that person's guide, wise older sibling, and role model. Someone with several decades of fundraising experience is teamed up with someone who is learning on the job. The person being mentored sees attributes, qualities, or abilities in the mentor that he or she wishes to learn or emulate. Whereas a trainer or consultant is hired for a specific amount of time and a particular piece of work, a mentor is usually a volunteer, and she or he may work with a person for years. Mentors are often in work situations with the people they are mentoring, which makes access to each other easy.

Coach. A coach can work with one person, several people, or an entire organization to help with the process of making decisions, imagining the future, and creating a plan to get there. In coaching, the starting point is the client's desire for personal and professional success. Coaching is not about how you came to be in the situation you are in, but rather about getting you from where you are now to a future that you want. Coaches clarify goals and help people through difficult or large transitions. Coaches are not generally used for how-to information or practical training, just as trainers generally don't help organizations deal with the death of a founder or help an executive director be a better manager.

Clearly, the lines among these roles are malleable and permeable, and the types of people who work in these fields will vary a great deal one to the other. This chapter deals mostly with how and when an organization should use a consultant; however, knowing the definitions of coaching, training, and mentoring may help you realize when what you need is not a consultant but one of the other types of helpers.

WORKING WITH A CONSULTANT

A consultant's work with your organization will be characterized by three things: it is time-limited (lasting either a few hours a week or a few days a month, or based on a contract for a specific number of months), the consultant is not involved in day-to-day operations, and there is more emphasis on advice and guidance than on doing hands-on fundraising work.

Partly because the services of a consultant are time-limited, the concept of employing someone in that capacity carries a negative meaning for many people. The jokes "A consultant borrows your watch to tell you the time" or "A consultant gives free advice for a price" are said only half in jest.

The problem of finding a reliable and competent consultant is compounded by the sheer number of consultants in business. As with nearly any profession, there are sleazy and unreliable consultants in the fundraising field, but a more common problem with consultants is that many genuinely think they know more than they actually do. Sometimes people ask me how they should go about becoming a consultant. When I ask what experience they have, they respond with a list of the books they have read and the trainings they have attended. They think consulting would be exciting because one can travel a great deal and they imagine they can charge a lot of money. They are also enthusiastic about the fact that consultants do not carry the ultimate responsibility of the fundraising success or failure of any organization.

What my inquirers fail to see, however, is that consultants carry a different level of responsibility: the advice we give must be correct. If implemented, it must work. Further, consultants must trust others to carry out plans that the consultant designed. This means that the plan must be communicated clearly and be appropriate to the level of skills and resources the people carrying it out have or have access to. Moreover, consultants must know the difference between what can be learned by teaching, guiding, and giving advice, and what can only be learned from experience. They must know what they can do for an organization and what an organization can only do for itself. If they fail in these aspects, they will not be consultants for long.

WHAT FUNDRAISING CONSULTANTS CAN DO

Here is a sample list of fundraising tasks for which it is appropriate to use a consultant:

- Create fundraising plans and help implement and evaluate those plans
- Research prospective donors (individuals, corporations, foundations, religious sources) and write proposals if needed
- Set up a database for keeping track of donor information
- Conduct feasibility studies
- Conduct direct mail campaigns
- Design (and manage) an online fundraising strategy
- Create a communications plan or public relations campaign
- Study and recommend structural changes in an organization to improve functioning and fundraising efficiency
- Help hire fundraising staff, including writing job descriptions and advertising for and interviewing candidates
- Organize special events
- Set up any other fundraising strategy that an organization has decided to use

If the consultant is also a trainer, he or she can do the following:

- Train and motivate people in all aspects of fundraising
- Help board members understand their responsibilities, and help organizations recruit and train good board members

WHAT FUNDRAISING CONSULTANTS GENERALLY DON'T DO

Fundraising consultants are not expected to do the following activities:

- Actually solicit money from individuals, unless they go as part of a team with someone from the organization.
- Use their personal contacts to raise money. Consultants often know a great deal about wealthy givers in the community; with discretion, they can share that knowledge in prospect research. However, consultants do not go from job to job with their own list of prospects.
- Actually raise money. If a consultant offers to do all your fundraising for you, run the other way. This is not an effective solution because, at best, it postpones the necessity of getting the board, staff, and volunteers involved in fundraising.
- Guarantee their work. There are no absolutes in fundraising. There is a body of fundraising knowledge, largely based on common sense, and there are many applications of this knowledge. No strategy will work every time for every nonprofit.

HOW TO CHOOSE A CONSULTANT

Once you have decided that your particular situation may be helped by a consultant, here are the kinds of things to look for in that person.

Track Record.   Ask how much fundraising he or she has done and with what success. Find out if the person has worked with organizations similar to yours in both purpose and strategy and in similar locales. A successful consultant for social change groups in Manhattan may be less useful for rural advocacy groups in North Dakota than someone familiar with rural fundraising. Superb consultants for large institutions may not be good for all-volunteer operations with budgets of less than $25,000. If questions of gender, sexual orientation, race, class, or disability are very important in your organization, ask the consultant what experience he or she has had working on these issues or with diverse groups of people.

Recommendations.   If you don't know the person by reputation, ask for a contact person at the last three organizations she or he has worked with. Then call those organizations and ask about the consultant. Was the person helpful? Did the consultant listen well and really understand the situation? Would this group hire this consultant again? You can also check references, but you may get a more candid evaluation from groups the person hasn't listed as references.

Compatibility.   If you envision a relationship with the consultant involving more than a one- or two-day training, you may wish to meet the person. The consultant should offer a preliminary half-hour meeting without charge. In the meeting, you get to see if you like the person and if you would feel good accepting his or her advice. It sometimes happens that an excellent fundraising consultant is not the right person for your nonprofit because the personalities will not mesh. If the organization dislikes the consultant, both the consultant's advice and your money are wasted.

Confidence.   Ask what the consultant will do for you or what they recommend. Avoid asking for long written plans. Elaborate work plans or proposals are often standardized; each one is essentially the same as the next, with the name of your organization substituted for the name of the previous organization. You can ask for a resume, if you find that helpful. By the time of the first meeting, you are not looking so much for proof of fundraising knowledge as for ability to put that knowledge across. Ask yourself, "Is this person believable?" "Is he or she enthusiastic about our mission?" "Will the people who will be working with this person like him or her?" "Do we have confidence in this person's knowledge and skill?"

Belief.   Finally, the consultant must be able to articulate the mission of your organization and believe that the work you do should be done. The consultant does not have to be a donor to your group, and she or he does not have to think that your group is the greatest idea since sliced bread, but the person needs to care about what you stand for and want to help you out of conviction as well as needing a job. This belief is particularly important if your work is controversial or challenges the status quo. Avoid consultants who advise you to "tone down" your message or broaden your goals "to make everyone feel included." A fundraising consultant's job is to help your organization raise money—not to water down the organization's message or philosophy and then help a newer, lightweight group raise money.

PAYING CONSULTANTS

There are no standards or guidelines for how much to pay a consultant. A high price does not necessarily mean better performance or more accountability, but a price that is too good to be true probably is. By hiring a consultant, you are investing in the present so you will have more money in the future.

Most consultants charge by the day or the hour, but some charge by the job. A person's daily rate is usually lower overall than if you were paying him his hourly rate for a full day; several days' work should average out to a lower fee per day than just a one-day job. Consultants also charge for all their expenses: hotels, meals, telephone, photocopy, and travel are the most common. You can cut some of these costs by offering to house the consultant in someone's home and by providing his meals, but if you do that, make sure the consultant is comfortable and can get a good night's sleep. I have often agreed to stay with someone only to discover that I was sleeping on a fold-out couch in the living room, which would be invaded by small children wanting to watch the cartoon channel beginning at 6 A.M. When you cut costs on comfort, you decrease the consultant's ability to be helpful by increasing his exhaustion.

Establish clearly what you are paying for. For example, you pay for the consultant's time, but when does that time start? In some cases, the time starts when the consultant reaches the office of the client or the training site. Even if it takes a day to get there, some do not charge until they are there. Other consultants start charging the minute they leave their house or office. Find out, too, if the consultant charges for all phone calls and e-mails, particularly those that are not substantive, such as setting up meeting times or confirming dates, and at what rate.

If you are hiring a consultant for several days or months of work, build in evaluation points. For example, you might say, "At the end of one month, we will evaluate progress and decide whether or not to continue or if the plan needs to be modified." This practice is best for the consultant, too, who may need to re-estimate the time involved or who may have run into some unforeseen obstacles.

It is important to have a written statement that you both sign spelling out your understanding of the consultant's role, fees, and expenses.

For the same reasons as discussed in the previous chapter, on hiring a development director, never hire a consultant on a contingency or commission basis.

NO MIRACLE WORKERS

Consultants play an increasingly important role in helping organizations increase their fundraising ability, solve problems, and get board members and volunteers to understand all the ways they can help raise money and why they should be involved in fundraising. However, like the results generally reported from personal psychotherapy, it seems that one-third of the groups do better, one-third do worse, and one-third stay about the same. Consultants cannot create motivation and cannot force people to change bad habits. Timing is key: Is your organization willing to change? Are you willing to try something new? Or do you wish you were willing to change but you are not really ready to do so? Are there major personality conflicts that need to be addressed before fundraising can begin? Are there other hidden problems?

During the first meeting with your organization, a good consultant should be able to help you figure out if consulting is what you need. If it is, he or she can also help you determine what the best use of his or her time would be. In the end, for a consultant's time to be truly useful, your organization has to be willing to hear what the consultant has to say.

Dealing with Anxiety

During the thirty-five years I have been in fundraising, I have observed that the greatest factor causing people to leave fundraising or to burn out is not the work itself or even the challenge of having to ask for money. It is the constant, gnawing anxiety that the money won't come in and the knowledge that once you have raised money for one month or one quarter you must simply begin fundraising for the next period of time. There is never a rest, success is short-lived, and lack of success shows up immediately. Fundraising can also be an isolating job, with the burden of producing money too often placed on one or two people.

Many paid fundraising staff have told me that they wake up in the middle of the night worrying and that they never really feel free to take a weekend off, let alone a vacation. Fundraising staff often watch their enthusiasm and self-esteem get eaten away by the constant pressure of a job that by its nature can never be finished.

Aside from psychotherapy or quitting one's job, there are five ways to deal with this anxiety.

Recruit Volunteers and Delegate.   Saul Alinsky, one of the most important figures in community organizing in the twentieth century, had an iron rule for organizing that also applies to fundraising: "Never do for someone what they can do for themselves." People like to help. When you are doing something that a reasonable, intelligent person could do with minimal training, find such a person and get him or her involved. This will decrease your isolation and increase your productivity. Having volunteers help you will not save time, as the time you save by having them do the task is used in recruiting, training, supervising, and then thanking them, but the goal of having the work spread over a larger number of people is accomplished, and the feeling that it is all up to you is diminished.

413

Keep Your Priorities Clear.   If your primary responsibility is to raise money, then every day that you come to work set your priorities around that goal. Ask yourself, "Of all the tasks that I have to do today, which one will raise the most money over the longest period of time?" Do that task first, then do the task that will raise the second-most amount of money, and so on. These decisions will call for some judgment on your part. For example, if you have the choice of writing a grant proposal for $10,000 or approaching a major donor for an additional gift of $1,000, you may decide to go to the donor because she is more likely than the foundation to give year after year. Or if you follow the advice to get others involved, you will try to get a board member to go to the prospective donor, freeing yourself up to write the grant proposal. Just remember that no one ever gets their whole job done. Make sure that the things you don't get done are things not related to fundraising. Here's an example.

In one organization, the director was the only staff person. Feeling responsible for everything, she did those things she knew how to do and that she could finish. She kept accurate and excellent books; paid bills on time; got out minutes and agendas for meetings; and wrote, edited, and produced the newsletter. The board did a lot of program work under her direction. Soon, the organization had little money and was in danger of going out of business. This director quickly learned to change her priorities. Now she works on fundraising at least four hours every day; the organization has outsourced the bookkeeping; board meeting minutes and agendas are handled by the board secretary; and at each board meeting, the director has a fundraising to-do list for the board. While some board members object that they would rather be working on a program than on fundraising, the director is teaching them that without money there is no program. The primary responsibility of the board and staff of any organization is to do work that fulfills the mission, which usually means active, ongoing participation in fundraising.

Detach from the Results of Your Work.   Not being able to do everything is not a condemnation of your worth as a person. A request turned down or an unsuccessful appeal does not mean that you are a failure as a person or as a fundraiser. If you make a mistake, it doesn't mean you are a mistake. Ask yourself whether it will be important in ten years whether you got the newsletter out today or next week. One person can only do so much. Do what you can do in the time allotted, and let the rest go. Too often, small nonprofits have fundraising goals that no one could reach. Instead of trying to live up to impossible expectations, evaluate your goal setting.

Recognize That There Are External Forces Beyond Your Control. You can do your job flawlessly and your organization can be effective and well regarded, and you still may not be able to raise the money you need. The rising gap between rich and poor, which every year reaches another record, and the depth and breadth of government cutbacks mean that more and more organizations scramble for money. In the United States particularly, there is plenty of money, but it is very unevenly distributed. Without a major restructuring of social policy that places people ahead of corporate profit and a priority on peace rather than military might, nonprofits of all sorts will continue to struggle. This state of affairs is not your fault. Dealing with these larger forces means opening up the time in your organization to join and work in coalitions of organizations addressing tax policy, the preservation of "the commons," and the role of the nonprofit sector in general. Your organization has to work on issues beyond its own mission. Getting perspective on the larger picture will help reduce your anxiety.

Some people have found it helpful to form support groups with others doing similar types of work—either informal gatherings over happy hour or more formal, structured meetings at a specific time and place. If you do use a support group, make sure it supports your work and helps with strategies. Do not use it as a gripe session to compare notes on how awful everyone's job is. That will only make you more dejected.

Take Care of Yourself. Don't always work overtime. Take vacations. Ask for help. Delegate tasks. The overall work of social justice is the creation of a humane and just society in which, among other things, work and leisure are balanced. If the culture of your workplace does not encourage balance, it is unlikely that your organization can have a positive role in creating social change. As the great contemplative monk Thomas Merton wrote:

> There is a pervasive form of contemporary violence to which the idealist fighting for peace by nonviolent methods most easily succumbs: activism and overwork. The rush and pressure of modern life are a form, perhaps the most common form, of its innate violence. To allow

oneself to be carried away by a multitude of conflicting concerns, to surrender to too many projects, to want to help everyone in every-thing is to succumb to violence. More than that, it is cooperation in violence. The frenzy of the activist neutralizes one's work for peace. It destroys the fruitfulness of one's work because it kills the root of inner wisdom which makes work fruitful.

Working with Your Executive Director

For many people reading this book, this chapter could be called "Working with Yourself," because as the only paid person, the title "executive director" describes you, as does the all-encompassing title of "staff." Nonetheless, even if you are a sole staff person, you may find this chapter helpful in avoiding mistakes once your organization is big enough to hire someone in the development role. Some organizations are lucky enough to have one or more volunteers who devote themselves to fundraising, being in essence unpaid staff. If you supervise people in this role, you will want to review this chapter. But mostly, if you are a development director working with an executive director, this chapter is about you.

As development director, the executive director can be your greatest ally or your biggest challenge, but rarely anything in between. The job of the development director is an odd one in the sense that you report to and are accountable to the executive director, yet your job includes organizing the executive director's time efficiently with regard to fundraising—which means telling your boss what to do. To work effectively with an executive director requires discussing early on in your tenure how the executive director wants you to present the fundraising tasks that he or she is to carry out and how the executive director intends to be accountable to that work. Here's how an ideal working relationship between an executive director and a development director would play out.

At the beginning of the year, the executive director and the development director create a draft fundraising plan. Perhaps the development director does most of the work on the plan and then brings it to the executive director to discuss, but the executive director is familiar with it and believes it is the appropriate plan for the year. These two staff go over the plan in great detail with the board leadership, such as the fundraising and finance committees. Board members' suggestions for changes are incorporated, then someone from the board presents the plan to the full board, ideally receiving enthusiastic buy-in (or at least willingness to do the job) from the full board. The development director feels supported by the executive director in all her efforts to work with the board and with the executive director. The executive director sees the development director as a partner in the financial future of the organization—a junior partner perhaps, but still someone she turns to for advice and whose counsel and instincts she trusts. The development director, in turn, sees the executive director as someone she learns from and whom she likes and respects. If not friends, at least these two see themselves as strong colleagues, interested in each other's opinions on a wide variety of topics related to running the organization.

Some co-workers develop this relationship naturally. They are usually people who are competent, not competitive and not controlling, more committed to the mission of the organization than to their own ambition, and able to delegate tasks and share information. Each appreciates the strengths and talents of the other, and they have complementary skills. These people are not without their struggles or disagreements, but they are able to be straightforward in conversation and listen to each other, and they are willing to take the time to work things out.

People who do not naturally subsume themselves to the work of the organization can still have a strong working relationship if they work at it a bit. These are usually people who are competent but can be controlling, who are committed to the mission of the group but wanting personal recognition, who are so overwhelmed with work that they have trouble sorting out what can be delegated and what cannot, and who keep information to themselves more out of sheer inability to find the time to share it than any real intent to conceal. Again, honesty in communication and a commitment not to harbor resentments will help this be an effective working relationship. It is also important to note that chronic overwork with no praise or recognition of effort can cause anyone to become difficult to work with.

Unfortunately, there are far too many situations in which the relationship between the executive director and the development director does not work. Although some of these poor relations may be primarily the fault of the development director, the majority have their roots in the work style of the executive director. Here are the most common reasons a productive relationship between executive director and development director fails to occur:

- The executive director's successes eventually mean that the organization grows past her ability to run it. Rather than admit that she has reached her limit of competence, the executive director becomes more and more controlling and may actually shrink the organization back down to a size she can manage. This dynamic is particularly prone to occur with executive directors who were founders of the organization.

- The executive director has been at the organization too long. He feels tired and has lost enthusiasm for the work, but he stays in the job because he can't imagine what to do next, or he is afraid he won't find another job. Mediocrity becomes the standard of work. Other staff, as well as the board and volunteers, follow the lead of the executive director and exhibit the same mediocrity.

- The executive director is sensitive to criticism, even defensive. She creates a work environment in which only total loyalty to her is acceptable and questioning her decisions or directions is perceived as insubordination. Creativity is squelched.

- The executive director is afraid to ask for money and will not help with fundraising from individual donors. Often this fear is disguised as "I can't deal with a bunch of little gifts. Let's just get a foundation grant."

- The executive director doesn't trust the board members or wants to retain power, so does not share decision making with them. Few if any boards will actively engage in fundraising if they are not involved in policymaking and other board activities, so the board is of no use in fundraising.

- The executive director is threatened by the development director's knowledge of fundraising and feels that his own lack of knowledge will be perceived as incompetence. He constantly belittles the development director's ideas or ignores them altogether.

- The executive director's job is too big. She works between sixty and seventy hours every week, which means she is often at the office on weekends; she rarely takes a vacation (and then is responding to e-mail and sending work-related text messages several times a day); she expects the same effort from the other employees, even though she will protest that she does not. Such people do not realize that they simply disguise the cost of doing business, and they wonder why they have high employee turnover.

- The executive director believes that the development director's job is to get the money. He wants the development director to bring in the cash, no questions asked. He is slightly embarrassed that the organization needs money at all.

There are many other variations on these themes, but these are the most common. If you are already working for an executive director who has one or two of these characteristics, it is possible to make a change in the staff dynamic, usually with the help of a coach or a consultant. If your executive director has several of these characteristics, it is more likely that you will need to find another job. To guarantee that you don't take a job where these dynamics prevail, make sure that you know what you have the right to expect from an organization and an executive director and what they have the right to expect from you.

One of the best ways to develop good working relationships is to be absolutely clear about your job. Your job is to coordinate the fundraising function of the organization. You are to make sure that all fundraising tasks are completed, one of which is to help the executive director complete his or her tasks. You lead by pushing others into doing the work, and your job is to get as many people involved in fundraising as possible so that the organization can raise as much money as it needs from as many sources as you can manage.

Given that these are your responsibilities, the executive director should expect that you and she would work closely together to create the executive director's fundraising task list and that you would have the authority to remind the executive director about her tasks and to hold her accountable for completing them. She, in turn, would expect you to provide the support she needs, such as materials, prospect information, strategy details, reports, and so on. Keep in mind that the executive director is the front person for the organization. Many donors will prefer to meet with that person rather than anyone else in the organization. The development director has to appreciate that the executive director balances many tasks, of which fundraising is only one—even if it is very important.

Sometimes the executive director will know a lot more about fundraising than the development director. In that case, the executive director should mentor the development director. More frequently, the development director knows more about fundraising than the executive director. The executive director should welcome this knowledge, recognizing that an organization hires staff partly because the executive director doesn't have the time—or necessarily the skills—to do the whole job.

Your job is also to coordinate the fundraising efforts of the board of directors and other volunteers. You should have access to all board members and be actively supported by the executive director in your efforts with the board. Both of you should work closely with board members, particularly on personal, face-to-face solicitation.

Both parties should know how the other likes to work. Questions of working style should be talked out early in the relationship. Such questions include whether interruptions are OK; how each feels about editing the other's writing (because the executive director needs to feel good about everything that comes out of the office, all written materials should be read and edited by other people); how much nagging about getting a task done is bearable; methods of dealing with conflict; the best way to hear criticism; and so on.

The way to have a good working relationship between development director and executive director is to be clear from the beginning what each of you thinks the executive director and development director jobs are and are not—and to agree on those job descriptions. In the end, the people in these jobs need to work as much as possible as partners in fundraising and to see the board as an asset to be developed. As development director, be mission-driven and know that your main loyalty has to be to the work of the organization. Know that you are not always going to see eye-to-eye with the executive director and that final decisions rest with the executive director. Above all, be honest and demand honesty in return. Your relationship needs to mirror the kind of relationships we want to see in the world: respectful, caring, nurturing, genuinely interested in the other, and joined in a mutual belief in something bigger than yourselves.

ON DEFENSIVENESS

Defensiveness is so important and so endemic that I feel it merits a short discussion on its own. Defensiveness, according to the dictionary, is "resisting criticism or attack." Defensiveness surfaces as the inability to be told that one's thinking or behavior either is or might be wrong—or even that there may be equally viable alternatives to one's thoughts or actions. Executive directors can be very defensive, as I mentioned earlier, partly because of the enormous responsibility they often feel for making everything go right so as to keep the organization afloat. Unfortunately, however, defensiveness can be found in all parts of an organization and needs to be addressed early and often.

There are several reasons why a person might be defensive, but one very common root of a defensive attitude is that many people equate disagreement with disrespect. It is impossible to have a discussion with someone with this misunderstanding and have conflicting viewpoints aired. Everything is taken personally, and the defensive person has a limited ability to separate action from personality. They hear "I disagree with you" as "You are wrong and stupid." I have worked with many people in leadership who demand their staff exhibit the kind of loyalty one expects of a dog to its owner. They can change, but such change usually requires intervention from someone they respect as well as some training in how to accept—and even use—criticism. Sometimes people (defensively) deny that they are defensive, but they truly may not realize the effect of their tone or body language. Simple changes can make a world of difference. For example, one harried executive director got this feedback from a facilitator hired to help with tension between him and his development director, "When the development director is speaking, you often interrupt her to explain why something happened the way it did, instead of letting her finish her point. This gives the impression you don't want to hear what she has to say and she also tends to lose her train of thought." The executive director was very surprised, and noted that he can't stand being interrupted by others. He now consciously waits until he is sure his staff person has finished what she wants to say before responding.

Another executive director got this feedback from watching a video one of her staff was making to post on YouTube about their mentoring program. Although the final video was only one minute long, the staff person had shot a lot of footage and the executive director got to see herself in several settings, including a board meeting. The executive director felt that the board was ineffective and offered little leadership to the organization. What she saw, though, was herself shooting down every idea that anyone proposed. "That can't work—no one will fund it" or "We did that a couple of years ago before you were on the board and it was a complete bust." She realized that she was so emphatic and dismissive that no one wanted to speak up. With the help of a coach, she has learned how to listen and to encourage ideas. Ironically, as she points out, she needed to learn the skills her organization looks for in finding good mentors.

For those who are not the executive director, defensiveness often arises out of fear of being perceived as a poor worker. "I disagree with you" becomes "You are a bad worker." These people overcompensate by posturing that they are always right. I know so many people like this that I have given them an acronym: "NIMF"—Nothing Is My Fault. One way a leader can counter this kind of defensiveness is to give honest credit and praise much more often than you levy criticism. Such balance will help your staff trust you enough to be able to hear disagreement or admit error.

Finally, of course, we live in a culture that is averse to conflict. When we read about things people are terrified to do, such as public speaking or asking for money, I sometimes think that at the top of that list would be "starting a conversation that might lead to conflict." Some organizations do in-house trainings on conflict and conflict resolution in order to strengthen their staff and volunteers' ability to be in creative dialogue with each other and to surface disagreements before they fester and become explosions.

None of the manifestations of defensiveness are good leadership qualities. Of course, all of us feel defensive from time to time. Thinking about what makes you feel on the defense and what helps you to let go of that defensiveness will help you deal with others. People who want to be effective leaders are always working on not taking things personally, and organizations that want to be healthy workplaces should put processes in place that encourage civil disagreement, that praise people for admitting mistakes and errors, and that teach people how to give and receive both positive and not-so-positive feedback.

Ethical Dilemmas Common to Fundraising

In our everyday language, we use a lot of words and phrases related to being a good person fairly interchangeably: a person might be honest, have a lot of integrity, always tell the truth; he or she might be highly principled, decent, fair, or just. Although philosophers and linguists (and the dictionary) can probably sort out the nuances of meaning among these words, I simply hope that all of us are doing our best to be all of the above. To behave ethically will have all these elements, and certainly an honest person will have a far easier time being ethical than will someone who is sneaky or deceitful. However, ethics are usually grounded in a large moral framework and involve issues of a broader nature than simply personal behavior. In this chapter, I look at some problems that can't be solved simply by applying accepted standards of honesty or integrity, but require in addition some broader ethical considerations.

Fundraisers often run up against dilemmas that test their honesty, but right and wrong behavior are still fairly obvious. For example, it is dishonest to tell a funder or a donor that you are engaged in a certain kind of program if you are not, no matter how much money that donor might give you if they thought you were. Similarly, it lacks integrity to take on a program area or a piece of work just because someone has offered to fund it. It is not fair to other employees or the mission of the organization to agree to hire your donor's unqualified son-in-law to be your organization's program director in exchange for a major gift. It is unprincipled to keep two sets of books—one for the public and a different, truer accounting that remains internal to the organization. Many of these issues are addressed in standard accounting procedures and in the excellent Association of Fundraising Professionals' "Code of Ethics" (see Premium Web Content).

Although we could also use the word *ethical* to describe appropriate behavior in any of the situations just described, there is a subset of ethical issues that fall into more of a gray area and that are usually the development director's job to navigate. These dilemmas often arise because the right or honest thing to do is not completely clear and because the development director has conflicting loyalties. Let's look at some examples, with you as the development director.

THREE MORAL DILEMMAS

A Question of When to Tell "the Truth" and to Whom. A think tank with a staff of five people is offered the opportunity to buy their office building. Their landlord suggests a reasonable price, but the building will need a great deal of work and the organization has never thought about owning property. The board chair and several board members are enthusiastic about buying the building, but the executive director and several other board members are not. They feel the building needs too much work and that owning and rehabbing the building could take staff away from the actual work of the organization. As development director, you agree with those who oppose buying the building; in addition, you think it would be hard to raise funds for something for which enthusiasm is not widely shared and for which the executive director, in particular, is not in favor. You talk over your thoughts with the executive director. At the next board meeting, the executive director announces that one of the organization's biggest donors, a banker, has expressed concern about the amount of work the building needs and has related that she has seen nonprofits get into financial trouble when they tried to own property. She has advised against buying this building. You know that no such conversation has taken place, even as the board chair recommends deferring to this donor's knowledge and the matter is dropped.

A Question of Being a Spy. A community theater is given $25,000 by a real estate developer who loves what the organization does and was approached by a board member for a gift. The entire organization is thrilled as this is the largest gift the theater company has ever received from an individual. About a month after the gift has come in, the real estate developer calls the development director and says that he will be building a gated community on a piece of land just outside of town, and he knows that some affordable housing activists are going to oppose this development. He asks if you would go to the public meeting on the proposal and report what you learn about their plans to him. Although it's not true, you say you are busy the night of the meeting. The developer agrees to find someone else to attend the meeting.

A Question of Conditions.   The chair of your board brings you to a meeting with her elderly aunt, who is interested in your organization's work. On the board chair's advice, her aunt has decided to offer the lead gift for a program your organization has wanted to launch; moreover, the donor is willing to give this same generous amount for three years. You and the board chair are thrilled. As your meeting with this woman is winding down she says, "I just have one question for you: Does your staff go to church regularly?" You do go to church, but your executive director is an atheist, and the two program staff who will run the program are Jewish. One is religious and one is not.

In these examples, there is one easy way out: let small fibs pass. So what if the executive director made up a conversation in order to end the discussion about buying the building? It avoided a big fight, and it was probably the right decision anyway; certainly, it was the one you agreed with. So what if you pretend you can't go to the meeting? He'll find someone else to do this for him. So what if you decide to give the impression your staff are more religious than they are? The donor probably won't pursue the question further. Your involvement as the development director in any of these three situations is relatively minor and your conscience can be pretty clear.

However, as the saying goes, giving in to any of these "so whats" leads you down a slippery slope. Each of these examples bears a deeper examination to ferret out the ethical and practical complications and to see if there is another way to respond.

THREE TOOLS

There are three tools that can help you avoid feeling the need to say or do something just to please a donor. First, follow the Quaker adage, "Assume good intent." That is, assume that people you disagree with may be acting out of positive motivation, and that they will want to know if you have concerns about what is happening. Second, follow a main principle of assertiveness training by making only "I" statements. "I felt," "I wonder," and so on. Third, use a "gut check." Does this feel bad or weird? What if this whole story were in the newspaper—would I feel proud of my role in the outcome? Using these three tools, let's look at the dilemmas in two ways: good endings and more difficult endings.

Good Endings

First, a look at how these situations could have good endings.

In the first situation with the executive director making up something a donor said, a gut check says, "This is weird." You need to talk with the executive director about his story. First of all, the board member may well know the donor whose name was invoked, and if she runs into her and thanks her for her clarity, your executive director will be found out and your board chair will be embarrassed. Second, if the board chair is a good person and good worker, why not see if she understands the fact that a capital campaign cannot succeed without total enthusiasm from everyone? Assuming good intent, you ask the executive director why he thought his story was the best way to solve the problem. Regardless of his rationale, you can then use "I" statements to make your position clear. For example, if the executive director explains that he didn't want to hurt the board chair's feelings and is quite certain she doesn't know the donor in question, you could say, "I would rather see if she understands the need for full staff and board support for a big project. Otherwise, something else may come up that she supports and others don't and we'd be in a similar situation."

Here's how such a scenario might play out: The executive director agrees to have a meeting with you and the board chair. He tells the board chair that he exaggerated a conversation with a donor to avoid hurting her feelings and now feels bad about it. He realizes she is perfectly capable of understanding why pursuing the building did not seem like a good idea to him. You offer support for his position, including telling the board chair how important she is to the organization and how no one ever wants to dampen someone's enthusiasm. She is understanding and, as is her nature, gracious. She does say lightheartedly as the meeting ends, "Don't worry about my feelings in the future. I'm tougher than I look."

In the second instance, being asked to report to the developer on what happens at a public meeting about his project, you say what you feel: "I don't feel comfortable in that role. I will feel like I am spying." He backs down: "That is not what I meant. I just thought the people at the meeting might speak more freely if I weren't there." You say, "If you go, they will know you really want to work something out, but if they find out that people are reporting back to you, they will think you are dishonest as well as against affordable housing and it will be much harder to come to a compromise that pleases everyone." He hasn't thought of it like that and thanks you for your insight.

The third example, concerning the religious behavior of the staff, is one in which "assume good intent" is the primary authority for your actions. You have no idea what the donor wants to know when she asks if you and other staff go to church. Perhaps she is just making conversation, and in her circle of friends, this is a common question. You would answer, "I am active in First Methodist. The two people running the new program are Jewish. One goes to Temple Emmanuel and I don't know so much about the other's life. Are you involved in a church?" You might be surprised when she answers, "I'm an Episcopalian. I think churches and synagogues might be interested in this program, and some of them might be able to provide some money and volunteers. Perhaps one of the program people can talk to my women's group and to their own religious groups once the program is up and running."

The lesson about ethics in these three situations is that we have a tendency to make up stories in our own minds about why other people do things. That habit in itself is, ironically, a form of unethical behavior. We don't approve of saying something that is not true and which could cause the person hearing it to behave in a way they wouldn't have if they knew the truth, but if we say something to ourselves that we don't know to be true and then act on it as if it were true, it has the same effect. Just as in donor negotiations, you need to stick with what the donor has said, and not add your own interpretation to it.

More Difficult Endings

Of course, all three of these situations could have gone another way. Let's look at how we might work with more difficult endings.

In the first circumstance, the executive director becomes quite defensive when you discuss his fabrication and refuses to talk to the board chair about it. He says that he has made up things before in order to "get things done" and that you need to be more practical. Your dilemma now moves to a different level: Do you want to work with someone who you know will make up stories (possibly to you) in order to get his own way? This would not be an easy decision, particularly if you like the organization or if jobs are hard to come by. Over time, however, the price of supporting someone who regularly exaggerates or fabricates to get his own way may be too great.

In the second situation, the donor might say that he is going ahead with this development no matter what, and that your theater owes him a favor. At this point you need to go to your executive director and get her or his support. Your organization can assure the donor that you will stay out of the controversy (if that is true), but his gift was to the mission of the theater and if it had any other meaning or requirements, he needed to have made that clear at the time. If necessary, you will have to offer to return the gift.

In the third case, the donor says she prefers to give money to organizations in which all the staff are involved in a church. Invite her to meet all the staff and hear from them personally before she makes a final decision.

By continuing to negotiate in any situation, you stay in a place of integrity but not self-righteousness. Having been in many serious moral and ethical quandaries with regard to fundraising, I have always felt best, and felt that the best outcome resulted, when I told the truth—that is, what was true for me—without insisting this was the only or even the complete truth. Offering options and asking to stay in conversation usually resolved the problem amiably.

As you can see, some of your willingness and ability to operate completely ethically will come out of having a diversity of funding sources so that no one person or source is so important to you that you are even tempted to compromise your values for the money.

It is also true that some things can't be resolved. Then the question revolves around your own integrity and what lengths you will go to to preserve it.

PART SEVEN

Budgeting and Planning

One of my more difficult clients was a longtime community organizer who resisted every suggestion I made. (He probably found me difficult, too). His board of directors, having learned of their fiduciary responsibility, asked to see a budget. He hired me to help put one together, and I suggested he also create a fundraising plan. As it turned out, he did not want to do either, finding both efforts a colossal waste of time. Finally, in exasperation he said, "We do what needs to be done with the money we have. That's my plan and that's my budget!" I often think of him when I think of planning. In many ways, he was simply more up-front about his method than many organizations I work with that operate the same way.

All nonprofits want to have enough money to do their work, but few can name what amount that would be. They certainly want to use the time and money of volunteers and donors wisely and make progress in accomplishing their goals, but the work of defining exactly what that would mean often doesn't get done. The founder, if she is still in the picture, and her friends are often working from a "plan" kept in their heads and revealed to others on a "need to know" basis. This is not an effort to be secretive so much as a failure to articulate the plan, rather than just operate from (usually good) instincts. The budgeting process is "We need money—whatever we can get. We'll spend what we have, but it won't be enough." The fundraising plan is "Help! Write a grant proposal, quick! Let's do an event—what's fast? Does anybody know anybody they can ask for a big dona-tion?" If you thrive on this chaotic, crisis approach to budgeting and planning, then don't read the following chapters. But if you think, "There has to be an easier way," you are right. In fact the time my client spent resisting me was about the same amount of time it would have taken to create a budget and a plan.

Because time is our most precious nonrenewable resource, all efforts that use time respectfully, efficiently, enjoyably, and with the greatest results accomplished for the time put in ought to be our top life priorities. Developing a financial plan—a budget—and a fundraising plan will let you use your time to maximum effectiveness.

Developing a Budget

The first step in developing a fundraising plan is to develop a working budget. In its simplest form, a budget is a list of items on which you plan to spend money (expenses) and a list of sources from which you plan to receive money (income). A budget is balanced when the expenses and income are equal; an ideal budget projects more income than expenses. Budgets are usually prepared from year to year, although organizations doing strategic planning usually prepare three-year budget projections.

There are many ways to prepare a budget. As organizations grow, they may change the way they prepare their budget a number of times before finding one that gives them the most accurate projections. In some organizations a single staff member prepares the entire budget and presents it for board approval, but this is a large burden for one person. Therefore, the method presented here assumes that a small committee will undertake the budget-setting process. This committee can be a standing finance committee of the board, which would then be in charge of monitoring the budget, or it can be an ad-hoc committee of two or three board members and a staff person. Many grassroots organizations lack expertise in developing budgets, so they recruit someone who has that experience onto their budget committee to help them create the budget. It is particularly helpful to have someone with financial expertise if you are switching systems or fiscal years or if you want to plan for more than one year at a time.

If you work with a committee, it should be limited to four or five members. Each should have some knowledge of the organization and be willing to put in the time it will take to do the job as thoroughly as possible.

There is a simple, two-step process for preparing a budget that most small nonprofit organizations can use effectively. The process takes into account the

433

largest number of variables without requiring extensive research and can be done using a simple spreadsheet, or even paper and a calculator.

STEP 1: ESTIMATE EXPENSES AND INCOME SEPARATELY

The budget committee should first divide into two subgroups: one to estimate expenses, the other to project income. When these tasks are completed, the subgroups will reconvene to mesh their work in the second step. If one or two people are preparing the budget, they need to figure expenses one day and income another day. Otherwise, the temptation is to make everything match up as they go along, which leads to inflated projections of income and inaccurately low projections of expenses.

Estimating Expenses

The people working on the expense side of the budget should prepare three columns of numbers representing "survival," "reasonable," and "maximum" expense figures, as shown in the example. The "survival" column spells out the amount of money the organization needs simply to stay open. If you are not able to raise this amount of money, you would have to shut your doors. Items here generally include minimum staff requirements, Wi-Fi access, postage, printing, and telephone. This column does not include the cost of doing new projects, salary increases, additional staff or consultants, or even office space, if you are able to work virtually.

Next, prepare the "maximum" column: how much money your organization would need in order to operate at maximum effectiveness. This is not a dream budget, but a real estimate of how much it would cost to have a real impact on the issues you are addressing.

Finally, prepare the "reasonable" column: how much money the organization needs to do more than survive but still not meet all its goals. These figures should not be conceived of as simply the middle of the other two columns. For example, an organization's leaders may feel that in order to accomplish any good work, the office needs to be larger or each staff person needs a laptop, or they must raise salaries to decrease staff turnover. Because an office, better equipment, and increased salaries may not be necessary to the organization's survival, they will not be included in the "survival" budget; however, they are imperative enough to the organization's work to be included in the "reasonable" budget, which would bring the reasonable and maximum budgets very close together.

The "survival," "reasonable," and "maximum" columns, then, give the range of finances required to run the organization at various levels of functioning. If you have a year or two of financial history, you can use the line items and costs from previous years to help in creating your budget.

The process of figuring expenses must be done with great thoroughness and attention to detail. For example, to estimate how much you will spend on printing, think through all the items you print and how many of each you will need. A simple mail appeal has at least three printed components—the letter, the return envelope, and the envelope the appeal is sent in. The budget for your online presence will need to include staff or consulting time for the person who updates the Web site, and the staff time required to respond to e-mail or to download donations or orders generated by the site. You may also want to hire a consultant to help you expand your online fundraising efforts so you can gradually phase out using a lot of direct mail. When you don't know how much something will cost, do not guess. Take the time while creating the budget to find out.

To ensure completeness and accuracy in budget setting, many organizations have found it helpful to send board and staff members to training sessions on financial planning.

Projecting Income

At the same time that the expense side of the budget is being prepared, the other half of the committee is preparing the income side. Crucial to this process is knowledge of what fundraising strategies the organization can carry out and how much money these strategies can be expected to generate. Much of this information will come from reports kept in previous years. As shown in the example, the income side is also estimated in three columns, in this case representing "worst," "likely," and "ideal."

To calculate the income projection labeled "worst," take last year's income sources and assume that with the same amount of effort the organization will at least be able to raise this amount again, unless you know that the effort expended was more than can be expected in future years or you were given some one-time-only gifts, or your community has plunged into a deep recession. In the case of foundation, corporate, or government grants it may be wise to write "zero" as the

Sample Expense Projections			
Item	Survival	Reasonable	Maximum
Personnel			
Executive director			
Development director			
Office manager			
Program coordinator			
Benefits and taxes (payroll, workers comp, health insurance)			
TOTAL PERSONNEL			
Professional development (seminars, classes, coaching)			
Staff travel			
Office rent			
Furniture and equipment			
Lease photocopier			
Computers			
Other (specify)			
Office supplies			
Telephone and Internet telephone service(s)			
Computer backup system			
Internet service provider			
Technology			
Software			
Web design			
Apps subscriptions			
Tech support for database			
Printing			
Design of print materials			
Brochures			

Sample Expense Projections *(Continued)*			
Item	Survival	Reasonable	Maximum
Annual report			
Mail appeals			
Newsletters			
Stationery			
Other			
TOTAL PRINTING			
Postage			
First-class mail			
Bulk mail			
Bulk mail permit			
Other (specify)			
TOTAL POSTAGE			
Other contractors			
Bookkeeping			
Event planner			
Training for board and staff			
Board and volunteers			
Board travel			
Annual meeting or retreat			
Volunteer appreciation			
Other (specify)			
TOTAL OTPS (other than personnel)			
GRAND TOTAL			

worst projection unless you have been promised or strongly led to believe that your grant will be renewed.

Draw up the "ideal" income projections next. These figures reflect what would happen if all the organization's fundraising strategies were successful and most grant proposals were funded. Again, this is not a dream budget. It does not assume events that will probably not occur, such as someone leaving you a million dollar bequest. The ideal budget must be one that would be met if everything went as well as it possibly could.

The "likely" column is a compromise. It estimates the income the organization can expect to generate with reasonable growth, hard work, most people keeping their promises, and expanding old fundraising strategies and having success with some new ones, yet taking into account that some things will not go as planned.

There are two ways to budget income and expenses from fundraising strategies: one is to show all expenses in the expense side and all income on the income side. For small organizations, this is probably the simplest. The other is to show net income in the master budget, with a detailed expense and income budget available on a separate spreadsheet for each strategy. For organizations that do a lot of special events or conferences or that have fees and products, this method will be much more helpful overall.

Both the income and expense sides of the budget are presented in columns of numbers, but each subcommittee should also include a narrative that explains some of the rationale behind the numbers and outlines goals other than financial that some fundraising strategies will be seeking to accomplish.

When the income and expense sides of the budget have been figured separately in this way, there is less chance of giving in to the temptation to manipulate the figures to make them balance. The committee should follow the old fundraising adage, "Plan expenses high and income low." If you follow this advice and your numbers are wrong (that is, if your expenses are lower or your income higher than projected), you will be pleasantly surprised. If you do what many organizations do, which is to boost income estimates to make the budget balance, you will soon be in financial trouble.

STEP 2: MEET, COMPARE, NEGOTIATE

When the entire committee reconvenes, you hope to find that the amount in the "reasonable" expense column and the "likely" income column are close to the same. In that happy circumstance, those figures can be adopted as the budget with no more fuss. Occasionally, nonprofits are pleasantly surprised to discover that their "likely" income projections come close to their "maximum" expense

Sample Income Projections			
Source	Worst	Likely	Ideal
Major gifts			
New			
Renewals or upgrades			
Monthly donors			
Donors giving less than $250			
New			
Renewals			
Special appeals			
Sale of products			
T-shirts			
Booklets			
Other (specify)			
Special events (define whether net or gross)			
House parties			
Dance			
Conference			
Board donations			
Fees for service			
Foundations (specify)			
Other (specify)			
TOTAL INCOME			

projections. However, compromises usually need to be made. Most of the time the expenses need to be adjusted to meet realistic income potential, not the other way around.

When no two sets of numbers are anywhere near alike, the committee will have to find solutions. There is no right or wrong way to negotiate at this point. If each committee has done its job properly, there will be no need to review each item to see if it is accurate. However, with more research, each subcommittee may discover other ways to delete expenses or add income.

As shown in the illustration, there are nine possible ways income and expense projections can match up.

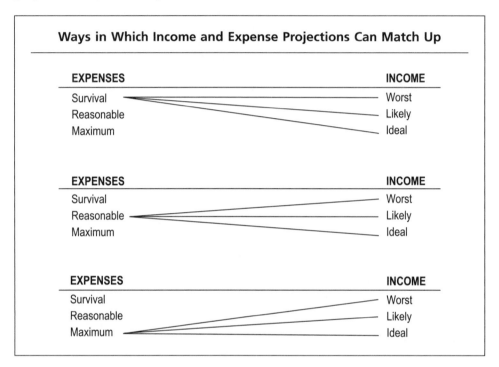

Ways in Which Income and Expense Projections Can Match Up

EXPENSES	INCOME
Survival	Worst
Reasonable	Likely
Maximum	Ideal

EXPENSES	INCOME
Survival	Worst
Reasonable	Likely
Maximum	Ideal

EXPENSES	INCOME
Survival	Worst
Reasonable	Likely
Maximum	Ideal

As an example, here are two case studies that illustrate different ways of reaching a workable budget using compromise and research.

THE MAKING OF A BUDGET

Community Arts Initiative

Community Arts Initiative was founded in the early 1990s. For the first ten years, it functioned as a small organization of mostly volunteers, with outside people brought in occasionally and paid for specific projects. Then it applied for Arts Council funding; for the past five years, the organization has received a grant of $50,000 annually, allowing it to hire a coordinator who, in turn, helped it raise more money. Last year, however, the Initiative was informed that Arts Council money was no longer available. Of its total budget of $150,000, this shortfall represented more than 30 percent. The budget committee developed the following estimates:

Expenses		Income	
Survival	$60,000	Worst	$50,000
Reasonable	$100,000	Likely	$75,000
Maximum	$150,000	Ideal	$100,000

All of their income projections were below their parallel expense projections. However, their "reasonable" expense projection was the same as their expense budget from the past five years without the Arts Council money but including fixed increases in line items. Their "survival" budget represented such significant cutbacks that several board members felt there would be little point in even staying open. After much discussion among the board and staff, the organization decided that it wanted to continue operating at the current level to avoid undermining morale completely and curtailing the program. The group agreed to adopt the "ideal" income and the "reasonable" expense estimates, and committed themselves to an intensive major donor drive in the first part of the fiscal year. That way they would have some certainty about whether they would be able to operate within this budget, and they wouldn't be cutting their coordinator before seeing if they could meet the budget. They also committed themselves to never being so dependent on one source of money again.

North Fork Watershed Protection

North Fork Watershed Protection had been functioning for only two years. The first year the program was run entirely by volunteers, most of them residents living near the watershed area. In the second year, in conjunction with the group incorporating as a nonprofit, some volunteers agreed to form a board of directors. They were able to raise enough money to hire a staff biologist. With this person's expertise, the organization proceeded to document the sources of the pollution entering its watershed, which generated a good deal of publicity and attracted the attention of the public health department. To keep the pressure on and to ensure that appropriate steps were taken to mitigate this pollution, the staff member now needed a half-time assistant to help with fundraising, administration, and dealing with the press. The board's initial successful fundraising represented a few significant financial contributions, but no one was certain that these gifts would be repeated. It was also difficult for the board to make income projections, because it had so little past experience to go on. A budget committee estimated these figures:

Expenses		Income	
Survival	$158,000	Worst	$160,000
Reasonable	$175,000	Likely	$175,000
Maximum	$220,000	Ideal	$290,000

The only difference between the "survival" and "reasonable" expenses was the cost of a part-time assistant. Even though the "likely" income could cover the "reasonable" budget, the board members elected to adopt the "survival" budget for the first six months, along with the "likely" income. They reasoned that although their track record for fundraising was good, their fundraising program was not well enough established for them to draw conclusions about the future.

Because the program had grown rapidly, the board members felt that taking on another staff person was ill-advised until they were sure of meeting their income goals. They decided that they would review their income after six months and hire the assistant if they had raised at least half of their "likely" goals. This strategy gave the board some breathing time and assured the staff person that the issue of her workload was being addressed and could be solved in a short time. In the meantime, board members and other volunteers committed themselves to helping out in the office and handling more of the media calls.

These case studies illustrate that budgets are designed to be flexible, to serve as measurements of progress, and to provide structures for the way money is spent and raised. Using a budget this way makes it a helpful document rather than a club hanging over an organization's head. Small organizations cannot know exactly how much money they will raise or spend beyond certain fixed costs, such as for rent or salaries, but they need the parameters that a budget can provide.

ONGOING MONITORING

Once the budget is developed and adopted, it must be monitored. Although you can monitor your budget using a spreadsheet, there are also inexpensive accounting software programs that can issue profit and loss reports that will be easier to understand and examine. (QuickBooks is the most commonly used program.) Every month, you note what you have spent or raised in each category of your budget as well as the amounts you should have spent and raised in that time, if all the money were being raised and spent equally over the twelve-month period (you will have more income or more expenses in some months than in others, which should make the budget work out at the end of the year). You can then make adjustments as needed and catch problems fairly quickly. Do not change your budget—use it as a learning tool. Compare what you projected would happen with what did happen and discuss the differences. This way, as the years pass you will be able to create more and more accurate budgets.

Creating a Fundraising Plan

E ven though I am a big fan of budgeting and planning, it is instructive to start this chapter with an old fundraising saw: "Fundraising is 10 percent planning and 90 percent follow-up calls." Although many people hate planning, I fairly frequently find people who take so much time to plan that they have no time to actually do the work. So this is a short chapter because, although planning has to be done thoughtfully and as thoroughly as possible, a plan that is not implemented is more problematic than working with no plan.

Planning for fundraising is not difficult to do. And even though planning should not be what you spend most of your time on, it is also true that one hour of planning can save three hours of work.

There are five steps to creating a workable plan.

Step 1. Set a Goal.   Your financial goal will come from your budget, which you can create using the principles outlined in Chapter Thirty-Eight.

Step 2. For Each Income Strategy, Attend to Certain Details.   The following details should be attended to for a workable plan:

- Tasks required to complete the strategy

- Due date for each task

- Who is in charge of each task

- How much the strategy is going to cost and how much it is going to raise

Now put the plan on some kind of "year-at-a-glance" calendar or spreadsheet so you can make sure that you have spread the work out over the course of the year as evenly as possible and that you have not made unrealistic plans (see also Part Five, "Fundraising Management").

Step 3. Plot Out Your Plans for Raising Money from Individuals. Your organization may raise money in any number of ways, but we are focused on your plan to raise money from individuals. You may need to also create other plans to show how you will raise money from foundations, corporations, or governments, or how you will market products or collect fees for service.

Given the amount of money that must be raised from individuals, determine how much will be raised from each segment of donors discussed in Chapter Three: first-time donors, repeat donors, and donors upgrading their gifts. Following the formula described in Chapter Twenty-One for major gifts programs, figure that 60 percent of the income will come from 10 percent of your donors, 20 percent will come from 20 percent of your donors, and the remaining 20 percent will come from 70 percent of your donors. The first number (60 percent of the total) is your goal for major gifts; the second number (20 percent of the total) is your goal for habitual donors responding to retention strategies, particularly from those donors who give several times a year; the last number (another 20 percent of the total) is your goal from first- or second-time donors giving through acquisition strategies.

Analyze your current donor base using the following questions:

- How many donors do you have now in each category—major gifts, habitual donors, first-time donors?

- What is your conversion rate? That is, what percentage of first-time donors give a second gift? (It should be about 40 percent.)

- What is your retention rate? That is, what percentage of donors who have given at least twice keep giving? (It should be around 80 percent.)

- What is your renewal rate? That is, what percentage of all donors who give in one year give in the next? (It should be about 65 percent.)

- What are the organization's strengths in working with donors?

- Do you do a good job of acquiring donors but have a lower-than-normal retention rate? Or do you have a strong base of very loyal habitual donors, with a higher-than-normal retention rate?

- Do you do a good job of identifying the top 10 percent of donors and regularly seeking upgraded gifts and major gifts from them?

- Has the number of donors to your organization grown, decreased, or stayed the same in the past three years? (If it has decreased, you are not doing enough acquisition and may also have a problem with retention of donors. If the number of donors has stayed the same, you are doing a good job with either retention or acquisition, but not both; otherwise, you would see an increase.)

Step 4. Decide on Numbers of Donors and Match Them to Strategies. On the basis of your analysis in the previous step, decide how many donors you need to meet your goals and match them with the strategies that work best for reaching those donors.

Step 5. Put the Plan onto a Timeline and Fill Out the Tasks. Voilà! A fundraising plan is created. (Two examples of fundraising plans are given in the case studies that follow.)

By using these steps, the planning process can be both simple and accurate. Once a plan is developed, working the plan should bring in the money you need.

FUNDRAISING PLANNING AT WORK: TWO CASE STUDIES
People's Theater

People's Theater is a community theater serving a city of 500,000 people. The theater performs works of local playwrights and works aimed at raising consciousness about or demonstrating the talents of children, seniors, and disabled people. It has a budget of $500,000 a year and four full-time staff: an artistic director, a development director, a program and marketing director, and an administrator. The administrator also helps with fundraising. The group has an active board of directors of thirteen people. This year they plan to raise $300,000 from ticket sales, small government grants, and fees from their acting classes. They will raise the remaining $200,000 from community donations, including making up for the loss of a foundation grant that has provided $50,000 for each of the past three years.

Using the formula in the third step of the budget-planning process, People's Theater sees that it will need to raise $120,000 from major donors, $40,000 from habitual donors, and the remaining $20,000 from its current fundraising program of three special events and an online campaign at the end of the year. The events focus mostly on acquisition: the online campaign brings in gifts from current and new donors.

The theater is highly visible in its community. It currently has one thousand donors, more than eight hundred of whom give less than $100, and one hundred of whom give between $100 and $249. Many of these gifts are given at the end of performances, when a board member comes out to the stage and asks people to make a gift above the cost of their ticket. The biggest gifts overall are $2,500 from a longtime major donor, five gifts of $1,000 each from board members and former board members, twenty gifts of $500 each and forty gifts of $250 each from regular patrons, and two gifts of $5,000 each from sisters who support all the arts programs in this community. Total giving from all donors is $85,000.

The donor attrition rate is more than 50 percent. For the past three years, the theater group has steadily lost donors, going from 1,500 to 1,250 and now to 1,000. Some board members have blamed this decline on the artistic director's choice of productions. In the past two years, the theater has put on a play about disability rights that some people complained was too strident, two avant-garde plays that some people found too obscure, and a play about an aging priest and his struggle with and eventual expulsion from the Catholic Church because of his views on sexuality, which some found anti-Catholic, others found anti-gay, and others found too pro-gay. Because the director mixes these productions with works appropriate for families and plays written and largely produced by children, other board members feel that the range of works is appropriate and suits the variety of people in the community. These board members also feel that since their mission is to raise consciousness, the plays that are chosen will necessarily raise hackles as well.

The board and staff have spent countless hours discussing these plays and audience reaction to them; by and large they have found these conversations helpful. However, fundraising has lagged. Now they have decided to focus first on fundraising and then to determine whether the plays they are producing are the cause of the decline in their donor base, since their audience numbers have not declined.

Applying the formula to their donor base of one thousand donors, they come up with the following figures:

- One hundred donors should give $250 or more, for a total of $120,000 (currently sixty-eight people give $250 or more for a total of $37,500 in major gifts)

- Two hundred donors should give $100 to $249, for a total of $40,000 (currently one hundred give in this range and their gifts total $20,000)

- Seven hundred donors should give less than $100, totaling $40,000 (currently eight hundred donors give small gifts that total $42,500)

- In addition, they must acquire at least three hundred donors to make up for a normal attrition rate of 30 percent just to maintain their base at one thousand donors.

Moving to step four, they draw up this outline:

Goal 1: Increase the number of donors giving more than $250 to one hundred and increase their total giving from $37,500 to $120,000. Meeting this goal will require asking for significant increases in gifts from current major donors and in moving some people up to be major donors. This seems quite doable.

Goal 2: Double the number of people giving between $100 and $249. Meeting this goal will require a big effort, both to acquire donors at this higher giving level and to ask about three hundred current donors to increase, and in many cases, double their current giving. This seems ambitious, but necessary.

Goal 3: Attract three hundred first-time givers and strengthen retention strategies to ensure that seven hundred of their current one thousand donors renew (many of whom will also be increasing their gifts). Achieving this goal, they will maintain their base of one thousand donors and not experience any more shrinkage. To reach this goal will require an intensive effort to convert single-ticket buyers to be regular donors.

To accomplish these goals, People's Theater will conduct two donor campaigns, one in the spring focused on major donors and one in the fall focused on getting current small donors to move into the $100 to $250 range.

Spring Campaign. People's Theater will create a gift range chart for major donors and seek to renew or upgrade its current donors as well as find thirty-two new donors, for which it will need one hundred prospects who could give gifts in the range of $250 to $1,000 (projecting both a 50 percent refusal rate and that 50 percent of the positive responses will give less than the amount requested).

Fall Campaign.   A well-written and attractively printed personalized letter, with a personal note from a board or staff member, will go out to all donors who have given between $50 and $249 for three years or more. The letter will ask for an increase in their giving and will be followed up with phone calls. All other donors who have given more than twice and who are not in these categories will be sent a personalized letter or e-mail, depending on how the theater corresponds with these donors currently, asking them to increase their gifts.

The theater's Web site will also feature the fall campaign and a thermometer there will show how the campaign is proceeding. With each online gift, the thermometer will rise.

To retain donors, the theater will approach current donors three times during the year, describing different projects and aspects of their work. It will also offer special receptions for donors who increase their gifts, regardless of the size of the original gift or the amount of the increase.

Finally, the theater will continue with the acquisition strategies that are working: asking for donations at the end of each theater show and holding three annual special events.

Moving to the fifth step, board and staff are ready to put their plan on a timeline. On a master calendar, they mark off when their plays are running, when their government grant proposals are due to be submitted, when their special events are scheduled, and when their quarterly newsletter goes out. Next, they schedule their extra appeals to take place just after the first three plays but at least three weeks before or after each special event. Finally, they schedule their major gift campaign in two small remaining windows of time: January 15 through February 15 and November 1 through Thanksgiving.

With this plan approved, the People's Theater board divides into three committees: acquisition, retention, and major donors and upgrades. With the help of the organization's administrator, each committee prepares a task list and divides up the work.

Affordable Housing for Working People

Affordable Housing for Working People is located in a small town about an hour away from a major urban area. Because the town is in a beautiful rural location surrounded by parkland, many of its homes have been bought as weekend and vacation places by the nearby urban residents. This influx has both driven the price of housing up and created a shortage of housing for people who actually work in the town. These people not only provide many of the services the second-home owners rely on when they are there, they also help maintain the rural and diverse flavor that is one of the town's drawing points. Affordable Housing seeks to purchase existing houses throughout the town and resell or rent the homes at affordable rates to local working people while holding the value of the land in trust for the community, as in the nationwide community land trust model.

After five years of building the organization, Affordable Housing has acquired its first property, which ultimately will house two families. Although it has launched a successful campaign to finance the purchase beyond what the rental income will cover, it needs to expand its member base in order to maintain a small operating budget of $42,000 for the current year. This budget supports two part-time staff people and a small office. The plan is to meet the budget with a repeat (final year) operating grant of $10,000 from the county, another grant of $10,000 from a local foundation, $500 from local businesses, and $500 from events. The remaining $21,000 of the operating budget is designated to come from membership income.

Last year Affordable Housing raised $12,000 in membership donations from 130 members. The renewal rate was low at about 50 percent. The organization realizes it needs to increase efforts to recruit new donors and retain old ones. Following the formula, it plans to raise $21,000 in individual donations as follows:

- 60 percent in major gifts from 10 percent of donors: $12,600 (average gift of about $500 from twenty-five donors, including board members)

- 20 percent from 20 percent of donors in midlevel gifts (both new and renewing), especially those giving more than one gift per year: $4,200 (average total annual giving of about $95 each from about forty-five donors)

- 20 percent from 70 percent of total donors in small gifts: $4,200 (average gift of $27 each from about 158 new and renewing donors)

The organization creates a fundraising plan for operations that includes goals, strategies, and actions; who will lead the effort; when each strategy will be implemented; and what expenses are involved (see chart). (See also Premium Web Content: "Creating a Fundraising Plan," by Stephanie Roth, *Grassroots Fundraising Journal*.)

Affordable Housing Fundraising Plan, 2011—Goal: $42,000					
Constituency	**Goal**	**Strategy and Action**	**Who Leads**	**When**	**Expenses**
Individuals:	$21,000				
Major donors ($250+)	$12,600 (25 at $500 avg.)	Board members pledge and make gifts. Clarify major donor contact people and make regular contact. Develop and implement special program for informing, interesting, and involving current and new major donors.	Fundraising committee	All year	Mailing
Midlevel gifts (new members and renewals)	$4,200 (45 at $95 avg.)	Renewals: Send up to three renewal notices. Monthly e-mail communication. Newsletter — 2x/year	Staff	Feb./March, May, Sept., Nov.	Printing, mailing

(Continued)

Affordable Housing Fundraising Plan, 2011—Goal: $42,000 (*Continued*)

Constituency	Goal	Strategy and Action	Who Leads	When	Expenses
Small gifts (new members and renewals)	$4,200 (158 at $27 avg.)	To recruit new members:		Nov./Dec.	Printing and mailing: thank yous; outreach
		• Each board, fundraising committee, and staff member will recruit five new members = 55			
		• 20 new members from: two house parties with follow-up contacts = 10	Fundraising committee; hosts; staff and board		
		• One annual event			
		• Outreach at Farmers Market, Town Fair			
		• Presentations to 2–3 community groups			
		• Boxholder mailing after completion of second-unit construction		July/Aug./ Sept.	Printing and mailing
Institutions:	$20,500	Awarded, to be received February			
County	$10,000	Solicit second grant	Staff		
Community foundation	$10,000	Solicit local bank; consider 2–3 other banks or businesses	Staff		
Businesses	$500				
Events:	$500				
	$100	Convert annual lunch to pie bake	Staff	July	Advertising
	$400	Fall event with local historian	Staff	Sept.	Advertising

What to Do in Case of Financial Trouble

First, don't panic. Like most people, organizations get into difficult financial straits from time to time. Panicking, searching for who is to blame, and whining will not solve your problem. What you must do first is carefully analyze the nature of the financial problem and how you got into it. This will help create a strategy for getting out of it.

Financial troubles range from simple cash flow problems to serious mismanagement or even embezzlement of funds. These major types of financial problems are discussed in the following sections. However, it is important to recognize that financial problems are usually symptomatic of deeper management difficulties. These difficulties usually show up first, and often most seriously, in the areas of fundraising and spending. The root cause may be the failure of the board of directors to plan the year thoroughly and thus anticipate the financial crisis, or it could be the reluctance of a staff person to discuss the finances of the organization honestly and fully with the board, leading the board to approve an unrealistic budget. Sometimes the deeper problem is that fundraising projections are inaccurate because not enough research was done to make reasonable estimates of income. Whatever the problem turns out to be, it must be addressed and solved. If only the financial problem is solved, however, and the underlying organizational issues remain unaddressed, the financial problems will recur, each time with increasing severity.

There are four main types of financial problems: cash flow problems, deficit spending, serious accounting errors or mismanagement of funds, and embezzlement of funds.

CASH FLOW PROBLEMS

A cash flow problem occurs when anticipated income is not coming in fast enough, creating a temporary lag in income in relation to spending. A cash flow problem has an end in sight. You know that when a certain major donation or grant payment comes in, or when a reimbursement from the city, county, or state is received, you will be able to pay your bills and say goodbye to your problem. Until that time, however, the organization has to draw on its reserves; once the organization exhausts any savings it might have, then it is in a bind.

You have several choices at that point. You can try to put a freeze on spending and even up your income and expenses by ceasing to incur expenses. You can attempt to stall your creditors by paying bills in installments and by postponing paying as many bills as possible. In that case, call creditors and explain your situation, giving them a date by which you will pay the bill. Many times creditors will allow you to postpone payment if they believe you will have the money soon. Another option is to borrow money to cover your expenses and repay the loan when your cash flow improves. Depending on the size of the loan, you may be able to borrow the money from a loyal board member or major donor who will charge little or no interest and create no publicity. Foundations and corporations in some communities have emergency loan funds to help groups through cash flow difficulties when those problems are not the organization's fault. A final option is to set up a line of credit at a bank and draw on it to cover expenses.

A cash flow problem is largely a logistical one and often can be avoided in the future by setting aside money in a reserve account in anticipation of such times.

DEFICIT SPENDING

A deficit is a chronic cash flow problem or, more accurately, a situation in which you are spending more than you are raising with no end of this discrepancy in sight. Irresponsible or short-sighted organizations finance their deficit with money from their savings, if they have any, or with money earmarked for special programs, a practice that is then problematic for the special program and may cause distress to the person or grantmaking source for the program. (And, depending on how you commingle funds from different sources, this can be illegal.) At some point, however, the organization will run out of money and no longer be able to finance the deficit.

There are only two solutions to deficit spending: create an ongoing way to raise more money or permanently cut down on spending. Examine where you are overspending and put a freeze on those areas. Besides the person who already has authority to authorize expenditures, designate an additional staff person or board member to look at all requests for more than $500 and, working together, see if you can identify a pattern of spending that can be cut. (As small organizations tend to be very frugal, this may be an impossible task.)

Obviously, the organization's fundraising plan and income reports will have to be carefully examined and strengthened. Raising more money, however, is the only viable long-term solution. Deficits require immediate attention because the longer they continue the worse they get. Once you are out of the deficit, avoid the situation in the future by spending only as much money as you raise.

SERIOUS ACCOUNTING ERRORS, MISMANAGEMENT OF FUNDS, OR EMBEZZLEMENT

In cases of even more serious financial errors, mismanagement, or embezzlement, the entire board must be notified immediately and the people responsible for the error or crime must be dealt with swiftly. If embezzlement has occurred, the person committing the crime must be fired; the board will have to decide whether to take legal action against the person or people responsible. In the case of serious error, some mitigating circumstances may be taken into account, such as if the person had never made an error before, the person admitted it immediately and took steps to remedy it, or the error was clearly a mistake and not indicative of carelessness or deception. Nevertheless, the person should probably be suspended until the situation is resolved.

Board members should prepare a brief statement on what happened and what the organization is doing about it. This statement can be sent to funding sources and used as a response should the story get into the media. Honesty and swift action are the best ways to ensure the fewest repercussions.

The more difficult problem to solve is how to make up the loss of money that such an error or crime has caused. Options include asking major donors who are close to the organization for extra gifts; seeking loans; and instituting spending freezes, vacation without pay, or pay deferments for staff. As a last resort, staff layoffs may be necessary.

If the financial situation cannot be improved by any of these means, the organization should consider closing. An organizational development consultant or a facilitator will be helpful in leading the board to a proper decision.

The most debilitating problem in the case of serious mismanagement or theft is the decline in morale of all the people involved. Very little work goes on when everyone in the organization is depressed and shocked. Morale will be boosted when the staff and board have decided on a course of action. If the organization is to stay alive, this must be done quickly and the plan implemented immediately. A crisis of this magnitude can pull people together and strengthen the organization as long as those who stay with it agree that keeping the organization going is of the utmost importance. (For more on this topic, see my book *Reliable Fundraising in Unreliable Times,* which provides much more detail about how to handle and survive a crisis.)

PART EIGHT

Special Circumstances

If I had a dollar for every time I have been told, "You don't know what it's like to raise money for _____," followed by a description of the place where the organization is located, or the issue it works on, or the people it encounters, or some other variable, I could endow every nonprofit I ever cared about. Of course, it is true that I don't know what it is like, but I can ask questions and learn, and that is usually why an organization is paying me to be there. What people mean when they tell me that I don't know what it is like is that I don't know how hard it is. No one says, "You don't know what it's like to have an easy time raising lots of money."

People in nonprofits often imagine that it would be easier to raise money for a different NGO from the one they are in. People in the arts think social service fundraising is a cinch, people in advocacy imagine that providing free legal services would really loosen the purse strings, environmentalists covet the fundraising jobs of labor rights activists, and so on. For the most part, people kid themselves that fundraising would be much easier in another setting, but occasionally special circumstances make fundraising more difficult for certain kinds of organizations or at certain times in an organization's existence. An accurate analysis of your fundraising situation is essential for planning long-term fundraising.

All problems in an organization will show up in its income, and they will often show up there first, leading an organization to think that funding or fundraising is its problem. However, it is worth a few moments of time to understand that fundraising is sometimes a symptom of a different problem, one that must be solved before fundraising (or even fundraising problems) can be addressed. The issue of analyzing your real problem is something I explore in depth in my book *Reliable Fundraising in Unreliable Times*. If you think fundraising may not be your organization's true problem, I advise you to check out that book.

Here are just a few ways organizations mistake what their real fundraising problems are:

- An organization that believes its board is inadequate or not well connected enough and so hampers the organization from raising money may in fact be hampered because its executive director is not well liked or well respected or because the executive director does not want the board to exercise any power.

- An organization may feel that it can't raise money because no one agrees with its program, when in fact it has failed to articulate a clear case as to why it deserves support, or its work is not generally known. If, in fact, no one agrees with what an organization does, that organization has no mandate.

- An organization that is losing donors and volunteers may believe the economy is to blame or that they need to use a new fundraising strategy. It may be, however, that the organization has drifted away from its mission, the programs it is engaged in don't really match what people think the organization is about, and donors are voting with their feet.

- A founder has built the organization past his or her ability to run it. Instead of stepping aside and taking pride in their creation, the founder stays and unconsciously shrinks the organization back to a size or focus he or she can manage.

Aside from how an organization's own myopia may affect its fundraising, external factors also play a much bigger role than organizations realize. An organization's fundraising may be diminished for any of the following reasons:

- When the local economy is in really bad shape, people just don't have that much money to give.

- A scandal in a large, well-known nonprofit can cause distrust of all nonprofits and decrease revenues temporarily. A series of scandals in a number of nonprofits, as occurred in the first part of this century, can cause an overall decline in public confidence, which takes a toll on fundraising.

- The sheer number of nonprofits asking for donations can contribute to donor fatigue.

- Natural disasters take attention and sometimes funding away from the day-in and day-out work of service agencies. In recent years, there have been so many natural disasters (compounded by poverty and racism) that organizations are in an almost permanent state of raising money for themselves while being supportive of efforts to address major crises.

- Wars take a bigger toll than is generally acknowledged. Financially, they absorb money that needs to be spent elsewhere, but they also wreak psychological damage, as the scale of wounded and killed overshadows a small, community-based organization's case for doing a piece of needed work in a local area.

- Issues come into style and go out of style; long after it has ceased to be popular to fund solutions to a particular problem, the problem will still exist.

In this section, I concentrate on five of the more common special circumstances that an organization may find itself in, either temporarily (being brand-new) or permanently (being rural). The fifth circumstance is one that all organizations face at different times, in which a question arises about whether to seek (or take) funds from a particular funding source—in other words, the question of clean and dirty money.

An entire book could be devoted to special circumstances, but these five should give you a sense of how to think through special circumstances of your own and make fundraising plans that overcome the adversity and take advantage of the opportunity the special situation presents.

Raising Money in Rural Communities

Along-standing belief in fundraising circles is that it is much harder to raise money in rural communities than in urban or suburban settings and that you probably won't be able to raise the money you need. This belief has some logic: there are fewer people in these communities, which means fewer people to ask. Although those people have fewer local nonprofits to choose from, there are still basic services that must be supported, and their tax rates may be higher to pay for a health clinic or schools or a library. Further, as studies by the National Rural Funders Collaborative have shown, nonprofits in rural communities do not receive foundation funding in proportion to their need, or even in proportion to their population. These facts support the belief that it is harder to raise money in rural communities. But harder does not mean impossible, and I have found it is not only possible to raise money in rural communities, it is sometimes possible to raise large amounts of money.

THE MANY DEFINITIONS OF *RURAL*

First, it is important to note that there are many different kinds of rural communities, and they will each have to look at their assets and challenges in creating stable fundraising programs. For example, our "American Gothic" image of rural people living and working on the same piece of land all their lives is more often than not an inaccurate perception. Many people living and working in rural communities do not make their living from farming or ranching. For example, some rural areas have become retirement communities, with many of the people living there not originally from the region and with little loyalty to it. Their charitable giving to that area will develop over time, but most of their donations will continue to be made to the organizations in the community they left behind.

Other rural communities, such as those within a few hours of major cities, are bedroom communities for commuters who work in the nearby cities. Even more people may telecommute, going to their business in the city only as needed. Their loyalty to their local community may depend on whether they are raising a family there and how strongly they wish to be accepted and involved. "Back-to-the-land" small farmers, vintners in boutique wineries, owners of bed-and-breakfast inns, and the staff of retreat centers, to say nothing of marijuana growers, are among the many types of people who can make up or contribute to rural communities. The finances and values of these people are extremely varied; the job of local nonprofits is to help people develop loyalty to their community and want to make it a better place.

There are many rural communities where people make their living (or once made their living) from mining or timbering. In others, people work on other people's farms or ranches, often forming large communities of migrant or semi-migrant workers. There are rural communities primarily built around a college or a prison. There are many rural communities whose populations vary seasonally, swelling with tourists and "part-timers" who own second homes or cabins or timeshares at resorts during part of the year. Many towns in popular tourist areas will host fifteen thousand people on a weekend who don't live there. Tourists are the main economy in many communities, in which case "locals" are often engaged in service provision for tourist destinations. Increasingly, there are rural communities where the majority of the population is made up of non-English-speaking immigrants or refugees from Mexico, Latin America, Russia, and Pan Asian countries. All of these sources of diversity add layers of complexity to any rural fundraising effort.

Nonetheless, there are certain things that must be taken into account when mounting fundraising efforts in any rural community, each of which is considered here.

Everything Takes Longer. There are two ways in which things take longer to accomplish: the obvious time involved in getting from one place to another when great distances can separate homes or towns, and the less quantifiable but equally important rural hospitality, which tends to be more extensive than that of city dwellers. For example, suppose you decide to visit a major donor on his or her ranch. You make an appointment, then drive one to three hours to the ranch. Once there, you do not chat briefly, ask for the gift, and leave in forty-five minutes, as you might in a city. The graciousness often customary in rural areas may lead your host or hostess to give you a tour of the ranch and invite you to stay for lunch or dinner. In remote communities, when you set up your appointment, you may have been invited to stay overnight. This graciousness is wonderful but time-consuming, and you disregard it at the cost of the relationship with the donor.

The Necessities of Ranch or Farm Life Can Limit a Donor's Availability. There will be times, such as planting, harvesting, lambing, or calving, when contact with donors will be limited because people are working almost around the clock. When none of those things are going on, the weather may make driving conditions so hazardous that volunteers cannot get to meetings, people cannot attend special events, and prospects cannot be visited.

Fundraising Costs Are Higher. The city dweller's idyllic notion that everything is inexpensive or free in a rural area is false. Almost all supplies and equipment have to be shipped in, adding freight to their cost; lack of competition among businesses can add another layer of cost. Consultants to help repair your computer or handle your bookkeeping needs are fewer and, lacking competition, may charge more. Although office space may be less expensive than in a city, there may not be any available. The distances between people and places make driving costs high, and there is rarely adequate public transportation.

Logistics Are Complicated. E-mail and cell phones have transformed many rural communities, enabling much faster and more reliable communication. However, it is still true that if you wish to print a newsletter, mail appeal, or flier in bulk, even though you can send it electronically to a printer in the nearest city, you may have to go there to pick it up. If you need an item sent or received quickly, there may be no overnight mail service from or to your community. And in communities where electricity often goes out in storms and cell phone signals are weak or nonexistent, these twenty-first-century conveniences may not always solve the problem.

Relationships Are Often Complicated. In some rural areas, people have known each other for many years; sometimes families have known each other for generations. Firing an incompetent staff person is more difficult when that person is your cousin's son or your friend's neighbor and everyone in the family or the town is going to hear about it. People are often involved in more than one organization. One development coordinator was puzzled that her two most reliable volunteers were reluctant to ask local businesses to take out ads in their adbook. Then she realized that all the business owners were close relatives of these volunteers, and that these same volunteers had asked these same business owners (sometimes over the dinner table) for an ad earlier in the year.

Moreover, people depend on each other for help in hard times or for assistance in emergencies. This interrelatedness makes them cautious about doing anything that might cause offense—including fundraising assertively or asking people for money directly. Rural people do not wish to seem pushy in their requests to a neighbor, partly because they know that if they have a medical emergency in the middle of winter and can't get their car started, they may need to call that person.

Cultural and Economic Forces Are Changing Rural Areas. Rural communities have been seeing a lot of things change in how they operate, and nonprofits working there must be able to adapt quickly. Many locally owned businesses have been forced to close as superstores such as Wal-Mart have opened nearby or as competition from Internet sales have lured customers with cheaper prices and direct shipping. Whole downtowns have been abandoned in favor of malls outside the town, which in turn may be closing due to high unemployment and young people leaving the area to find work. Many family farms have been bought up and put out of business by agribusiness concerns, and in many places suburbs and ex-urbs have replaced farmland altogether. For fundraising, this can mean that the people who live in these communities don't know each other and are fairly isolated. Finding who the donors are, let alone who might donate to your organization, is challenging.

YOU CAN RAISE THE MONEY YOU NEED

The first step in fundraising in a rural community is to reflect on the characteristics of that community. How big is the permanent population, and what do most of those people do for a living? What other local nonprofits are you competing with? If you have a part-time as well as full-time population, who are the part-timers—weekenders, tourists, students, farm workers? What is their giving potential, and how might you capture their gifts?

The second step—or more accurately, a simultaneous step—is to set a goal. How much do you need to raise? People have told me, "We can't raise millions of dollars here in Green Valley like you can in a city." If you don't need millions of dollars, then it doesn't matter that you can't raise it. It may be that you can't raise what you need, and there are some solutions for that, but first, know your need. It is possible to raise substantial amounts of money in rural communities. For one thing, there are people in every community who have the means and will understand the need for larger gifts.

Here's an example. There are a number of communities called "colonias" that span the borders between Mexico and the states of Texas and New Mexico. These communities often lack running water or electricity. Their community facilities—schools, roads and local government—are in poor condition or nonexistent. The people in these communities tend to work in factories or farms nearby. Many people have lived in these communities for years. Raising money for nonprofit work is not easy in a place where so many people have so little, but some organizations in these areas have done well. In addition to setting up food booths and collecting small amounts of money from residents, groups have identified a few people who care about the community and who can afford to give more. In one instance, a staff person of an organization working with teenagers identified a small farmer they thought could give $100. When they asked him for that amount, he misunderstood the question. "Yes, I can give that every month," he said, to their surprise. He has been helpful in identifying other people who can also give substantial monthly or yearly contributions. Further illustrating the relationship between fundraising and organizing, he has helped several community groups petition local government agencies for improvements to roads, sewage systems, and public schools. He has helped people understand that because they pay taxes, they have the right to services that taxes are meant to provide.

Second, even relatively small communities can raise large amounts of money for a variety of big projects over time. In a town of two thousand people in Northern California, for example, the Friends of the Library decided to expand their public library facility. To do so, they needed to raise $35,000. Everyone involved in the nonprofit part of the community agreed that such an amount would drain the community and make other large fundraising drives impossible. Nonetheless, many in the community supported the idea, and the Friends of the Library decided to proceed because the expanded facility would be so well used. They raised the $35,000 they needed. Soon after, leaders at the community center in town decided they desperately needed a new space and set out to raise $750,000 to build a new community hall. Between grant monies, county subsidies, and individual donor fundraising, they succeeded. Now the common wisdom of the community was that there certainly was no more capital money in the community. Nonetheless, two years later the health clinic had no choice but to launch a capital campaign to modernize and expand its facilities. This fundraising effort was also successful.

Each of these fundraising drives took place over a number of years and used several different strategies in their individual donor campaigns: special events, major donor solicitations, and direct mail. They all took a lot of hard work and the volunteer efforts of dozens of people. To be sure, this community has a number of wealthy retirees, and many of them made significant gifts to these campaigns. But the entire community participated, and some money was even raised from tourists. A poorer town with no wealthy retirees and no tourism would need to raise this kind of money from government or foundation grants, but it would still need to be open to the idea that a few people in their community could make significant gifts and the rest of the community could give significantly with a number of smaller gifts.

The lesson here is that in any community, but more obviously in a rural community, fundraising is not a zero-sum game. There is always more money, and it is not diminished or used up by big campaigns. Organizations in rural communities will want to time their campaigns—for two organizations to run a capital campaign at the same time will rarely be as successful as running them sequentially. In addition, the need has to be well established, and the community has to agree with the goal of the campaign. But it must be remembered that money grows back and produces more money.

PROSPECTS

There are three populations from whom a rural organization can raise money: locals, part-timers, and people in nearby towns and cities. Let's begin with the last group.

If you are located near cities with populations of ten thousand or more—and where there is not another program like yours—focus attention on raising money in those towns and cities, where the financial base is strongest. Form support groups with people living in the town or city by asking existing donors in those communities to host a small party for you, or by contacting sympathetic churches, synagogues, service clubs, and the like. Sometimes even getting an article in the local newspaper will bring interest. Hold special events in these larger towns, and use direct mail and your Web site to recruit donors there. If local people have contacts in these nearby towns and cities, use those contacts to introduce your local needs to this population and to cultivate potential major donors.

Next, try to discover ways to raise money from people who pass through the community, particularly tourists and visitors. Some communities mount events primarily to attract tourists. For example, many communities have county fairs or various kinds of festivals, such as the Garlic Festival in Gilroy, California, the Ramp Festivals in many communities around Tennessee, Georgia, and Virginia, and Shakespeare Festivals in Ashland, Oregon, and many other communities. These events attract tourists who spend money to attend the event and also to buy things that are sold at the event and in the town hosting it.

If you live where tourists come to see the natural beauty or to vacation (such as along the coasts or near national parks or monuments), consider developing products that tourists will buy. Local crafts and homemade jellies and jams are always appealing. Photography books and calendars, guides to the local sights, and collections of stories of people who live in the community have all proved to be steady income streams for rural organizations. In some communities, the history museum will have a gift shop featuring items from a number of nonprofit organizations. A for-profit bakery or grocery store may also carry calendars, woodcarvings, and the like whose sale benefits local nonprofits. Imagination and cooperation are key to the success of these endeavors.

If you live near a freeway or a frequently traveled road, set up a rest stop where truckers and tired drivers can buy coffee, doughnuts, fruit, or other treats. Such an enterprise can be very lucrative in the cold winter months, particularly at night. It is also a community service that helps keep people from falling asleep at the wheel.

At the local level, focus on finding a few people who can give larger gifts. Every community has generous people, and a few of those will be able to give major gifts, if asked. Whenever possible, ask current donors for the names of other people who could also give. People tend to be friends with people who not only share their values but are also in a similar economic situation. Someone who gives your organization $500 will know two or three other people who could give $500 and one or two people who could give $1,000. They, in turn, will know people who could give $2,500.

You can also raise money from the community at large. Even in the poorest and most remote areas, churches, volunteer fire departments, rescue squads, and service clubs are supported by local residents. Even the smallest, poorest towns in the Bible Belt, for example, support at least two churches; even if they do not have paid clergy, the people manage to support a building.

Money can be raised locally through special events. Providing a way for the nonprofit to give something in return helps counter the reluctance rural people have for asking for money directly. Events such as raffles, auctions, and bake sales can be good moneymakers. Many times people from rural community groups simply stand with buckets at busy crossroads and ask drivers to drop in spare change. Three hours at a crossroads on a shopping day can bring in $300 to $500. Flea markets are also popular. It is often easier for rural people to donate items rather than cash, and people always seem willing to buy each other's castoffs. In Sitka, Alaska, on Baranof Island, there is a thrift shop run by volunteers called the White Elephant Shop. Between purchases from locals and in the summer months, tourists, the store averages $100,000 in profit every year, which it donates to a variety of nonprofits on the island. Often a prom dress or fancy suit will be sold two or three times before being retired to rags. On the other side of the country, on the Outer Banks off the North Carolina coast, the Outer Banks Hotline Crisis Intervention and Prevention Center has developed a store called Endless Possibilities that helps support the operating costs of their domestic violence program. (For more on entrepreneurial funding for domestic violence programs, see Premium Web Content, *Funding Domestic Violence and Sexual Assault Programs in North Carolina,* by Kristen Dubay and Joel Rosch, Center for Child and Family Policy, Duke University.)

STRATEGIES FOR RAISING MONEY

Keeping in mind the six factors described earlier, let's look at the most common fundraising strategies available to rural communities and how they are similar to and different from those in their urban counterparts.

Special Events

Everyone is familiar with the large golf tournaments, award luncheons, and black-tie dinner dances that raise at least $100,000 and as much as $1,000,000 in urban areas. These events cost thousands of dollars to put on and require paid staff and dozens of volunteers working for months to be successful. Most rural communities can't pull off something like that. However, the special events that small nonprofits can put on often form the basis of the social life of small towns and rural communities.

A rural organization can raise $1,000, $5,000, or even more with three or four months' lead time and a handful of volunteers. Start with an event that people would like to come to and might even travel into the nearest town for, and do your best to put it on in your community.

Take, for example, a dinner dance. The dance can be held in the community center or the school gymnasium, which in many places can be used for free or for a minimal fee. The food can be provided by members of your organization, but to make it more fun, turn it into a competition. Community cooks then pay a small fee to "enter" the food competition in various categories, such as main course, salad, and dessert. Each is asked to bring enough food to feed fifteen people. People coming to the event get a small sample of each entry and then vote on which ones they like the best. They can then pay for a larger portion of the dishes that they liked. In reality, most people will be full after the tasting, so the group will not run out of food. A cash bar serving smoothies, soft drinks, and juice can provide extra income. (Be cautious about serving alcohol to people who will be driving home. If you want to have alcohol for sale, be sure to get permission if your event is in a publicly owned building and check that you have adequate insurance.) Later, dance music can be provided by a local band that is trying to become more well known and so will perform for a small stipend or for free. Or music can be provided by a DJ who is a friend of one of the members.

Marketing and advertising for the event are done largely by word of mouth, radio public service announcements, and posters hung in the post office, general store, library, and other places around town. Each board member is expected to sell ten tickets. If your event is the only thing going on that Saturday night, getting a hundred people to attend should be easily done. If the ticket price is $10 to $25 per person and many people pay $10 or $15 more for extra food or drink, and the food competitors each pay a $5 entry fee, an organization can easily gross

$3,000 to $5,000. If you have T-shirts or other items to sell, you can add a small income stream from those sales with little effort.

Expenses will include buying drinks to sell, printing nice-looking certificates or ribbons for the winners of the food contests, and mailing thank you notes after the event to volunteers and participants. Of course, some drinks can be solicited as donations, and perhaps a member of the organization knows how to print the certificates from his or her home computer. Even with expenses as high as $1,000, the group could still net $2,000 to $4,000 from a "good time had by all." As the years pass, more and more people will want to enter the food contest, and more people will want to come to the event.

A Chocolate Lovers Festival put on by an organization with a total budget of $75,000 in a college town of eight thousand people—including students—was organized along the lines of the dinner described above. By the fifth year, the festival netted $40,000! Eventually, it attracted top chefs from restaurants in nearby towns in addition to lay people entering their favorite brownies or best hot chocolate. Pictures of the festival posted on the group's Facebook page and video highlights on YouTube become the best advertising of the festival for the next year.

The dinner dance is just one example of how malleable events are. Each aspect of the event should be conceived of as a separate component, and components can be added or subtracted according to the number of volunteers and the amount of time available. A silent auction can be added to the dinner dance, or a live auction could replace the dance or be added to it. An afternoon barbecue at the beach could replace the dinner, and games could replace the dance. That kind of event would focus more on families with young children. Tea and dessert followed by a lecture would appeal to a more academic or older crowd. Silent auction items that can be easily shipped can be auctioned online as well by opening the auction to online bidders first. One organization whose staff is technologically sophisticated is experimenting with a simultaneous live and online auction in which it tweets initial bids to its followers, then posts higher bids as they come in from responding tweets on the items for those at the auction in person to see and bid against.

The secret to all of these events is to do as much as possible for free or very low cost and to charge for as many things as you can without having people feel that they are being nickel and dimed to death. Advertising must be effective so that the maximum number of people who might be interested in attending are attracted to the event at minimum cost. Word of mouth is the cheapest and most effective advertising and marketing vehicle, and the organization's board should talk up the event everywhere they go; but e-mail blasts, Facebook postings, announcements on community TV and radio, and articles in the weekly paper are important as well.

Using Web 2.0

Using the Web to bring your rural community to the computer screens of people living in urban areas has been a boon for many organizations, particularly those doing environmental work. Pictures, video clips, and articles posted with "donate now" icons on every page bring former residents, regular visitors, and even people who have never been to your community into your reality, and some of them may donate. Using a message board, blog, or other way to solicit comments also allows for dialog and questions and answers and gives your organization a sense of what people want to know. (See also Chapter Fourteen for more on Web 2.0 and fundraising.)

Personal Solicitation

Personal face-to-face solicitation is the most effective strategy for all organizations, big or small, rural or urban. Your rural organization may not have a lot of name recognition outside your immediate community, and you may not have famous people on your board. But your board members and volunteers have integrity, and donors give $500 or $1,000 because their friend, Terry, is on the board and says that the group does good work.

Personal solicitation is both the easiest and the hardest strategy for almost anyone. It is the easiest because volunteers just have to talk to their friends, who are, presumably, easy to find and comfortable to talk with. There is no real cost involved, except for the time of the volunteer and perhaps the cost of taking a friend out for coffee or lunch, and the meeting can be set at the convenience of the volunteer and his or her friend. It is the hardest because it requires asking for money and running the risk of rejection or of offending the friend. Because you will see your friend often, you don't want to do anything that will harm the relationship. Your request may be more low-key than in a more urban culture. Instead of saying, "Will you help with $500?" and waiting for a response right then, say, "I'd love it if you gave in the $500 range. Take some time and think about it." Follow-up will be important, but giving the prospect some room to turn you down without having to tell you no directly will help preserve your relationship.

CONCLUSION

Whatever strategy you choose, don't assume that the people who did the work or gave the money know that you appreciate their help. Make the time to thank donors, volunteers, colleagues, and anyone else who supported your project. It's not only the right thing to do, it's the best public relations available. Thank people in person whenever possible. E-mail works for thanking people, but in this Internet age, a handwritten note or an actual phone call works better. You know from experience how good you feel when someone thanks you personally.

When all is said and done, the essence of rural fundraising is the essence of all fundraising: building relationships. Successful fundraising of any kind requires ingenuity, commitment to the cause, love of people, common sense, a willingness to ask for money, and an understanding and deep appreciation of human nature— especially of the natural desire of all humans to be appreciated.

Fundraising for a Coalition

There are hundreds of organizations whose board members are representatives of nonprofits that have joined together for the benefits that a coalition of organizations can bring. Churches that want a presence on college campuses and that are aligned theologically will form an ecumenical "campus ministry" that may represent several denominations, and the board will be made up of representatives of the churches involved. In federated funds, members of the federation hold the majority of seats on their board. Almost every state has a coalition against domestic violence, for which directors of local domestic violence or sexual assault prevention programs serve as board members. Most regional associations and national organizations operate the same way, with most of those on the board of directors drawn from the member organizations.

There are obvious advantages to this type of board. A regional or national organization whose mission is to strengthen local chapters as well as raise overall visibility for an issue will be best governed by those most affected by the decisions made. Sharing resources, working collaboratively, developing joint projects, and seeking to expand the reach of the work will all be done best by a coalition made up of people with power at their local level. A board or staff member of a local chapter will be in the best position to represent the concerns of the local organization to a regional or national group. This person will also well understand the need for a regional or national umbrella, engendering a commitment to the coalition as well. Ideally, this person will be the best qualified to make policy and help plan for the umbrella group and to translate the work of the umbrella group to the people at the local level.

There are differences between coalitions that are made up of local chapters of a national organization and those that are made up of separate freestanding organizations that come together for some purpose, but the fundraising challenges to all of them are similar. With a coalition representing local chapters, the umbrella group's executive director or development director is working with board members whose primary loyalty and main fundraising commitments lie with the organizations they represent. Sometimes people have not actually chosen to serve; they may be appointed to a coalition board by their organization and such service may be a part of their job description. In that case, with a job that is often more than full time, tasks related to coalition board service can get short shrift. Getting such a board to raise money requires patience, perseverance, and a degree of maneuvering. However, if you are the person in charge of that fundraising, keep in mind that it can be done.

EXAMINE THE PROBLEM

The first step is to examine the problem. Evaluate the excuses coalition board members offer for not being able to raise money. Most will say they can't participate in fundraising because they have to raise money for their local group. They will say that they can't ask the same people to give money to the umbrella group as well as to the local group, and they will claim that the local work has much more immediate appeal to donors. Next, they will point out that fundraising strategies other than face-to-face asking are difficult for a coalition to carry out. Special events, for example, require a local presence to generate interest in the event. Direct mail is not a good way to sell an umbrella group because the service is too complicated and local representatives are reluctant to provide names of possible donors. An aggressive online fundraising approach will confuse the donors to the local groups. When I have worked with board members of coalitions, they were often able to offer these or similar cogent, sensible explanations as to why every strategy I suggested would not work. Yet they would claim that they were committed to the coalition—they just couldn't do anything to help with fundraising.

I puzzled over this conundrum for many years, until I happened to work with a local organization that was part of a coalition. In a casual conversation, the board chair of the local group said, "Part of our problem is that the executive director does so much fundraising for the coalition that he doesn't have enough time to do the fundraising he needs to do here." I was surprised to hear this, as I had worked with the coalition of which this executive was a part and knew him to be one of the most strenuous objectors at the coalition meetings about how fundraising responsibilities at his organization kept him from raising money for the coalition.

When I looked more closely at the people who complained most about how difficult it is to raise money for an umbrella organization, I realized that many were like this executive director: not effective at raising money at the local level or for the coalition. In fact, perhaps not so surprisingly, people who are very effective at their local level, with active fundraising committees and well-executed fundraising campaigns for their local organization, often make the best fundraisers at a regional or national level.

The reality of fundraising is that some individual donors, foundations, or corporations prefer to give locally; others have no preference and will give locally, regionally, and nationally; and still others would rather be part of a regional or national strategy. Further, as we have noted before, the vast majority of donors give to several organizations, so the notion that if they support the local chapter they will not give to the state organization is not true. The only way to know if a donor to a local organization would also give to the regional association is to ask that person. (I may have mentioned this insight earlier!)

Local organizations are in the best position to identify sources of funding that are based in their communities but that might be more interested in regional or national work. Those sources should be solicited for the umbrella group. It also happens that a donor will find and donate to an umbrella organization but is in fact more interested in supporting local work. The coalition should let all its donors know of all the local affiliates. Further, some donors will give to both the local group and the larger coalition, understanding the importance of both organizations to the overall cause being served.

Another common excuse from local people is that they don't have time to raise money in addition to all their other responsibilities for both the umbrella board and their local group. This is a legitimate problem; however, these same people will spend hours debating personnel issues, discussing policy and program problems, and poring over the budget to see what can be cut. By shaving a few minutes off of each of those tasks, they would have some time for fundraising.

To be frank, you will fight an uphill and pointless battle if you spend all your time trying to get executive directors or active board members of local groups to raise money for the coalition or umbrella group. It is better to spend time recruiting and developing other board members who will raise money specifically for your umbrella group.

SOME SOLUTIONS

There are a number of ways to approach fundraising for a coalition or umbrella group. First, every board of an umbrella group should have at least three slots reserved for at-large members—people who are not associated with a local group. These can be former staff or former board members of local groups, or they can simply be people committed to the cause who don't happen to work for a local version of the cause. Ideally, they are people who prefer to work at a regional or national level. Their primary loyalty should be to your umbrella group, and their primary task should be fundraising, although they will take part in all other discussions and decisions of the board. When they are recruited they understand that raising money is going to be the main task they perform for this organization.

Second, umbrella groups usually call for a representative of each local group to be on the umbrella board. This person does not have to be a staff member or an active board member at the local group. A person who has previously been a staff person or a board member or who is a key volunteer but not on the board can do a good job of representing the local organization. These people will have more time to devote to the umbrella board.

One federated fund requests that member groups send as their representative someone who "does not have major responsibility for the health and well-being of the local organization." Its board is active in fundraising, and board members do not have the problem of divided loyalties. They are clear that they represent their local organization, yet their primary task is to promote the umbrella organization. Further, they understand that they work best for their local group by being part of a strong umbrella organization.

Third, coalitions perform a vital service for their members and need to create some kind of income stream, such as a dues structure, that reflects the value of the work they are doing. In several coalitions I have worked with, the member groups paid no more than $50 per year; in some groups no membership fee was charged. These token payments reinforce the idea that no part of the budget of the coalition needs to be produced by the board representatives of the local organizations. It also raises the question of whether the local organization that pays dues that amount to less than the cost of dinner and a movie is going to see the coalition as important. Dues can be structured so that groups with larger budgets pay more than smaller affiliates, but dues should constitute at least 20 percent of the income of the coalition, unless there is some compelling reason that makes that goal impossible. (In thirty-five years of fundraising, I have not yet heard such a reason.)

Working closely with individual board members, lobbying with member groups for the most appropriate people to be nominated, and creating an organizational culture in which everyone participates in fundraising will enable an umbrella organization to get maximum use of its board for fundraising. The following case study provides one example of a successful coalition's fundraising effort.

A LOCAL ARTS COALITION RETHINKS ITS FUNDRAISING

A statewide coalition of thirty-five arts and culture organizations struggled for years to get the funding it needed. The board was made up of one representative from each of the local groups; very few people on the board had ever helped with fundraising. The coalition had three staff members. The executive director spent most of her time on the road giving speeches, talks, seminars, workshops, interviews, and the like on the critical importance of arts and culture to the quality of life in any community. She was an inspiring speaker and did an excellent job of promoting the arts. Her deputy director did most of the fundraising as well as providing technical assistance to local affiliates on financial management, evaluation, marketing and promotion, and fundraising. The affiliates appreciated both of these staff and were quite loyal to the coalition. The third staff person did the administrative and financial management for the coalition.

The three staff people were stretched to the brink. They worked far more than full time, and the deputy director developed a number of stress-related health problems. They could raise the money they needed to maintain their budget, but they desperately needed at least two more staff people. They were so shorthanded that they had to turn down several arts organizations that wanted to join the coalition because they couldn't provide services to them. They also turned down an invitation to be part of another coalition of public schools and related programs that was lobbying for more state funding for art and music programs, libraries, and sports in schools, even though everyone involved in the coalition agreed that this work would be helpful in fulfilling their own missions. The staff and board agreed that they were missing a number of opportunities and that the workload was far too burdensome. However, most of the board members maintained that they could not be involved in fundraising in any serious way because of their fundraising responsibilities in their own organizations.

With the help of a consultant, the coalition members rethought their entire fundraising approach. First, they instituted an annual dues structure on a sliding scale from $100 for the smallest arts groups to $2,500 for the largest. All members agreed on the necessity for dues and concurred that what they got back was well worth the money. Next, the group set fees for technical assistance to member groups. Because most of the thirty-five members used about four hours per year of technical assistance, the coalition continued to offer four hours without charge; hours after that were billed at $125—at or below the prevailing consulting rate.

The board then decided to shrink itself to eleven members from the original thirty-five, with a quarterly meeting to bring all the members of the coalition up to date and to elicit their concerns. This much more manageable board not only saved the coalition the expense of carrying a larger board (in travel, communication, and time), it also was better able to focus on fundraising and governance.

The thirty-five-agency membership then divided itself into five groups of seven representatives each; each group chose one or two months in which it would be active in fundraising, focusing on one of five agreed-to strategies: a corporate honorary membership drive; an art show; a major donor campaign; a phantom event appeal; and an online directory of artists, art supply vendors, galleries, classes, teachers, and the like called "ART: Art-Related Things," in which anyone who wishes to be listed pays a yearly fee (later this was taken over by a staff person). Although some of the subgroups have been more effective than others, over the past five years this system has worked well and become part of the organizational culture. Although the member groups are paying much more money, they are receiving far more time, attention, and other benefits, and no one questions the dues structure or the fees for technical assistance.

With the added income from fees, the coalition was able to take on new staff: a development director to work with the deputy director, a membership coordinator to work more closely with the member groups, and another support staff person. In the first two years, there were a number of rough moments, but five years into this new structure, staff workload is manageable and the organization has grown a great deal. Further, the staff have high morale and good camaraderie. Like all the staff in this coalition, they work many more hours each week than they are paid for, and with increasing tax cuts to the arts, they have added another staff person to coordinate their advocacy efforts. The decision to add this position was made by the member organizations, which raised the money for this position beyond their dues.

The successes and growth of this coalition demonstrate the importance of everyone feeling that they are pulling in the same direction, regardless of whether they are working locally or statewide.

When Everyone Is a Volunteer

Hundreds of thousands of successful nonprofits are run entirely by volunteers. Most service clubs (Rotary, Lions, Ruritan, Shriners, and so on, as well as PTAs, hospital auxiliaries, "friends of" groups, and neighborhood organizations) have no paid staff. In many rural communities, even the fire department consists of all volunteers. Many of these organizations have run effectively for decades. They are designed by volunteers and designed to be run by volunteers. Other organizations may prefer to have paid staff but cannot afford them, so they too run on the energy of volunteers. Finally, there are untold numbers of short-term projects that are run by volunteers from beginning to end. Examples include building a new playground; organizing a demonstration, a conference, or multiblock sidewalk sale; or organizing local political campaigns. If your group or project is an all-volunteer endeavor, here are some pointers to help you function smoothly and effectively.

The goal for any organization, but especially one run entirely on unpaid energy, is an environment in which people do what they say they will do and do not take on any more than they can do. In an all-volunteer organization, the volunteers should think of themselves as unpaid staff. An organization should not tolerate incompetence and lack of follow-through from a volunteer any more than it would from a paid person.

Like staff, volunteers have lives beyond the organization and should be encouraged to set boundaries around their work with the organization. Suppose you know that Sally Jones would make a great treasurer but she says she doesn't have the time. Finally, after you implore her several times, she agrees to take the position. Don't be surprised when Sally turns out not to be as good a treasurer as you had expected—and that she truly does not have the time to follow through on the tasks. As part of showing respect for each other's time, it is imperative to create and support an organizational culture that allows people to take on fewer tasks if it also encourages them to finish the tasks they do agree to. Moreover, some people have more open time than others and may be able to take on more work than others. These differences need to be accepted in the group; people with less time to volunteer must not be made to feel that they are not doing enough if they don't put in as much time as those who have more time to devote to the organization. Ironically, one of the best ways to create this type of supportive work environment is to make sure that no one or two people take on most tasks. When you have "uber-volunteers" who get everything done, accomplishing more work than anyone else, everyone else's enthusiasm to pitch in to the work is dampened.

Volunteers should use their own and other people's time respectfully. Meetings should start and end on time. There should be an agenda. A facilitator, the chair of the meeting, or the group as a whole should agree on how long each agenda item will take and try not to take longer on any item than agreed to. There is usually more that can be said on any item and one more way of looking at things, but unless the group is an academic think tank, don't try to explore every possibility.

People should take on particular responsibilities. Someone should be the treasurer, someone should prepare the agenda for meetings, someone should be the chair. Organizations working in a collective model can rotate these responsibilities (which need to be rotated occasionally in any structure). No one in the group should have to wonder, "Who has the checkbook?" or "What's the password to get into the database?"

Think of the people working in your organization as being like a sports team. On a team, everyone has a place and they play their place. Everything is time-limited, rules are clear, and violations of rules have penalties. At any given time, some players are out on the court or in the field and others are resting on the bench. No one plays all the time and no one rests all the time. Discuss this team metaphor from time to time in your organization; examine how your organization is most like a team and where it needs to improve.

For an all-volunteer organization to succeed over time and over generations of new volunteers, it is particularly important to write things down. In decades-old successful all-volunteer organizations, there are handbooks that discuss almost everything a volunteer might be called on to do. Part of the job of current volunteers is to keep this information up to date. Every event, mail appeal, campaign, and so on should be evaluated so that next time it can be done better and more easily, even by new people, on the basis of the records kept. Turnover in all-volunteer organizations is often high, and knowledge easily gets lost, particularly if there is no central way to store information. If you do a special event, send an appeal, or write a proposal, keep track of everything someone else might want to know about it in order to do that same fundraising task faster and more easily the next time. Any systems used should be documented. Err on the side of keeping track of too much rather than too little information. Imagine a graduate student in one hundred years reconstructing your organization from a box of dusty files, real or virtual. Would it be possible? It should be. If yours is a group that is coming together for a one-time project, this level of detail is not important. However, if your intent is to exist for several years or indefinitely, you will need to set up Web-based information storage and retrieval systems, including backup systems to prevent data from getting corrupted and central storage sites such as Wiki pages or Google Docs that everyone can access. You can also store information on flash drives, but those have to be kept in a place everyone has access to.

Preparing reports and narratives for the use of people who will come after you is the best way to ensure that your organization can continue to function well using volunteers. In fact, developing such a history helps to ensure that your organization can grow.

EFFECTIVE ORIENTATION OF NEW VOLUNTEERS

The two most important elements in creating a culture of accountability are making sure people know, understand, and accept their tasks, and making sure that people who do their work are rewarded with appreciation and with time off and that those who don't do their work are gently but firmly called to task.

In my own experience working with thousands of people over the years, I feel confident saying that most people do most of what they say they are going to do. When they say they are going to, they come to meetings, show up at events, bring food, pick up or deliver people or items, and so on. A few people almost never do anything they say they will do, and all of us fail to meet commitments from time to time, but the organizational lament that board members and volunteers don't do their work fails to note that the reason for such malfunction is often a failure to orient them to the work required and to make sure they have agreed to do it.

We often think of orientation as acquainting someone with the organization itself: going over the case statement, budget, number of meetings, and obligations of being part of the group, along with the projects currently being worked on. Although accurate, this is only half the story. When we end our orientation with the question, "Are there any questions?" or "Is everything clear?" our novices nod their heads with more or less enthusiasm. They understand what they've heard; they have no questions. But what we haven't asked is, "Of the tasks we have outlined, which ones could you see yourself doing right away, Terry?" "Of the tasks we have discussed, which ones would you like to have more training on or more time to think about, Marge?"

The best way to use new volunteers is to get them to agree to do something immediately, and the tasks they agree to have to make sense to them and they have to feel that it is something they can do.

Agreeing in theory that something should be done, and wishing I were the kind of person who would do it, or even thinking that maybe I could do it even though it sounds scary, tedious, complicated, or embarrassing, is not the same as saying, "Yes, I will do it." People show up for tasks that they are familiar with and know how to do: get to a meeting, pick up pizza, text directions to an intern. Seeking ads from business owners for the adbook, asking friends to attend a fundraising house party, calling a current donor and asking for another gift— these are not things everyone knows how to do, and while someone may talk themselves into doing them at a meeting, they rapidly talk themselves out of doing them after the meeting is over.

The orientation has to include how people are going to be trained to do the tasks and what latitude they have in choosing tasks to focus on. There have to be deadlines and goals. In other words, the orientation is run as though it is the beginning of a campaign.

FINDING VOLUNTEERS

Organizations should constantly seek to expand the number of volunteer workers. There is so much work to be done that a few initial dedicated volunteers will burn out quickly. You should be drawing new people into the organization all the time so they can help share the work and broaden the organization's thinking and its access to funds.

All-volunteer organizations are not that different from many grassroots organizations that have one or two paid staff people. In fact, in many grassroots groups there are two kinds of staff: low-paid and unpaid. In all other grassroots groups there is one kind of staff: unpaid. The work is still valuable, and people's time is still invaluable. Keeping these points in mind will ensure that your organization is able to do the useful and important work it has set out for itself.

The case study examines some of the pitfalls for all-volunteer groups.

HOW MARY MORPHED FROM TEAM CAPTAIN TO ONE-WOMAN SHOW (AND BACK)

A PTA starts out with twenty active parents. Mary, the chair, is a full-time volunteer. Everyone else has a paying job in the work world; some of the parents have two jobs in order to make ends meet. When the PTA first starts meeting, everything seems to go well. Mary does more of the work because she has more time, and neither she nor anyone else seems to mind. However, after a short time, Mary starts to volunteer to do things that others could easily do. For example, someone always brings snacks to the meetings, which are held right after work. José offers to bring them to the next meeting, saying, "I'll grab some stuff at the supermarket right after work." Mary says, "You don't need to do that. I have time. I can bake something healthy and delicious." After that, Mary always makes the snacks.

The meetings are always at someone's house. People can bring their children, who play with each other while their parents meet. Sharon offers her house for the next meeting as long as no one is allergic to dogs, as she has two friendly mutts she adopted from the Humane Society. No one is allergic, and several people say that they love dogs, but Mary says, "Why don't we just have the meetings at my house?" Mary does have the nicest house, with a playroom for kids and no pets. No one ever volunteers their house for a meeting again, and from then on all the meetings are at Mary's.

The PTA decides to have a "white elephant" sale to raise money. Bill and Tiffany are excited and offer to chair. They find a space, send out e-mails inviting people to donate stuff, and create a fun flier advertising the event. Bill stores the items in his garage. At the meeting two weeks before the event, Bill and Tiffany announce that they have gathered a lot of really good stuff, including a place setting for six with only one fork missing, some wonderful antique bookshelves, some interesting fabric, and two quilts. Tiffany has invited some antique dealers who she thinks will pay top dollar for some of the items. Bill has set aside time the evening before the sale for people to come over and put prices on things, which he knows is often a fun task. Mary says, "Oh, no. We need to research prices and I think it should be done this week. I can do all that—just give me a key to your garage." Bill reluctantly agrees that a more thoughtful approach might be better. The sale goes well. The antique dealers pay the prices Mary has set, and almost everything sells. Afterward, Tiffany, Sharon, and Bill volunteer to count the money, write a report, and make the bank deposit. However, Sharon and Bill can't do it until Tuesday, three days after the sale. Mary steps in. "Tiffany and I will do it today and get it in the bank right away." Sharon reluctantly agrees that getting the money in the bank sooner might be better. Although Bill is beginning to find Mary's controlling ways annoying, he doesn't feel he can criticize her, as she does get a lot done.

At the next meeting, Mary has baked a lovely cake that says, "Thank you Bill and Tiffany." The five parents who come to the meeting are grateful to Bill and Tiffany, who feel appreciated. However, the cake is so excellent and extravagant that, ironically, the focus goes back to Mary, and everyone thanks her profusely for her thoughtfulness. Bill announces that he can't come to meetings for a while because of work.

At the next few meetings, a new parent, Mimi, is present. She has just moved into the district and her son is starting school halfway into the year. She is an organizational development consultant by trade and notices immediately the dynamic between Mary and the rest of the parents, now down to eight others. She soon hears grumblings from other parents—a mixture of admiration for Mary's indefatigable energy and resentment of her seeming need for control. Mimi invites Mary to dinner and asks her how she feels about doing so much for the PTA. Mary admits she is getting stretched thin, but points out that she is the only one without another job. Mary says she tries to make up for the fact that she's the only one not working by doing as much as possible to make it easier for the other parents to participate. She also expresses puzzlement that so many parents have dropped out over time.

Mimi tells her that she imagines many of the parents feel that Mary is such an incredible volunteer that nothing they do can come close to matching her accomplishments, so they just give up. "Kind of the way kids will stop cleaning their room altogether if a parent never praises the attempts that they make," Mimi explains, "even if those attempts do not result in a perfectly clean and tidy room." Mary understands that metaphor immediately. "What can we do to get people back?" she asks. "You have to do less, and you have to ask some people to do more," Mimi advises. "For example, ask José to bring snacks next time."

A year later, the PTA is back up to twenty active parents. Mary is still the chair and still does a lot, but she is careful not to volunteer for everything. With Mimi's help, the parents have had some honest conversations about how they work together and have begun to work much more like a team.

Starting Out Right

Organizations that have just been started are often operating on the donations of their founding members and the energy and enthusiasm these members bring to the cause that has propelled them to action. Soon, however, they realize that they must reach further for support or they will burn themselves out both financially and emotionally. Someone goes to a fundraising class or reads a book such as this one. Newly inspired to develop a membership base or raise money through any of the strategies presented, she or he can also be newly baffled. "But where do I start?" is often the next question. There are many possible starting places for raising money, but there is little money to meet startup costs. She or he now knows something about what will attract money, but there is not much room for making mistakes. This chapter provides some tips on where to start.

Of course, your group will make some mistakes. Challenge yourself to make new mistakes and not to fall into predictable and avoidable traps.

Figure out how much money you need for your organization to begin functioning smoothly. Once you have drawn up a budget for a year, break it down into what you need for this month and then the month after. See everything in the smallest possible time frame so that you don't get discouraged. If you can raise this much money for one month, then you can continue for that month. Then go on to the next month. Sometimes in the early days of an organization, you may even go week to week. Although this is not a sustainable practice for more than a few months, there is nothing inherently wrong with it.

You have probably started by raising money from the founders of the organization—yourselves. Each person should pledge a certain amount per month or per quarter and should pay that money to the person designated as treasurer. This practice will begin the important habit of developing a culture of giving money among all who work with the organization. Next, each founder or core volunteer should assess how much money he or she can raise from friends, family, and acquaintances.

Each person should make a list of all the people he or she knows without regard to whether these people believe in your cause or give money away. Just list the names of people who would recognize your name if you phoned them. Next to that list, mark all the people who you know believe in the cause your new nonprofit represents. If you don't know, put a question mark. Next, for all the people who you know believe in the cause, mark all those who you know for a fact give away money. Now, for all the people on the list who you know believe in the cause and who you know give away money, note how much you are going to ask each of them for. If you are not sure what to ask them for, keep it small. Is it $50? $100? $35? Keep in mind that some family members and friends will give you money just to be supportive of you. Finally, note what method you will use to solicit this money. Will you hold a house party? Send a personal letter and follow up by phone? Set up a personal meeting? If a meeting, will you bring someone else from the new group with you? (See Chapter Seven, "The Logistics of Personal Solicitation," for detailed information on identifying and approaching prospects for gifts.)

The chart shows what your list might look like.

Potential Donors to Our Group				
Name	Believes in Cause?	Gives Money?	Amount to Request	Method
Francisco	yes	yes	$100	meeting
Edward	yes	?	?	invite to house party
Marianne	?	yes	$35	mail appeal
Gloria	no			
Charmaine	yes	yes	$50	phone call

People sometimes object to raising money for a brand-new effort in this way by saying, "You can't just ask people for money without giving them something. We don't have a newsletter or a program or even an office. What are they giving to?" At this point, people are giving to an idea and to the people involved in making the idea an organization—you. They will give for the same reasons you are giving time and money—they agree with you and they think you are the people who can do this job. Some people enjoy—even prefer—to give money to new organizations. (In fact, many organizations find that the people who gave them money in their first five years do not continue to give—they move on to other new groups.) Those who prefer to give to more established groups won't give to you right now, but that will not be everyone's response.

The next step is to identify a few people or foundations that will give larger amounts of money ($1,000 or more) for startup costs. Use the methods described in Chapter Seven for this step. For information on approaching foundations, go to your local Foundation Center collection (see Premium Web Content, Foundation Center Cooperating Collections Network). You will need to develop a case statement, including a preliminary budget. Although your organization has no history, the people who are forming it have history. Each of the founders should be briefly described in order to show that knowledgeable and experienced people are behind this idea.

From the beginning, appoint someone to keep records and ensure that they are accurate. Always write thank you notes, even before you get organizational stationery. Start an e-mail list and get on Facebook so you can keep people posted on what you are doing. Using social media gets your message out much faster than you could do otherwise and gives you a base of people to start raising money from.

Being a brand-new organization gives you a chance to do your fundraising the right way from the very beginning.

The Perennial Question of Clean and Dirty Money

O ver the years, I have received dozens of questions about a problem that surfaces at some point in the life of almost every organization. The problem was nicely laid out in the following e-mail:

> Dear Kim:
>
> My group is struggling with what I understand to be a perennial problem: dirty money. We have two questions: Should we take dirty money, and how do we decide? A corporation has offered us a large grant for operating expenses, but several people in our group have problems with this corporation because of the way they treat their workers (badly). On the other hand, we need the money and not many places give money for operating expenses. What shall we do?

I responded that this group had stumbled on the subject that has probably taken up more time in progressive groups than almost any other topic one could name. In fact, had some organizations held a "dirty money discussion-a-thon" and sought pledges for each minute they spent discussing the very questions the writer raises, they would be handsomely endowed by now and could change their discussion to "dirty and clean investment policies." However, the writer raises serious questions that are not easy to answer, which is why this debate is perennial.

Let's divide the questions into two parts: the idea of "dirty" money and the consequences of taking such money.

I don't subscribe to the idea that there is "dirty" money and "clean" money. Money is a tool. Similarly, a hammer is a tool. A hammer can be used to help build a house or it can be used to bludgeon someone to death, but we never talk about clean and dirty hammers. Because we don't credit hammers with power they don't have, we are able to see just what a hammer is and to separate the hammer itself from what it might be used to do. We need to get that kind of perspective on money. Money can be used wisely or squandered. It can be raised honestly or dishonestly. It can be earned, inherited, stolen, given, received, lost, found—and many combinations of all of these ways of getting money. It is not in itself dirty or clean.

If you let go of the idea of dirty and clean money, you can focus on the real questions in accepting money, which are these: How does it make you feel to accept money from a corporation whose labor practices you find appalling? How does it make you look to others to accept this money? What will be the cost in goodwill, faith in your organization, or even actual money given to your organization if you accept this money?

I have seen organizations answer this question in various ways. The most sensible one I've seen was adopted in 1980 by a group in San Francisco called the Coalition for the Medical Rights of Women during a marathon discussion about accepting free printing from the Playboy Corporation. The Playboy Corporation had always been a strong supporter of civil liberties and reproductive rights groups. In those days it offered to print stationery, envelopes, invitations, newsletters, and the like for nonprofit groups working for those causes. Any nonprofit using such money simply had to put the statement "Printing donated by the Playboy Corporation" somewhere on the printed piece.

The Coalition, which was the first place I worked as a development director, had occasionally accepted Playboy's services to get some of this printing. Although this was a big help financially, the group, which by definition was fighting against sexism in many areas of society, always had great uneasiness about taking advantage of Playboy's program. As a collective, we discussed whether to continue taking the free printing. We argued back and forth, with those in favor saying, "Playboy made its money off of women and we're simply putting that money to good use; we deserve it." Those against argued that Playboy exploited women and promoted sexism and we would help it in its sex-for-money pursuit by taking its free printing. Late one night, after we had made and remade every argument several times, one person finally said, "I don't know whether it is right or wrong to take this money. All I know is that the idea of taking Playboy's money or its free printing makes me want to vomit."

From then on, in questions about taking money, we applied the "vomit test." If a person who was important to the organization—staff or board member, volunteer, longtime friend—said, "Taking money from such-and-such would make me want to vomit," we wouldn't take it, because that person and her continuing contributions to our group were more important than any money.

I have never found a more rational approach to the question, "How does it make us feel to accept money from a source whose practices we do not condone?"

The second question, "How does it make us look to the outside world to take this money?" is a more practical one. Sometimes a source of money will pass the vomit test but fail this second test. For example, a board member of a tiny health center in rural New Mexico was a fraternity brother of the vice president of a large uranium-mining operation that is polluting the entire area around it with radioactive uranium tailings. Through his contact, the board member secured a grant from this mining corporation, which so outraged several major donors to the health center that they stopped giving. The ensuing bad publicity and loss of donations was a major factor in the demise of that organization the following year.

When an organization accepts money from a source that is controversial, it needs to think about how its other donors or contributors might react. Of course, others' reactions are sometimes hard to judge, but people are likely to be shocked or offended if an organization accepts money from a source that is perceived to be in conflict with the values or goals of the organization. So when a mining corporation whose irresponsible practices are causing serious health problems donates to a health center, accepting such a donation can be predicted to cause outrage. Had the corporation donated to the public library, there might have been less of an outcry.

The other factors in accepting money from a controversial source are the amount of money relative to the budget of the organization and what kind of recognition the source wants for the gift. Though this may have happened, I have never heard of an organization spending hours debating whether to accept a $50 gift from a corporation with even the most foul practices or from one of that corporation's employees, because that amount of money cannot buy any influence. Similarly, I rarely hear of an organization refusing to accept even a large gift from an individual who may have made his or her money from a corporation with horrible practices, because the corporation will not receive any glory for that gift. Certainly, I have never heard of an organization turning down a foundation grant, even when the source of that money might also be problematic.

Sometimes an organization will accept money from a corporation if it does not have to publicize that gift, but will refuse the gift if it requires public acknowledgment. Examining the hypocrisy of that position can be helpful to groups sorting out whether to take that money or not. Ask yourself, "If this gift from this source were to be headline news in our local paper tomorrow, would we be happy, would we feel embarrassed, or would we be nervous about the consequences?" If happy, take the money. If you would rather people didn't know about the gift, then don't take it.

The issue of clean and dirty money generally comes up in relation to corporations. Since corporations are only responsible for about 5 percent of all the money given away in the private sector, and only 11 percent of corporations give away any money at all, organizations are simply better off focusing their fundraising efforts on building a broad base of individual donors. When an organization receives most of its funds from individuals and those individuals ask no more than to be thanked for their gifts and kept abreast of the work, there is no need to worry about clean or dirty money.

INDEX

B

C

development director working relationship with, 417–421

Expenses: capital campaign, 343–345; estimating, 434–435; of fundraising in rural communities, 465; matching income and projected, 440; projecting income to cover, 435, 437–438, 439; sample expense projections, 436

F

Face-to-face opportunity fundraising, 247

Face-to-face prospect meeting: etiquette issues of, 98–99; following-up after the, 101–102; prospect's possible responses during, 99–101; rural community fundraising and, 473–474; tips for preparing for, 97–98

Facebook, 384

Fact sheet enclosure, 176–177

Faith-Based and Neighborhood Partnerships, 19

"Famous people": direct mail appeals, 188; phone-a-thons promotion by, 206

Feasibility studies: description of, 355; increasing your chance of success with, 359; the information provided by, 358; making the decision to conduct or not to conduct, 356–358; who conducts the, 355–356

Financial mismanagement, 457–458

Financial needs: annual, 27–29, 339; capital, 27–29, 52, 339–341; endowment and reserve funds, 30–33; matching donor giving to, 34

Financial problems: accounting errors, mismanagement, or embezzlement, 457–458; cash flow, 456; deficit spending, 456–457; keeping calm when facing, 455. *See also* Budgets; Fundraising challenges

Financial statement, 47, 48

Fiscal accountability, 51

501(c)(3) status: description of, 8, 22, 49–50; "one-third rule" and risk of losing, 22

Foundation Center, 13

Foundation funding: comparing corporation and, 16–17; myth of, 9–10; realities of, 15–16

Franklin, Ben, 298

Franklin Institute, 298

Friends of the Library, 467–468

Friends of Progress, 149–150

Funding Domestic Violence and Sexual Assault Programs in North Carolina (Dubay and Rosch), 470

Fundraising: board of directors' role in, 55–57; budgeting for, 47, 48, 113, 114, 431–443; for a coalition, 475–481; ethical dilemmas common to, 425–430, 495–498; foundation and corporation giving myth of, 9–10; for new nonprofit organizations, 491–493; paid staff role in, 57; in rural communities, 463–474; understanding that anyone can do, 25–26; when everyone is a volunteer in, 483–489. *See also* Development directors; Money; Nongovernmental organizations (NGOs)

Fundraising barriers: fear of asking for money, 76–80; fear of consequences of "asking a friend for money," 81; fear that "the person will say no," 80–81; quid pro quo fear, 81–82

Fundraising challenges: clean versus dirty money, 495–498; fundraising for a coalition, 475–481; identifying any

Fundraising challenges (*Continued*) real and serious, 460–461; mistakes in identifying nonprofit's, 460; of new nonprofit organizations, 491–493; of raising money in rural communities, 463–474; when everyone is a volunteer, 483–489. *See also* Financial problems

Fundraising events: adbooks, 138–145; annual dinner, 126–132; house party, 119–126; phone-a-thon, 194–209; raffles, 132–138; special events, 103–118

Fundraising management: managing donor data, 379–386; managing your information component of, 365–369; office issues of, 363–364; time management component of, 371–378. *See also* Volunteer management

Fundraising office, 363–364

Fundraising plan development: step 1: set a goal, 445; step 2: include certain details in each income strategy, 445–446; step 3: plot out plans for individual donors, 446–447; step 4: match numbers of donors to strategies, 447; step 5: write out the timeline of tasks, 447

Fundraising plans: Affordable Housing for Working People case study on, 450–453; case statement section on, 46–47, 48; creating, 445–453; developing a budget role in, 433–443; importance of, 431–432; People's Theater case study on, 447–450. *See also* Budgets

Fundraising principles: diversifying sources, 21–22; understanding that anyone can fundraise, 25–26; understanding why people give, 22–24

Fundraising strategies: available in rural communities, 470–474; getting comfortable asking for money, 75–82, 280; matching financial needs with, 27–37; organizational importance of having, 1–2; organizational learning to correctly use, 35–36; personal solicitation of prospects, 83–102; religious organizations' successful, 19–20; retention of donors, 35, 150–151, 240–242, 287–291; working smarter at, 37. *See also* Acquisition strategies; Large-scale fundraising; Upgrading strategies

G

Garlic Festival (Gilroy, CA), 469

Gates, Bill, 13

Gaywill.com, 302

General bequest, 299

GIFT (grassroots-fundraising.org), 401

Gift Pyramid, 282

Gift Range Charts: calculating a major gift, 282; Capital Campaign Gift Range Chart, 345–347; Endowment Campaign Gift Range Chart, 331; major gift prospective donors, 284

Gifts of assets, 340

Gifts of income, 340

Giving and Volunteering in the USA, 13

Giving contributions: challenges of collecting data on, 10–13; corporate funding share of, 16–17; foundation funding share of, 15–16; myths of foundation and corporate, 9–10; power of individual, 17–20; sources of 2009, 10; uses of 2009, 18

Giving motivation: understanding individual, 22–23; understanding multiple reasons for, 23–24

campaign planning by, 450; spring campaign planning by, 449–450

Personal solicitation logistics: approaching the prospect, 92–93; ask a prospect, 83–87; e-mail or letter contact, 93–94; face-to-face, 97–102; phone call contact, 95–97; steps in creating a prospect list, 87–92

Philadelphia Foundation, 298

Philanthropy: definition of, 7–8; funding myths of, 9–10; funding realities of, 15–16

Phone call contact: issues to consider for, 95; when you do reach the prospect, 96–97; when you don't reach prospect, 95–96

Phone-a-thon letters: to people with questions about nonprofits, 200–201; for people who say yes to donating, 199; as a reminder of your pledge, 205; "sorry we missed you," 199–200

Phone-a-thon steps: step 1: prepare the list, 195–196; step 2: create way to record results of calls, 196–197; step 3: set date for phone-a-thon, 197; step 4: write a script, 197–198; step 5: prepare three letters and appropriate enclosures, 199–201; step 6: determine number of phones and volunteers, 201–202; step 7: find a place, 202; step 8: recruit volunteers, 202

Phone-a-thons: description and advantages of, 194–195; "famous people" promotion of, 206; getting publicity for your, 205–206; on the night of the, 203–204; preparation steps for, 195–202; recruiting and training volunteers, 201–202, 202–203, 207–209; tasks for after, 204–205. *See also* Telephone fundraising

Planned giving. *See* Legacy giving

Playboy Corporation, 496–497

Pledge card reply device, 310

Pledge programs: advantages of setting up monthly, 271–272; collecting donations from monthly, 275–276; introducing monthly, 273; marketing monthly, 273–275; sample pledge reminder form for monthly, 277; tracking pledges from monthly, 276–278; two don'ts of monthly, 278

Pledging: capital campaign pledge agreement form, 351; monthly donor programs for, 271–278; two different meanings of, 271

Premiums, 180–181

Programs. *See* Nonprofit programs

Prospect contact: deciding method of, 92–93; direct mail, 147–161; e-mail, 93, 122; face-to-face, 97–102; identifying any contact of prospect with organization, 84; letter, 93–94; phone call, 95–97

Prospect Identification List form, 88, 90–92

Prospect list: creating the, 87–92; Master Prospect List form, 88–89; Prospect Identification List form, 88, 90–92; Prospect Record form, 91

Prospect Record form, 91

Prospective donors: ability to give, 86–87; approaching capital campaign, 349–350; audience for online strategies, 215–216; beliefs and values of, 84–86; contact with, 84, 92–102; endowment campaign solicitation of, 332–337; invited to house party, 121–122; issues of consideration related to, 83–84; keeping action plans on, 377–378; legacy, 295–305; major gift campaign,

Segmenting donors: benefits of, 267–268; criteria for, 266–267; to facilitate staying in touch with donors, 268–270; understanding your donors by, 265–267

Service fees. *See* Voluntary service fees

"Shadow question," 100–101

Shakespeare Festival (Ashland, OR), 469

Sharing mailing lists, 159–161

SMART objectives, 44

Social networking: Facebook, 384; LinkedIn, 384. *See also* Web 2.0/Web sites

Special circumstances. *See* Fundraising challenges

Special event committees: creating, 111–112; developing a timeline, 114–115; Master Task List for, 112–113, 114; preparing a budget, 113, 114

Special Event Evaluation Form, 118

Special event planning: checklist of commonly forgotten items for, 115–117; committee tasks for, 112–115; creating a committee for, 111–112; evaluation step in, 117–118

Special events: consistency, judgment, and appropriateness of, 106–107; criteria to consider when choosing, 105–106; front money required for, 108; major gifts campaign, 314, 315; organization image reflected by, 107–108; planning, 111–118; and repeatability, timing, and the big picture, 109; rural community and, 471–473; three goals of, 103–104; types of people who attend, 104–105; volunteer energy required for, 108

Sponsorship (or underwriting) committee, 129

Staff: board of directors' responsibilities for, 52; canvassing done by, 233–234, 238–239; capital campaign and cost of, 344; dividing volunteer work from work by, 390; executive director, 417–423; fundraising roles of, 57; major gift solicitation by, 286; post-capital campaign celebration for, 352. *See also* Development staff

Standard and Poor's, 13

Statement of agreement, 53–54

Stories. *See* Nonprofit stories

Strategic plans: board of directors' role in, 51; components and functions of, 47–48; differences between case statement and, 47–48; SWOT test of, 47

Structure section: description of, 46, 48; key to accountability, 46

T

Tax issues: adbook rules, 139–140; rule on recording gifts, 384; rules on value of gift benefits, 285; tax return data on giving, 11, 12–13; UBIT (unrelated business income tax), 139–140; value of major gift benefits, 285. *See also* Internal Revenue Service (IRS)

"Teaser copy," 166

"Technological natives," 215

Telephone calls: after a mail appeal, 209–210; opportunistic fundraising through, 247; thank you, 258–259; as time sink, 373; voluntary fees for services delivered by, 231–232

Telephone fundraising: Do Not Call Act (2003) impact on, 193; history and advantages of, 193–194; opportunistic, 247; phoning after a mail appeal, 209–210; phoning for renewals, 210–211; voluntary fees for phone-delivered services, 231–232. *See also* Phone-a-thons

participate, 388–389; matching volunteers to strategies they are comfortable using, 389–390; orienting volunteers to your fundraising program, 389; showing appreciation to volunteers, 390; understanding that perfection isn't necessary, 390. *See also* Fundraising management

Volunteer nonprofits: effective orientation of new volunteers, 485–486; finding volunteers for, 486–487; PTA one-woman show (and back), 487–489; special challenges facing, 483–485

Volunteers: allowing time off to, 391; annual dinner events, 128; to augment board members' work, 71; canvassing done by, 233–234, 238–239; dividing staff work from work done by, 390; fundraising issues when all are, 483–489; major gift program solicitation by, 286; major gifts campaign solicitor, 311–312, 314–315; phone-a-thon, 201–202, 203–204, 207–209; post-capital campaign celebration for, 352; raffle, 134; showing appreciation to volunteers, 390; special events and required energy of, 108; taking pressure off of staff by recruiting, 413; three different types of, 389–390

"Vomit test," 497